Storms, Ice, and Whales

Willem van der Does

STORMS, ICE, *and* WHALES

The Antarctic Adventures of a Dutch Artist
on a Norwegian Whaler

Written and illustrated by

WILLEM VAN DER DOES

Translated by

RUTH VAN BAAK GRIFFIOEN

Introduction by

JOOST C. A. SCHOKKENBROEK

William B. Eerdmans Publishing Company
Grand Rapids, Michigan / Cambridge, U.K.

First published 1934 by the Board of the Representatives and
Directors in the Dutch East Indies

Wm. B. Eerdmans Publishing Co.
255 Jefferson Ave. S.E., Grand Rapids, Michigan 49503 /
P.O. Box 163, Cambridge CB3 9PU U.K.

Printed in the United States of America

08 07 06 05 04 03   7 6 5 4 3 2 1

Library of Congress Cataloging-in-Publication Data

Does, Willem van der, 1889-1966.
[Storm, ijs en walvisschen. English]
Storms, ice, and whales: the antarctic adventures of a Dutch artist on a Norwegian whaler /
written and illustrated by Willem van der Does; translated by Ruth van Baak Griffioen.
p.   cm.
ISBN 0-8028-2125-1 (alk. paper)
1. Voyages and travels. 2. Whaling. 3. Does, Willem van der, 1889-1966 —
Travel — Antarctica. 4. Antarctica — Description and travel. I. Title.

G545.D613 2003
919.8904 — dc22
                            2003060134

www.eerdmans.com

Contents

Translator's Preface

Willem van der Does was born in Rotterdam on April 20, 1889, and died in Zeist on February 3, 1966. The son of a sea captain, he had lived in the Dutch East Indies for some time even before his great Antarctic adventure of 1923-1924, which he describes in this book. After World War II, as Indonesia's battle for independence from the Dutch grew fiercer, he left the Indies for the last time and returned to the Netherlands. He lived in Schiedam first, then moved to Zeist in 1957. He was a professional landscape painter and book illustrator.

Over Christmas of 2001, a signed, dated copy of Van der Does's book, *Storm, IJs, en Walvisschen*, surfaced out of a family attic into our lives. My father immediately recognized the author as his mother's cousin. One of Willem's paintings — appropriately enough, a Dutch winter landscape — had hung for years over my father's desk, a gift from Willem in thanks for care packages sent from the American branch of the family to the Netherlands during Europe's lean years after World War II. Since my father happened to be writing a history of his mother's family, the Van der Does clan, and since I happened to know Dutch, my father asked me to skim the book for clues to the personal character of its author.

Our family had actually met Van der Does in 1961 in his retirement home in Zeist. Although Willem's relation to us might seem distant, my father's family had for some generations been unusually small in numbers; both Willem and my father could count all their known living relatives on two hands, and thus were eager to meet each other. The two had a pleasant visit in Willem's art studio; though by then an old man, Willem was still an active painter. Regrettably, the subject of Antarctica never came up. (At the time, we were unaware of this part of his life story.) The visit was brief, with children left in the car outside lest they overwhelm the quiet artist. On the way out, my father posed for a picture with Willem, whom he strikingly resembled — apart from the age difference and Willem's smart goatee. I had grown up seeing that picture, but not until my parents enlarged it for me while I was working on this translation did any of us notice that far down in the corner of this dark print was a two-year-old, the third person in the photograph. I was that toddler. Imagine if someone could have told Willem that this little American baby would grow up to learn Dutch, live for a time in the Netherlands, and someday translate his book into English.

Though, being only two, I missed my chance to meet Van der Does properly then, I thoroughly enjoyed getting to know him a little bit, four decades later, by translating this marvelous book about his Antarctic journey. The character my father was looking for shines out on every page: Willem was adventurous, clever, omnivorously curious, keenly observant and at the same time very generous in his estimation of others. He had that rare combination of qualities that earned him the respect and friendship of both the sailors and the officers onboard the *Sir James Clark Ross*. He worked very hard, had a good sense of humor, and was so persistent in the pursuit of his goals that, as he put it when describing his dogged attempts to talk himself on to any whaler heading south, "I became so annoying that I even began to annoy myself!"

He shared the spirit of his era in his admiration for his strong, stalwart Norwegian companions, continually exulting in their descent from pure Viking stock. His artist's eye took in a rush of visual details throughout the voyage; you can always tell when he's been carried away by the beauty of a scene because his otherwise delightfully straightforward prose waxes frothy and turgid in classic Victorian style. His views on the world's peoples were not always enlightened by modern standards but typical of his time; his views on the whaling industry in which he found himself were, I think, more than a little ahead of his time. As much as he admired the sturdy whalers' skills, the artist in him cried out against the creatures' slaughter, and he ruefully concluded that at the rate things were going in the 1920s, the whales would be completely wiped out within just twenty years. How Greenpeace would have surprised him.

Van der Does's story picks up just as the Heroic Age of Antarctic exploration had come to a close. Roald Amundsen was still alive, Robert Falcon Scott's disaster was only a decade old, and Ernest Shackleton had died just the year before. The master of Van der Does's ship was C. A. Larsen, who had captained whalers for nearly forty years already, and had been not only the first person to discover fossils in Antarctica but also the first to chart whole coasts of the Southern continent. (The rapidly disappearing Larsen Ice Shelf on the Antarctic Peninsula is named for him.) Although the expedition that forms the subject of this book was no great voyage of discovery, it was significant for several reasons. First, it was one of the earliest attempts to establish an Antarctic factory-ship whaling industry. Second, when Van der Does stepped on to the Ross Ice Shelf (or Great Ice Barrier, as it was then known), he was apparently the first Dutchman ever to set foot on Antarctica. And third, Van der Does's paintings and drawings arising from this expedition belong to the extremely small genre of Antarctic art done by professionals.

Thanks to all my Van Baak shipmates on this voyage of discovery: to Tom, for the laptop that made work possible in ridiculously peripatetic circumstances; to David, for many hours of help in matters nautical, geographical, historical, scientific, and so on, and for assistance with the glossary of nautical terms; and most of all to my parents, Edward and Frances Van Baak, for starting it all off and encouraging me at every rotation of the propeller.

Storm, IJs, en Walvisschen was first published in the Dutch East Indies in 1934 and saw a second printing in 1935. These were beautiful half-folio tomes with superb reproductions of the book's numerous pen-and-ink illustrations, and formed the basis for this translation. The book was republished in Amsterdam in 1947 in quarto; a third edition, a paperback with no illustrations, was issued in 1955. My thanks to Eerdmans for recognizing Van der Does's book for the historical gem that it is and agreeing to publish this first translation.

RUTH VAN BAAK GRIFFIOEN
Williamsburg, Virginia, 2003

Foreword to the 1934 Edition

Shortly after the return to the Dutch East Indies of our famous Indies maritime painter Willem van der Does, I had the pleasure of marveling at an exhibition of his works, one that exclusively featured sketches of his visit to the South Pole.

The somber natural world of the ice, the tremendous masses of snow depicted — these awoke in me and many others not only great wonder at his abilities, but also the wish to hear about the adventures of his great voyage to this inhospitable place.

But Van der Does is a very reserved and also fairly modest man, and it is not easy to get him to talk. And so for the time being it remained a wish.

A few years later I visited him once in his studio — he had settled in Malang in the meantime — and saw a few of his ice paintings. Again I asked him about the great adventures he had experienced. In the peaceful atmosphere of his cottage he described a few incidents, and he did it so fluidly that in passing I mentioned that it would be a good idea to turn his story into a book. And if this story could be illustrated with his famous pen-and-ink drawings, it could, I thought, be a very fine and interesting book.

But, however attractive this idea was and however much interest he himself might have had in it, a writer he was not.

So I proposed to him that he try to expand his observations, clarified by the drawings, and then we could try to make whatever we could out of them.

That's how I got him to write, after we had agreed that his work would appear for the time being as a serial in the monthly magazine *Nautica*. And the first attempts already went so well that in our circles the desire arose immediately to put the whole thing out in book form.

We got much support and complete cooperation from our printers, the firm of Albrecht & Co., and the results, dear reader, you now hold in your hands.

WILLEM VAN DER DOES is, as far as we know, the first Dutchman to visit the South Polar area, and, after the famous Dr. Wilson of Scott's storied expedition, he is also the only one to make drawings of that region.

The kind reader will notice that the adventures he went through — one could even say struggled through — are described very simply, but it is precisely this sober account that is doubly instructive for us.

And although people might not ascribe any literary merit to this book (although I think it does have it), it remains in any case a satisfying work for those who want to enjoy an old-fashioned, exciting travel story.

It is precisely in these modern times of traveling with great speed and in great luxury that this story can be a light and pleasant change, and in our humble opinion both young and old can enjoy it. So we send this book out into the world with great confidence, and we trust that those who are entitled to judge it will acknowledge that for our part we have made an effort to enrich our Dutch literature with an unusual work, one that begins on and remains on an intriguing level.

We give Van der Does our thanks for the effort he was willing to make to produce this book, which lay far outside his usual line of work, but to which he clearly devoted great love, as he does with everything that comes from his hands.

May this book take its place, a humble place, in our literature, one that I believe it undoubtedly well deserves.

C. M. BAKKER

Foreword to the 1947 Edition

Storms, Ice, and Whales was written by the painter Willem van der Does, who lives in Java. In this book he describes an unusually interesting whaling expedition to the Antarctic Ocean, which he experienced as a working member of the enterprise.

For this painter-writer-sailor, the adventurous voyage began as no more than a study trip that would give him the opportunity to examine the environment of the polar regions, to round out the knowledge he had already gained in nature studies via years of activity in tropic and temperate climates. On many pages it will be clear that a true artist is speaking. That the author himself made the drawings which illuminate the book also makes this clear, of course.

We must not fail to mention that Willem van der Does was the first Dutchman to set foot on the unknown sixth continent of Antarctica, the legendary Southern Land, which still glitters on the globe as a huge, empty, white mass.

The voyage described here was unusually interesting because the expedition ship, the *Sir James Clark Ross* (named after the great English polar explorer), was the first normal freighter that dared to penetrate the seemingly impenetrable barrier of the fearsome polar pack ice. Previously, all ice experts had considered this possible only for vessels that had been specially built for that purpose.

This was without a doubt a very risky undertaking — to drive a vulnerable steel ship like the *Ross* through the Antarctic pack ice. But the undertaking was successful, although it often looked as if "the pack" had completely blocked passage to the Ross Sea. Thanks to the courage, persistence, and seamanship of the stalwart Norwegians, however, the heavy sea ice was splendidly overcome, after which they reached the famed Great Ice Barrier, in the heart of the South Polar Region.

The Bay of Whales, an inlet in this tremendous glacier, the harbor in which they had hoped to find safe anchor for the mother ship and the chase boats, appeared to be unapproachable after all. In this bay, which Roald Amundsen had used as the departure point for his famous sledge-march to the geographic South Pole, the winter ice still sat like a wall, meters thick, even though according to the calendar it was the middle of the summer. This gives readers a mental snapshot of the temperature that reigns there at the end of the earth.

In unembellished language, with, as it were, the briny ocean breeze wafting through it, Van der Does gives a thrilling report of the vicissitudes of the expedition in the lonely regions of the Eternal Ice. In lively fashion he describes the many dangers and difficulties that the rugged pioneers had to overcome in the wide, white wilderness of silent emptiness and deadly desolation. He writes entertainingly of the hunt for the leviathan, the whale, which despite its prehistoric dimensions is as defenseless as a lamb.

But above all the author succeeds in painting a picture of the majestic expanse and the stern beauty of the South Polar Region, where the violating hand of man has not yet been able to defile the grandeur of the Pole's barren environment.

Along with the author, readers feel the irresistible attraction that emanates from the vast white kingdom of the Eternal Quiet, which extends around the southern end of the earth's axis in all the lofty beauty of the first days of creation.

The hunting and business methods Van der Does describes are not as ultra-modern as those of today; in this area too technology has advanced rapidly. So, for example, on the *Sir James Clark Ross* the huge whale carcasses still had to be processed by men who had to stand perilously on the lurching, decomposing cadavers as they lay alongside the ship in the sea. Nowdays, by contrast, these dead giants of the sea can be taken wholly on deck, where all the necessary procedures can be performed without regard to weather conditions. Spotting these enormous ocean mammals also presents fewer difficulties than it did in the past, now that men can follow the trail of the whale under the ocean's surface with the help of airplanes. Earlier, the hunters had to search with eagle eyes for the *blååst* — the beast's expelled breath — a rare cloud of vapor that quickly dissolved into the atmosphere.

Now that the Netherlands, after sitting out for several centuries, is resuming its place among whaling peoples, we decided to include this interesting travel tale in the "Library of the Seven Seas." The publisher is convinced that this Dutch ocean epic will be heartily welcomed by all those who cherish the life on the long swells.

The first edition of *Storms, Ice, and Whales* appeared in Batavia, where the book was published by the Board of the Representatives and Directors in the Dutch East Indies. The author then retrieved the copyright and had meanwhile returned to the Netherlands. Here the publisher considered the work so important, particularly in connection with the revival of the Dutch whaling trade, that we proceeded immediately with this revised edition.

Another stimulus no less strong was that this book so convincingly demonstrates that the ancient spirit of enterprise lives on in our people just as strongly now as in earlier times. For although the author may have pursued his unusual study trip with, as he puts it, a purely artistic goal, it would be ungrateful of us if we did not mention that he has simultaneously shown his countrymen the way to the Antarctic Ocean, where a great task no doubt awaits our merchant fleet. We are convinced that the resumption of whaling under the Dutch flag will herald a promising new era for them. And so we must regard the painter-writer-sailor Willem van der Does as the man who first devoted his full attention to the great possibilities that stand before us in the icy, little-known seas that lap the shores of the Antarctic.

It seems fitting that the author has dedicated this new edition to the Board of the Dutch Society for Whaling in Amsterdam, thereby bringing honor to the men who took the initiative to revive Dutch whaling.

INTRODUCTION

Willem Jan Pieter van der Does (1889-1966): Whaler, Author, Artist

—⟨ø⟨ø⟩⟩—

T he first Dutch edition of this book saw the light in 1934, ten years after
Willem Jan Pieter van der Does had returned from his whaling voyage in
the Ross Sea.[1] At the time he was writing the book, he was living in Malang,
Indonesia. With a keen sense of drama he referred to the tropical atmosphere
that surrounded him while he wrote the final lines about his sojourn in the
freezing-cold Antarctic waters:

> Writing this travel memoir, I was often struck by the extreme contrast
> between the natural scenes I was describing and the richness of the tropi-
> cal environment that smiled on me as I wrote. While I was trying to con-
> vey what an Antarctic blizzard was like, I saw the crowns of the fruit-
> laden coconut palms shining in the bright sunshine and the tops of the
> high bamboo stalks, fine as lace, waving next to them in the sultry
> warmth of a tropical morning. And the same day on which I recounted
> the desolate desertedness of the land of the Pole, where not even humble
> mosses can live, I saw the king of the night blossom, the cactus with the
> huge, beautiful flowers, a sublime example of the sumptuous splendor
> with which Flora has adorned the tropics.

For almost seventy years the Dutch-speaking world has had the opportunity
to read Van der Does's stunning firsthand account of this highly important

1. *Storm, ijs en walvisschen: een moderne Vikingtocht, met Noorsche walvischvaarders naar de
Zuidelijke IJszee* (Board of the Representatives and Directors in the Dutch East Indies, 1934).
The second edition was published in 1947 by C. de Boer Jr. in the series Bibliotheek der
Zeven Zeeën (Library of the Seven Seas).

whaling expedition under the Norwegian flag. The English-speaking community, however, has had to content itself with the narrative of the same voyage by the well-known mariner Alan Villiers.[2]

Villiers and Van der Does should not be considered competitors. I rather see their work as complementary, in style as well as in content. Both men served on the factory ship the *Sir James Clark Ross* (formerly the *Custodian*)[3] — but that's where the commonality ends. In his writing Villiers tends to follow the more traditional way of keeping a journal. In a rather dry, not very vivid manner, he provides information about the weather, the number of whales that have been caught, and, occasionally, life onboard the ship. In contrast, Van der Does paints colorful pictures — both figuratively as well as literally — of his experiences during the same expedition. But Villiers' work is widely known, widely acclaimed, and often cited, while Van der Does's work has remained unknown — until now.

At the time of the expedition, the *Sir James Clark Ross* (8,223 tons), named after the Englishman who had discovered this sea in 1840, was the largest whaling ship ever built. This floating oil factory, which was able to process the whales after they were captured, was accompanied by five catchers. From these fairly light, slim boats, which weighed one hundred tons at most, the whales were harpooned. This Norwegian whaling expedition was the very first to enter the Ross Sea to check the whale population and test the feasibility of whaling activities there. Many of the hunting expeditions of the five catchers can thus be considered voyages of exploration. In addition, much of the natural wildlife in this area was described for the first time. For instance, the first recorded attack of a blue whale by killer whales (orcas) is described by the whalers onboard one of the catchers.

Thus both Villiers and Van der Does participated in this truly historic adventure and created valuable records of it. Both have contributed immensely to our knowledge about life near the South Pole; both have left their legacies. Now Van Der Does's record has the opportunity to become as prominent as Villiers'. His tribute to this all-important voyage now lies in front of you.

2. Villiers, *Whaling in the Frozen South: Being the Story of the 1923-1924 Norwegian Whaling Expedition to the Antarctic* (Indianapolis: Bobbs-Merrill, 1925).

3. In 1923 the Ross Sea Whaling Company purchased the *Custodian*, an old steamer originally christened the *Mahronda*. While converting the steamer into a factory ship, the company named it the *Sir James Clark Ross*.

Willem Went a-Whaling

Van der Does was an experienced seaman by the time he mustered on to the *Sir James Clark Ross* (or the *Ross*, as he himself refers to the ship). He made his first voyage on a ship at the age of eleven. Later, he sailed for the Royal Dutch Shipping Company as a helmsman. During the 1920s, the author lived in Schiedam, close to his native town of Rotterdam. Here, many a whaler came into the harbor to unload its cargo of oil, and Willem became fixed on the goal of getting onboard a whaler and seeing the South Polar Region for himself.

But the path leading to the *Ross* was not an easy one. In 1922, Van der Does visited every whaler that docked in Rotterdam, Antwerp, and Bremen, desperately trying to get a place onboard as a painting passenger — or should I say as a passing painter? Finally he was offered a place on the Dutch ship *Sultan van Langkat*, a tanker destined for the Kerguelen Islands (about 48-55 degrees south latitude).[4] But this ship wasn't venturing far enough for Van der Does's taste. So he returned to the Netherlands with an even greater ambition to realize his goal.

During the summer of 1923, the author left for Norway onboard the *Thor I.* This ship first went to Sandefjord to pick up sufficient crew to sail to South Georgia for a whaling expedition. Because Norwegian law prohibited non-Norwegian crew on ships flying the Norwegian flag, the foreigners on board — three Dutchmen, one Englishman, and one Lettlander — were let go. The others went home — but not our determined Van der Does! He stayed on, doggedly searching for another ship, eventually spending a few nights at the Hotel Atlantic, the very same place where Carl Anton Larsen and his wife were staying. The sixty-four-year-old man was the father of Antarctic whaling and the leader of the expedition with the *Sir James Clark Ross.*[5] Van der Does finally had Fortune on his side when he managed to smooth-talk his way

4. This steel tanker, 3,150 registered gross tons, was built in 1897 for the N.V. Scheepvaart Maatschappij Palm-Lijn.

5. For an excellent account on the development of whaling (and sealing) in Antarctic waters and C. A. Larsen's contributions, see Ian B. Hart, *Pesca: The History of the Compañia Argentina de Pesca Sociedad Anónima of Buenos Aires: An Account of the Pioneering Modern Whaling and Sealing Company in the Antarctic* (Whinfield, 2001). See also J. N. Tønnessen and A. O. Johnsen, *The History of Modern Whaling,* trans. R. I. Christophersen (Berkeley and Los Angeles: University of California Press, 1982), especially pp. 147-306. Finally, see Richard Ellis, *Men and Whales* (New York: Knopf, 1991), especially pp. 337-70.

onboard the factory ship — in large part because his dogged efforts earned the sympathy and influence of the shipowner's wife, Mrs. Rasmussen. Van der Does certainly wasn't the only one who longed for Antarctic adventure: on the factory ship and the five catchers, there were 200 crew members in all.[6]

Finally, after traveling many thousands of miles, the fleet reached the 77.5th parallel. Although this statement is almost impossible to verify, I dare to say that Van der Does's participation in the Norwegian expedition made him the first Dutchman to reach the Ross Sea! He started the voyage with the rank of "guest cablemaker." Later, in the cold Antarctic waters, he rose to the rank of boatswain. He also regularly replaced the steersman on shifts on the catchers.

Upon their arrival, the whalers found an abundance of whales, and the first two whales — a male and a female blue whale — were shot. These were the very first of many that would die in their wake between the 1920s and the 1960s.[7]

Very important from a whaling historian's point of view are the author's descriptions of the actual whaling: he describes thoroughly and vividly how the crew of a catcher struggled through the ice while on the lookout for whales. Once the huge mammals were in sight, all hands got ready. The captain/gunner — on catchers the two roles were almost always a combined responsibility — prepared the harpoon gun with its deadly load. Once the whales were shot and killed, they were inflated with compressed air to prevent them from sinking.

The catchers then brought the dead whales alongside the factory ship, where men on platforms stood ready to flense the whales. The 90-foot blue whales, with their weight of approximately 90 tons, were peeled like apples. Huge pieces of blubber were hauled and heaved onboard the factory ship, where meat and blubber (and also bones) were processed in boilers.[8] The work on the platforms was particularly dangerous, as Van der Does points out. The hard-working men first of all had to deal with the icy, slippery surface they were working on. And whenever a whale was flensed, hungry killer

6. The crew of the catchers consisted of 60 men, 12 on each boat. A total of 140 men were employed onboard the factory ship.

7. Between 1923 and 1930 — just seven years — 6,111 whales were killed. Only 270 of these were *not* blue whales!

8. This very same technique was used by American whalers throughout the late eighteenth and nineteenth centuries. But they didn't hunt the blue whale, the fin whale, or the minke whale. They went after the largest of the toothed whales, the sperm whale or cachalot.

whales turned up to eat away parts of the floating leviathan. With their huge mouths with dozens and dozens of deadly teeth, they proved to be a serious menace to the unprotected whalers, who more than once had to use their flensing knives to keep the killer whales away from their feet. It wasn't until a year later, in 1925, that the first factory ship with a slipway — a big hole in the hull through which the whales, regardless of their size, could be hauled on deck with steam winches and processed — set sail for the Antarctic. The ship, with a slipway in the bow, was appropriately named the *C. A. Larsen*. (Larsen had died on his second expedition to the Ross Sea in 1924.) Later, the impractical slipway in the bow was replaced by the slipway in the stern.

The *Ross* continued its whaling activities until the first days of March 1924. Never before had anyone stayed in the Ross Sea for such a long time! Already at an early stage, however, it was clear to all the men involved that the voyage would not turn out to be an overwhelming economic success. Only about 25 percent of the ship's cargo capacity was used. While the tanks were designed to hold about 60,000 barrels of oil, only 17,000 barrels were transferred from the whaling grounds.[9]

On the return voyage, Captain Larsen decided to leave the five catchers behind at Patterson Inlet in New Zealand. They could (and would!) be used again during the following season. The crew from the catchers joined the 140 men onboard the *Sir James Clark Ross*. Via the route around the much-feared Cape Horn, the factory ship headed for Europe. Near the Canary Islands, the ship received orders to unload its cargo of oil in Rotterdam. After almost nine months of continous sailing, the ship dropped anchor at the Wilhelmina Harbor in Schiedam. Here the author disembarked.

Prose and Paint

Van der Does is without a doubt a fine author. I sat on the edge of my chair while reading this book in manuscript form. It really made me wonder whether I was reading a ship's journal, a tantalizing autobiographical novel, or — if at all possible — a combination of the two. The story is greatly enhanced by Van der Does's illustrations, which are excellent and exquisite in

9. Roughly speaking, one big blue whale would yield a hundred barrels of oil. A standard barrel in the U.S. contains 31 ½ gallons.

detail. Not only does Van der Does provide an astounding wealth of informa-tion about the flora and fauna of the areas he visited during his voyage to the Great Ice Barrier. He also describes with a very sharp eye everything that has to do with the sailing of a ship — be it the large *Sir James Clark Ross* or one of the relatively small catchers. Even while writing about the numerous techno-logical aspects of the ships, the author never failed to capture my attention and my imagination.

In his descriptions of natural phenomena, Van der Does more than once goes on and on, raving about the light in the sky, the colors of the ice, and the colors of the sea. He also describes all the characteristics of the differ-ent species of penguins, and devotes many sentences to the albatross. At one point he deviates from the subject of modern whaling and writes a whole chapter on Dutch whaling during the seventeenth and eighteenth centuries! Even an uninformed reader will find out soon enough that the book is writ-ten with a paintbrush, not a pen.

All this praise is not meant to suggest that Van der Does is a man with-out flaws. If modesty is considered a virtue, then Van der Does shows a lack thereof when referring to his talent for painting and sketching. On the other hand, it wil be clear to all that the author had every reason to be proud of his gift to represent what he saw on paper, with only ink and oil colors at hand! More serious are his occasional comments about life onboard. Now and then he refers to the "manly" life of the sailor and the "manly" aspects of his work. One may find legitimate reasons to crown Van der Does, in retrospect, with the negative epithet "male chauvinist."

But these aren't flaws that significantly interfere with the great story that Van der Does is telling, and as he tells it, once can glimpse other admira-ble traits in him. His sense of humor is delightful, and plays through many of the chapters. He is also clearly a compassionate man. His description of the death and burial of "Old Hans" in one of the last chapters is quite moving: one can feel shivers running down one's spine while reading about the sober ceremony, presided over by Captain Larsen. Moreover, in this chapter Van der Does reveals his own belief in God in a subtle way, as an excerpt shows:

> After that [the crew's singing of a farewell hymn] Captain Larsen read the burial service, ending with these words: "For dust thou art, and unto dust shalt thou return, and in the earth shalt thou be buried." With this he took a scoop of sand and sprinkled it over the dead man's bier. Out of a

feeling of piety the men had filled the sand chest with Norwegian scouring sand, which they had managed to locate somewhere after a long search. And thus was Gamle Hans buried, if only symbolically, in Norway, his fatherland.

A little later, Van der Does continues:

> No one moved, and the reverent silence remained unbroken. There wasn't a man there who wasn't deeply aware of the presence of a power before whose might his own flourishing life was like grass before a prairie fire. All those men stood there with taut faces and stared ahead with unseeing eyes, filled with distant, serious thoughts. No one had peeked curiously overboard when the long, flag-covered parcel shot out to sea. They weren't thinking of Old Hans anymore — that was past. Their thoughts had turned inward, and with the eyes of the soul they saw their loved ones in the far-off fatherland. These were holy moments.
>
> No sound disturbed the sacred silence other than the sighing of the wind and the splashing of the waves, which made the silence seem even greater.
>
> Then with great gravity the captain began the "Our Father." With this, the spell seemed to be broken. Everyone returned to reality. There was a nod to the bridge, the telegraph rang, and the engines began to turn again. Soon the ship resumed its course; life resumed its rights.

Later Years and Legacy

In 1946, after World War II, Van der Does returned from Indonesia to Schiedam, the city where he had lived during the 1920s. In the same year, Dutch whaling, which had come to a complete standstill in 1875, was resumed again. The Nederlandsche Maatschappij voor de Walvischvaart fitted out the factory ship *Willem Barendsz* (formerly the Swedish tanker *Pan Gothia*, 10,409 registered gross tons) for a whaling expedition to the South Pole.[10]

10. The factory ship was named after the famous Dutch explorer Willem Barentsz (active in the late sixteenth century), rightly considered the father of Dutch Arctic whaling. In 1955, after the launching of the *Willem Barendsz II*, the ship was renamed *Bloemendael*.

The officers onboard the factory ship as well as the crew on the accompanying catchers were Norwegians. A second, much larger factory ship was launched in 1955 under the name of *Willem Barendsz II* (26,830 registered gross tons). In 1957, Van der Does moved away from the rivers and harbors. He left Schiedam and set his course for Zeist, near the city of Utrecht. He lived here until his death on February 3, 1966, at the age of 76.

Van der Does's artistic oeuvre is not limited to the numerous illustrations in the two editions of his *Storm, ijs en walvisschen*. A few years after this book was first published, he illustrated the *Gedenkboek der Vereeniging van gezagvoeders en stuurlieden in Nederlandsch-Indië, 1912-1937* (Batavia, 1937). This book presents an overview of Dutch captains and first officers in the Dutch East Indies. Van der Does also illustrated the Dutch translation of Richard Henry Dana's *Two Years Before the Mast,* originally written in 1840.[11]

In addition to being an avid illustrator, Van der Does must have been a frantic photographer and a patienceless painter. In my quest for silent witnesses of Van der Does's work, I found eight photographs in the collection of the Maritiem Museum Rotterdam. The Nederlands Scheepvaartmuseum in Amsterdam harbors three photo albums containing work by Van der Does. These albums had been presented to two employees of the Koninklijke Paketvaart Maatschappij (KPM).[12]

The same museum collection contains six of Van der Does's paintings. Five of these are portraits of ships related to the Dutch East Indies: the M.S. *Overstraten* (KPM), the S.S. *Sawahloento* (KPM), the S.S. *Nieuw Holland* (KPM), the passenger liner M.S. *Tjibadak* (Java China Japan Line; painting dated 1935), and Hr. Ms. *Valk* (in the service of the Gouvernementsmarine; painting done in or after 1951).[13] The Marinemuseum in Den Helder owns a portrait of Hr. Ms. *Poolster*, like the *Valk* employed by the Gouvernementsmarine (until 1942). Finally, there is a painting by Van der Does depicting the harbor of Tandjong

---

11. *Twee jaar voor de mast* (Amsterdam, 1954). The book was translated by P. Verhoog and published again by C. de Boer Jr. in the series Bibliotheek der Zeven Zeeën (Library of the Seven Seas).

12. Mr. Baron S. van Heemstra received one album, and Mr. L. J. Lambach received two on the occasion of his farewell as president of the KPM in April 1916.

13. "Hr. Ms." stands for Hare Majesteits ("Her Majesty's"). The Gouvernementsmarine (literally, "the Governmental Navy") was established in the late nineteenth century. It was put in charge of the defense and safe-keeping of the waters within the Dutch East Indies.

Priok (Indonesia) in the collection of the Nedlloyd Shipping Company.[14] Oddly, there is only one painting by Van der Does with a whaling subject. In the painting, part of the Dutch maritime collection in the Nederlands Scheepvaartmuseum in Amsterdam, Van der Does depicts a Norwegian catcher in the Antarctic ice. The back of the painting reads "Zomerdag in Antarctic" ("A Summer's Day in the Antarctic").[15] In addition to these maritime works, there are two landscapes and one portrait of a woman by Van der Does in the collection of the Tropen Museum in Amsterdam.[16]

It is praiseworthy that Eerdmans Publishing Company has decided to share Van der Does's description of the woeful yet wonderful world of whaling with a much larger audience via this translation. Willem Jan Pieter Van der Does was a man of many talents. Up until now, many of you who wanted to appreciate them would have had to travel far to enter his world of experience. However, through this English edition of his thrilling and significant journey to the frozen world of the Antarctic, Van der Does now enters your world instead.

JOOST C. A. SCHOKKENBROEK
Curator, Nederlands Scheepvaartmuseum
Amsterdam, The Netherlands
Advisory Curator, New Bedford Whaling Museum,
New Bedford, Massachusetts

14. Here I would like to express my appreciation to Mrs. Irene Jacobs, Curator at the Maritiem Museum Rotterdam, for pointing this out to me. Reproductions of several paintings by Van der Does were recently published in *De kunst van het handel drijven: 4 eeuwen maritieme verbeelding/Art Inspired by the Sea: Four Centuries of Maritime Art*, ed. A. Oosthoek (Abcoude/Rotterdam, 2002), pp. 191-92.

15. In all likelihood the painting depicts the catcher (one of the five that accompanied the *Ross*) that got stuck in the ice sometime around New Year's Day of 1924.

16. See *Indië omlijst: Vier eeuwen schilderkunst in Nederlands-Indië*, ed. K. van Brakel et al. (Amsterdam, 1998), pp. 146-47.

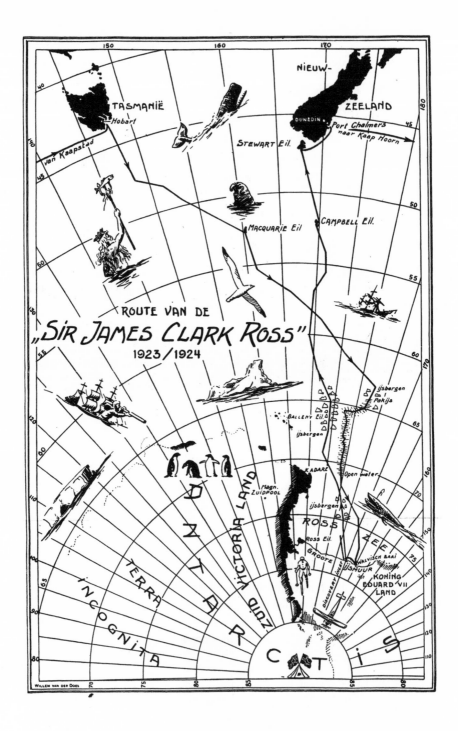

ROUTE VAN DE
„SIR JAMES CLARK ROSS"
1923/1924

WILLEM VAN DER DOES

CHAPTER ONE

First Contact with the South Polar Region

Deception

M y plan to make a trip to the polar regions wasn't an altogether new
one. But in the East Indies, where I had lived for several years, it isn't so
simple to get a feel for the frozen ends of the earth; there isn't a single connection between the tropics and the poles. And, given such extreme contrasts,
that isn't surprising. I decided that it might well be easier to find some contact
with the polar regions in Europe. Wasn't there a Dutch company that ex-
ploited coal mines in Spitsbergen? Not to mention other nations with interests in the polar areas. So the Russians might find fossil ivory on the New Si-
berian islands of the North Sea: stony bones and teeth of mammoths and
other extinct mammals. And those nice, thick polar-bear pelts that one sees
here and there in Europe must also, after all, come from the polar regions.
Stories also circulated about American sealing and whaling ships, which in

the past century dared to enter the pack-ice boundary that rings the South Polar area. So there were indeed ways to get to the polar regions.

My long, unbroken stay in the Indies played no small part in strengthening my desire to get to know the coldest places on earth. Every man appears to be born with the desire for change and the need for stark contrasts. Still, in my case, it was the artist in me that was most drawn to the pole. Day after day for years I had enjoyed the beauty and richness of nature in the Indies. And after struggling daily with the strong, vivid tropical light, so difficult to capture with paint and color, I began to long to test my powers under a wholly different light and with completely different colors. In addition to my desire to depict the frozen, barren polar landscape, I should also admit here that my strong desire for adventure increased my longing to see the polar region.

These things and more drove me to make a study trip to the wild, white, empty outer reaches of the earth — or at least attempt to do so, for it quickly became clear to me that it's much simpler to make such a plan than to carry it out. At that time — this was in 1922 — I lived in Schiedam. The varied activity in the Rotterdam harbor nearby especially attracted the sea- and ship-painter in me. With a sketchbook and a box of pastels, I often wandered all day long around the harbor, where I could always find plenty of subjects, and in all weather conditions: fog, sunshine, storm, and rain.

There, in the famous harbors of Rotterdam, I had my first contact with the polar regions. It was known that ships bearing cargoes of whale oil sometimes docked in certain Western European harbors, and there was an undeniable connection between oil and the poles. This is just as true today as it was in earlier times, when the Dutch whalers brought wealth from the waters around Spitsbergen into our northern seaports. In those neighborhoods, the many old "whale ribs"[1] that can be seen bear witness that the Hollanders used to be successful whale-hunters.

Schiedam and Vlaardingen were once also destination points for such oil-laden ships. The oil was headed for soap production or found its way to the margarine factories.

The oil ships sailed mostly under the Norwegian flag, and several had on the bow and the stern curious constructions whose function was hard to determine. These turned out to be floating oil factories — *flytende kokerier*

---

1. Van der Does puts the phrase in quotation marks because these bones were whale jawbones rather than whale ribs.

Silhouette of a flytende kokeri (floating boiler)

[floating boilers] the Norwegians called them, the so-called mother ships, to which a number of smaller chase boats belonged. The chase boats did the whale-hunting and brought the captured animals alongside the mother ship, where the carcasses were processed for oil. The unusual shape of the ship was due to the portion of the oil-producing installation onboard that was visible above deck.

But, whether it was a mother ship or a normal tanker that came to unload a cargo of oil, they always came from the Antarctic Ocean[2] or from the islands on the edge of the South Polar Region: South Georgia, the Kerguelens, the South Shetlands, or the Strait of Magellan — names that are inseparably linked with notions of grim and stalwart romanticism; names that evoke images of islands of bare rock covered with snow and ice and surrounded by tempestuous gray seas, strewn with threatening icebergs and blockaded by endless, deadly ice-fields.

And what wouldn't a man of imagination be able to see from the great black-and-white crow's nest that all the strange ships had high atop them? Wasn't a high *tönne* [crow's nest] like that the most wonderful lookout post? Not only to sight the approach of a whale from a great distance, but also to offer an unobstructed view over the whole polar world — bleak, desolate, forsaken. How fascinating it would be to look around undisturbed at the white chaos and ponder just what God had in mind when he created the immense ice wilderness, bare and uninhabitable. Standing in such a lookout post, peering out over the wide, white horizon, one might discover land that no man's eye had ever rested on before. The unknown!

2. The Antarctic Ocean, referred to here and elsewhere in the book, is, in Dutch, the poetic *Zuidelijke IJszee* — literally the "Southern Sea of Ice."

It is precisely because it is unknown that daring men are so powerfully drawn to the vague, legendary Antarctic. This mysterious southern land, whose existence the ancients already surmised on theoretical grounds, was sought after for ages without being found, because it is a secret protected by an impenetrable ring of ice fields and icebergs.

Now, in our twentieth century, as the empty white places on the globe are growing fewer and smaller, Antarctica still glitters as just about *the* only virgin white spot on world maps. It is all still terra incognita. Only a few bits of the capricious coastline and a few islands are known. Those great, mysterious, silent voids are what have drawn men like Ross, Scott, and Amundsen with irresistible force.

I BOARDED every whaler that docked in Antwerp, Rotterdam, and Bremen. On all these oil ships there was an unusually unpleasant smell of rancid oil; they really reeked. And yet that scent always wakes raw, strong, romantic memories. It's a good sort of romance, the kind Herman Melville and Jack London know how to portray.

Aboard such ships, I felt as if I already had one foot in the polar region, and it took no small amount of courage for me to try to convince the captains to take me on as a passenger on the next trip poleward. But they always stubbornly refused to give my request and reasons a hearing. In retrospect, this doesn't seem so surprising, because even though I was bound and determined to head toward the Pole, I made the mistake of introducing myself only as a painter wanting to go along as a passenger, with the goal of taking every opportunity to paint. That there would be no shortage of subjects I knew very well. The typical activities of the whale hunt and life onboard — these alone would offer plenty of rewarding study material, enough to keep me busy the whole trip. But especially the polar region itself, with its grim, completely untouched landscape, would demand to be captured on paper and canvas, while the ever-changing beauty of air and water on the long trip to the far south, the wonderful wealth of color of sky and sea at sunrise and sunset, wouldn't leave much time to let palette and pencil rest. And then there would be the wild splendor of the ocean swept up in stormy weather. There is for the painter no more gratifying subject than the sea, the full ocean in bad weather, as the primal forces of air and water are let loose. Storms that test men also make them — and frequently kill them.

No, not a single one of those whaling captains thought for one second of taking a painter along. Men who are accustomed to the hard life of the polar seas and earn their bread that way mostly tend to be so down-to-earth and practical that they must consider an artist to be a completely useless and incomprehensible being. The life of the mind of such Viking types is poles apart[3] from that of artists, so different that mutual understanding is out of the question.

These stalwart lads never said it, but their whole bearing clearly implied that they wouldn't even think of being cooped up for the whole trip to the hunting fields with a nuisance like me. Such an artistic type would naturally be always and everywhere in the way, seasick the whole time, and, worst of all, constantly asking the most inane questions and saying crazy things about subjects that nobody had the slightest interest in. I would be an endless irritation, and a foreigner to boot, who didn't know a word of Norwegian.

So, not surprisingly, they all let me know that there could be no possibility of taking me along, even if they were too polite to give me the real reasons for their refusal.

ONE DAY a four-masted ship, the *Fortuna*, docked in Schiedam. It came from Deception Island, off the coast of Graham Land, far to the south of Tierra del Fuego, where it had taken over a cargo of oil from some whale hunters. It was a cold autumn day when the ship arrived in Holland, and some of the crew had their polar gear on: jackets of sheep and seal fur, fur hats, and Laplander *finneskoë*, tall seaboots lined with fur. These fellows — tall, blond Norwegians — could have stepped right off the ships of the Norse sea-kings who once plundered and pillaged the coasts of Western Europe.

The tall masts and the tangles of piled, coiled rope were deeply fascinating, and the sturdy chaps would have inspired Kipling to write a Viking novel. There was certainly a romantic aura about the whole ship. What wouldn't I have given to go along to the far south with them! But I was no luckier here than I had been with the other ships, although I might have had a chance had I been able to speak Spanish. At least the captain asked me about that. He himself seemed to have some problems in that department. He didn't know the language of the *caballeros* either, though the ship was from the Compania de Pesca Argentina, and its home port was Punta Arenas. So he

---

3. This pun is regrettably not in the original, but is actually the closest English image to the Dutch word Van der Does uses here: *hemelsbreed*, "wide as the heavens."

The drunken captain

would gladly have had someone onboard who could speak Spanish. I thought I might be able to make myself useful by finding him a laundryman, a baker, and other tradesmen. But that was no good. There wasn't a chance that I was going to feel the deck of this ship rock under my feet. If only I had known Spanish!

Another time I found a four-masted schooner laid up in a quiet corner. It turned out to be an oil carrier too, which had last carried oil from Grytviken in South Georgia. The ship was chartered by Lever Brothers Ltd., the makers of Sunlight soap, who had a factory in Vlaardingen. The ship was almost deserted; only a watchman was on board, and I found the captain drunk in the galley. He wasn't in any condition to talk, and in any case the ship was laid up for the time being.

By persistent searching and inquiring, I also found out that there was a Dutch ship that sailed regularly to the Kerguelens, where it fetched elephant-seal oil. There's a land station on those islands where these colossal seals are captured and processed into oil. The owners of that ship, a tanker named the *Sultan of Langkat,* gladly gave me permission to take a trip with them.

Since the Kerguelens are French, it would have been simple to get permission to go along on the seal hunt from the French consulate in The Hague. But there was a problem: these islands lie on the edge of the South Polar Region, and at this point I had really set my sights on seeing the land of the Pole itself. So I declined the owners' friendly offer, although with some hesitation. I didn't know then whether I was actually going to manage to find a whaler that really would be willing to take me along to the true Antarctic Ocean. But usually "slow and steady wins the race."[4]

When by the summer of 1923 I had unsuccessfully tried every whaler that docked in Antwerp, Schiedam, Vlaardingen, Bremen, and Liverpool, I decided to put my head in the lion's mouth and go to Norway. The whole of modern whaling is in the hands of Norwegians, and they sail from a number of harbors on the southeast coast. It occurred to me that if I could go there and talk to the owners myself, my chances of success would be considerably greater.

4. Here Van der Does uses the phrase *de taaie aanhouder wint wel:* "The tough customer gets the best deal" or "The persistent player wins the game."

CHAPTER TWO

Mustered on a Whaler

Whalers in Sandefjord

S hortly thereafter fortune smiled on me when the *Thor I* came to Rotter-dam.

After this whaler had unloaded its oil for a margarine factory, it needed a crew to sail the ship on to Norway. This sort of mobile oil-factory needs a much larger crew for oil-processing and for whale-hunting than is normal for an ordinary tanker. It's customary, immediately upon arriving in the destination harbor, to discharge almost the entire crew and send them back to Norway. This is done for reasons of economy. After the tasks of unloading and making necessary repairs are completed, only a skeleton crew is kept to take the ship to Norway, where it is prepared again for the next trip to the polar sea.

Other than the officers, not a single member of the crew of the *Thor I* was kept on. I wasn't much interested in why this happened; what interested

8

me was that the ship needed a new crew to get to Norway. I didn't let this chance pass me by, because from Norway the *Thor I* was headed to South Georgia to go whale-hunting to the south, around the Sandwich Islands.

I signed on as a sailor for the trip from Rotterdam to Sandefjord via Cardiff and eagerly took the opportunity to do active service on a ship that was really going to the Antarctic Ocean. And gradually I came to imagine that since I was now, after all, mustered on, there would be a good chance that I could also stay on and go along on the trip to South Georgia, most certainly if the officers were pleased with my work as a deckhand. I didn't worry about this; once you've been a seaman — as I had — you know what needs to be done on board, and on the high seas you learn to use your hands.[1]

Mustering on and departure went rather quickly, so there was no time for me to assemble respectable polar gear. That might in any case be better done in Norway, I thought. So I went to sea on the *Thor I* outfitted very primitively; only my painting supplies, as my first priority, were completely in order. I said long-term good-byes to family and friends, for I would certainly not be seen in Holland again anytime soon.

The trip to Sandefjord proceeded uneventfully. I made friends with the captain, who quickly realized that this Dutch sailor wasn't just another ordinary seaman. Long before we set eyes on Norway, he had promised to arrange for me to go along to South Georgia. This suited me just fine. Once in South Georgia, I was sure I would easily find the opportunity to push on farther toward the Pole. That was a matter to deal with later. Unfortunately, the captain couldn't keep his word to me; he got sick in Sandefjord and had to give up his command to someone else. But, however things might turn out later, on this ship I already felt as if I stood with one foot in the polar world. Naturally, conversations were mostly about subjects having to do with hunting in the ice, and there was much to learn on board for the man who kept his eyes and ears open.

ARRIVING IN Sandefjord, the primary Norwegian whale-hunting port, one became enveloped in a place whose very atmosphere was permeated with oil and ice. Several large whalers were docked there, either ready to begin the

---

1. As Van der Does notes in Chapter 26, he had worked for some years as a helmsman in the Dutch Merchant Marine, plying the well-worn colonial route from Amsterdam to the Dutch East Indies (now Indonesia).

To sea as a sailor

long trip to the south or bustling with people making final preparations. But all had as their destination somewhere in the Antarctic. Modern whaling is almost completely concentrated there, and no more in the Arctic, as was once the case.

The earlier hunting-grounds in the far north have been fished completely empty, and whales are so scarce there nowadays that for the large modern whalers it isn't worthwhile to ply their trade there. So everything having to do with whale oil now heads south, where the whales have for eons been able to breed undisturbed.

At anchor in the fjord lay the whalers, with their tall oil-kettles on the fore- and after-deck, and also a number of large sailing ships that were going to fetch cargoes of oil barrels from the Antarctic.

But a wrench got thrown into the works. The crew that came on board the *Thor I* in Rotterdam had been mustered to Sandefjord, and according to Norwegian law, once we reached that destination harbor, those of us who weren't Norwegians had to be sent home again by the ship's owners. No jobless foreigners were allowed in Norway.

After the discharge, the three Dutchmen, the Lithuanian, and the Englishman were taken into custody by the police, who were to provide us with further transport to Oslo. I didn't resist being sent there. In the capital, I laid out the whole story to the Dutch consulate, and with their help I received permission to stay in Norway for two weeks. I used this time to visit all the owners in Larvik, Tönsberg, Sandefjord, and Oslo who had whaling ships. Nowhere did I succeed in my quest. But meanwhile the news reached me that the biggest ship of the year, the 12,000-ton *Sir James Clark Ross*, was being prepared for an expedition to the Great Ice Barrier,[2] beyond the almost impenetrable barrier of the pack ice, which up to now had called an inexorable halt to every normal vessel. In a few weeks the ship was to begin its voyage to the almost unknown Ross Sea, in the heart of the South Polar Region.

Once I heard of this unusually rare opportunity, I was bound and determined not to leave Norway except on that ship — as a stowaway, if need be. One way or another, it just had to bring me to the Great Ice Barrier, that immense natural wonder.

I set up camp in the Hotel Atlantic in Sandefjord, where the leader of the expedition, Captain C. A. Larsen, was also staying. Immediately I buttonholed him and explained my plans — and also spoke with the owners, the consulate, and countless others, even those who might have only a little influence. But none of it did any good. I was told that the whole expedition had been planned long ago, down to the smallest detail, and there wasn't a single place left onboard. But it wasn't in me to let myself be knocked off the playing field just like that. Every day I made my arguments again, until I became so annoying that I even began to annoy myself, and I almost lost heart because of the consistently negative results of my quest.

I must have seemed like a hopelessly irritating and unusually tenacious fellow. I even tried to convince the owner's wife — and there I was in luck. Maybe she took pity on me when she saw how all my attempts had been ship-

2. What Van der Does nearly always names *De Groote IJsmuur* ("The Great Wall of Ice") is today called the Ross Ice Shelf. It is the world's largest body of floating ice, the size of France (about 500,000 square kilometers or 200,000 square miles). First seen by ship — by the British explorer James Clark Ross in 1841 — it appeared as a great white barrier wall of ice up to 60 meters (200 feet) high and 800 kilometers (500 miles) wide, and was named accordingly: The Great Ice Barrier. But in the early twentieth century, the shelf was climbed and served as a gateway for explorations of the Antarctic interior, including the famed polar journeys of Shackleton, Amundsen, and Scott. The shelf is fed by glaciers on the East Antarctic polar ice sheet, and changes shape constantly by calving and melting as the shelf advances northward. Despite being on a ship full of Norwegians — and Norway being the nation whose skiing expertise had made the Ross Ice Shelf a "highway to the Pole" rather than a barrier — Van der Does uses the British-tinged name of "Great Wall of Ice," common at the time.

wrecked and had left me in despair. That night I had tried once again to soften up Captain Larsen, but again to no avail. So I had decided I would leave Sandefjord and try once more in Tönsberg, where maybe I stood a small chance of mustering on the *Örnen,* which was sailing for the Falkland Islands.

But the following evening, as I was heading for the train, Captain Larsen intercepted me. He said that Mrs. Rasmussen, the owner's wife, had convinced him — against his inclination — to take that Dutch painter along on the *Ross.*

"Will you work?" he asked.

"Of course, captain," I assured him. "It doesn't matter to me what I do, just so long as I can come along."

"Then in God's name muster on as a laborer," answered Larsen.

Not an hour later I had already signed the contract to work as a laborer on the *Sir James Clark Ross.* I would make the trip to the Ross Sea at a wage of 130 kroners per month and with a bonus of 2 öre per barrel of any whale oil that might be processed.

Imagine my unbridled joy! An hour before, I was at the point of leaving, with all my hopes dashed, and now I suddenly had full certainty of reaching my long-envisioned goal! I took the contract that guaranteed me all this and stowed it safely in my wallet.

I cabled the news home right away with the request that my baggage be sent immediately to Sandefjord. It was urgent because we were to leave in just a week.

OBVIOUSLY a strong, healthy body is the first requirement to be able to live and work successfully in the polar regions. And so the crew of a whaler is examined very carefully. Here things nearly fell apart for me, because the medical examiner found that my spleen was enlarged, the result of a long-ago bout of malaria. Fortunately, he approved me, laughing, when I said that this voyage would provide the long-sought-after opportunity to freeze the last of the malaria out of me.

Mustering on went without a hitch, and then it was just a matter of waiting for the departure, which was set for September 22, 1923.

A few days beforehand there was already work to be done onboard. The equipment for the long trip through the ice had to be loaded and stowed away. That was all unusually instructive and interesting. The whole tween-deck of the forward hold was set up to store the hunting tackle: the harpoon cannons, the harpoon lines, and the harpoons.

Nowdays whales are no longer caught by manually launching harpoons, the method our forefathers employed; cannons are used. This makes the hunt much simpler and safer, albeit at the same time less romantic. The harpoon lines with which a captured whale is secured are made from the best manila rope, which need not be heavy but is still sufficiently strong. A cannon-launched harpoon can travel a remarkable distance with such rope attached to it without its direction changing. A harpoon like this is something quite different from a bent pin or a fish-hook — what my friends and I used as schoolboys to try to catch minnows and roaches. They're heavy, and it isn't pleasant to drag them around on your shoulder all day, especially if you aren't fortunate enough to own a shoulder callus.

I surveyed from all angles and with more than usual interest the pieces of equipment for sledge trips across the ice: the ingeniously constructed sledges, very light but strong; the long skis; the ski poles; and the light tents. Later we would probably become much more closely acquainted with all these things. A whole packet of boards and beams would be very useful if we found it necessary to overwinter and build quarters on land or on ice. Why long bamboo poles might be needed on a polar journey was not so easy for me to guess. Not surprisingly, a great number of provisions were loaded on board, since they had to last two hundred men for two years.

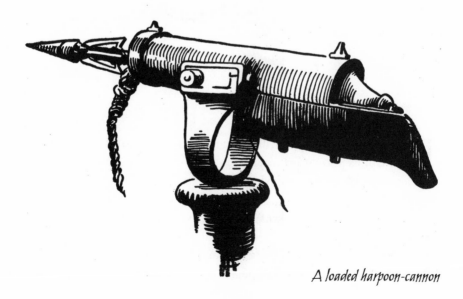

A loaded harpoon-cannon

CHAPTER THREE

The Expedition's Ship and Crew

The Sir James Clark Ross at the wharf in Sandefjord

The background of the expedition, whose story will be told in the following chapters, is of little importance to the reader. I just want to say here that Captain Carl Anton Larsen was the father and organizer of the expedition.

Captain Larsen, who was already over sixty years old, had long since earned his stripes, not only in whale-hunting but also in polar research. For many years now he had not actively taken part in it. But he knew that the hunt for oil was a rich source of wealth for his fatherland, Norway. He also knew that he had only a few years left to live. He suffered from heart disease, which was bound to send him to his grave soon. But before the end came, this valiant descendant of Vikings wanted to perform just one more great service for his country by opening up a rich new source of income. As the known hunting grounds came to yield less and less bounty, he wanted to open up a larger and richer area for whaling and at the same time put whale-hunting on a broader and more modern footing.

The reports of the Ross and Scott expeditions had convinced him that in the Ross Sea, at the foot of the Great Ice Barrier and beyond the formidable barrier of pack ice that separated that sea from the open ocean, whales were more plentiful than anywhere else in the world. A careful study of the expedition diaries had also convinced him that the Ross Sea must be largely ice-free during the very short Antarctic summer, in January and February. In addition, he was certain that with a sturdy steel ship with sufficiently strong engines it wouldn't be impossible, as had always been thought, to clear a way through the dreaded pack ice.

Supported by this conviction, he cultivated the necessary interest and raised the funding indispensable to carrying out his plan: a hunting expedition to the Great Ice Barrier. So in the spring of 1923, the *Mahronda* was purchased, a 12,500-ton, 150-meter-long English freighter. It was rebuilt as a tanker while also being transformed into a *flytende kokeri*, a floating oil-factory. So that the ship could better withstand the great pressure of the ice, heavy iron crossbeams were laid in the bow, and the whole front of the ship, above and below the waterline, was covered in a heavy oaken ice hull to take the direct force of the ice and to prevent it from penetrating the steel hull-plates.

Experience had taught that wooden barrels were less suitable for transporting oil from the poles via the tropics to Europe, because they would start to leak from the great temperature changes, and much oil would be lost. So the below-decks were transformed into watertight tanks to store the captured oil.

The ballast tanks could hold about 2,000 tons of fresh water. That was reckoned on an average usage of 80 to 100 tons per day. This was the quantity necessary for the oil boilers. Because it probably wouldn't be possible to find fresh water in the hunting grounds, two evaporators were built in, which could convert about 60 tons of fresh water out of seawater every day.

The ship also got a wireless station — three kilowatts Marconi. At departure we didn't have high expectations of the wireless: we doubted whether we would be able to remain in contact with the inhabited world from deep in the South Polar Region.

But the equipment turned out to be better than we had dared hope. Although the nights at 78° S latitude are very clear during the polar summer, and thus significant disturbances occur, we were able, for instance, in the Bay of Whales, under the Great Ice Barrier (78° 26′ S and 195° 45′ E), to make contact with Awarua Station in New Zealand (46° 30′ S and 168° 23′ E) over a distance of 2,034 nautical miles. At the 78th south parallel we also heard Sydney and received telegrams over a distance of 2,855 miles. Under the Great Ice Barrier we were able to synchronize our chronometers to the time signal from Nauen [twenty miles west of Berlin], which came from a distance of 9,248 miles.

It is of incalculable worth to be able to maintain contact with the inhabited world when a ship is separated from it by such an expanse of sea and ice. Although we weren't able to transmit over such great distances, we were able to receive, and thus we stayed up-to-date with the most important world events. Almost daily we had our bulletin, copies of which the radioman put up in the cabin, the mess room, the crew's quarters, and the *pinguinleie*, the "penguin deck," as the workers' quarters were so colorfully called. You can just imagine with what interest everyone read those bulletins. But I still vividly remember how we often turned away annoyed if the world news turned out to contain nothing but the results of a boxing match.

THE "penguin deck" was where I and my fellow laborers — about forty men — lived. This area took up the front half of the tweendecks of the forward hold, which had been specially built for this purpose and fitted out as living quarters. The name "penguin deck" arose thanks to the striking similarity it bore to a penguin colony. It was as crowded as a penguin colony, and during lunchtime or on nights off it was also as noisy. The only difference was that there are several hundred thousand penguins in a breeding area which cause all the ruckus, while the forty fellows in this camp created a rather higher volume of sound. Sometimes the racket was really deafening, if people were in high spirits and the harmonica — the sailors' organ — entered the mix, and the "penguin deck" resounded with sailor songs (usually not very chaste), or if a free-for-all broke out, which usually happened if the men had managed to get their hands on hard liquor.

At the head of the expedition stood Captain Larsen, who wasn't only the spiritual father of the undertaking but also in all other respects like a father to everyone. This was partly because of his age, but much more because of the outstanding gifts of head and heart that he possessed. He was a Norseman of that fine old make: courageous, energetic, self-confident, and completely honest. As the leader of the expedition, he was perfectly equal to his task. He knew everything that had to do with whaling; since childhood he had been familiar with the Antarctic and with navigating in the ice.

When he was still in the prime of his life, he was in command of a hunting expedition to the Antarctic (1892-1894) on the *Jason*, the same ship that the dean of scientific polar research, the great Nansen, took to the east coast of Greenland, from which he began his famous trip across that island. On this trip with the *Jason*, Larsen discovered, in addition to a number of islands, King Oscar II Land. He also penetrated past 68° 10′ S, an achievement of legendary proportions for that time which caused great amazement.

Larsen was always keenly interested in all the scientific questions posed by the polar regions. His special scientific contribution was being the first to bring fossils from the land of the South Pole, Antarctica, by which it could be proved that sedimentary layers existed there. This love for scientific research led him, in his forties, to take the nautical command of the Swedish South Pole expedition under Otto Nordenskjöld, from 1901 to 1903. This was an unusually adventurous voyage during which the expedition ship sank in the Antarctic Ocean, a voyage as rich in romance and adventure as usually occurs only in fables and fantasy novels (Nordenskjöld, *Antarctic: Two Years in Ice and Snow*).

So Larsen felt completely at home in the middle of the ice and on the tempestuous seas that had managed to keep Antarctica untouched for so long and warded off the ever-further advances of *Homo sapiens* and civilization. He was one of those Viking types that don't come our way much these days, and only very rarely occur at all, with an irresistible iron will, the type that needs danger and adventure to live, the true breed of explorer, whose greatness and strength only grow as the difficulties increase.

We all watched the 64-year-old with wonder and affection as he manned the ice lookout on the foretop night after night and gave orders when the ship was laboriously picking its way through the pack ice. This was a man who had already retired ten years earlier and had lived the good life on his country estate in the middle of fields and woods. Now his inner drive had propelled him to take up the mighty struggle with the polar region in order to offer with his final powers one last, great service to his country.

And how that man could tell stories, he who had lived through so much and had so many tales to tell! He had a most unique and unusually exhilarating way of spinning out yarns, which pulled everyone along thrillingly as if in a strong current. It didn't matter whether he was recounting how as a lad of nine he saw his first whale, or was painting with pithy and powerful words the wreck of the *Antarctica* when that ship sank under the sea ice in February of 1902.

SUCH A MAN was Captain Larsen, the *bestyrer* (leader) of our expedition, a position that compared with that of Merchant in the days of the East India Company. The actual nautical pilot was Captain Alf Kaldager. He was no polar expert like Larsen, but he was an unusually good sailor and also shared the captain's special interest in science. This quality in the two leaders was all to the good for the expedition's scientific results, although both men were required to ensure first of all that the expedition reaped financial rewards. The whole purpose of the expedition was economic: scientific research was allowed only if the monetary interests of the shareholders were not harmed thereby.

Kaldager, although a very different sort than Larsen, was an open and agreeable man, and highly educated. Although after the trip to the far south our paths diverged widely, we met each other again from time to time. He became a captain on ships in the Klaveness line, and he would let me know in advance when he was coming to Surabaja, and

Captain C. A. Larsen

then we would dig up all sorts of memories from our time on the ice. Even though during that voyage he had been a captain and I a simple laborer, polar travel brings men in close contact with each other, and difference in rank exists only in connection with work.

The first mate, Olaf Wegger, was a committed whaler with plenty of experience in hunting and a very good seaman, even by Norwegian standards. So it was all the more the pity that he was such an unusually close friend of Bacchus, which caused serious problems from time to time. Later his love of drink even cost him his life. On another expedition a year after ours, he fell overboard in a drunken stupor and drowned. Despite his failures, Wegger was everyone's friend because of his intrepid and cheerful nature. He was a fine fellow, and there wasn't a man on deck who wasn't at his beck and call, especially because in every circumstance where courage and resolution were needed, he was first in line and knew no difficulty or fatigue.

Our second mate, Gjertsen, was a captain of the Norwegian navy. Because of his exceptional gifts he had received special leaves of absence several times already, such as he had now as well. When Roald Amundsen made his legendary trip to the South Pole, Captain Gjertsen was the pilot on the old *Fram*, the ship that brought Amundsen's expedition to the Great Ice Barrier. So Gjertsen had already twice braved the wide barrier of the pack ice that encloses the open Ross Sea, and thus was the designated man on our expedition to do service as ice pilot. Gjertsen was one of those many men who was irresistibly attracted to the poles. Later he became governor of Spitsbergen, the modern Svalbard.

Andersen, the third mate, was an experienced old pole-rat who had battled both the Arctic and the Antarctic oceans many times. He most liked to tell of his trip on the *Stella Polare* to Franz Josef Land, under the Duke of Abruzzi.

Then there was my friend, Dr. Ludwig Kohl, the expedition doctor, nicknamed "The Pill." He was German and the son-in-law of Captain Larsen. Besides being a doctor, he pulled teeth when it was required, healed wounds, put frozen hands, noses, and feet back in shape, and if need be prescribed excellent brandy for those who needed a pick-me-up. He was an all-around learned man; his specialties were geology, zoology, and meteorology.

He had the restless heart of a wanderer; he had been to the Antarctic Ocean with Filchner on the *Deutschland*. He spent the World War in Mesopotamia after being taken prisoner by the Japanese on Yap, the cable station in the

Painting in the doctor's laboratory

Pacific. He wrote about his various trips, and with pleasure I illustrated his interesting books about Lapland and the South Sea Islands.

Unfortunately, after the trip on the *Ross*, we quickly lost track of each other. Recently, though, I heard from him again, when he made the great flight with the *Graf Zeppelin* — just the thing for him.

The second scientific member of the expedition was the Swedish zoologist Sten Vallin, a charming young fellow and a pleasant companion. His special fields were plankton and oceanography. During the voyage he made zoological collections for Swedish universities. I spent many of my free hours in the laboratory where the two scientists on the *Ross* were set up. There I often found a safe refuge to be able to paint undisturbed.

It did happen sometimes that the whole ship was in an uproar because Bill — the name I answered to then — was nowhere to be found, and the men were convinced that "the Hollander" had fallen overboard. Eventually they learned where they could find him when he wasn't in any of his usual haunts, but usually they left him there in peace. Then they would say that his assistance was required for the cause of science. Actually, that was frequently the case, but at the same time, the number of my painting studies grew, right along with the number of specimens preserved in alcohol and the stuffed penguins and the deep-sea creatures. The products of the combined zeal of these men of science eventually so filled the laboratory that art was hard-pressed for space. Finally there was no place left for me to paint; all the room on the tables was taken over by microscopes, bottled specimens, and interesting but foul-smelling whale parasites. That was bad enough. But when "The Pill" compounded disaster by hanging a pair of undressed albatrosses from the ceiling, which boxed my ears left and right with every roll of the ship, it got to be too much, and I fled to the salon. I had already moved my finished painting studies there some time earlier, because penguin feathers and other less identifiable parts of the collected sea creatures would get stuck in the wet paint, which wasn't exactly flattering for the studies.

ABOUT MOST of the men onboard there's not much to tell. All of them were driven by a lust for adventure, and many had had highly unusual careers — as, for example, Pisani, the Norwegian with the Italian name, who was the national wrestling champion of Norway. It's not my intent to write about all that, although the men of the *Ross* could have provided the fodder for many a novel.

One of them I'll never forget, because his life was so dominated by the South Polar Region, and at the age of 54 he still dreamed day and night of seeing the mysterious Antarctic one more time. This was the German Karl Klick, who was in charge of the two oil-boilers in the afterdeck. There, under high-pressure steam, oil was coaxed from the tremendous whale jaws. In his youth Klick spent several years in New Guinea. He went with Drygalski as the cook on the *Gauss,* and went back again to the South Pole area as the cook on the *Deutschland* under Filchner. On both expeditions he turned out to be an indispensable jack-of-all-trades. In normal life he was a customs agent and paced the treadmill of daily routine. But he actually had a sort of double life. In the one, he did his daily duty as an ordinary citizen: cared for his family, showed up at the office on time, and went home right when the clock struck closing time. But in his other and probably more real life, he was a completely different being, burning with an adventurous spirit. His South Polar dream was finally fulfilled when, near the end of 1923, we left the pack-ice barrier behind us and neared the Great Ice Barrier, which had beckoned him in dreams so often and so urgently.

The ship, which had been rechristened the *Sir James Clark Ross,* after the famous polar explorer by that name, had in addition to the normal crew before the mast an even greater number of men onboard whose special task it was to process the whales and man the oil-refinery installations. These were the oil boilers, the flensers or blubber cutters, and the blubber grinders.

These men lived in lodgings under the portside, along with the smiths, the bosun, and the carpenter, who was also a diver and for whom a complete diving outfit had been taken along. There was always the possibility that the ship might spring a leak while in the ice. Then the damage had to be exam-

In the slop chest

ined underwater before it could be repaired. There, far in the south, men are entirely dependent on their own resources. And indeed, the *Ross* did suffer a nasty leak during the trip through the ice, and the carpenter-diver had every opportunity to show his expertise. Farther back on the "penguin deck" lived the gang workers, whose job was to do whatever came up. The usual complement of deckhands and machine workers lived in back on the poop deck. And, last but not least, the officers were lodged amidships, as was customary.

An unusual crew member was the ship's clerk. I never really figured out what his duties were, exactly; I think that he was something like an administrator. But he was a companionable fellow, and popular, even if most valued as keeper of the slop chest that we had onboard with us, which hearkened back to the days of sailing ships. The slop chest was a warehouse in business format — or, more precisely, ship format — where those aboard could buy, at reasonable prices, practically everything that a sailor on a polar expedition might need. This meant first of all smoking materials — tobacco, chewing tobacco, pipes, cigars, and cigarettes — and all sorts of sailors' clothing and gear: woolen underwear, sweaters, work clothes, blankets, oilskins, Icelandic sweaters, caps and other headgear, socks, seaboots, knives, and so forth. One could even buy needles, buttons, thread, shoe leather, and nails, as well as reindeer fur for sleeping bags.

This miniature warehouse may have been called a slop chest, but it was no chest. On the *Ross* a few empty cabins were set up as the slop chest, and every day the store was open during certain hours. They're a very useful in-

stitution, these "slops"; I've gotten many an outfit and countless sweaters, oilskins, and mittens
from them, and many a piece of leather to repair
seaboots. Oh yes, you learn all kinds of things as
a whaler: not only do you quickly learn to speak
Norwegian, albeit Norwegian with a decidedly oily
finish, but also, in addition to all the other useful
things, clothes-making and shoe repair. Experience has shown that a slop chest is essential on
a whaler, because it's a peculiar sort of person
that is drawn to whaling. On the long trip to
the south and during the hunting season, the
crew earn a lot of money without having any
way to spend it. But once they get back on land
with a full purse, there's no stopping them. Then
the fruits of their labor are laid out long and well
until they're all gone, and they land completely
bankrupt on another whaler, and everything they
own for a trip toward the Pole usually fits in a red
handkerchief.

The tönne (crow's nest) on a whaler

That's when the slop chest serves a good purpose, and the guys aren't so particular about the
size of their seaboots. If, for example, they're a few
sizes too big, then a few extra pairs of stockings
fill up the extra room quite effectively; a spot of
caulking also does some good. If a pair of pants
is too long, they simply cut the legs to fit. And
an overly large cap or southwester is taken up
with a bit of sailor's thread.

The entire crew of the *Sir James Clark Ross*
numbered 140, but the whole expedition con-
sisted of nearly 200 men. The other 60 formed the crew of the five chase
boats that accompanied the mother ship. These chase boats were named *Star
1*, *Star 2*, *Star 3*, *Star 4*, and *Star 5*. Two of these had already gone out to Hobart
in Tasmania; the other three went there from Seattle in the United States. The
trip to the south would start from Hobart. The chase boat is a small but very
seaworthy vessel weighing about 90 tons. It hunts whales, harpoons them

with a harpoon cannon that's positioned far forward on the prow, and then brings the dead animals alongside the mother ship, where they are processed. A crow's nest hangs high on the mast, and from there the movements of a whale are carefully observed by a lookout. The captain, who is also the gunner, always mans the harpoon cannon himself.

The real whale-hunters are the men on these small chase boats, who brave all sorts of weather. They are a breed apart: raw, strong, and fearless. They do the hardest work under the worst conditions, such that only fellows with iron constitutions and muscles of steel can stand up to the hard life on these chasers. You can't imagine how hard life is on this kind of chase boat unless you've experienced months on turbulent seas, and being hurled to and fro so violently that you have to be lashed into your berth, and having to brace yourself in a corner somewhere to wolf down a bowl of hot soup. On deck your life is in danger all the time, and you always run a good chance of having a wave wash over you. That by itself is fairly unpleasant, but it gets truly disagreeable when it freezes hard, and your clothes freeze into a stiff suit of armor around your body. I have a great deal of respect for the fellows on the chase boats; they are completely fearless and tough as steel.

With a few exceptions, all the members of the expedition were Norwegians. For a long time now the whole whaling industry has been in Norwegian hands, and an entire category of men has developed who make their living exclusively by whaling and are very experienced at it. So whaling has become a thriving and very profitable business for Norway.

CHAPTER FOUR

From Sandefjord to the Cape of Good Hope

The departure

———∽∾∽———

On the 22nd of September 1923, the *Sir James Clark Ross* glided out over the still water of the bay of Sandefjord. It was a peaceful, still evening, with no wind. Slowly, almost imperceptibly, the light disappeared, leaving delicate pastel tints in the hazy west. Distant lights popped up here and there from solitary houses along the fjord, winking farewells and casting flickering strands of light that seemed to creep toward the ship as if they wanted to give a last, silent greeting. As the darkness finally fell, and the contours of hill and dale were obscured by the night, all of us, some more consciously than others, took final leave in thought of everyone we had left behind.

The great voyage had begun.

Although the ship wasn't completely ready, the leader of the expedition didn't want to delay the departure any longer, and rightly so. He knew that already toward the end of October the whales began to migrate southward from the warm coasts of South Africa and Australia, and our trip to Tasmania would take about two months. It was from Tasmania that the trip to the Antarctic Ocean would begin.

According to the old sea-hands, we left Sandefjord under good omens. Once we were offshore, two cats were discovered onboard. And when, moreover, on the second day at sea three little kittens were born, it was irre-futably clear to the superstitious seamen that the trip would be a success in every way. They were completely sure of this, just as much as they would have been convinced of an unlucky trip had the *Ross* set out to sea on a Friday. Not a single whaler ever sets sail on a Friday. Sailors are always very superstitious, and whaling is without doubt a very risky business, especially in the Antarctic.

The first few days at sea one could easily have thought that the ship still lay undisturbed alongside the wharf at Sandefjord, due to the deafening din of riveting and hammering that rang out everywhere onboard, on the fore-, aft-, and tweendecks.

Due to our hasty departure, a number of details were no-where near ready, and the wharf had sent the necessary bosses and workers along as far as Cardiff, where the *Ross* would pick up its load of coal. In Barry, where we began taking on pit-coal, the ship was first set in dry dock. This was necessary because, while lying still at the wharf in Norway, the part of the ship's hull that lay under the waterline had developed such a welter of fauna that the voyage would have been considerably hindered, as the stretch from Sandefjord to Barry made very clear.

In dry dock, the whole army of laborers went to work scrubbing, slicing, and scouring, so that in less than a day the whole ship's hull under the waterline was not only cleaned but sported a nice new coat of growth-resistant paint.

Good-luck cat

The reporters in Cardiff

Meanwhile, the newspaper reporters had sniffed out a lead and streamed over the ship, looking for copy. Everyone onboard who spoke English was accosted to give information and details about the expedition, and already the following day there were articles yards long about us in the papers. That's when we realized that we had some pretty serviceable jokers among the crew of the *Ross*, who had managed to convince the reporters of the most ridiculous nonsense.

In Barry Dock we loaded 9,200 tons of coal; the tanks and the holds were full to the brim, and the rest stayed on deck.

You can just imagine the nightmare of loading coal. Day and night, with irregular breaks, the black gold was taken up into the ship by the ton with a thundering uproar. Amid all that the men called, shouted, and cussed, as the black shadows loomed up and disappeared again in the thick clouds of coal dust. You can imagine how eventually absolutely everything turned black, and the coal dust penetrated everywhere, every nook and cranny stopped up and filled in. By the end, men not only walked all over the ship covered in coal; they slept in it and ate it. The white crew turned completely black; with blinking white eyes they spooned black soup out of their mess tins and ate black bully-beef and black hardtack.

Luckily there's a nice beach among the rocks near Barry Dock where we could go roll off the extra coal dust now and then, and you can bet that's just what we did.

It's understandable that Captain Larsen wanted to take along as much good, cheap Cardiff coal as possible. We would need an unbelievably huge amount of it, and there also aren't any coal bunker stations in the Antarctic.

And so, during the coal-loading, although they hadn't specially intended to, the men quickly began to paint the outer hull, especially amidships, where the Plimsoll lines were hidden under the weight of a huge layer of the black stuff, so that the harbor authorities wouldn't be able to see that the *Ross* was loaded about a foot over the legal limit. Finally, the ammo dump on the poop deck was also crammed full of ammunition for the harpoon cannons, along with other explosives.

ON THE SIXTH of October the last purchases were made, and that same evening the *Ross* began her long journey to Tasmania, around the Cape of Good Hope: a trip of sixty days between sky and water, without putting in at a single harbor.

For anyone who loves the sea, such a long ocean voyage is exhilarating. It is an endless pleasure to observe the play of wind and waves, the floating clouds, along with the life of the creatures in the sky and water. Don't think that we had much time to notice this. On the contrary, there was work in

The sailmaker

abundance. Everything had to be put in order for the hunt. Once we were in the Antarctic, there would be absolutely no time for that. During the very short polar summer, we would be busy with nothing but whaling and everything that had to do with it, day and night without stopping.

So a great but cheerful busyness reigned over the whole ship. The boiler kettles were completely cleaned and tested, as were the cannons. The harpoon ropes were cut to size and spliced. The flensers sharpened their knives and spades, the workers trimmed the coal from the deck to the bunkers, and the swabbing and scrubbing of decks was unending, after the plague of coal in Barry Dock.

At first I was a guest cable-maker, after the pilot discovered that I had a handy way with nails, cloth, and sail needles. This ropemaking ability is largely thanks to the basic instruction I enjoyed on "De Zure," the "Pief," and the "Manus," up in the rigging attic of the Maritime Training School in Amsterdam.

In the cable locker there was plenty of work to be found. The contents of the sail room had degenerated into an unusually chaotic state. This was not surprising, since the *Ross*, when she was still called the *Mahronda*, had sailed to British India and had a crew of Lascars. Weeks went by before the sails and awnings were all usable again and neatly stacked in their places in the sail room. Most of all, many new things had to be made.

When I was finally lord and master of the cable locker and was in charge of the materials, I used the opportunity to make a nice sleeping bag out of a heavy tarpaulin cover. Such a thing might well be useful in the polar regions — and indeed, it frequently did come in handy. And not only there in the far south, but also later in the Indies, on mountain-climbing trips. The sleeping bag was very useful on Semeru and Arjuna as well as in the hut on Kawah Ijen.[1] Up there in the mountains of Java it is of course nowhere near as cold as on the Great Ice Barrier, but it can get pretty brisk there at night, because the body gets used to a rather high temperature in the tropics.

---

1. Gunung Semeru (Mount Semeru) is an active volcano 30 kilometers (18 miles) southeast of Malang in East Java. At 3,676 meters (12,000 feet), it is the highest peak in Java. Gunung Arjuna is 30 kilometers northwest of Malang, a dormant volcano 3,339 meters (11,000 feet) high. Kawah Ijen (Lake Ijen) is a turquoise-colored sulfur lake that is 2,148 meters (7,000 feet) above sea level inside the active volcanic crater of Gunung Ijen, on the east coast of Java. Gunung Ijen's last major eruption was in 1936; Gunung Semeru's in 1994.

FROM THE English Channel our course lay in a wide arc along the Canary Islands to the Cape of Good Hope, and from there across the Indian Ocean to Hobart, the capital of Tasmania. A lonely route, only rarely traveled.

It was already October, and in the Bay of Biscay we ran into real autumn weather, raw and wet, with much wind and rain, so that we couldn't take sights for our position. That wasn't much of a problem; our course lay far away from any other. The only thing we saw in the Bay — besides the gray, close sky and the drab, surging water — was a cable-laying ship, which was just riding out the rough weather.

At the latitude of the Portuguese coast, it began to clear up. The sea and sky turned blue, and with the better weather things got busier on deck. During the raw, wet weather everyone had sought as much shelter as possible to work in, but with the nice warm weather, the deck got more and more popular: on the tanks and the hatches you'd see clusters of men sitting, making rope, cozily chatting, pipes in their mouths. By now everyone had adjusted themselves to the long sea voyage. Sailors are at their best in such conditions. And no wonder — everything starts with a clean slate. Nice warm weather; pleasant work with no unusual haste. The men are in a good mood, it rains jokes, and every once in a while the sound of laughter chimes from one of the groups on deck. Others, working alone in a bosun's chair high on the mast or in a boat that needs to be cleaned, sing to themselves. A cheerful, truly pleasant air pervades the whole ship.

The surrounding environment is happy and full of joy: gleaming white summer clouds sail in the wide blue sky, and frisky little crests of foam romp on the ultramarine blue waves. Porpoises speed past the ship, springing and snorting. Portuguese men-of-war (*Nautili*) spread their transparent sails in the swelling wind, and now and then a North Cape whale blows in the distance. Needless to say, these whales attracted special attention, and one could learn a great deal about whales in the ensuing conversations. My knowledge of the huge mammals was remarkably expanded this way, whereas formerly I knew little more than what I had seen and, most of all, smelled. That was in my youth in Holland, in a sort of traveling museum, where a beached whale was on display for the curious public.

WE STEAMED steadily southward, and soon enough we picked up the northeast trade winds, and schools of flying fish shot rustling over the waves forward of the bow, frightened by the roar of the approaching ship. We usually

Heavy northeast trade winds

think that these fish leave their element out of pure *joie de vivre* to go gliding, but nothing could be further from the truth. If you watch closely, you generally also see that a school of flying fish is being pursued by a dolphin or other hunter, and then you understand that hurtling into the air is the flying fishes' last desperate attempt to escape the certain death that waits for them in the hungry jaws of their pursuer. The hammerhead and other sharks, which are plentiful in these areas, probably wouldn't turn up their noses at a flying fish either.

For a painter in the trade winds area, it is a pleasure daily renewed to see the sun rise and set. The lightly clouded sky is overrun for a short time every morning and every evening with a flood of rich, beautiful hues. A colorful world and a wealth of warm light are things that men always eagerly drink up in deep gulps. As the falling evening washes away the beauty of color from the sky, and the night spreads its dark mantle out of the east over the high dome of the heavens, the stars begin to twinkle one by one against the dark velvet. Then it's good to stand against the rail in the cool evening wind, wrapped in the peaceful stillness of the night, feeling the deck rolling rhythmically, while the ship steadily rises and falls on the light, even swell, and the bow thrusts forward a rustling band of foam, which lights up green in the

black water. Anyone not completely estranged from nature would never tire
of this peace, which seems to come over a man when he gives himself over to
the harmony of the twinkling stars and the murmuring, phosphorescent water.

At night in the trade winds, all is peaceful on the bridge. The pilot on
watch leans quietly over the railing. The helmsman stands silently behind the
wheel, his face faintly lit by the compass in front of him. There is no sound
other than the regular stamping of the ceaseless engine and sometimes the
dreamy humming of the man on the lookout in the foretop.

On such lovely evenings when it was truly a sin to sleep, I often came
out on the bridge.

Usually not much was said; it seemed irreverent to disturb the almost
sacred silence of the night. But often someone soon came by — the captain,
the professor, or the doctor. Then it usually wasn't long before we'd all be
wishing on a star that had just become visible, and wanting to know its name.
If nobody knew, someone would go look it up in the chart room. Soon that
star-hunting became a sort of night-time game, and the most diligent player
was the professor, who had never been so far south. Every evening there were
new stars in the sky. The old familiar constellations disappeared below the
horizon, while new stars rose continually in the south.

I've never been able to fathom how some people can find a long ocean
voyage monotonous. The exact opposite is true, at least for those who can
satisfy their eyes with true virgin beauty, whose ears are still able to hear the
great rhythms of the endless ocean in her vast, bewildering compass.

So, during a silent trade-winds evening on the wide ocean, one is happy
to leave the narrow confines of civilization behind. Forgotten is the unnatu-
ral formality that a large community enforces. On a long sea voyage, people
quickly get to know each other through and through, so that it makes no
sense to play-act for anyone. You call and treat everyone for exactly what he
is. And reigning above all is the voice of nature, which echoes in the continuous song of the waves. Men feel free and strong, even though they feel insig-
nificant and small in the endless space that surrounds them. In fact, it is precisely because of this space that they feel strong. To be thrown back on their
own resources awakens mighty powers that lie slumbering in men. In the
middle of civilization a man cannot develop all his capacities; he is hemmed
in on all sides and limited to being only himself.

Unwearied, unceasingly the engine drove us farther, day after day and night after night, uninterruptedly farther southward, through endless expanses of water without land, without our seeing a single other ship. The *Ross* moved over an immeasurable sheet of water, blue as the high, pure vault of heaven, in which it tried to mirror itself.

Sighing and groaning, the ship sliced through deep valleys of water, dark as indigo, then dove again, quivering and shaking, from long-loping water hillocks, which heaved up their white-wigged heads but rolled bellowing under the ship without doing any harm.

The restless screw ceaselessly propelled the *Ross* forward toward the equator, toward the mysterious, almost sacred silence of the tropical night — the nights with their enchanting silver moonlight and their sparkling hosts of stars. On such nights the regular working of the engine no longer sounds like the pulsing of a machine made by human hands. Instead, the rhythm seems to become one with the pulse of life that is all around, even in the infinity of the heavens above, where the great, silent heavenly bodies shine. Only those who have felt such things and taken them deep into their souls know what it means to dream silently, peering over the wide ocean and learning to fathom ever deeper the life of one's soul.

The best hours at sea in the tropics are those when the moon stands motionless in the velvet-blue night sky, and a broad, trembling band of liquid silver flows over the rolling water, a glowing path that seems to lead from the ship to the dark, mysterious distances beyond the horizon. The stars try to mirror themselves in the rising and falling waves, but the water breaks their reflection into flickering points of light. These are the children of the stars, who play tag on the waves, hiding themselves in the wave troughs, then suddenly springing up again, chasing each other, hopping and dancing, zigzagging over the slow swell of the sea.

Equally lovely is daybreak in the tropics, as the new day is born in glory and majesty. First there appears a faint, pale light above the eastern horizon. Very quickly afterward, the fine fray of cloud above the horizon begins to lighten, and the gleaming light rises up visibly into the eager clouds, after which the whole eastern sky bathes in a rosy glow, which spreads out along the edges of the clouds to high in the zenith.

Immediately thereafter a blood-red slice of sun appears above the horizon. The sun climbs quickly and in a very short time stands above the horizon as a glowing ball. Still climbing, the sun rises above the night mists that hang over the sea; the light is already so strong by then that one can no longer look at it with the naked eye. Meanwhile, the color of the sea has been transformed imperceptibly from a deep inky black to a deep translucent blue.

In these early morning hours one is completely fresh in body and mind. But toward midday, as the sun stands at the zenith, when the whole iron ship seems like a glowing oven, and the heat covers everything like a heavy veil, the men have lost a great deal of their energy. Then it is still and listless onboard. The hammer blows in the ship's smithy sound far less heavy, and their speed slows. The sailmaker's needle and the sailor's broom move with longer pauses, and the wake, which is otherwise a straight, blue-white strip right behind the ship, is an irregular, meandering line. Yes, the man at the helm isn't as observant as usual, and the pilot has to ask him whether he's busy writing his name on the ocean with the ship.

ON THE 16th of October we passed the Cape Verde Islands, although at such a great distance that there was no trace of land to be seen. The nearness of dry land was betrayed only by flocks of seagulls, which, coveting the spoils, followed the trail of a school of killer whales (*Orca gladiator*). But the professor, who had never seen a palm tree in his life, was determined to get a glimpse of the wondrous world of the tropics, which he had read so much about and which he had always dreamed of. So he spent the whole day peering through his binoculars, and from time to time he would excitedly proclaim that now he really was seeing land. Everyone who walked past him had to look through the binoculars, but what he took in his enthusiasm to be palm-crowned mountains always turned out to be a dark mist-bank or a whimsically shaped cloud. He peered and peered so long that his eyes got very tired, and he really couldn't see much of anything anymore. But that gave his imagination an even better opportunity, so that in the end he was really sure he had seen land and swore to us that he had definitely seen mountains covered with palm trees and natives who were cake-walking on their hands. To prove it to us, he even made a drawing of it. A gentle land breeze actually did waft toward us rare scents of damp earth, exotic flowers, and strange spices; these odors probably heightened the professor's powers of imagination.

That same day, broad, reddish-brown channels in the blue seawater indicated that here was the mouth of a great river, the Niger.[2]

---

2. It must have been the Senegal rather than the Niger River.

IN THE TROPICS it's so warm that the men stay on deck in the afternoons when their work is done. They often try to catch fish, even though this usually isn't very easy on a steamship that travels fairly fast. Besides, the fish are frightened off by the action of the grinding screw. But you can see so many fish everywhere that the desire to catch them just grows naturally. In earlier times, on sailing ships, men had much better opportunity and a greater chance of success in fishing below the waterline. As a rule, sailing ships didn't lie very high in the water, and with the irregular, weak winds in the doldrums, they frequently made little or no progress through the water. Most important of all, the fish weren't chased away by the thumping of the screw.

The best-loved sport was catching sharks — and that went fairly easily. A strong iron hook with a piece of salted meat on it, splashed up and down in the water, is enough to attract a shark. As is well-known, sharks are enormous gluttons, and usually they blindly guzzle anything that's in front of their snouts. The strangest things are hauled out of a shark's stomach: not only fish, but just as often pieces of coal, empty bottles, boots, pieces of cork, jampots, and broken lanterns — and also, once in a while, human limbs. Everything that falls off or is thrown off a ship seems to be a welcome prize for the sharks.

If sharks are spotted, then you can count on all sorts of grisly tales of bitten-off arms and legs. Without a doubt, no single creature is so thoroughly hated by seamen as the shark. Most of them actually have direct or indirect knowledge of the voraciousness of this predator.

At anchor in Olehleh, I once saw how an Inland quartermaster was eaten up by sharks. We were there in a Royal Dutch Merchant Marine steamer, unloading along the coast. The ship was rolling, and it swung a bit. This caused a breeches-buoy that had just been hauled up to make a long sweep and knock the quartermaster overboard, onto the edge of the outrigger platform that lay alongside. He fell from

Man-eating shark

the platform into the sea, and instantly two sharks shot off after him. Evidently they had been lying in wait under the platform for something like this to happen. The strong current quickly pulled the drama away. There wasn't the slightest chance to help the man. A boat was launched in great haste in the hopes of fishing out some of his remains, but nothing could be found.

The north and west coasts of Sumatra swarm with sharks. At the Bencoolen anchorage I witnessed another horror: a few times water buffaloes fell into the water while being unloaded off a rolling ship, and they were immediately swallowed up by sharks. I emptied many a revolver into those sinister beasts, but unfortunately never with much result, because bullets immediately lose their power upon contact with the water.

When a shark is caught on a ship, it's remarkable to see how the sailors give vent to their hate. Even when the shark is stone dead, they can't resist kicking it and jabbing their knives into it. I've even seen them in a blind fury literally hack a shark to pieces.

On the *Ross* the smith was quickly put to work making shark hooks, but the sharks didn't come close enough to be caught. So then some hand harpoons were forged to try to catch porpoises, which sometimes frolicked forward of the bow in great numbers. To do this, the men stood outboard on one of the anchors and tried to harpoon the romping, torpedo-like fish. But on a heaving, fast-moving ship, this doesn't work all that well; not a single porpoise could be hauled onboard. Catching flying fish went much better, especially at night, when they came leaping onboard all by themselves, attracted by the lights. In the dead of night you could hear them floundering all over the place, wherever they had fallen. Baked flying fish make good eating. A couple of times so many

Harpooning porpoises

Flying fish

were caught that for a whole day on the whole ship nothing was served but flying fish in every form: baked, cooked, put into soup, and made into meatballs.

One day the second mate rigged up an ingenious device that he had made: an old awning, positioned just above the waterline with outboard spars. A large hold-lamp above it would serve to attract the winged sea-banquet. When he came on deck at the dogwatch, he of course made straight for the custom-made net to see if there were a lot of fish in it. Fish he did not find, but he did discover a large merman with a big blond beard who reeked of liquor. The merman lay snoring heavily with an empty bottle in his hand, ready to fight off a robber, when he was rudely startled out of his dream and ordered to get out of the fishnet with all due speed. This sailor had disguised himself more or less as a siren with some pieces of sail, but unfortunately to precious little effect. As advance reward for his troubles, he had "found" a bottle of aquavit at the steward's.

IN THE TROPICS it was too warm at night in the cabins and bunks. Everyone slept in the open air — in a corner on the bridge, in the boats, in the powder magazine, or on the awnings. Under the port-side awning it was always nice and busy at night: some men played cards and played songs on the har-monica, while others sat or lay on the clean-

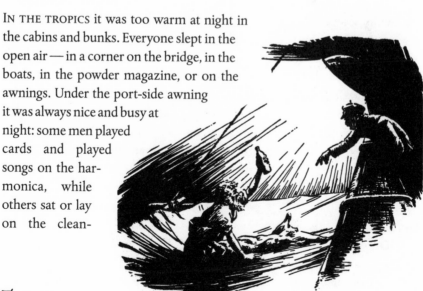

The merman

scrubbed deck or rocked in handmade hammocks. The soft tropical nights were usually very peaceful and still, and, gently rocked by the slow swells, the men quickly became less rowdy, the harmonicas eventually fell silent, card players put their games away, and soon enough silence reigned in the half-darkness under the awning, broken only by sounds of sleep here and there.

But it isn't always so calm and peaceful in tropical seas. Although always brief, violent storms also occur. One night we were overtaken by a storm while we were sleeping on deck. We were bolted awake by the banging of the awning, which the storm was trying to snatch away. An instant later the cover ripped off, and everyone knocked themselves out trying to find a good place to hide from the ravages of the slapping canvas and breaking awning battens. I was dumped onto the deck along with my hammock and got tangled up in its lines. I couldn't get away very fast, and since I didn't care to be thrown overboard by flapping tatters and battens, I crept under the drum of the anchor winch, the closest safe hiding place.

The storm died down as quickly as it had arisen, and when I turned up among my shipmates again, I was greeted by a flood of good wishes. I took that as proof of great affection. The fellows had been anxious about the Hollander, and when they hadn't found him right away, they thought that Bill had been pitched overboard with the deck awning.

The squall had come upon us so suddenly that we had no time to stow the awnings, and they all went promptly overboard. By day you can see a tropical storm coming soon enough, but not by night. In a dead calm you can hear a hissing, rustling sound over the water, which quickly comes closer, and before you really know what's happening, the wind has already reached the ship, and the awnings go flying in tatters through the air.

Such typical tropical storm-squalls are so short and so localized that the ocean has no time to roughen up, and they move so quickly on their course that they don't push any swells before them that would announce their approach. A tropical storm disappears as quickly as it arises, and right after the wind comes, the rain descends in sheets.

THE CROSSING of the equator!

On whalers this event is still celebrated as splendidly as it was in the great age of sailing. But who would have thought that even the old, rugged god Neptune had modernized! But he obviously had done just that, and he seemed to find it natural, just like a normal mortal, to make use of the most modern technical discoveries. Apparently he had the use of a radio installation! On the day that the *Ross* was to cross the equator, he sent us a radiogram in which he announced the arrival of himself, his consort, and his retinue, in order to baptize the neophytes in the ancient, formal manner. The radioman hung up this radiogram just like all the other news reports in the usual way — in the salon and cabins.

Already days beforehand the men before the mast were busy with the preparations. It is above all the ordinary seamen who cling most to the old traditions, and these are the men who always keep celebrating the Neptune festival with as much childlike pleasure as they are given opportunity. For days, things were being done in secret, and the men went around in a mood of happy expectancy, like children getting ready for the Feast of St. Nicholas.

The God of the Seas had announced that he would arrive on the *Ross* at two o'clock in the afternoon, and precisely at the moment when the helmsman on the bridge struck four bells, Neptune and his retinue appeared on deck all the way up at the prow. It was supposed that the old sir had clambered out of his briny domain through the hawseholes on deck. (Actually he and his retinue came up through the forepeak hatch.) First appeared the royal orchestra, consisting of a solitary harmonica-player in peasant disguise: he didn't make a very royal impression in his ordinary work-clothes. He had even forgotten to get himself dripping wet in order to at least suggest that he belonged to Poseidon's procession and had just surfaced from the ocean. But people don't get too particular about these things, and anyone who's bothered by such minor points is a killjoy.

After the music, the rest of the company hoisted themselves up through the narrow hatch, and the parade lined up. In front was Neptune, dressed in canary-yellow oilcloth and tall seaboots. He had fantastic fluttering yellow hair made of frayed rope, and a beard of the same that reached all the way down to his waist. His chest was hung full of insignia cut out of tin, and around his muscular neck hung a nice little pair of binoculars — very cleverly made from two bottles lashed together — and a megaphone. Although these items were not of irrefutable mythological origin, the general opinion was that they significantly improved the overall effect. The threatening trident that the sea god clasped in his left hand was more in the proper style. Heavily smeared with red paint, the thing was supposed to suggest that Neptune was a real bully and a tyrant who didn't let himself be trifled with.

The dolphin and the seaweed that decorate the trident in all illustrations were, for lack of anything better, replaced by a cod and some rope-yarn. If you didn't observe him too critically, the old ogre made quite an imposing impression with his robust, athletic form. Pisani, our engineer, was the national wrestling champion of Norway, and was for that reason the person chosen to play the lead role in this production.

On Neptune's right arm was his illustrious consort, a portly matron. High on her hemp hair waggled a cast-off straw hat, held under her chin with a bit of lamp-wick. That was no superfluous luxury, since the fresh breeze that blew constantly threatened the tottering finery. Mrs. Neptune also had chic accessories. She was wearing very long gloves (actually black stockings) that provided necessary camouflage. Without these coverings, her muscular, hairy, heavily tattooed arms would have greatly damaged the intended feminine impression. In addition, the goddess wore an elegant short dress and an old shawl, with a towel wrapped around her robust waist. Out from under that peeked a pair of solid sea legs covered in long stockings, which were fastened under the knees with red handkerchiefs serving as suspenders. This was of course thought to be just gorgeous, along with the firecracker-red blush (dried paint powder) that made the cheeks of the Goddess of the Seas glow. She was a smashing success, as one can understand when in the middle of the ocean a feminine creature suddenly appears onboard, even if it's only an imitation of a woman. And, despite her divine origin, Mrs. Neptune appeared to be far from prudish and not at all averse to risqué jokes. The decidedly immodest remarks and observations she heard, she gave back with interest — even with usury.

Then followed the divine writer of secrets. For unknown reasons he had rubbed dry red paint on his face, painted his eyebrows black, and donned a big sombrero. The great hunchback he bore clashed completely, as did the long, close-fitting cotton coat, made in a style worn by Polish Jews.

Evidently he himself felt that his appearance didn't entirely match his important function, and so he had painted "Secretary" on his hat in big letters. He carried a huge wooden book in which were written the names of all those onboard who had not yet crossed the equator, and thus were to be formally baptized. Along with the book came a giant pencil; it looked like a weaver's beam. Quite a cargo, all these writing implements.

After the secretary came the doctor. On his head was a skullcap on which was painted not only a red cross but also a skull and crossbones, so that the nature of this worthy personage was impossible to miss. A big blue pair of snow goggles sat up on his nose, and he had doused his whole face with rouge — or with what had to pass for it. When the boys made themselves up, they evidently figured it had to be done well, and they weren't frugal with the paints they used. Especially Mrs. Neptune. A pinch of rouge can sometimes come in quite handy, but she hadn't been content with a pair of fire-engine-red cheeks, and had done up her nose the same way, which ended up looking like an overripe tomato.

This was perhaps all meant to be taken as a hint to the steward that she, a woman, would thus not be averse to a good swig from the barrel of aquavit, to which the steward would have access after the party, as everyone well knew. With that tremendous red nose and her ludicrous would-be womanly bearing, she was absolutely the most feminine creature that one could possibly imagine.

The doctor, like the secretary, had wriggled himself into a skintight jacket. His legs were thrust into wide, baggy trousers, and with the colossal barges he had on as shoes, he moved around like Charlie Chaplin. He had put his medicines and medical instruments in a dilapidated valise: all sorts of bottles with highly questionable mixtures in them, like brews of vinegar, syrup, machine oil, ketchup, mustard, petroleum, shoe polish, and whatever else he had managed to rummage up in the galley and the engine room. Rolls of bandages, strips of sailcloth, and medical instruments bulged out of all sides of the battered medical bag. The instruments had all been fash-

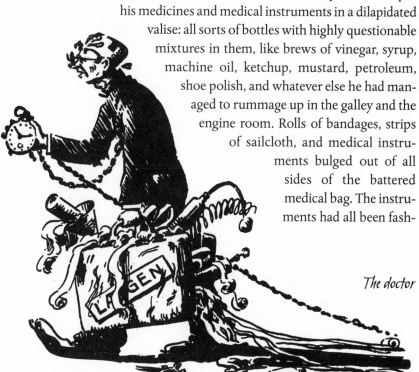

The doctor

ioned out of rope, empty bottles, and wire, and the most important one of all seemed to be an old paint funnel with a piece of rubber hose on the end — at least it was the one used the most often. To check the pulse of those about to be baptized, the doctor had an old watch with him, fastened to a solid chain, which hung rattling behind him.

The barber was dressed up pretty much like the doctor, and these two, the comics from the "penguin deck," made sure with their wisecracks and jokes that the audience lurched from one laughing fit to the next.

Then there was the surgeon's assistant, who was armed with a shaving razor of improbable dimensions, and the barber's helper, who had disguised himself with the help of a pot of black paint. He looked like he stepped out of a minstrel show.

Finally, there was the master of ceremonies, or the chief of police, followed by his eight henchmen, dressed in oilcloth and sporting police hats made of sailcloth. Together they would have to hunt down the novices who had to be baptized and keep order during the baptismal ceremony. The police chief himself was decked out in a white tropical outfit, complete with helmet. Who would have thought to have brought clothes like that on a polar expedition? The onlookers were properly amazed, and the wearer of the outfit was as proud of it as he was of all the tin insignia and stars with which he had decorated his chest in an effort to give himself an air of authority.

As soon as Neptune and his train had appeared on deck, his own flag had gone up the mast: a black shark on a white field, and starfish in the four corners.

Now they made a circuit of the ship while the gruff God of the Seas reviewed, with knitted brow, the seaworthiness of ship and tackle. He announced his critique thereof in full voice, and not always gently — not by a long shot. Both captain and crew left a lot to be desired, nautically speaking. After the inspection of the entire ship, the whole procession went to the bridge.

Neptune had clearly grown truly angry. He stood below on the steps, and with his megaphone he summoned Larsen in a thundering voice to come stand next to him. When the captain showed up, Neptune[3] asked what the

3. Twice in this passage the author writes "Neef Teunis" — "Cousin [or "Nephew"] Theunis" — for Neptune, evidently an old sailor's nickname or misunderstanding of the Dutch "Neptunus." In a heavy Dutch brogue, "Neptunus" and "Neef Teunis" sound remarkably similar. Thanks to Kees Olthof for this suggestion.

devil of an unheard-of impertinence was this, to sashay across the equator without first asking permission from the Lord of the Ocean. Who in the world did Larsen think he was? The ship would in no case be allowed to proceed before all the formalities were properly observed! "Stop immediately!" commanded the infuriated sea-god, and without waiting to see whether his command was followed, he climbed the stairs of the bridge, walked over to the telegraph, and set it ringing to rest on "Stop." . . .

The man at the wheel gasped in surprise at this over-the-top impudence. It was, after all, just the engineer who was playing the part of Neptune. (The *Ross* actually just kept sailing calmly on its way; the telegraph that Neptune had taken over was only the one for the poop deck, not for the engine room.) But on this particular day it seemed that he was in an unusually foul mood, and the stopping of the telegraph hadn't cooled his wrath. After having his secretary present himself and his consort to the captain and the officers, he ordered the captain to show him the ship's papers and log immediately.

The ship looked very suspicious to him. What were all those big boilers doing in the fore- and aft holds, and what was the meaning of all that strange machinery on deck and amidships? It was explained to him, and he was shown several pieces of wastepaper masquerading as ship's papers.

I take it that old gods like this don't have much understanding of modern printed letters. Neptune held the sheets of paper upside down while he carefully studied them, grumbling all the while. He seemed to me more or less satisfied with the result, and he gave the papers back, growling. He rightly supposed that among such a huge crew there must be many who had not yet received their equatorial baptism, and he commanded the pilot not to steam ahead any farther before he had completely investigated this situation and all required formalities had been completed.

Then the whole retinue descended to the foredeck, where thrones — empty oil vats — stood ready for Neptune and his wife. A tarp filled with seawater stood by as the baptismal font. The secretary called the names of the victims out of his book. Those who didn't come forward of their own accord were hunted down with the trident and led by force, if necessary, before the puffing sea god. They were hauled before him from the farthest nooks and crannies — the aspiring seals had hidden themselves everywhere. A whaler is in fact an ideal place to play hide-and-seek; you can find an overabundance of excellent hiding-places.

The baptizands had crept off in all directions. A couple of them were plucked out of the sail room; one lay rolled up in a hawser in the forepeak; another had entrenched himself in the crow's nest high on the mast. The ship's boy was found in a boat under the deck covering, and a trimmer was pulled backward out of the tunnel into the daylight. Two others had stuffed themselves backward under the oil boilers; they kicked and fought like lions, so that their shoes had to be taken off before they could be dragged off to appear — unspeakably filthy and like floundering rubbish — before the sea god. They put up a struggle not so much because they were so resistant to being baptized, but because they wanted to give the show a sort of circus-like magnificence and glory.

Once a victim was finally set down on the platform, he was personally interrogated by Neptune in a gruff voice while the grim old god let a string of salty curses flow. And naturally, of course, it came out from the hearing that the defendant was in dire need of being baptized and with all possible speed, in order to be made worthy of being allowed to continue sailing on a ship through Neptune's kingdom.

The findings were written up by the secretary in his enormous book, after which the sea god with a magnificent gesture indicated to the doctor to investigate whether the patient was physically fit for this honor. This upholder of the Hippocratic Oath then hauled up his watch, felt his patient's

The doctor in action

pulse, doubtfully shook his head, and randomly administered some medication: a dab of petroleum, a mixture of lubricant and mustard, or something of that sort. The awful face made by patient after patient was taken to indicate serious symptoms, and prompted a shampooing with shoe polish or an injection of ketchup over their backs. This resulted in more doubtful grimaces, which in turn led to a fearful thumping of the patient's chest or served as an excuse to wrap the patient up in some frightful cast that bound both feet together, or other such illogical treatments. The inevitable conclusion of the physical examination was the enema.

For this the patient was unceremoniously dumped on his head, and the doctor and his helper wielded his funnel with the rubber hose on the end so convincingly that the proceedings looked perfectly real, to the huge delight of the onlookers. The cheering was especially loud when it was the professor's turn: he was naturally the star attraction on the baptismal-feast program.

Without exception the doctor delivered all his patients over to the barber as hopeless cases. His helper planted them without much fuss on the barber stool — an empty chest — and with a big cement-brush soaped them over generously with a mixture of soot and oil out of the crankcase. Then the barber himself shaved them with a huge wooden knife. To get the baptizands washed off, a quartet of henchmen packed them off and plopped them into the improvised swimming pool. And with that the ritual of equatorial baptism was brought to a full and final end.

The baptized, who crawled out of the barrel spluttering and snorting and unrecognizable from being knocked around, were taken on the spot into the worldwide circle of real seamen. As a preventative against catching cold, they were allowed to get a little heartwarmer from the steward, and they made a point of not neglecting to do so, even if it wasn't exactly in order to avoid catching a cold. And since, due to the ministrations of the doctor and the barber, they had all become unrecognizable, the craftiest ones saw a chance to relieve the steward of a whole series of drinks by coming forward with a new number each time.

During the whole party, the doctor and the barber especially outdid themselves with jokes and pranks. Those two had long since been the leading jokesters onboard who kept making people laugh, and on this unusual occasion they had put their best feet forward and scored such a roaring success that the shouting and cheering never quit. The noise escalated when the professor and the ship's clerk were brought before Neptune. The first man in particular had aroused Neptune's wrath because of the many samples of plankton and liters of water that he had taken from the sea god's kingdom out of scientific curiosity.

These two were submitted to an especially thorough inspection and given a choice of vile potions to swallow. All sorts of jokes were made about their personal qualities, raising a storm of applause. A loud hooray went up from the gallery — in this case, the tall blubber-kettles in the forward hold — when the two gentlemen, who under normal circumstances were treated with respect, were tossed into the bath just as unceremoniously as the rabble had been.

Near the end of the show, things got more than ridiculous. Neptune and his consort had totally lost their divine dignity. It was awfully warm by then; we were sailing over the equator in the heat of the day, and the whole farce took place on the blazing-hot iron deck. So is it so surprising that when Neptune — accustomed as he was to being in his cool element — got too warm, he not only took off his oilskin jacket, but also took his very luxurious but equally heavy golden locks and flung them overboard?

People laughed themselves to tears as Mrs. Neptune, who had also found it stifling in the scorching sun, started taking off her masquerade clothing piece by piece. The first thing she took off was her headgear. Her artistic hat made of hemp must have weighed several kilos and must have been stifling in the burning tropical sun. Next she took off the very pronounced feminine bulges under her clothes that were made of old junk — certainly not items that made her feel cool or comfortable. In fact, the poor fellow posing as Mrs. Neptune had been so stuffy that he threw off all his feminine finery. When he was done, he sat there puffing — without a trace of femininity anywhere on him — next to Neptune, who was puffing even harder, both of them in their net-shirts. The goddess didn't have to take off her shoes; she hadn't worn any, lest her feet look even less like those of an elegant lady.

When the last rookie crawled, filthy and sneezing, out of the water, the Neptune party was over. The retinue reassembled, and the God of the Seas gave the captain permission to turn the telegraph back on full power again, as if the *Ross* really had lain still all that time. The shark flag was struck. As a conclusion the crew got their mandatory ration of gin, and so afterward the fun was extended a little while yet. The lady most of all had to pay for it: without the slightest pretense of respect, she was pinched in the rear. And even Neptune as he passed by was dunked under in the improvised baptismal font, after which he led his attackers on a wild chase as he tried to spear everyone with his bloody trident.

It was remarkable how well the whole party went, without any roughness. All around what one heard and saw was nothing but authentically boyish, open-hearted fun. It was a party of childlike — almost childish — naiveté.

THE SOUTHWEST trade winds stretch northward of the equator in this season of the year, with a steady breeze, which made the temperature fall markedly. Once we were in the cold Benguela current, things got even more brisk. This sort of cold ocean current is easily recognizable from the green color of the water, which stands out very strongly against the deep dark blue that is the characteristic feature of a warm current. This greenish coloring is due to the greater abundance of plankton in the colder water.

At the fifteenth parallel south latitude the first albatross was sighted, a harbinger of the still-distant great South Polar current, which we would first reach once we passed the Cape of Good Hope.

This albatross for its part had ended up in very warm parts. The real territory of these remarkable birds of the high seas lies much farther south, in the area of the Great West Wind. Farther south we saw steadily more albatrosses, not only the most common *Diomedea melanophris* but also the wandering albatross (*Diomedea exulans*) and another species with a greenish-yellow-colored beak (*Diomedea chlororynchus*).

The closer we came to the southern tip of Africa, all sorts of storm birds announced the proximity of the Great West Wind, the "Roaring Forties": sea swallows, Cape doves, and sometimes a much larger species that among seamen is known by a number of unkind names, but in Latin bears the mellifluous name of *Majaqueus aequinoctialis* [white-chinned petrel].

Albatross

CHAPTER FIVE

The "Roaring Forties"

In the "Roaring Forties"

———❦———

We didn't visit Capetown; we were in too much of a hurry to waste precious time there. We hailed a fishing boat, which took our mail and left its catch on the *Ross*. Table Mountain, with its broad, flat top, loomed up in the distance out of the ocean, and the whole day we could still see South Africa's mountains. But already by the following day there was no more land in sight.

From here to Tasmania, we would doubtless see only sky and water around us, along with maybe a couple of albatrosses and a few petrels. It was possible that we might see New Amsterdam Island or the St. Paul Rocks, about halfway along our route, but only if it was by day that we happened to pass these little islands lying lost in the ocean.

For the first few days after we left the Cape of Good Hope, the westerly Agulhas windstream still kept the air and water temperature high. But a long, high swell out of the southwest indicated ugly weather in the area of the Great West Wind, the "Roaring Forties," farther south between the 40th and 50th parallels.[1]

There a steady, strong westerly wind blew; it was often — or rather, always — stormy. In the days of sailing ships the skippers often gladly made use of this wind to go a good ways eastward quickly on their voyages to the Indies. Around the latitude of New Amsterdam Island the ships let themselves be driven by this powerful wind right up to the Sunda Strait.

In the "Roaring Forties" the sea is usually high with long rollers. Nowhere in the world have I seen such huge waves as in these parts. And it's no wonder that the seas are so unusually high here. At this latitude the course of the Great West Wind spans the entire globe, and as the waves stretch out entirely to the south of the northern continents, they are unbounded by any coast and thus have the chance to rise ever higher.

On the many stormy days the churning ocean offered a great show: the sight of waves swept up high as if by mighty giants at play is somber and powerful but also majestic and beautiful. The long, thundering foam crests that crown the mountainous waves have given the name of the "Roaring Forties" to this storm-tossed part of the great Southern Ocean, the *Sydhavet* in Norwegian.

If you want to see the ocean in all her beauty, power, and glory, then take a good, seaworthy ship to the region of the Great West Wind. Here Neptune reigns supreme, in his pure element. The house-high waves look like dark, pursuing clouds, the storm's companions, that chase the wild gray billows higher and higher, wrenching the tops off and scattering them in a shower of clattering droplets. The powerful masses of water in their furious onrushing are mighty and imposing, as dark and gray as the colossal scudding clouds. The tremendous waves roll out broad and wide, one after another, so great and full that, when seen from the ship, the long ranges of water-mountains look as if they're proceeding only moderately fast, and the broad, rushing foam crests seem to approach slowly.

1. Van der Does uses the English phrase "Roaring Forties" throughout the book.

Very often in the "Roaring Forties" I stood astern to enjoy the savage beauty of the whipped-up ocean. The *Ross* was running with the waves, and thus the speed of the rushing billows was visibly lessened by the ship's progress. So, at a certain distance, approaching waves didn't look so very large. But as they came closer, they rose higher and higher above the stern with their fluttering white manes, roaring and lowing, while the wind ripped off a pelting rain of flying water that hit the face as painfully as hail. Just as a tremendous wave towered high above the stern, threatening to bury it under the weight of tons of water, the *Ross* began to rise on the wave, higher and higher, until she was carried to the very top. Then the whole, enormous, seething mass of water, howling and hissing, rolled under the ship with a deafening roar. The ship glided slowly down the other slope of the wave-mountain.

As this storm approached, the ship was quickly made secure. In the high swells, the ship lurched strongly, which made everything work loose. The rigging and the funnel-stays had to be shored up, or the masts and funnels could snap off and go overboard. The boats and lifeboats were lashed down extra tight, hatches battened firmly down, ventilators removed, and all

Water on deck

sorts of things cleared off the decks. It was hard and dangerous work, because heavy seas were soon washing over the ship. Soon such huge surges of water were breaking over the bulwarks that the men who worked amidships were in danger for their lives. Ropes were tied around their waists and fastened to the bridge to prevent a wave surge from washing them overboard. Anyone flung overboard under such conditions is hopelessly lost and given up for dead.

In such weather, seaboots and oilcloth don't do any good; the overpowering seas drench you to the skin in an instant. A sailor engaged in such dangerous work not only pays attention to what his hands are doing but also never lets the sea out of his sight for a moment, so that as soon as he sees and hears that a heavy wave is going to wash over the ship, he can immediately run to safety. He always keeps in sight a ladder-way, the rigging, a deck house, or some other such life saver that he can spring toward at the first sign of danger.

You can imagine, though, that accidents still occur sometimes. A man can't always escape fast enough, and once seized by a wave washing over the ship, he is frequently torn away from whatever it was he was holding onto for life. Once the water violently hurls a man against something, he stands a high chance of breaking a couple of bones. The chances of injury are increased by the fact that everything on a modern steamship is made of hard iron.

On my first sea voyage, when I was but a lad of eleven, there was very foul weather in the Bay of Biscay. I really don't remember much more about it than that. For me it was a vacation, but I was so dead seasick (nearly unconscious) that the captain had laid me down in the card-room, high and dry. But I still remember very well what a deep impression it made on me when I later heard that two sailors had broken both their legs and had to be transported to the hospital at Gibraltar. My respect for the power of water dates from that time.

Many a sailor has died in the "Roaring Forties," and many ships have been lost with all hands,[2] although this happened more often in the past than nowadays. The last great naval disaster in that region was that of the Danish training ship the *Kjöbenhavn*, a five-masted bark that sailed in December 1928 from Buenos Aires to Melbourne, and from which nothing more was ever

---

2. In Dutch, the charming phrase is *met man en muis vergaan:* "sunk with [to the last] man and mouse."

heard again. Not so much as a shipwrecked board was ever found of that beautiful, 4,000-ton ship. With one blow the ship and its crew were swept off the world stage. One can scarcely guess how the drama played out. The world will probably never know. The sea doesn't give up its secrets — and they are uncountable.

Those who know the Great West Wind understand all too well that a ship runs a substantial risk of wrecking; just one unusually strong storm surge can so swamp the ship that the hatches collapse. Then as a rule the ship is done for. And it is precisely in the "Roaring Forties" that it isn't out of the question that a ship might break in half. It sails uninterruptedly over such a long stretch, for days at a time in practically the same direction and over heavy seas, that the same points on the ship repeatedly endure very strong stresses. At a certain moment that wrenching can become too great, and the ship simply snaps. It is also possible that the *Kjöbenhavn* foundered on an iceberg, for wandering icebergs have more than once been reported in these parts.

Before the wireless telegraph existed, it wasn't unusual for a ship to sail out and disappear without a trace, without anything ever being heard from it again. Nowadays, when nearly every ship is furnished with wireless equipment, that's nearly impossible. Thanks to Marconi's brilliant invention, thousands upon thousands of human lives have been wrested from the waves.

The *Kjöbenhavn* had a wireless onboard, and this makes the mystery of her disappearance all the murkier. The answer to this riddle is yet another one that the gray waves will forever hide in their bosom.

FOR THE coal crew, it was — all things considered — pretty nice work on the *Ross* in the "Roaring Forties." The men on this crew had the task of carting

The "Kjöbenhavn"

the necessary quantity of pit coal from one of the forward holds to the coal bunkers. This was work that could only be done on deck, which Neptune was busy washing so energetically and thoroughly. The men hauled the coal up in baskets and carted it in wheelbarrows to the coal bunkers amidships. When in bad weather heavy seas occasionally broke over the ship, coal-trimming became life-threatening work, although sometimes it made for great hilarity when the sea god went bowling with the lads and their wheelbarrows. If any one of them was knocked off his feet by the sea and came crawling out from under his empty wheelbarrow sneezing, wet, and black, he became the target of good-natured ribbing from the others — until they themselves were washed toward some other corner of the floating deck in just the same way. It's really a wonder to report that no serious accidents occurred during such miserable work as this. When the weather was truly too terrible, then coal-trimming naturally had to be stopped, not only for the sake of the men but also because too much water would otherwise pour into the opened hatches. Still, it had to be truly wretched weather before the coaling crew would give up its battle against the oncoming water.

Now of course at the stoke-hole they needed the normal quantity of coal to keep up a good head of steam, which is all the more necessary in bad weather, and it can't be made up by working harder the next day. So if the weather stays ugly day after day, the ship loses substantial steam power and eventually becomes uncontrollable.

After a day of trimming coal like this, being bowled around the deck by playful Neptune, the men were really glad when the day's work was done and they could wash up. Then, mess pails in hand, with black faces and naked to the waist, the whole troop besieged the cook. Everyone tried to get some warm water from the galley kettle to bring to the bath-house to clean off the stubborn combination of coal dust and seawater that was plastered all over their bodies. The bath-house wasn't built for such a rush, and so there was naturally an awful stampede. Since I was used to the large, open-air bath-houses in the Indies, I preferred to bathe on deck. Poseidon usually took care of the rinsing, and because of his playfulness I often had to make a long, uneven chase around the inundated deck before I could snatch my pail from his grasp. My bathing on deck in the wind and the weather surprised people, and for good reason, but I considered it a necessary toughening-up process. I was looking ahead to the cold that we would have to withstand once we got to the far south.

I had been living in the Indies for years and was completely unused to low temperatures. So a little toughening up seemed appropriate to me, and the future bore me out on this point. Once we were in the polar region, I turned out to be able to manage the cold as well as the others could.

Now robust health is naturally an important factor in this respect, but I still believe that without this rigorous training I wouldn't have been able to bear the cold this well. I kept up this tempering process until later, farther southward, when it was -5° C [23° F] on deck during my daily bath. After one such brisk bath, the professor sneered that I looked more like a boiled lobster than a Hollander. In none of my sunset studies that I had painted in his laboratory had he ever seen such a bright red as on my anatomy after my open-air bath.

Practically speaking, it wasn't possible for me to bathe on deck once we reached lower temperatures. When it got that cold, we were already within the boundaries of the pack ice. There the ocean left me in the lurch and didn't provide the seawater I needed. That had to be hauled up from overboard, and nine times out of ten, the bucket clattered on the ice instead of landing in the water.

In milder areas, when it was still good weather, men sat on deck and on the hatches. In the "Roaring Forties" that was no longer possible, and after dinner, when the ship's boys had cleaned the long mess-tables on the "penguin deck," the men sat around on the benches around the tables. There were always storytellers galore. Most of them had lived through so much in the years they had wandered all over the seven seas on all sorts of ships that they had stored up more than enough material to spin out interesting yarns for nights on end. Remarkably, hardly anyone ever managed to tell a story all the way through. Rather, the tale was interrupted from all sides with remarks and observations, and the talk leaped from one subject to the other, becoming a sort of mixed pickles — and often heavily peppered ones at that.

Others sat playing cards and smacked their trumps down on the table with sharp sweeps of their arms. They're all veteran cardplayers, these whalers; you can see it in the way they so deftly manage the well-thumbed cards. The cards quickly get dirty and smeared on the mess tables. In bad weather it sometimes happens that the contents of a soup kettle pour over them when the ship makes an unexpected lurch. Usually the mess-hall benches were lashed securely to the buttress that ran down the middle of the tables, or were held together with some shaving razors stuck here and there in the table, but that wasn't always enough. Sometimes the ship made such a dangerous lurch that the contents of the kettles spilled over the edge, and a couple of times it happened that the ship rolled so far that it not only tipped everything off the table to the leeside, but also dumped the men off the long benches and tumbled them over each other in a heap on the low end, between plates and buckets. Sailors don't easily lose their balance on a heaving ship, but at mealtimes they're at a severe disadvantage when the ship rolls. Then they have to hold on to their plates with one hand and their coffee mugs with the other, if they want anything to stay in them. So it was a sight to behold when a whole row of men would slide off the bench, one right on top of the other, plate and mug in hand, sprawling on the floor to leeside, where of course the entire contents of the cabins also sailed out.

They never played for money in the sailors' quarters; nobody had any. The bids consisted of things that had real value onboard, such as tobacco and packs of cigarettes. These could be purchased on credit from the slop chest. Toward the end of the trip, when the store of smoking materials was nearly used up, there were furious card games lasting nights on end, each of the players desperate to be the one to walk away with a single carton of Capstan cigarettes or something of that nature.

Others made themselves usefully busy repairing their clothes. There were those among us who whipped up entire work-outfits out of old sails and potato sacks, and others repaired their seaboots and shoes with leather from the slop chest. Some old salts busied themselves in the old manner of the sailing ships by making little models of the *Ross* or small buoys, constructed out of packing boxes, with the ship's name on them. This presented me with an unexpected opportunity to put my painting talents to work. Many sailors were keen to have a little rendering of the *Ross* painted on their buoys. The honorariums I would be offered for doing this were unusual. One man offered to resole my seaboots in exchange for a painted buoy; another was willing to wash my clothes for a month; yet another promised to give me his ration of cheese for awhile. Here was yet another instance that made it clear that talent is recognized everywhere, even in the form of very useful items; that true art is valued even among whalers, and will sometimes even be paid for with a luxury article like a good old ripe cheese.

Because I came onboard speaking English, I was taken for an expert, and there were eager students among my fellow workers who wanted to learn the language of Albion, the international language of the sea, and asked me to give them lessons. I had nothing against that; for me it was a not-to-be-missed chance to learn a little more Norwegian, since of course I had to explain everything in Norwegian. For want of English textbooks, a few old magazines took their place. Giving lessons wasn't very easy, since there was an incomplete knowledge of English on the one hand, and a superficial knowledge of the Scandinavian language on the other. This often led to a Babel of confused tongues, where every possible language came to the fore in an effort to make one thing or another clear. German, Spanish, Russian, and Swedish were hauled in, but usually without success. It made me think of the Indonesian sailors on leave, who in Genoa held forth in Malaysian to pure Italians, because Malaysian and Italian sound a little bit like each other.

ANYONE WHO doesn't want to sit in the noisy cabins and is looking for a quiet corner to be able to read or write has to head for his berth. That's the only place that a seaman before the mast can have for himself. It isn't much; he doesn't have his own cabin. The middle of the "penguin deck" is taken up by the mess hall, with its long tables and benches. Around this, built against the hull of the ship, are cabins, one for every four or five men. In these the men have stashed all their worldly goods.

The sea chests are lashed in front of the bunks, and everywhere hangs sailors' clothing and seaboots on nails, which, obeying the law of gravity, describe endlessly repetitive arcs along the walls with exasperating regularity. The bunks stand above each other, two high along the bulkheads, and it is by no means a matter of indifference which sort of bunk one chooses, upper or lower. Most prefer an upper bunk, because then you don't run any danger of having something fall on your head from up above you — or even the whole bunk, contents and all. A lower bunk has the disadvantage that the man living one story above you has to set his not-always-tidy feet on the edge of your bunk to perform the gymnastic feat necessary to land himself in the upper bunk. On the other hand, the lower bunks have the advantage that the sea chests sit in front of them and provide rather decent places to sit, and are in fact used very often.

The upper bunks are actually freer; they are so high that you can't just look right into them, as is the case with the lower ones. Most men correct that defect by hanging a little curtain, or running a line with handkerchiefs and pieces of clothing hanging from it to bring about the same effect. This

Sailor's bunk

can be effective in an upper bunk, but in a lower bunk, any sense of personal privacy is utterly and completely illusory, as can be imagined.

Everything a seaman needs to keep at hand for immediate use he will store, for lack of any other storage space, in his bunk; it is his sanctuary. A variation on the well-known saying that one could use onboard is, "Show me your bunk, and I'll tell you who you are." For instance, a student in the cabin adjoining mine had a whole collection of medical texts in his bunk. They stood on shelves that he had hammered into the bulkhead. He had brought such an overabundance of learning along that there was barely any space left for him. When he stood up, he invariably bumped his head against it, but when the ship was heaving, he could stow himself nice and watertight with the big, heavy volumes and sleep so safely that he didn't need to worry about falling out of his bunk.

By the way, it is truly amazing how soundly a sailor can sleep in bad weather. He takes precious little notice of what he hears of the storm, whistling and howling through the rigging, and he peacefully lays his head down, even if the seas are breaking thunderously over the ship or half the ocean sloshes over the deck above his head. This great peace comes not only from being used to danger, but also from a deep trust in the seaworthiness of the ship, and from a strong belief in the capability and the seamanship of the men on the bridge, whose abilities the men have learned to trust under any circumstances.

It was another matter entirely when the men had to leave the safe protection of the cabins to go up on deck. Then it was a job to open the door at the top of the ladder-way at just the right moment, between waves, and shut it again quickly before the next wave had the chance to crash in.

But there were days when the decks were so constantly flooded that it was impossible to leave the "penguin deck" without a huge quantity of water coming in.

Those were bad times for the ship's boys, whose work was to bring the kettles of food from the galley to the bunks. Not only did the oncoming waves often overturn them, kettles and all, so that they got spilled on the deck along with the soup and potatoes, but on top of that they got an earful from their hungry clients about their clumsiness when they came back, dripping and limping, without food or with kettles where the meat bobbed around in seawater. This was not an enviable time for those poor boys. All of them had to cross the seething decks at one time or another, but none of them had their hands free to steady themselves if the water threatened to knock them off their feet.

On such raw days a box of hardtack was lashed to the mess tables, and anyone who felt like it could grab a handful. The ship's boys usually managed to bring a kettle of coffee safely up front, even if the black drink was pretty salty through and through, since the sea almost always found a chance to add a dash of salt water to the mix.

One time a ship's boy had managed to get a kettle of food safely all the way to the door of the sailors' quarters. But just as he opened the door to come down, a hefty wave whipped across the deck, tossing him, kettle and all, down the ladder-way. Luckily, he got off without injury.

In such weather it is definitely no pleasure to be on deck. And any work there is done only if it is crucial — for instance, if something comes loose because of the ship's heavy going. Under these conditions, everything on deck has to be tied down tight as a drum. As the ship rolls, any loose objects are sloshed violently through the water from one side to the other, and they can cause serious damage to the ship — not to mention the danger they pose to the men.

If the bunk of the student was obvious from the knowledge that spilled out of it, then the painter's bed was easy to find because of the paintboxes and sketchbooks that lay about.

Other bunks contained (besides their owners) carved model ships, cobbler's tools, and all sorts of other interesting things. Typically, none of this attracted anyone's attention. But this was not the case with the bunk of my neighbor the *daeksgütte* [ship's boy]. This fellow was always the one who had to go fetch the eating tins. He was evidently a cautious type, liked to plan ahead, because even if in bad weather he might turn up with only cans full of seawater for our supper, still he'd go sit in his upper bunk and set to work on all sorts of things that as far as we could hear tasted good to him. This incited envy, and upon closer inspection it turned out that the little sneak had stashed his bunk full of all sorts of canned food. Wandering about in the galley and the pantry, he had apparently found these items lying around unguarded and decided to take them. In case he reached his cabin some days without soup or stew, he would still have the necessary provisions stored up in his bunk — at least enough to get himself through unscathed, at any rate, and not have to survive, like most of the rest of us, on a diet of hardtack and black coffee for as long as Neptune's bad temper lasted. When his wickedness was discovered, he naturally didn't have a ghost of a chance of ever squirreling away another can, at least not all for himself.

Beyond all that, the men used all sorts of means to make their bunks as homey as possible, because for a sailor his bunk is the one small spot that is completely his own, where he feels at home.

Most men have portraits of the wife and kids or of their intended hanging on the wall, and those who haven't gotten that far have usually satisfied themselves in that department with illustrations from magazines featuring film stars and society beauties. But it vouches for their identity as sailors that many have also decorated their walls with pictures of ships, especially sailing ships, where the heart of the true sailor still really lives. Smoking materials are also important to Jack Tar, and in nearly every bunk one finds pipes neatly hanging in a row on a handmade rack. A box for the tobacco is nailed up next to it, with an empty milk bottle serving as an ashtray. A shaving razor sticks out next to the pillow, under which one can find nails, a piece of sailcloth and other sailor's tackle, along with knots of cleaning rags, chunks of hardtack, laundry lines, and shaving and sewing materials. Sometimes writing pads and bottles of ink nestle themselves among the other items, although this happens only occasionally. Between the boards and the mattress you can find the motliest assemblage of hidden things: from supplies of tobacco and matches, soap, flashlights, belts, hats, shoes, bandages, and bottles of alcohol, to boxing gloves, revolvers, and even rifles. Dirty clothes also find

Saturday afternoon

a place somewhere in the bunk, while the dandies among the whalers have neatly spread out the outfit they'll be wearing when they go ashore under their mattress to keep the folds in their pants nice.

Saturday afternoon is completely devoted to household chores. Then the cabins have a definite Saturday feel to them, and if the work onboard allows, the men are free to do their washing and sewing. In good weather all the hens sit on deck doing washing and other housewifely things. The old-timers have made washbuckets from half-barrels that once contained oil or salted meat, and they can use them to wash and splash in to their hearts' content. Whoever's fast enough might be able to get hold of some warm water from the cook. When that doesn't work, he might try to get hot water by making a little vent in the steam pipes and getting the steam to go through his laundry. Even using deck brooms and steam, it's quite a feat to get clothes more or less clean that are pitch-black with a mixture of coal dust, oil, and salt water. It would be a frightful thing on a Saturday afternoon for your average Dutch housewife to see the "clean" wash flapping on the line of the *Ross*, the fine clothes of the officers all brotherly next to the smeared workshirts of Jack Tar.

A couple of industrious fellows had specialized as laundrymen in advance and earned some spare change doing wash for the officers and those of their colleagues who didn't consider themselves cut out to be washerwomen. In the delicates department they did wonders with bottles filled with glowing ash. They managed to do collars and jackets together, and it more or less worked. After a washday like this, the whole ship was decked out with the products of the wash-happy crew, which waved like flags everywhere. In bad weather, not much of this laundromat system worked, and then the men tried — to the great annoyance of the machinists — to hang their wet laundry in the engine room. The stoke room attracted some attention too, but although the wash got nice and dry there, it didn't come out again much cleaner.

FOR ABOUT four weeks on the stretch from the Cape of Good Hope to Tasmania, we got little good and a lot of very raw weather. It doesn't make the mood onboard more pleasant when it's bad weather like that for weeks on end. But if anyone's mood might suffer under these conditions, it's clearly not that of the albatross. These are storm birds par excellence. At these latitudes we always saw them around us, and in stormy weather they came so close to the ship that people could practically grab them off the bridge with their hands. Why the birds did that has always remained a mystery to me.

The albatross loves a stiff breeze; its special niche is the band of the Great West Wind, and it avoids places where it doesn't blow hard. Like no other bird, and far better than men, the albatross understands the art of gliding. It doesn't flap its wings, as other birds do; rather, it uses the power of the wind to keep gliding, which it knows how to do expertly, making tiny adjustments in the position of its long wings in order to direct its flight. Serene and stately, it skims over the tops of the waves with its wide, outstretched wings. Its flight lasts so long that it doesn't actually fly but *sails* in the true sense of the word. You can stand and watch an albatross for hours on end, floating in great arcs over the ship, without seeing it make a single flap of its wings; whether going with the wind or into it, all of it goes calm and sure, without a single wingbeat. It's a joy to see these birds gliding over the high seas, searching for food, closely following the profile of the waves, sometimes with a wingtip almost touching the water. They are princely birds: their bearing is thoroughly regal, and the whole far-flung stretch of the "Roaring Forties" is their kingdom. *Sydhavets kongen*, the King of the Southern Ocean, the Norwegians call them.

Without any effort the albatross covers enormous distances. Near Capetown we caught one that we let go again after we had banded its neck. We kept seeing the same bird circling the ship, and not until we began to approach land, the coast of Tasmania, did we lose sight of it.

Albatrosses are pre-eminently flying birds that feel most at home in the air. They set foot on dry land only during mating season. They breed on the many uninhabited and inhospitable islands that lay scattered here and there in the Southern Ocean. They are as clumsy and awkward on land, and even on water, as they are graceful and confident in the air. They probably sleep mostly in the air. Seldom do you see albatrosses floating on the water, and if they splash down once in a while, it's obviously a great deal of trouble for them to get those huge wings neatly folded up again. Taking off out of the water is even harder for them, chiefly because their wings have three joints instead of two.

A few stately albatrosses fell prey to science during our trip. One stormy day when they kept sailing above the ship, the doctor shot them down to do some scientific research on them.

In the air an albatross looks much smaller that it really is. The body itself is scarcely as large as that of a goose, but a specimen of average size has a wingspan that measures 2¾ meters [9 feet] from tip to tip. It's a pitiful sight to see such a proud ruler of the Westerly Storm lying lifeless in a heap with broken wings. The seamen have an instinctual respect for these stately, regal gliders that so boldly make the formidable Great West Wind their servant. They believe that the deliberate killing of an albatross brings bad luck. According to sailors' superstition, the spirit of the Westerly Storm demands the soul of a man for every albatross killed intentionally. This follows Old Testament form: an eye for an eye, a tooth for a tooth, a soul for a soul.

Luckily, in this case the punishment didn't follow the sin, probably because the birds weren't shot wantonly but for scientific research. Or should the death of that old salt Gamle Hans be attributed to this after all? Some of the old sea-seals pronounced this conclusion with great conviction when Gamle Hans died on the voyage home of complications from a frostbitten foot and found a sailor's grave in the wide, wild, watery wilderness between New Zealand and Cape Horn.

On the dead birds the scientists found all sorts of parasites, which they preserved in alcohol: bird lice, worms, and other interesting creatures. You could make nice cigarette holders out of the wingbones.

OFF THE Australian coast, with a somewhat more northerly course, we came into better weather. After weeks of being able to see neither sun nor stars, we could walk around on deck warm and dry, an unfamiliar sensation after such a long period of stormy weather and flooded decks.

At night the Southern Cross again shone high in the black heavens. After almost a month of seeing only rushing gray water, and the uncertainty of feeling the deck always heaving and rolling under one's feet, the sight of land, the vast, immovable earth, was a peculiar and almost unbelievable thing to see.

You might almost believe that you were living in the time of The Flood, that the whole earth was one endless ocean, without any human life other than that on your own ship, which, like a modern Ark or like the *Flying Dutchman*, drifted aimlessly over the ever-onrushing waves, with a fearful endlessness of surging water below and pouring rain above.

The longing to see land after such a long sea voyage is great and universal. It still seems to have a wonderful attraction for one and all. Everyone who has even a little bit of time stands peering at the still, vague outlines of mountains whose peaks rise just faintly above the horizon. Especially if it is unfamiliar land, this gives the sensation of discovery.

And discovery it is, insofar as one will see people and things that are completely new, in a certain sense, although fantasy plays a large role in such experiences. It must have been something quite different for Columbus, when he saw for the first time the coast of the supposed Indies, than for us when we saw the top of Mount Wellington rise up out of the seas. We knew very well what we were going to see, while Columbus set foot on a world totally alien to him. But the approach of land still always gives rise to a certain happy, excited anticipation. Anyone who had binoculars stood for hours staring out of them as if he hoped to see who knows what, even though all he might be able to discover were the outlines of mountains that present practically the same view that can be glimpsed everywhere else in the world. But interest rises proportionally higher as one nears the coast and it is more clearly delineated, and becomes still greater when the destination harbor becomes visible.

Ours was Hobart, the capital of Tasmania, named after Abel Tasman, the Hollander who discovered the island. (Incidentally, the names of numerous Dutch explorers are preserved in the geography of these parts.)

For many onboard, Tasmania was nothing other than the last point of contact with the inhabited world. We had already left two oceans behind us, the Atlantic and the Indian, and after Hobart, a third awaited us, one of a wholly other sort: the Antarctic Ocean. Once past that, we would enter the grim and secret polar world.

Land

CHAPTER SIX

In Tasmania

Rocky coast

On November 24, 1923, the *Ross* arrived in Hobart. Early in the morning the ship rounded the high cape made of basalt columns at the entrance to the long fjord where the city lies.

For the inhabitants it was a very unusual event to see a flotilla of whalers in the harbor. Yet to a great extent the city had whaling to thank for its rise, for that trade had blossomed some eighty years ago in the waters around Tasmania. In those days it happened that twenty, thirty, sometimes even forty whalers stood at anchor at the same time in Storm Bay, the wide arm of the fjord that connects Hobart to the sea. In those days it wasn't Norwegians who went whaling but chiefly Americans, and it was mostly sperm whales that were caught in these waters, just as in the whole of the Pacific.

The population of the land had grown up with the stories from these boom times still in living memory. For them, whaling was synonymous with riches and prosperity. No wonder, then, that the whaling industry interested them and that they greeted our expedition enthusiastically as well. During the short time that we lay in Hobart, thousands came daily to visit the strange ship that was headed to the unsailed polar sea to go hunting for the swimming gold.

It was the little male *spes patriae* that showed the most and the noisiest interest. Before and after school one could find them gathered on and around the *Ross* and the five chase boats. The crow's nests high on the mast were especially attractive to the boys, as one can imagine. It made me think again of my boyhood years in Rotterdam, when my friends and I also wandered around by the ships in the harbor if we could find even a little free time. The Hobart schoolboys were very dutiful. In our time, we just played hooky if there was a strange ship to be seen, or if a circus was being set up, or if something else interesting was happening.

In the lands to the south of Australia, the name of the Ross Sea doesn't sound as foreign as it does to us. Roald Amundsen lay in Hobart with the *Fram* when he returned from the South Pole, and in nearby New Zealand people talk every day about Scott, Shackleton, and Mawson as if speaking of old acquaintances.

Our five chase boats had all arrived already when the *Ross* itself entered Hobart. Three of them had departed from Sandefjord before we did; the other two came from Alaska, where they had been hunting.

It was the beginning of the summer when we were in Tasmania, when nature is at her most beautiful. It is a land richly blessed with natural beauty that is only slightly threatened by civilization. It is young and only scarcely populated. There are about 250,000 inhabitants in an area of 679,000 kilometers, thus not even half a person per square kilometer.[1]

The flora looked subtropical, with many tree ferns that made me think of the mountain country of Java. Among the trees, those of the eucalyptus variety dominated, as they do everywhere in Australia. The climate is mild — so mild that when, as a curiosity, people showed us photographs with snow and snow-covered tree ferns, it seemed really unbelievable.

---

1. This is very unlike the Netherlands, whose population density is nowadays a thousand times greater.

Chase boat

A good highway runs from the foot of Mount Wellington, the mountain that dominates the city. Streams on the slopes provide Hobart with drinking water, and the road ends at a large reservoir. Here begin untouched woods. The whole island is for the most part covered in virgin forest.

We visited the botanical garden, which was very beautifully laid out, to get to know the fascinating Tasmanian flora better. And almost every day we went to the museum, not only because one could see there the skeleton of the extinct giant ostrich, the moa, but even more because the bird life of the far south was very well represented in stuffed specimens. It was nice to be able to study the bird species that we would be coming across in the polar region so that we would be able to identify them more readily once we were there.

Part of the museum is devoted to ethnography. There you can find, among other things, what has been preserved of the original Tasmanian population: photographs, pieces of clothing, and the skeleton of King Trucacini, the last native of the island, who died in 1876.

The aboriginal population of Tasmania has disappeared completely. The race appeared unfit to withstand the blessings of civilization, but it was also to a great extent willfully exterminated. This actually began in 1803, when the first European settlement was established on the island. For thirty years the unequal conflict raged between whites and aborigines, during which much occurred that doesn't bear inspection by the clear light of day. Bounties paid for the capture and killing of aborigines, and human hunting-parties made for many black pages in the book of white civilization. Now all of that is nearly forgotten; the huts of the aborigines have disappeared, along with their hide-covered canoes. Offices, country houses, and river steamers have taken their place on the Derwent River, and only the artifacts in the museum remain to prove that the Tasmanians ever existed.

But the earth doesn't stand still, and the lovely spring adorns the beautiful island with the same wonderful colors as before. The flowers smell just as sweet, the birds rejoice and sing in the warm sunshine, and the kangaroos jump just as heartily as they did just one human lifetime ago. The eucalyptus and kaori trees have survived the drama of the vanished natives, only now their tremendous trunks stretch out even higher above the blossoming land.

We made many excursions in the vicinity — to Belle River or Brown River — on the passenger boats that connect the outlying areas quickly and inexpensively with the capital. These were happy, sunny days, when a trip over the smooth fjord, with a string ensemble playing onboard as the boat went past green, blooming hills, did us a lot of good after the weeks of beastly weather we had endured in the "Roaring Forties." Spring scented the hills with orchids, roses, and countless other flowers whose names we didn't even know.

One peaceful Sunday we took such a trip on the small Brown River, which takes its name from a little brook that empties into Storm Bay. On either side stretched a wide, sandy beach. How different it was from our huge bathing beaches, which are so full of people that you can see neither sea nor sand. Here it was calm, not crowded; everyone could enjoy his fill of sea, sun, and sand. In Europe in such a paradisaical spot there'd be a top-notch bathing resort and all that comes with it, but Tasmania is still a land on the rise.

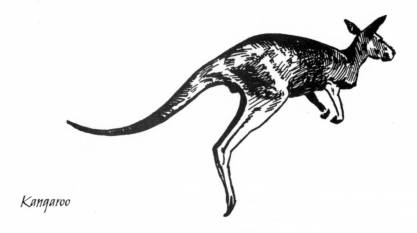

Kangaroo

The countless machines and factory smokestacks that people build with such frantic haste in Europe don't exist here yet. And so Brown River can remain a wonderful place, where people can come after a tiring day and take a refreshing dip in the sea, and drink their five o'clock tea in the light surf in the middle of nature's beauty.

For us these were our last days in the inhabited world, where the sun was warm and where trees grew. Just a few more days and we would be on our way to the far south, far away from all these things that make life so pleasant. Conscious of this, we enjoyed to the last drop everything that friendly nature offered us with her gentle hand.

All told, we spent six vacation days in Tasmania. But the men onboard didn't sit idle. A wooden flensing deck was built in the forward and rear holds, a foot above the normal iron deck. This was done to make it easier to work the whale meat, should the hunt bring success once we were in the Antarctic Ocean. The huge strips of meat would be hauled on deck and there cut with flensing knives into pieces to be cooked in the oil boilers. On an iron deck, the knives would quickly become uselessly dull, but that isn't the case with a wooden deck, which also makes it possible for oil, blood, and all such filth that comes from processing whales to flow out underneath.

The chase boats were furnished with coal, a sizable supply of fresh provisions were stored up, and in addition six fairly young men from Tasmania were mustered aboard to serve as laborers on the voyage to the Antarctic Ocean. We also waited one extra day for the New Zealand mail boat, which had a representative from the New Zealand government onboard, the marine captain Hooper, who went with the *Ross* because the little-known lands around the Ross Sea, the goal of our expedition, Victoria Land and King Edward VII Land, are New Zealander — or rather, English — possessions.

For all of us, these spring days in Tasmania would always be unforgettable. We enjoyed them to the fullest, each in his own way, but with the restlessness of men who have a higher goal in sight.

Now the real trip was finally about to begin. The last preparations for departure were made, the last mail was sent home, and the last handshakes were exchanged with newly-made friends. The cabins were full of flowers when on November 30 the hawsers were let loose and the *Ross* swung slowly out of the harbor.

CHAPTER SEVEN

To Macquarie Island

Heavy seas

Ahoy! The gangway went up as if to the beat of a jumbled, incoherent song, the anchors were hauled into the hawse-hole, and the clamps set on the chains. Then the telegraph jingled, the flag gave its last wave, and the *Ross* sailed with calm dignity over the smooth water of the fjord to meet the ocean and the polar sea.

From the seamen's cabins still wafted the notes of a melancholy harmonica tune, a memory of Jack Tar's shore-leave pleasures. Now that was all over. On the long trip from Europe to Tasmania, the fellows were full of the fun that they promised themselves onshore in Tasmania. And to judge from the unsteady gaits, the partied-out faces, and the stained clothes, many a man had tasted the pleasures of Hobart's harbor district to the full. But now the

70

pleasures of bars and dance halls, gaudily painted ladies, theaters, and police stations were behind them. Now they had to focus on the more serious matter of life. The Antarctic Ocean with her storms and threatening masses of ice, her whales and hard work that awaited, now beckoned in command. Not with the come-hither gesture of the brightly lit, nightlife neighborhood, but with an urgency that was inescapable. Every turn of the screw drove the *Ross* southward toward the polar sea and to the whales that had to provide these men's living for a full year.

From then on, the whale hunt was almost the only subject talked about. Those who weren't completely sober yet would quickly be called to order by the Great West Wind, by all appearances.

It was a soft, dreamy evening when we saw the lights of Hobart disappear behind us, but a veil of clouds for the most part hid Mount Wellington from our sight, and above its high peak a flock of fleecy clouds painted a pale lilac against the dark sky. That signified stormy weather and promised us trouble with our towing. Three of the chase boats — the *Star 1*, the *Star 2*, and the *Star 3* — had already left three days before, en route to Macquarie Island to see if the whales had already begun their migration to the south. We had the other two, the *Star 4* and the *Star 5*, on a towline. They would just delay us otherwise, because they couldn't go nearly as fast as the *Ross* itself, and the idea was to sail through the Antarctic in convoy, in light of its many and unforeseen dangers.

The boats were towed with a long steel cable that was fixed to the anchor chains onboard each of them. The cable was then let out, thus giving it enough weight to hang in a sturdy but flexible curve.

It was more or less certain that we would run into nasty weather before we actually reached the Antarctic Ocean. Our course to Macquarie led us once again through the "Roaring Forties," and although the waters to the south of Tasmania are only rarely sailed, we knew all too well that every expedition to the polar seas had had to reckon with heavy weather in those parts: that of Ross as well as those of Scott and Shackleton and also, most recently, that of Sir Douglas Mawson. And so on the *Ross* we were prepared for storms.

Out on the open ocean it wasn't blowing yet, but there was already a high swell, and heavy seas ran nearly straight across our east-southeast course. Storm and waves picked up quickly. The ship rolled heavily to the side with wind and waves at her flanks, and soon enough water poured over fore and aft. Coal-trimming had to be halted, not only because the work became life-threatening, but also because too much water poured into the open hatch-covers, while both air and water promised driving weather.

The chase boats being towed behind us found it hard going, although it was quite a show to watch their struggles. Even though the big ship had slowed down, the chase boats were flung violently through the mounting seas, because just as they tried to raise their bows as they climbed up the back of a wave, they were yanked down by the heavy towing cable, so they couldn't ride over the tops of the waves as usual but were dragged straight through them.

From the *Ross* we had a good view of the wild spectacle. First we would see the mast and funnel of one of the boats rise up behind a house-high mountain of wave, and just as we expected to see the boat appear on the crest of the wave, it would disappear completely in a cloud of flying foam. Every wave that came its way whipped over the harpoon cannon onboard and washed the whole deck clean, after first streaming over the poop deck. The men onboard had to exercise great care and seamanship to keep from being thrown overboard in such weather.

The barometer stood at 742 millimeters [29 inches]. When the mercury is that low, life at sea is usually no great pleasure, and for the lads on the battered and flooded chasers, it certainly was a stark contrast to the merry days of luxury in Hobart.

During these raw days both the *Ross* and the chase boats suffered storm damage on deck. The doctor suffered serious damage too, although not of the material sort. When he came up on the bridge to read his thermometer, he brought with him a whiff of alcohol so strong that not even the storm could waft it away. The bad weather had surprised him in his sleep, and before he was fully awake or knew what was happening, everything that he had piled up in his cabin began to slide. In the process a large bottle of pure alcohol meant for specimen preservation had broken, and the powerful fluid had lent his clothes an odor that would have garnered an approving smile from Bacchus. Naturally we knew better, but ever after that we often kidded him by hinting that he must be a secret lush who offered himself up to the God of Wine in the solitude of his cabin.

At night the sea rose even higher. The towing cables, although they were let out even farther, turned out to be unequal to the tremendous wrenching they had to endure, and both of them snapped, one shortly after the other. The masthead lights of the jettisoned chase boats soon vanished from sight, and the *Ross* was forced to heave to until dawn finally broke so that she could go searching for her lost sons. We just had to hope that they weren't in trouble, although it was hard to tell. But, after all, weren't the two captains of the chase boats true and worthy descendants of the Vikings?

By daybreak the sea had already improved markedly, and after a brief search the smoke of both chase boats came into view. Not long after that we sighted the vessels themselves, fighting gamely against the sea with undaunted gallantry. They were moving much more easily and smoothly now than they had when they were being towed. No effort was made to haul out new towing cables; the ocean was still wild enough to make that practically impossible.

Being towed makes murderous work for the crew of a chase boat. A vessel that is being pulled by the nose through the waves is no vacation spot when the seas run high, and it runs a great risk of being swamped by the onrushing water in such wild, thrashing seas. Our chase boats had to go on under their own power, and they held up well, the valiant little things. One of them managed to exert itself so much that it looked as if it wanted to outpace even the *Ross* herself. The other one, however, was in no condition to keep up with the *Ross*, even though the mother ship was sailing at half speed so as to stay in the vicinity in case anything should happen.

In the course of the day the weather steadily improved, and although a heavy swell remained, it was no longer necessary to stay quite so close together. The three vessels steamed onward, each in its own way, to Macquarie Island, the next goal. We had gotten another strong challenge from the power of the "Roaring Forties," and it did us good to prove that the chase boats too were able to withstand that test splendidly. They hadn't come to Tasmania via the Cape of Good Hope like the *Ross* had. Precisely in order to avoid the Great West Wind, they had taken the path via Insulinde.[1] But now their seaworthiness was clear for all to see. That reassured us, for we knew all too well that the chasers and their crews would have much to endure once they reached the polar seas.

1. Insulinde is a poetic name for the Dutch East Indies, coined by the nineteenth-century Dutch author Multatuli (the pseudonym of Eduard Douwes Dekker, 1820-1887). My thanks to Henk Vreman for the loan of the century-old Dutch dictionary that solved this and many other puzzles in Van der Does's Dutch.

The bad temper of the "Roaring Forties" meant that it took us almost four-and-a-half days to cover the 900 miles that separate Macquarie Island from Hobart. By the time the island loomed up on the horizon on the evening of December 5, the weather was manageable. Already by daybreak, great flocks of seabirds had signaled that land was near. These were mostly skuas (*Megalestris antarctica*), albatrosses, and whale birds (*Prion banksi*). You can imagine with what curious eagerness we took in the raw, rocky island when, toward midday, the anchor dropped on the lee shore, at a respectful distance from the countless reefs whose black tops reared out of the foaming breakers. Although it was discovered in 1810, Macquarie Island — which forms a connecting link, as it were, between New Zealand and the land of the South Pole — remained for a long time almost unknown.

Now and then only a few pirates paid it a short visit. Bellingshausen, Wilkes, Shackleton, and Scott also mentioned brief stops there, but only with Sir Douglas Mawson's expedition did the island join the set of fixed points from which the challenge of the South Pole was addressed. A detachment from that expedition spent two years on the island, chiefly functioning as a radio connection between the main party of the expedition in Antarctica and the outside world.

We searched with binoculars for the radio masts, but they were no longer to be found. Storms had no doubt blown them over long ago. We did see still standing the hut where the Macquarie detachment had done their work during their voluntary "Robinson Crusoe" stint, under the direction of Tinsworth. Bauer's hut was also still standing. Bauer, a German New Zealander, had been the last to visit the island — in 1916. He and a few others had lived off the hunt for elephant seals and penguins, from which they extracted oil.

Since then the island hadn't been visited again; during our visit in 1923, it was totally uninhabited. Its isolated position in the middle of the storm-battered ocean made it a very undesirable place to live.

The climate there — at 55° S and 159° E — is unusually raw and not especially attractive to people, but apparently fine for elephant seals and penguins, who have chosen it as a place to live, probably precisely because it is absolutely deserted. To prevent the total extermination of these animal species, the whole island has been declared a nature sanctuary. It has been left entirely in its natural state, and the hunting of seals, penguins, and seabirds (who breed there) is now forbidden. Now it wouldn't exactly be weekend

hunters who might want to brave the "Roaring Forties" to go shoot a couple
of seals or penguins, but the government of New Zealand, to whom the island belongs, no longer grants any concessions for seal-hunting. And so
Macquarie Island has become a haven for subantarctic fauna. Elephant seals,
penguins, albatrosses, seagulls, and all sorts of other petrels can reproduce
there in peace, untroubled by *homo sapiens*.

This is thanks to the dedication of Sir Douglas Mawson, who was so
struck by the wealth of fauna on Macquarie that after his return he managed
to persuade the government of New Zealand to proclaim the island a national reserve.

Not surprisingly, the doctor and the professor burned with desire to get
a look at this wealth of nature and to collect material for study.

Elephant seal

CHAPTER EIGHT

A Paradise for Penguins and Elephant Seals

Fighting elephant seals

N eedless to say, I hankered just as much as the doctor and the professor did to go ashore and see the completely unfamiliar subantarctic world up close. But the chance that an opportunity would present itself was slim. Because of the previous days' bad weather, which had seriously hampered the coal-trimming on deck, the coal bunkers were nearly empty. So that work had to be tackled head-on. In addition, the five chase boats had to be provisioned with coal again. And, because in the meantime I had been promoted to second bosun, it became my personal duty to see that the whole coal business was put in order. I could do no more than look at the island from the deck during the noon watch, and had to be content with that.

Most of the men peered over the sea searching for whales, but for the time being they interested me less. Later on we'd see whales enough. From the ship there actually wasn't much to see. Macquarie is a mountainous island. It looks desolate and inhospitable. No trees grow on it because the climate is far too raw.

It was already summer when we arrived, and the temperature was good, but in the winter it must get very cold because of the continual snowstorms that ravage the island; it's not the kind of place you'd want to live.

The steep, rocky coast is sown with rock reefs whose threatening heads protrude everywhere out of the white surf. A difficult place to land, especially in the weather we were having, so I figured it was unlikely that a landing would be attempted. I put such thoughts aside and decided instead to enjoy myself with the black gold of the tweendecks.

But not long afterward the pilot called through the hatch down below: "Hallo, Bill! Where are you? Come on up — you're going with the Prof and the Pill to shore!" The pilot didn't have to call me twice. I quickly turned the work over to Björne, who also spoke a little English and would make sure that the new Tasmanian crew would get the coal in the bunkers and not in the provisions hold or in the chief engineer's cabin.

There was no time to spruce up, and in any case there was nobody ashore who would take offense at my unkempt appearance. In all haste I grabbed my sleeping bag, matches, gun, and sketchbooks. The two scientists came with blankets, cameras, and some empty gas cans.

We didn't have to take provisions along; we knew that food aplenty was to be found on shore in the form of fat elephant seals.[1] But the steward evidently thought otherwise. All stewards are of the same mind: that the primary goal of life is to have food and drink with you. True to this principle, he had prepared a large basket of delicious provisions for us.

When the Prof came out of his cabin, a cheer went up. In complete contrast to the Pill and I, who had on sloppy getups — which, incidentally,

---

1. This — and further comments about captured penguins and the possible taking of some young seals — may sound strange, given what Van der Does says in the preceding chapter about the island's having been made a sanctuary. However, the *Ross* was presumably granted an exception by virtue of the presence of its two staff scientists (Drs. Kohl and Vallin); they must have had the blessing of the government of New Zealand. (Chapter Six closes with the mention of the presence onboard of its representative, marine captain Hooper.)

went wonderfully well with the ragged wildness of the island where we were going — he had put on an exquisite polar outfit, made of polar bear fur, that he had dug out of his trunks. It was magnificent indeed, no doubt a masterpiece made by one of Stockholm's leading tailors. In that fantastic costume, good old Dr. Vallin looked exactly like Santa Claus on a Christmas card. But in place of the old bearded face was the blushing young one of the genial professor. The general opinion was that he looked unusually smart and very seductive, and he was gravely warned not to turn the heads of all the lady penguins on Macquarie. In fact, he was teased so mercilessly that his expensive suit ended up lying at the bottom of the boat long before the line was let loose.

We used a flat-bottomed skiff to attempt the landing. A regular boat wouldn't have been manageable for three men in the breakers, and a flat boat is really more usable in wild water. In bad weather on the Dutch coast, many people have been rescued from stranded ships by flat-bottomed boats.

The greatest difficulty in landing would prove to be the thick, heaving belt of kelp that drifted in a wide mantle around the rocks. Kelp is a giant seaweed with thick, flat stalks, as wide as a hand, which can reach a length of thirty meters or more. At this latitude the drifting seaweed forms an impenetrable barrier around all the rocks, both above and below the water. It simply isn't possible to get a boat through it.

Fortunately, one of the chase-boat captains was kind enough to tow us right up to the surf. At this point our little boat lay a scant two miles from shore, but it was still quite a stretch to row, especially for the scientists, who weren't sea types. They had to row as well as they could while I, the sailor in the company, handled the tiller in back. There was no opening to be seen among the rocks. At the cost of huge blisters on their hands, the learned rowers reached the dangerous breaker zone, and there between the rocks where the foam flew overhead we could see a small stretch of beach, covered with pebbles.

Here we found an opening in the chaos of rocks and seaweed. It was really a narrow passage, but big enough for the boat.

We dashed through on the back of a roller, which deposited us high on the gravelly beach a little later. The shock of impact knocked the scientific rowers right off the bench. Meanwhile, I leapt overboard to keep the retreating wave from dragging the boat away, and for a moment I saw nothing but their waving limbs. Together we hauled the boat high onto the beach beyond

On the back of a roller

the reach of the tide so we didn't have to worry about it and could go exploring to our hearts' content, which was our unspoken goal.

A nice Robinson Crusoe feeling came over us as we stood there on the deserted island, eager at the prospect of being able to wander about for a few days through this environment that was still new to us. There was space in abundance. Macquarie Island is one great mass of rugged rocks, ten kilometers long and three kilometers wide.

Over the whole beach lay elephant seals by the thousands. We had apparently landed by chance right in the middle of a harem; there were only females and young animals. They lay sleeping in hordes, all over on top of the stones and among the rocks, enjoying the summer weather. Colossal! How splendidly those seals can sleep. Never have I seen another living creature that surrendered itself with such devotion to the art of sleeping.

The snorting, hawking, and snoring noises that rose up out of all these fat, lazy bodies formed a raucous but impressive Morpheus Symphony. Stretched out in sophisticatedly slothful positions, they soaked up the watery sunshine, sometimes hanging half over each other, now and then scratching their flat flippers with their long claws. You might expect that these animals, living in their natural state, unfamiliar with humans, might quickly take flight at our approach. Not at all. We apparently made no overpowering impression on these unwieldy bags of bacon. They only resented the fact that we disturbed their precious sleep. Only when our footsteps on the pebble-strewn beach awoke them did they show any interest. With drowsy, bulging eyes they looked at us, confused and drunk with sleep, and as they caught sight of these strange beings, they made a feeble attempt at frightening us by pulling their red muzzles wide open to show off their huge eye-teeth. They also hissed like cats, with as little success. These female elephant seals are harmless. With the far larger males, one has to be more careful; some of them can be formidable. Farther on we saw the carcass of one such lordly beast. He had such an enormous girth that from a distance we took him for a beached whale. That specimen must have weighed a good twenty tons.

The males have a remarkable way of fighting, as we later observed. In the male elephant-seal colony, titanic fights occur — over the females, of course. It's the same all over creation. When elephant seals fight, they rear themselves up bellowing so that they can let themselves go thudding down with their full weight onto their opponents. With their big eye-teeth they try to rip open their enemy's flanks. All the older males bear the signs of such battles, these long, broad scars — although they might also be attributable to killer whales, the only creatures who dare take on these giant seals in a fight.

Sometimes we got in trouble with a big elephant seal if we wanted to sketch or photograph an especially nice specimen. We preferred to immortalize the gentlemen in a lively, fighting pose, roaring and upright, rather than lazily sprawled out over the stones like sacks of salt, snuffling and snorting as they slept. A couple of well-aimed stones were usually enough to get these animals into the desired martial posture. Still, we had to be careful not to get crushed. Elephant seals always try to fall on their tormentors with their full weight.

Sitting pretty

WE EVENTUALLY left the seals on the beach to enjoy their *dolce far niente*[2] undisturbed. We fastened the boat a little more securely to a boulder with ropes that we hauled out of a rotting seal-hunters' oil processor that stood a ways farther on.

The rocky, stone-strewn beach presented a sorry sight: it lay full of washed-up wreckage. We saw the weather-beaten remains of a shattered longboat, hundreds of decaying oil barrels, the mast of a schooner, and all sorts of other things that spoke silently of a tragedy at sea that must have taken place there. Might these be the sad remains of the Australian schooner that disappeared with all hands onboard in this area twelve years before?

There was no trace of men on the island. Shipwrecked souls would in any case have immediately signaled upon the approach of a ship and would certainly have shown themselves when we landed. Of the schooner's crew, twenty-six heads strong, not a single sign of life had ever been seen, despite a lengthy search. Not even a piece of wreckage had ever washed up anywhere. But that didn't mean it was out of the question that the remains of the vessel had finally been thrown up on land here.

For a seaman it isn't particularly pleasant to stand by the wreckage of a ruined ship, and we stood in silence to remember the unknown companions who had been claimed by the ocean. We thought about all the miseries that the twenty-six men had probably endured before the cold waves had mercifully closed over their heads. Poor fellows. Poor wives and children who were left behind. Without speaking, we walked between groups of lazing elephant seals to the hut where the seal hunters had lived. The building, made of wood with a galvanized roof, stood at one end of the beach, under a rock wall. If it were still usable, it might make a nice *pied-à-terre* for us. We hoped to stay for a few days, but that would depend on instructions from the mother ship: we had arranged onboard that the hoisting of a yellow flag on the *Ross* would signal that we had to return immediately.

The hut didn't look all that badly decayed yet. The roof was solid, and the single window and the door were shut. The key still sat in the keyhole, but it was so rusty that we had to ram the door open with the butt of a rifle. The hut had evidently been left in haste. Everything stood exactly as if the place had been lived in the day before: dirty dishes on the table, clothes all over the benches, and an oil lamp on the wall. It was still inhabited, albeit not by hu-

2. This is Italian for "sweet do-nothing," Van der Does's favorite phrase for a nap.

mans. They rustled in every corner and hole — rats, of course. We poked around, hoping to find something that would slake our romantic thirst a bit. The wild, deserted island so strongly conjured up feelings of raw, primitive, romantic adventure that we were really a bit disappointed when we didn't immediately find ourselves landing in the middle of such a tale.

We weren't so young anymore that we required a genuine blood-drenched pirate's nest, but we thought we could do with a little real adventure. The seal hunters appeared to have been fond of a hearty meal. A large number of bottles of assorted pickles stood neatly in rows on shelves along the wall. But it seems they didn't need all that hearty an appetite to have a yen for whiskey. Whiskey bottles lay in great numbers in the corners, empty. A chest full of guns and ammunition indicated what line of business the earlier inhabitants had been in. A large first-aid kit contained mostly a wide assortment of splints. No wonder, since the rocks and reefs that lay all along the coast were piled up so haphazardly that there was a good chance of breaking an arm or a leg.

The hunters' work was naturally confined to the coast where the elephant seals stayed exclusively. Beyond the tools of that trade, the hut had little more than the things necessary for a very primitive way of life: tins of food, fish hooks, decaying foul-weather clothing, seaboots, and the like.

There was still one can of petroleum. Maybe there was an outside chance that we could fill the lamp and save ourselves the trouble of making a campfire from wreckage wood, as we had thought we would have to do. The hut also had a bedroom where, in ship-style, bunks had been built into the wall one above the other. It appeared that every rat on the island had found shelter in the beds' rotting straw. We threw out the reeking filth to get ourselves a more or less usable place to sleep so that we wouldn't have to spend the night under the open sky.

WE DIDN'T spend a lot of time cleaning up the hut, actually. We quickly got our things out of the boat and set out toward the northern point of the island, where, we knew from Tinsworth's reports, there used to be a colony of penguins. On the way we passed the hut where the radio crew of the Australian South Pole Expedition had lived years before. When this group left the island, they apparently neglected to shut the doors of the hut, and now a number of young elephant seals used it as their playground, while their mothers lay about blubbering and grunting contentedly. The whole beach swarmed with elephant seals. Behind every clump of rocks lay a group of these lard-balls, sleeping, always sleeping. The island seemed to be a paradise for the creatures. We kept seeing more and more elephant seals; the water's edge was literally strewn with them. What looked like a pile of stones in the distance turned out to be, as we got closer, yet another group of seals.

We soon reached the penguin colony. Look! A couple of them hopped up on that pile of weather-beaten rocks. The birds had obviously already heard, or smelled, that something strange was afoot, and tripped up onto the rocks to get a better look. They appeared to be Victoria penguins, a rare species. It is the smallest kind of penguin, and the most beautiful. This bird, which is no bigger than a half-grown chicken, is, like all penguins, black on the backside and white on the belly — an unusually decorative coloring. But the Victoria penguin also has as extra ornamentation above its roguish, curious, beady eyes — a row of long green eyebrow-feathers, which wave coquettishly in the wind.

The birds were completely unafraid of us; they did not yet know man. But their first acquaintance with *Homo sapiens* turned out to be decidedly to their disadvantage. The professor dearly wanted two specimens for his collection. A chloroform-drenched cotton wad in the beak killed the victims quickly and painlessly.

The actual colony lay somewhat farther on among the rocks. It was easy to find because of the well-trodden path over which the penguins busily toddled up and down, from the breeding grounds to the water, to take a bath or to look for food, which consisted of small sea creatures. The hens sat brooding in clefts between the stones, sheltered places among the tufts of long tussock grass that grew there. They remained calmly sitting on their nests as we approached. Only if we came a little too close did they peck at our legs, although that shouldn't be taken as an indication of an especially hostile disposition toward humans, because they snapped just as much at any of their fellow penguins that came within their reach. Beyond that, they took precious little notice of us. They looked sideways at us, as if to say, "Hey! What kind of queer customers are these?" Then they exchanged a few words with their neighbor ladies next door, who really didn't think we were worth all the trouble.

The hens showed almost no interest in us whatsoever. The other birds were attracted to us even less — if that's possible. They were far too busy. Energetically they scampered over the stony path on their way to the sea to get food, or returned with their craws full. They were in such a hurry that they calmly walked right over our feet if we were standing in their way. They were much too busy to trouble themselves with us. Unfortunately, night was already beginning to fall; it was time for us to get back to our part of town before dark. We would gladly have observed these interesting birds in their comings and goings for much longer. We consoled ourselves with the thought that later, on the polar continent itself, we would get many more opportunities to study penguins. I quickly made a couple of sketches, and we put the captured penguins in a sack to be prepared later in the laboratory onboard.

On our way back to the hut, Professor Vallin explained some interesting things about antarctic fauna, but especially about our new acquaintances, the penguins. They are wholly aquatic birds, so much so that they move rather clumsily on land. On their short little feet they waggle awkwardly like old ladies out of breath. But they are remarkably supple and speedy in their true element, the water. There they are all elegance and grace itself, and unbelievably fast. Penguins don't move like ducks or geese on the water; they swim in it like fish. Penguins are a good example of a species' adaptation to changed living conditions. Long ago, in an earlier era of the evolutionary history of the earth, when the land of the South Pole really was land and didn't yet carry its measureless layer of glaciers as it does now, the ancestors of penguins must have been actual birds that could fly. Antarctica has actually not always been the endless wilderness of ice that it is today. There were times when this now-inaccessible, barren continent was covered with rich plant growth. The coal-bearing layers of earth that have been found there prove this. But as the climate grew colder and colder, all plant growth eventually disappeared. As a consequence, flying made no sense anymore, so the penguins' ancestors completely lost the ability to do so. With the advance of glaciation, all animal life that had still managed to survive was slowly but surely forced into the sea. The penguins too had to learn to get used to life in the water, since they hadn't adjusted to life in the air like other sorts of birds. And it is truly amazing how wonderfully they have adapted to the watery element. Wings, quills, and feathers have vanished. Their tiny feathers resemble scales more than feathers, and they've developed fins. Thanks to these fins, the penguins are able to move superbly through the water. It is with the greatest of ease that they can hunt and catch their prey (consisting of small fish and shrimp) under water and ice.

ON THE BEACH we had the chance to learn more about another bird of the subantarctic regions, one that had not lost the ability to fly: the skua gull, a true thief and freebooter among the many peaceful bird species of this region. The skua gulls constitute the municipal sanitation department: they clean up all the garbage and corpses. They are pretty, dark brown birds with white bands on their quills, and we had seen them many times circling high in the sky, like true birds of prey. On the beach, several of them were diligently at work cleaning up the washed-up carcass of an elephant seal, and they were so absorbed in this unsavory work that they weren't quick to notice us. Once they did see us, they were reluctant to interrupt their feast. So we left the skuas alone with their gamey elephant seal. It was getting dark, and our stomachs began to protest our long fast. Thanks to the tender care of the steward, we had better things than the skuas did to silence our hunger — although of course that's a matter of taste.

Wandering farther along, we met another inhabitant of the island: a donkey penguin, easy to recognize from the white triangle over its eyes. We had been surprised how comparatively few penguins we had seen, since as far as we knew, the island had been a paradise for all sorts of penguins.

The colony of Victoria penguins numbered only several hundred, very few for a penguin town. So we were sure that there were more penguins on Macquarie — and we were right. The next day we found the other breeding grounds. But on this first evening we encountered only this solitary donkey penguin, who trudged along so indifferently looking for a bite to eat that we immediately christened him "The Beachcomber."

Over dinner we were visited by a couple of Maori fowl, who stood in the open doorway, looking inside curiously. We had seen several more of them on the walk to the penguin breeding grounds. These fowl or their ancestors were certainly among the things that the seal hunters had left behind in their overly hasty departure, along with the two horses that followed us at a distance the whole time without daring to come closer. Once we'd lit the lamp and stoked our pipes, we felt nicely at home in the crude hut, which for years had sheltered some real adventurers.

All sorts of peculiar noises sounded outside, coming from the elephant seals, which lay everywhere among the nearby rocks and in the tall tussock grass. Sometimes they sounded like pigs, which made us feel as if the hut were in the middle of a huge pigsty. Then we'd hear a sound like a barking dog. Sometimes it sounded as if a whole bunch of babies were screeching, and other times it seemed as if a couple of fellows were getting into a big fight somewhere. The whole atmosphere made us feel like voluntary Robinson Crusoes on this deserted island, completely shut off from the outside world. Only the lights of the *Ross,* visible through the window, belied this romantic conception. But with our backs to the window, it was very pleasant to think of ourselves for awhile as genuine pirates.

The professor declared, completely contrary to all tradition, that he didn't give a fig about civilization and cared even less about the accursed shackles that it placed on a man. He swore that he really wanted to spend the rest of his life like a modern-day Pan on Macquarie. What did he care about women, who in any case gave a man nothing but all sorts of misery and commotion? "Nothing! Absolutely nothing!" he assured us. He made these and other nonsensical pronouncements with such fiery conviction that anyone who didn't know this happy, vivacious chap might almost have believed him. He also didn't think much of the miserable situation in Europe, which made a man feel like a slave, a number, reduced to nothing. There, in the civilized world, he had always felt as if he were shut up in a cage with bars on it. So hooray for Macquarie with its unlimited freedom!

Unlike the professor, the doctor and I felt that we would be content to live for half a year on the island. That would give us more than enough time to get to know everything about it. After six months of being alone, it would be nice to sit in a real café again, drinking a mug of beer and watching life walk by in full display like a brightly colored movie. A loud, complaining screech by the door jolted us out of these hermit's meditations, which ought always to be interrupted at just the right moment like that, because they never lead to a reasonable conclusion anyway. It was another Maori fowl, which paid its respects and then entered the hut with elongated strides. It had undoubtedly been lured closer by the strange human sounds. The bird disappeared again into the darkness a moment later. We had been too absorbed in our discussions to catch the bird in time, either for the sake of science or for soup. This event made us think of getting to bed. To do that, we first had to wage formal war against the rats, which had re-occupied the beds we had cleaned up and didn't fancy surrendering their reconquered territory just like that.

Lying in our bunks, lit pipes in our mouths, we talked a good deal longer. Because of the lowing, sneezing, and snoring of the elephants, the conversation turned back naturally toward the seals, about which the doctor,

who dabbled in all the sciences but especially in biology, had a lot of important things to say. But when he started telling us with a momentous air that
the elephant seals formed a transitional species between land and sea mammals, that with their fin-like feet they could move easily in the water but only
with difficulty on land, and that their rear extremities had been transformed
into a sort of tail-fin — when he kept going on and on about all this stuff that
the professor and I had noticed all afternoon, then we tried to impose silence
on him in the form of a well-aimed rat.

But you don't know Dr. Kohl if you think that such a simple means
could shut him up once he had gotten onto one of his hobbyhorses. He
tossed the rat back on his attacker's bunk and calmly went on lecturing about
elephant seals. In ancient times, he told us, when the glacial cover over
Antarctica spread out further and further, elephant seals — along with their
relatives, the sea leopards, sea lions, Weddell seals, and crab-eater seals —
must have been forced into the sea, like penguins, by the persistent and
steadily advancing ice. Back then they were probably land predators, and in
their new element, water, predators they remained. Like all fish-eaters, they
now also had pointed teeth, separated from each other by open spaces.

But when he also wanted to tell us how the male sea elephant came to
have a tapir-like nose, which gave these seals the name of elephant seal, a
swift and succinct end was made to the doctor's lecture by putting out the
light and dumping the sack of penguins on his head. Once we assured him
that the elephants only have this protuberant nose in order to be able to turn
it up against the cause of science, he turned over and went to sleep.

Soon enough all three of us were busy snoring along with the choir
outside.

THE NEXT morning found us on the path again very early, after a hasty breakfast. We had no time to lose and wanted to get as many impressions of the
place as possible in the very short amount of time available to us. Our stay on
the island couldn't be long in any case. Captain Larsen was in a hurry; he
didn't want to miss a single day of the very short polar summer in the Antarctic Ocean, and we had stopped at Macquarie for no other purpose than to investigate whether the whales had already left to go southward.

The doctor wanted to take a few more pictures of the colony of Victoria
penguins. The previous day it had already been too dark for that. Now as
then, groups of elephant seals lay everywhere along the path, sleeping, al-

ways still sleeping. Skua gulls were busy at their clean-up work; Maori fowl puttered about with a self-important air, searching for their morning meal among the rocks.

The Victoria penguins waggled back and forth to the sea, busy as housewives beginning their daily chores. Every now and then they stood still a minute to chat with an acquaintance, but they didn't have much time to spare, and soon enough they wiggled and hopped on down the uneven path. It is a pleasure to observe these remarkable birds for a while; they are always oh-so-busy and their behavior is so very human that they always engage one's attention. Also, their very erect posture and the way they walk with their short little feet are very reminiscent of human beings.

Near the penguin village, on a steep rock sticking up out of the sea, we discovered a colony of cormorants. Their excrement had plastered the whole rock white. Unfortunately, the rock was unreachable: a wide moat of sea-weed waved all around it. The wide brown stalks looked very much like enormous living serpents. With the waves they heaved regularly up and down, and with the incoming and outgoing rollers they glided constantly to and fro, sliding steadily past each other in graceful convolutions and in unbroken, rhythmic movement.

Coming back to the hut, we found that our romantic pirate quarters had been commandeered by a detachment from the *Ross* that had been sent out to catch some young seals: fresh provisions. The meat of the young animals is indeed very tasty. Our food stores, which consisted mostly of cans and bottles of high-quality stuff, very luxurious for whalers, had led the men into temptation. They made up for their theft by catching a few nice donkey penguins alive for the scientists.

Looking for more penguin colonies, we followed the beach southward, armed with knapsacks, cameras, and sketchbooks. The beach was almost entirely covered — literally — with elephant seals. At first we saw mostly females, which weren't more than 3½ meters [11 feet] long, and yearlings of 1½ to 2 meters [5 to 6½ feet], easily recognizable by their fine, very dark hides, which shimmered like velvet. The older animals were the same brownish-gray color as the rocks among which they lay. Many of the larger animals displayed both old and new wounds on their fat bodies, tokens of fierce battles among themselves. Others had thick pus flowing out of their noses; we couldn't figure out why. Maybe they had colds.

The way these animals act can make a novice somewhat anxious. Their movements have something alarming about them, but one quickly notices that their abruptness is nothing other than an expression of fear, caused by their own unwieldiness. By suddenly rearing up their upper bodies and distending their muzzles, blowing and spluttering, they try to frighten the disturbers of the peace. But they give up their attacking posture immediately; it's all bluff and no guts. If you approach them undaunted, they quickly retreat among the rocks or try to scramble to the sea.

In the water the seals move with distinct ease, in contrast with the difficulty that marks their movements on dry land. Sea lions and sea leopards can still use their four limbs to move about on land, but not elephant seals: their rear extremities are positioned directly behind them and have turned into a split steering-tail. Out of water the animals move like caterpillars, with undulating contractions of their long, rounded bodies. Their front limbs assist awkwardly. And yet they managed to move faster than we could over the beach strewn with pebbles and piles of rocks.

There was one giant specimen that we guessed was about 20 feet long, the largest seal that we encountered alive on Macquarie; we called him the king of the seals. He seemed to be an old grump. He lay all alone, yawning and sniffing, while in general these animals lay cozily about each other in groups of twelve to fifteen. A few pebbles were not enough to wake this old codger from his sweet sleep; he only scrabbled dully with his wide rear paw. A small barrage was necessary to recall him to reality and get him to assume a fighting stance for a moment, which the photographer and the artist extended on his behalf. But immediately thereafter he let himself collapse with a heavy sigh and resumed his disturbed *dolce far niente*, without troubling himself further about the invaders. He had probably taken the upright-moving beings for nothing more than overgrown penguins. Little bunches of

Beach scene on Macquarie

donkey penguins waggled among the seals on the beach, which grew flatter as it sloped away from the sea. A few birds fished diligently for food in pools and puddles. We saw many penguins and Maori fowl in the immediate vicinity of the elephant seals, and often we even saw the penguins peacefully stepping on the fat seals' bodies and picking things off of them, probably little crabs or mussels. The two species seemed to be friendly with one another — a sort of symbiosis, perhaps. Much choosier than the elephant seals, who in a certain sense are the proletarians of their type, are the fur seals, of which we saw a few. Fur seals don't care for the company of penguins, and actually seem to prefer to move away from them. It is known that fur seals retreat from a stretch of beach where penguins appear, and then actually avoid that place for years afterward.

In contrast to the good-natured elephant seal, the fur seal is easily irritated, perhaps too sensitive to endure the chatter and twitter of penguins, especially during mating season. The doctor thought that the unpleasant smells that rise out of the penguins' breeding grounds might drive the seals away. But that really isn't likely, because the smells that surround the seals don't exactly offer competition to Coty, Houbigant, and Pinaud, either.[3] I think it's obvious that the cause is to be found in the availability of food. Penguins live together in such huge numbers that their presence means food shortage to the seals. So then it's simply the struggle for existence that forces the seals to retreat.

In any case, it's a fact that the fur seal, the source of the expensive sealskin jacket that is in such high fashion among the ladies because of its lovely shine and velvety softness, is very sensitive. Some little thing — a cast-off match, for example — left behind by people in a place where fur seals try to stay is sufficient to drive the animals from that place, sometimes for a year or two. Seal hunters know this and so have to take this peculiarity into consideration.

To watch the donkey penguins close up, we laid on a flat piece of sandy beach between a pair of elephant seals, who only looked lazily about and then went on sleeping soundly when they saw that we meant no harm. The penguins, who had uncertainly kept themselves a little ways off, huddled together in groups. They appeared to be conferring over what attitude they should adopt toward the strange visitors. At last four of them stepped up to us, more or less shy and hesitant — a sort of welcoming committee.

3. These are the names of perfume-makers.

The deputation

Two paces distant they remained standing, and they took a good look at the aliens, stealthily and half-afraid. Avoiding sudden movements, we said Good Morning to them, whereupon they answered with soft throat sounds. After that they evidently asked us something, but of course we didn't understand them, and they didn't understand our answer, either. Obviously disappointed, they gave it up, looking at each other in puzzlement. After wandering about inconclusively, they waggled away again. Our whistling brought them back, listening curiously, so that we had another chance to immortalize the deputation on film and paper. But when they couldn't make themselves understood, the penguins preferred to give up further attempts to approach us.

The young penguins were comical in their rough, sloppy down coats. The largest one scampered behind the older birds, chattering loudly, begging for food. An amusing sight, an agitated ball of fluff like that, lurching to and fro on too-short feet like a sailing ship in the doldrums. The young birds didn't go to the water of their own accord to forage. Instead, they accosted whichever grownup penguin first emerged from the sea with a full gullet, and they walked howling and twittering behind her, until she, just to get rid of them, spit out a piece of her meal, which the young vagabonds then gulped up greedily.

From the penguin beach we climbed up the steep hill covered with tussock grass and Maori cabbage. Underneath the slope, under overhanging grass, lay the nests of several donkey penguins. They were nothing more than shallow holes in the bare earth. In some of the nests lay eggs; others sheltered clumsy fledglings covered in gray down. Narrow, curving, beaten-down paths led from the settlement to the beach. Above the hill, which was about 200 meters [650 feet] high, stretched a sort of plateau. Farther on in the south rose the highest peak of the island, Mount Elder, which still obviously exhibited its original volcanic character. The old crater was clearly recognizable.

For a little ways we followed the high ridge up which we had just climbed. The surface was marshy and damp here, full of puddles and holes, making the going difficult. The plateau dipped in the north-south direction, and a little brook streamed through it. There were no remaining patches of snow to be seen; the island was already decked out in spring attire. In this valley the plant growth was fairly luxurious. The round leaves of the Maori cabbage were large and fresh here, and the tussock grass grew strong and high. Large, light-green clumps of *azolla* ferns, liverworts, and other ferns gave a little variety to the otherwise monochromatic, treeless vegetation; especially common was a plant with long, green stems and reddish-brown flowers.

After being together with others on a ship for months, a man is usually drawn instinctively to go his own way, without there being any unfriendly motivation behind it. That's how we lost sight of Professor Vallin. The rest of us had passed through some very swampy places in which we unexpectedly sank up to our waists, and that made us worried about the wanderer, who naturally was off somewhere collecting plants. Our concern was heightened when the weather turned stormy and our calls received no answer. Finally we concluded that he was looking for another penguin colony, just as we were. Soon afterward we saw the bird city, like an irregular, white-speckled band, weaving about over the dark-colored landscape, and we headed in that direction.

Amid the dark, forlorn mountains, the colony looked so tremendously large that we first thought we were seeing millions of birds together. Coming closer, we contented ourselves with a census of several tens of thousands. But most certainly we stood before a truly great penguin breeding ground. And, sure enough, there at the edge of the settlement sat our friend the professor, already taking pictures. At this distance we could already hear the tumult that the thousands upon thousands of birds made. As we approached the settlement, we saw what appeared to be a breeding ground for king penguins. These penguins have a canary-yellow crest that stands up when they're excited, just like the crest on a cockatoo.

The king penguins are almost two feet high, much larger than the Victoria penguins. Here, as at the donkey-penguin settlement, our company was officially welcomed by a distinguished delegation. Here too the delegates departed disappointed, shaking their heads at our stupidity. We were apparently not "penguin-capable," and we were dismissed without further thought. One of the delegation went so far that, as he went his way grumbling and grousing, he walked right over our boots with a dismissive gesture, splashing his webbed feet. The traffic in the colony was heavy. Long processions worked their way continuously up and down, and in such a regular and orderly fashion that it looked as if they were directed by an invisible police force.

Each penguin followed along without looking to or fro, muttering to itself, completely occupied with its own weighty pursuits. Only the hens remained calmly sitting on their nests, on their eggs, or by the downy chicks. The animals didn't mind us visiting their city at all. In fact, we had to watch where we walked. The penguins hadn't gone so far as to develop a community sanitation service, although their society was sufficiently well-ordered to have one, and the nests lay close together. As with most animals, the mothers with young were more alert than the others, and they would peck our legs if a seaboot came too close to the nest.

The behaviors of the penguins show a very striking similarity to those of humans. There is the same fuss over little things, the same jealousy and envy. You notice this immediately if you take the trouble to observe the life of these birds a bit more closely. And that's precisely the greatest attraction that a penguin colony has for us: it is in many ways a mirror of our own society. All polar explorers mention this with amazement and affection about their friends the penguins, who in the loneliness of the polar region are seen almost as equals.

The nests of the little Victoria penguins were already simple enough, but the camps of these penguins seemed to be true proletarian housing, despite their royal name. They lay close together and were nothing more than deep holes clawed into the stony surface, so every family could peek into the nest next door. This naturally led to all sorts of complications. People also get testy when they're housed together so closely that the neighbors can see everything. So in the penguin city, disputes and disturbances were the order of the day. And our presence that day provided extra inducement to all sorts of quarreling. If we threw a stone among the animals, the one penguin blamed the other for making trouble, and at the same time other families took the opportunity to get in their neighbors' hair, and so the unrest spread like a tide throughout the whole colony. There was an unholy ruckus, and while we stepped through the settlement, our seaboots received many a vicious gash from a beak. Eventually such a battle arose among the penguins themselves that it looked like a civil war.

On nearly all the nests sat hens with downy gray young, which looked unusually well-fed with their tight, round bellies. These chicks looked just like gray balls of wool with loosely dangling heads and little sticks for wings and feet. After a long search we even found some eggs in various stages of brooding: study material for the scientists.

Meanwhile, the weather had gotten worse. Reluctantly we left the penguins' enjoyable city and climbed up the mountain's spine to see what condition the sea was in. The weather appeared to have broken, and we wondered if the quarantine flag would be flying on the *Ross*, the sign to return to the ship. And sure enough, even before we could see the ship, we heard the steam whistle giving its impatient hoots, with short pauses in between.

It was clearly necessary for us to return immediately. When we reached the ridge, coming out from the protected valley, it was blowing hard out of the east. It couldn't get worse than that. It meant that wind and water would now fill the beach where we had landed the day before. It would probably be impossible for us to get through the high breakers with our flat-bottomed boat. The yellow flag beckoned impatiently and urgently on the ship. We hoped that the windy conditions wouldn't develop into a storm that would hold us prisoner for days on the island. By itself that wouldn't have bothered us. Quite the opposite, in fact: we wouldn't have minded a long stay on Macquarie. But we also knew that Captain Larsen's intention was not to stay here an hour longer than was necessary. He wanted to force his way through the ring of pack ice as soon as possible so as not to lose a single day of the very short polar summer.

It was a hasty return — over the rocks on the narrow, rough beach, over stones and alarmed elephant seals, after we first went down the mountain head over heels along a fresh cleft in the earth. We could have started an avalanche of stones running after us, but we were in a hurry, so we chanced it. That sliding party shortened our way back quite considerably.

We didn't concern ourselves anymore with the countless elephant seals that were still sleeping and growing bacon for the sake of future seal-hunters. If they lay in our way, we simply jumped and ran right over them. They looked up a little and roared at our intrusion, but resumed snoring just as hard right afterward. We frightened countless elephant seals as we hurriedly ran over the rocks, sending stones jarring loose to plop onto the snoring blubberbags. This made them start fighting among themselves, since one would think he'd been attacked by a neighbor, and so on. We stirred up a real commotion among the membership of the seal elephant club, but we had no time to enjoy the furious beasts. The steam whistle of the *Ross* kept on blowing with short pauses, insisting on greater speed.

We reached the hut dead tired and gasping, but a rest was out of the question. It was late in the afternoon, and we had also gotten fearfully hungry from our strenuous march. So, while we gathered our baggage together, brought it to the beach, and stowed it in the boat, we polished off a couple of tins' worth on the run. The sea was already so high that we left behind all the food and other things we didn't need so that the boat would float as well as it could. It was still going to be heavy, difficult work to get it through the rising surf. The two scientists weren't sea types and wouldn't know just the right moment to try, if such a moment came.

We tried several times to get the boat into position on a high, incoming roller, but the maneuver didn't work, and over and over again a following wave would smack the thing back sideways and half full of water. And there we sat! We couldn't get away from Macquarie!

The *Ross* had already left her anchorage, which had grown unsafe. She had steamed around to the lee of the island and had dropped anchor there. Luckily, she had left behind one of the chase boats, the *Star* 2, to help us if necessary.

In our battles with the boat, all three of us had gotten soaking wet. And it was cold in the biting east wind. The doctor and I had to laugh at the profes-

A dangerous resting place

sor, who gave up the whole show. He knocked off the top of a bottle of port on a stone, drank half of it down to stay warm, and wormed his way blithely down onto the leeside of the biggest elephant seal on the beach, right up against its fat, lazy body, which undeniably radiated some welcome warmth. The poor soul was exhausted, and it took some trouble to convince him to seek a more sensible place to rest.

On the chase boat they had seen our useless attempts to leave the island and understood that it was impossible for us to get away without help. So the captain brought the chase boat as close to the coast as the surf and the rocks allowed, about 400 meters [850 feet] from the beach. To our relief, we saw a fully manned boat lowered into the sea. Through an opening between the rocks they approached as close as they dared, after which they sent a line to us on an oar. Swimming out to it, I managed to grab it and fasten it securely to the painter of our boat.

Quickly the two scientists clambered in, and our little cockleshell was pulled carefully through the dashing surf toward the sloop — luckily without getting full of water, although it wouldn't have mattered much. The benumbed professor and the doctor, his teeth chattering, were quickly helped into the sloop, wrapped in blankets, and put in a safe corner. And I was happy to be able to take an oar in order to get warm by rowing. The half-drowned flat-bottomed boat was taken in on a towline.

It was strenuous work to row the sloop against wind and sea through the high incoming breakers. It was a good thing that the stubborn chase-boat captain handled the steering oar himself. Without mishap we reached the chase boat, which lay thrashing heavily at her anchor. The flat-bottomed boat had meanwhile filled with water. Before it sank we had just managed to fish out our things; otherwise this chapter would have remained unillustrated.

Later on our little vessel was hoisted onboard via the painter, to spare us the bailing. The chase boat now looked like a luxury steamer to us. Captain, pilot, and engineer willingly offered us their places for the night. But we contented ourselves with sleeping on their mess table and benches, though we gratefully accepted dry clothes and whiskey.

Returning to the mother ship was out of the question for the evening. However, the Star 2 did immediately weigh anchor, in order not to be caught on the lee shore in this stormy weather. She had in fact been ordered to join the other ships on the leeside of the island.

Snoring elephant seal

The short journey around the north side of Macquarie put our seaman-ship strongly to the test. Even if you can stay as frisky as a kitten in all kinds of weather on a big ship, that doesn't by any means guarantee that you'll stay equally frisky on a smaller vessel, which makes completely different kinds of movements. We found this out the hard way. First Sweden put his pipe away and flew hastily down the stairs to pay his toll to Neptune. Then Germany followed hard on his heels and bent next to him over the railing. Holland held up a tiny bit better, but went white and red in the face by turns. But one thing is certain: whiskey is an outstanding medicine for complaints of this nature.

Long ago, when the Batavian Yacht Club was still near Pasar Ikan,[4] we often sailed on the *Penguin* in the roads of Batavia.[5] In the monsoon season there would be such a short, choppy sea that half the crew, all sailors, felt the need to feed the fish from time to time. But there was always a crock of the Schiedammer liquid kept ready so as to stop such generosity toward the *kakap*, *tongkol*, and *tengiri*.[6]

4. This is Indonesian for "Fish Market."

5. Batavia was the Dutch colonial name for Jakarta. "In the roads" is a nautical phrase referring to partly sheltered areas of water near a shore in which vessels may ride at anchor.

6. These are the names of species of Indonesian fish.

CHAPTER NINE

Icebergs

The first iceberg

The next morning we transferred from the chase boat to the *Ross*. From the chase boat's bridge we could jump over the railing of the mother ship. We had to do that very carefully, keeping an eye on the waves. The sea was running high, and the little vessel was tossing and rolling heavily. An anchor on the ocean floor kept it free of the big ship. Just when the doctor, coming last, had jumped over, the railing of the bridge, on which he had just been standing, tore off into splinters against the side of the *Ross*.

The chase boats were supplied with coal for the rest of the journey southward. This was done in a peculiar fashion. The chase boats lay prancing alongside the ship like tempestuous horses, so the sacks of coal couldn't be loaded the usual way, with the winch; too much precious coal would be lost. Such a luxury wasn't allowed; nowhere in the Antarctic was there coal for sale. So we threw the sacks from the *Ross* onto the decks of the chase boats, one sack after another, every time a wave wafted the boats high alongside. Later we became very adept at this unusual method of bunkering. When we were in the open sea in the polar region, the chase boats were always supplied with coal in this manner. It couldn't be done any other way. Still, we knew very well that in raw weather, it often happened that more coal landed in the sea than on the decks. Sometimes the pieces flew about if a wave smashed a chase boat against the *Ross*.

All five chase boats got roughly enough fuel and provisions for the rest of the trip to the south. Most of all, they got good advice: to stay within sight of the mother ship. Before we reached the pack ice, at latitude 60° to 65° S, there was still a lot of bad weather to be feared. Icebergs could be expected soon, and sea ice. Things would look pretty bad for a chase boat that got lost in such an ice field if it was far away from the others.

While the chase boats were provided with the necessities, we used the time to drag-search the ocean floor. Only various sorts of seaweed and a mass of shells were brought up. Fishing with hooks from astern yielded similarly slim results. I caught a hideously ugly fish, full of prickles and warts, which turned out to be a hitherto-unknown species, and the professor threatened to name it officially after me, out of revenge for the mockery of his fanciful polar costume, naturally. It offended my aesthetic feelings as an artist to think of my name being linked forever to such a monstrosity, and so I threatened to immortalize him in his reviled outfit if he followed through with his threat.

Luckily, he didn't do it, and consequently I am also not allowed to let you see how chic the professor really looked in his costume made of polar bear fur.

Nowhere in the waters off Macquarie was there a single whale to be seen, so there was no reason to stay there any longer. When all the chase boats were ready, the whole flotilla went anchors aweigh that same evening and headed southward, towards the ice and the unknown. While we sailed along the coast, the island lay there like a long, stretched-out giant whose head carried a yellowish fiery glow in the south. Only there was the view open and limitless. A couple of lemon-yellow clouds shone at the zenith. Other than that, the sky was completely covered with clouds, just as it had been during previous days.

While we were near the coast, the ship was followed by Cape doves, skua gulls, and countless albatrosses. A multitude of king penguins romped in the water and, just like dolphins, popped up lightning-quick and then disappeared again. The grace and liveliness with which they moved formed a startling contrast to the calm and clumsy thoughtfulness that they had displayed the previous day on land.

Now southward, to the Ross Sea! Many might not even know the name of this ocean, and that of its counterpart, the Weddell Sea. And yet these seas are larger than, for example, the North Sea. And both have a characteristic unusual for the polar regions: they are "open" — that is to say, nearly ice-free, once the seafarer manages to break through the broad ring of the pack ice that separates these seas from the Pacific and the Atlantic Oceans.

Until now, only a few South Pole expeditions had pressed through to the Ross Sea — and only those ships that had been specially built for a trip through the ice. The *Ross,* on the other hand, was scarcely different in any way from an ordinary freighter.

During these days, of course, all the names that are linked to the history of the Ross Sea came up for review. Balleny and Ross, both Englishmen; next the Norwegians Bull and Borchgrevink; and then Scott, Shackleton, and the Japanese Shirase. The last ones who sailed before us into the Ross Sea were Scott with the *Terra Nova* and Amundsen with the *Fram.* Both reached their stated goal, the geographic South Pole, but the valiant Scott, alas, never returned.

It had been eleven years since the bow of the *Fram* cleaved the waves of the Ross Sea. We all knew the histories of the various South Pole expeditions, and they formed the main topic of our discussions. How would the *Ross,* a ship that had never sailed anywhere but the Indies, hold its own in the ice? Many, especially those who already had more experience with ice, would have felt more comfortable on a small but genuine ice-ship.

THE DAY after we left Macquarie, the mist grew thick and the steam whistle sounded continuously, not only so that the chase boats wouldn't wander off but also so that we could "hear" possible icebergs. Sounds are thrown back from the walls of icebergs, and in conditions of poor visibility the echoes often reveal their presence.

The chance of encountering icebergs already at this latitude wasn't especially great, but so little is really known about the extent of the ever-changing ice zone in these parts that we preferred not to take chances. In the mist we also sailed at half-throttle in order not to risk collisions with any ice there might be. Also, from that time on there was always a man on watch in the *tönne* high on the foretop.

When the mist lifted, all the chase boats turned out to be nearby. There was no ice to be seen, but a couple of whales were spouting in the distance.

It isn't water that whales spout, as many people think. When a whale comes to the surface to take a breath, it forcefully blows the warm breath out of its lungs: it's air, in other words. Since a whale is a mammal, it can't stay underwater for more than about a quarter of an hour without drowning. The warm breath is exhaled as a visible stream of water vapor, drifts for a moment like a little cloud, and then dissolves in the atmosphere.

The first two days after leaving Macquarie, there was no cause to complain about the weather. The third day also began with a wonderful, radiant morning. The deep-blue ocean waves rolled peacefully in long, slow swells, as in the tropics. The atmosphere was clear as glass, the sky blue and white — not, as was usually the case, obscured by

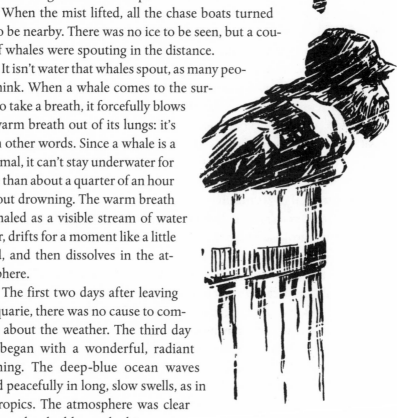

The lookout

leaden, formless haze. But by midday the weather had wrapped itself in the same gray shroud again, and the wind picked up. In the evening a hailstorm chased over the ship with short, sharp wind gusts, followed by a thick snow-storm out of the southwest. There could be icebergs in the area, and we couldn't even see a hundred meters in front of us; from the bridge one could scarcely see the deck.

Between pelting snow showers, the sign was given for the chase boats to stop when night began to fall. With such poor visibility, it was too risky to sail farther. Meanwhile, a sharp eye was kept out for icebergs, which the storm might well have driven out forward. Soon there was nothing more to be seen of the chase boats.

From all previous expeditions we knew that we had to reckon with heavy storm weather upon reaching the ice zone. But that night was the stormiest that we had experienced since leaving Norway. Especially for the sake of the chase boats, we heaved to and faced the ship seaward. That way, when both wind and sea came head-on, the ship didn't take on as much wa-ter as before. Even so, such great sheets of water came over the *Ross* that things grew dangerous. The forward and rear holds became impassable ter-rain. A few ventilators had already been swept away, and the resultant open-ings had to be quickly closed. On the bridge deck, a couple of doors were stove in, and — more serious — one of the lifeboats was very badly damaged. Meanwhile, water poured into the engine room from the sloop deck through the sheared-off ventilators.

Bit by bit the storm intensified, until toward midnight a hurricane raged. Having come around, the ship rode nicely over the onrushing moun-tains of water. It was a great and wonderful show of the power of wind and sea during that stormy night. The whole ship trembled and shuddered like a hunted animal in fear for its life. The steel rigging, stretched taut as harp strings by the hurricane, buzzed and shrieked under the enormous wind pressure. If you stuck your head a little above the bridge railing to see how the phosphorescing water flowing like liquid fire washed over the foredeck, your breath was cut off as if by a knife, and the flying foam hit you in the face as hard as hail. Ola, the man at the wheel, even claimed that the hurricane had shoved his teeth into his throat when he stood up to look at the compass, but that Ola was a jokester.

Everything that wasn't nailed down was ripped loose and flew over-board. With a crack the coverings of the sloops ripped off. The ship rolled so far to the side that the masts and funnels threatened to snap off, and the rigging and funnel stays quickly gave way.

The dull thunder of the breaking waves drowned out every other sound. The whole creation seemed filled with the mighty voice of the hurricane: it howled through the rigging, and cried and clattered in the foam that the sharp wind ripped off the tops of the waves. The wildly tossing sea boomed like a rumbling thunderstorm, and the waves, whipped up ever higher, broke with a roar. One could already hear the great breakers approaching from far away, even before their white crowns were visible. Coming nearer, one of these graybeards hefted its ragged, tousled top ever higher in the rushing firmament, until it was as high as a living mountain, and came hurling at the quivering ship. But the *Ross* always kept climbing faithfully up against the dark, flowing hills of water.

We were happy when day broke and in the weak gray light we could see again. By then the show was, if possible, even greater. As far as the eye could see, the wild, swept-up ocean was covered with long white bands of foam, left behind by the breaking rollers. We couldn't see very far, because the storm pushed up a thick haze of dashing water, which even from a distance of just a few ship-lengths obscured everything from sight.

Nobody got much sleep that night. I lay in my bunk in foul-weather clothes and seaboots; I might be called at any moment. Unluckily, my bunk lay athwartships. One minute I slid with a jerk toward the foot of my bed and ended up on the lower level, only to be dashed against the head end shortly thereafter as the ship leaned over toward the other side. No wonder that the greater part of the rigging was destroyed that day.

At breakfast everybody had something to say. One seaman claimed that he'd slept like an elephant seal, but of course nobody believed him. Another thought that a storm like this was something wonderful, a revelation of nature's grandeur, but really was better viewed with solid ground underfoot. He sounded like a retired sea-captain who, as it storms and hails outside, presses his nose against the window but then goes and nestles snugly in his armchair and tells stories about the bad weather that he once experienced. A third said that his cabin had been transformed into a swimming pool, in which he and all that he owned had bobbled about. Still others were in bad moods and cursed. It had really been an unusually awful night. But by day people usually see things in a more cheerful light. In fact, during the course of the morning it cleared up a bit, and as the mercury rose in the barometer, so did the grumblers' mood.

Two of the chase boats had been driven off in the storm. There were only three to be seen at daybreak, but several hours later the smoke of the other two appeared above the horizon. Lucky thing! They might well not have survived the hurricane.

Now that the flotilla was again complete, we immediately resumed our course.

In the afternoon the wind died down, the sky cleared again, and the sea quieted down remarkably. Steaming southward, we had apparently left the storm band behind us, and by evening the sun set in beautiful weather in such a glittering glow of color that one would think that bad weather could never happen there.

When at midnight it was no darker than at twilight, it was clear that we had already reached a rather high latitude. It began to get quite cold, and the central heating that was furnished to all the living quarters was turned on.

FIVE DAYS after leaving Macquarie, we paused in beautifully calm weather and a very quiet sea to restock the chase boats with coal. But this time it was somewhat easier and quicker than the first time. It was advisable to provide the chasers with fuel. At any moment now we could expect ice.

Above the horizon in the south there was a pale glimmer of light. Was it iceblink? Iceblink is what they call the light, cloudless atmosphere that usually hangs above an ice field. Over open water, evaporation usually occurs, leading to cloud formation. If the water is covered in ice, however, the atmosphere above it is relatively devoid of water vapor, and clouds don't form. Iceblink is usually visible from a great distance, and from its brightness one can estimate the thickness of an ice field. Above open, loose ice, the iceblink is rather weak; a bright, strong shining indicates thick ice.

Many birds flew around the ship, although only albatrosses and whale birds. These latter were so named by whalers because they often follow whales. Also, when the whales dive, they follow their trails and thus give the chasers an indication of what direction to go looking for the prize. Apparently it's not always exclusively the trail of whales that they follow, because although a great many of us searched for whales, we saw nothing more than two humpback whales (*Megaptera boops*) the whole day. The flight of the whale bird is unusually busy and nervous, compared with the calm and stately soaring of the albatross, for whom a single flap of the wings appears to be enough to brave the force of a storm, and a slight contraction of the wingtips enough to alter its balance.

We now frequently saw albatrosses alight on the water. They always managed to keep their heads into the wind. As they descended in a flawless glide, they stretched out their feet like rudders and kept their beaks into the wind, as befits any good flier. To take off, they skittered several meters over the water, and then, the outstretched wings set a little aslant, they lifted into the air.

THE DAYS continued to lengthen as we neared the Antarctic Circle. The nights were like muted days, and stars ceased appearing in the heavens. The temperature of the seawater indicated the nearness of ice. One day the thermometer read about 5.1° C; the next, no more than about 1.7° C. Excitement onboard rose in proportion as the temperature sank. Where was the ice? At night above the eastern horizon lay a clear white strip of light. Above that drifted a few loose cumuli.

If you looked just long enough, you thought you saw land. Ice! No, it wasn't that, either. It was *Smörland* (Butterland), said the Norwegians. This is land that exists only in the imagination, and it melts away like butter in the sun whenever one tries to approach it.

The sky was overcast the whole day: heavy, dark, and gray. The somber picture changed completely toward midnight, when a welter of warm colors blossomed up along the entire horizon. Gray, formless clouds quickly became transparent, and their edges turned a radiant gold. Gradually flowing and shifting, the delicate mists played their happy game with changing tints, in every nuance between faint blue and flaming purple — a delight for the eyes.

The following day brought a new sign of changes at hand. The color of the ocean gradually grew green, the characteristic color of seawater in the far south. This peculiar color is caused by the plankton, which for some time now had displayed a considerable increase in diatoms.

Great industry reigned on the *Ross*. Finishing touches were made to all sorts of preparations for the hunt. But where were the whales hiding? The past few days we'd seen only one single "blow." That wasn't worth the trouble. We had expected to meet great schools of whales by now.

By searching for whales, we had nearly forgotten about the ice, so it was

Tabular iceberg

actually a surprise when at 63° S we encountered our first iceberg. No, it wasn't some huge, dangerous iceberg that stirred up memories of the *Titanic* and other such sea dramas. The situation wasn't anywhere close to that. The weather was fine, the sea calm, the visibility excellent, and there wasn't the slightest danger that we would come upon anything unexpectedly.

The first iceberg that we came across was an old leftover from last year. In its youth it had probably been an imposing colossus of ice, but now it was no more than a melted-down, crumbled ruin. Sea, wind, and sun had robbed it of its greatness and girth. It lay lurching about on the waves like a disabled, rudderless ship. Icicles of frozen seawater hung from its protruding edges. It froze quite hard at night, while during the day its temperature fluctuated around the freezing point.

Shortly after the first, worn-down iceberg, a second one came into view, a much larger one. It was three hours later before we were alongside it. It was a typical Antarctic iceberg, a so-called tabular iceberg, with a completely flat top and nearly perpendicular sides.

These tabular icebergs occur only in the Antarctic Ocean. They are the so-called calved-off pieces of the Great Ice Barrier. The barrier itself is in fact nothing more than one immense ice shelf, formed by the ice pack that has slid off Antarctica and been forced out to sea, where it continues to drift without breaking off the continental ice. Very slowly, a few meters every year, this land ice slides out to sea, year after year; each winter deposits a clearly visible layer of snow.

On a tabular iceberg these annual layers are easy to distinguish on the top portion. Lower down it is less clear, because the snow is condensed into a homogenous mass by the heavy pressure of the layer lying above.

All icebergs consist of glacier ice, which is white, not transparent, as opposed to frozen water, which can be as clear as glass.

When people talk about icebergs, they automatically link them to highly dramatic circumstances. They think of the terribly tragic accident of the *Titanic,* which at the time sent a shock wave of emotion throughout the entire civilized world.

As it turns out, the icebergs in the North Atlantic Ocean are actually much more dangerous than the ones in the Antarctic. This is the case because they lie on a heavily traveled route, but even more because the cold current that pushes the icebergs to the south collides with a warm sea current at around the latitude of the Newfoundland banks. The temperature differences that occur as a result often cause extensive fogbanks to arise, and therein lurks the greatest danger. The fog can so hinder visibility that a ship first sights an iceberg when it is already too late to avoid a collision.

After the *Titanic* disaster, the American government set up an ice-patrol service, which gives ships radio reports on the presence of icebergs and their precise location. Particularly large and dangerous icebergs are blown up with dynamite by this service. Nevertheless, it can still be frightening to sail these waters. I can remember crossing the Atlantic at the latitude of Newfoundland in the summertime, when the ship had fallen into dense fog and was sailing cautiously, feeling its way through the thick, chill mists, while the steam whistle's agitated, gloomy wail was heard incessantly. That sound cuts through to the bone and gives you goosebumps.

On the *Ross,* however, icebergs didn't cause any anxiety, and they weren't accompanied by frightening circumstances. The weather was clear and bright, and the sea was quite calm. The sun shone happily on the steep

Whimsically shaped icebergs

walls of the ice monsters, which drifted by calmly and majestically. Naturally we kept a respectful distance — not so much out of fear of running into that portion of an iceberg that lies underwater, but because very often the sea around an iceberg, particularly on the windward side, is covered with chunks of ice debris, large and small, that the force of the waves has broken off the ice mass.

The invisible part of an iceberg is not as large as people generally think. We all learned in school that the specific gravity of ice is 0.9, but that holds only for compact, clear ice. Glacial ice is markedly lighter because it contains much more air. So the portion of an iceberg that lies underwater is about four times as great as the visible portion, and not nine times as great, as is usually thought.

But although on the *Ross* there were no ominous circumstances, the first appearance of an iceberg was still generally experienced as a great event. We had stepped over the threshold of the polar region. Moreover, each new discovery brought happiness, insofar as beauty goes — even for us Westerners, whose senses require such strong stimuli. The lively conversations proved how moved the men were as they stood in groups, staring at the white giants gliding by.

Truly great and unusually beautiful they were, these shining white mountains of ice. The flat tops, fresh with snow, glittered white and clean in the bright sunshine. Millions of ice crystals shimmered out of the walls, which were like hewn marble. The gentle swell sloshed and gurgled in the holes and hollows that the water had carved out at the foot of the ice.

Several completely white snow petrels hovered over the shining top of one ice mountain in the thin azure. That was a vision never to be forgotten: an iceberg gliding past, so stately, so white and undefiled in the full, glistening sun, so distinguished and worthy in its unconscious grandeur.

It often happens that important things are pushed into the background by trifles that come up unexpectedly. And so a humpback whale that suddenly popped up between the ship and the iceberg attracted all our attention. First we would see its dark upper side, then the lighter side of its long fins, which looked like enormous, threatening swords as they struck out high above the water and then waved back. The animal was probably just playing — but such playing! Its tremendous body sometimes came almost completely out above the water.

Evening brought no darkness, but it did bring more whales of the same

species. When some blue whales and fin whales also arrived to pay their respects, the merry mood onboard reached its high point. Every member of
the crew had a share, in accordance with his wages, of the profit that the
whale harvest would bring. So it was oil and golden kroner they saw dashing
about there in the water, and they imagined themselves already as capitalists.
Never had the crew on the *Ross* been so excited. Oil fever is no less severe than
gold fever, and naturally it finds its victims especially among whalers.

The night — which really wasn't night anymore but rather an open,
clear dusk in which one could see as clearly as in broad daylight — brought
still more icebergs. Another one of these had the typical tabular form. Its
height was an estimated 30 to 35 meters [around 100 feet], and its length, 400
meters [1,300 feet]. The iceberg displayed a large cave in its side above the waterline, washed out by the waves. The sea, which was pushed into the cave by
the swell, compressed the air in it with such force that the water was blown
out again like a cloud of dust.

All the other icebergs we saw had been greatly altered in appearance after all their wandering, eaten away by the wind and the sea, and some had already been completely overturned. The young icebergs had fresh fractures;
the older ones showed their weather-beaten sides. And the ancient bergs
looked like huge, drifting balloons, so smooth and round had they been
washed by the sea. It was striking that even through the binoculars we saw
no moraine streaks — or any other stony deposits — on a single iceberg.

The temperature of the seawater had gradually dropped — it was already below freezing — and the bird world was being represented by new
species, chiefly two kinds of petrels, one of which closely resembled the Cape
dove. The pure white snow petrel (*Pagodroma nivea*) also occurred more frequently now.

The next day it was no longer solitary floating icebergs that brightened
the view of the sea. Now they seemed to blossom out of the water like mush-
rooms. By the dozens they towered above the bright horizon, their white
flanks shining in the sun wherever you looked.

Now it was freezing both by day and by night, and the weather remained fresh and lovely, making us feel uncommonly good. Such steely,
healthy weather chases the blood forcefully through the arteries, a source of
energy and lust for life.

CHAPTER TEN

In the Pack Ice

Open pack ice

—◦◦◦—

The brisk cold and the unusually clear atmosphere indicated that there was a great deal of ice in the immediate vicinity. And sure enough, toward midnight on December 14, the ice pilot in the lookout announced that there was pack ice ahead — thick in the southeast, but thinner toward the south. A short while before this we had sailed through several small stretches of brash ice, chunks of ice that have been ground up by the waves.

My watch was asleep when the *Ross* entered the actual pack ice, and I woke up from the unaccustomed sensation of the ship lying still. Coming on deck to see what was happening, I was taken aback by the spectacle that has always been preserved in my memory as a nearly divine revelation of the glory of creation, of the unspeakable beauty of nature that is still completely untouched.

It was around four in the morning, but the sun stood clear and bright above the horizon in the wide, open heavens. The ship, surrounded by its chase boats, lay still in a large hole in the ice, shut in on all sides by ice fields, which covered the sea like an endless, widely folded, rolling cloak, as far as the eye could see. In the distance, shining icebergs rose up out of the white ocean. But it was the light that lent such an enchanting charm to the grandeur of it all. Tender, delicate hues tinted the wide expanse of the sky and the white, rocking ice floes. Diamonds sparkled on the brightly lit walls of the icebergs and on the cobalt-blue shadows in the ice holes and caves.

The entire space around us, from the one distant horizon to the other, was flooded with the most tender, fairy-tale-like hues, while the whole scene gave the impression of emitting pure light.

It is totally beyond me to paint with words the utterly joyous purity of that spectacular scene. Even with colors it isn't possible to reproduce more than a faint impression of it. Even with pure light on his palette, no master of the canvas could do justice to the incomparable beauty of light and color. With just a drawing pen it's completely out of the question, of course. So, to my great regret, I am unable to share with you the joy of this bewitching sight that so enraptured us that day.

Several great blue whales played calmly among the ice floes. Unafraid, they surfaced close to the ship, took a couple of breaths, and then silently glided down again into the unruffled, deep blue water. Icy-white snow petrels glided and skimmed over the leviathans' spouts. One of the giants swam up alongside us, not ten meters away from one of the chase boats. It was a Tantalus-like temptation for the gunner, who stood by the harpoon cannon. That's because orders had been given not to shoot any whales. Surely we first had to figure out how to break through the pack ice, since the tremendous carcasses couldn't be dragged through it.

To the gunner it seemed like a challenge from the audacious whale to size it up. Furiously he rained insults on the giant's thick, dark hide. His wrath earned him enthusiastic applause from the crew of the big ship, which sent him quickly back into his chart room.

On the *Ross* a ship's council was held. Was it advisable to go through the ice now? Dead reckoning established the place where we first encountered pack ice to be at about 64° S, 179° E. A long swell rolled out of the west, which kept the ice in motion, and there's a great risk attached to navigating through moving ice, especially for a ship like ours, which on the whole really wasn't prepared for it. Even though that swell formed the only perceptible connection to the outside world, we would still rather have done without it in this case. A storm out of the west would put the ship in a very dangerous position, sitting there in the middle of the ice. Imagine if we were overtaken by a storm like the last one! The furious waves would ram the thin steel sides of the ship with such sharp ice floes that, quite probably, there would be nothing left of her. At the very least, the ship would spring leaks in numerous places.

But the barometer was rising; there was thus no immediate danger of a storm. And should bad weather come later, it wasn't so much to be feared then, since we would probably already find ourselves in the middle of thick ice. Firmly compacted ice acts as a damper against the ocean and completely subdues the swell.

The winds were favorable. A weak, cool breeze out of the south stretched over the ice, shining in the sun.

After brief deliberations it was thus decided to enter the ice without delay. Southward!

AT FIRST it was no more than pleasure-boating. The narrow lanes of light ice didn't offer the least hindrance. On a crumpled ice-floe sat a solitary emperor penguin; like a sentry stationed at the front, she guarded the borders of her domain. But she didn't order us to halt. Without a trace of wonder or fear, she calmly let us pass.

Amazing! As soon as we reached the pack ice, everyone seemed to consider himself called upon to predict the ice conditions that we would encounter. One seaman was certain that we wouldn't come up against enough ice to fill the bay in Oslo. Another shook his head thoughtfully and spoke of a heavy year for ice, impenetrable. They all missed the point, these assertions. The most reasonable men were those who said, "Let's just wait. We'll see soon enough how it's going to go."

A little farther to the west a storm was brewing. A high swell arose, and the ship rolled heavily. Risking going into the thick ice now would be reckless. We turned around and tacked toward the north again, back toward open water, steaming slowly back outside the pack ice to await a more favorable opportunity. Overall the conditions were excellent: bright sunshine and deep blue water, with the barometer showing no inclination of falling. We didn't fear a storm; we were just waiting for the swell to recede.

We passed by an iceberg that had a large cave where the swell broke in with thundering force, like cannon shots, heaving out in a cloud of glistening water drops, a rain of diamonds.

By night the swell had gone down so much that we could enter the pack ice again. There was iceblink everywhere except in the north. So the bow was pointed southward again.

Meanwhile, since the first appearance of whales, a typical character trait of whalers had become obvious. Their interest in these oil-suppliers has a far greater effect on their happiness than does a glimpse of the endless world of ice. If they see whales, lots of whales, they laugh at the world, and the future looks sunny and happy. (They had a similar reaction during the hunting period. If a small whale was brought alongside, then their faces grew long. But if a large one was shot, then their faces brightened immediately, and joy reigned.)

The next morning we spent sailing through light, broken ice that covered the sea in long, narrow lanes, separated from open patches where lots of snow and icy slush was floating. The strips of ice, which actually were nearly flat, looked in the distance like a mirage of hilly islands, and the remains of icebergs they contained gave the impression of steep mountain peaks. Everything went very well. The five chase boats followed easily through the channel that the *Ross* left behind.

In the afternoon the swell picked up, and when we reached relatively open water again, the prophets of the meager ice-year appeared to be proven correct. But a little later the lookout reported heavier ice, especially in the west, which forced us to turn the bow more southward.

Everywhere there were icebergs in a great variety of shapes. And whales, which surfaced now and then among the ice floes, awakened happiness and hope in the hearts of the men. They came right up close to the ship. Evidently they hadn't yet learned that death and destruction threatened them there. But we couldn't even think about shooting them, since we still had the great mass of ice before our bow. Our next goal was the Bay of Whales[1] at the

---

1. The Bay of Whales was a large indentation in the Ross Ice Shelf. First seen by Sir James Clark Ross in 1842, it was the base for several important journeys into the Antarctic interior, including Amundsen's. Then more than 10 miles (16 kilometers) wide, the bay

Great Ice Barrier. The men hoped that the bay wouldn't betray its name. If we could believe the reports of earlier scientific expeditions, then countless whales awaited us there. We could thus better save powder and shot for that "oil-dorado."

Toward night we came into heavier ice. While I lay in my bunk, I heard thundering and cracking in front of the bow, and I was glad that it had been provided with a sturdy ice-hull. Sometimes the ship shivered and shuddered down to its last seam as it overturned a heavy chunk of ice that sat frozen among the looser floes.

In the ice, Captain Larsen was in his element. He usually did the lookout duty himself up in the *tönne*, and from there he gave orders to the pilot on the bridge. There, so high in the air, one can see much farther than from the command bridge, and can sooner find the open channels that one prefers to use.

Pack ice is a very complex, constantly changing formation of ice in the open sea. As the temperature falls a good ways below freezing and the sea is nicely flat and still, the first thin layer quickly develops, a couple of centimeters [an inch] thick, which as a rule isn't destined to last long. The wind, which puts the water in motion, quickly splits the layer and breaks it up into smaller pieces. The waves constantly scour these pieces against each other until they form flat, round slices with piled-up edges made of ice fragments. This formation of young ice is called pancake ice.

Of course, it can also happen that the conditions are so favorable that a much thicker layer of ice forms immediately, one that can offer more resistance to the thrust of the waves. Indeed, a strong swell doesn't break up fresh ice right away; it's fairly flexible. In the long run, however, a layer of ice does break up, and the thicker the layer, the larger the loose pieces will be. Wind and sea currents drive the floes apart, then shove them back together again later or push them over one another. In addition, the whole pack is constantly in motion, and its appearance constantly keeps changing.

Shackleton painted a very good picture of it when he compared the pack to "a gigantic and interminable jigsaw-puzzle devised by nature." He writes,

---

was narrowed over the decades by the movements of the advancing ice sheet. By the early 1950s it was nearly obliterated, and it ceased to exist entirely when in 1987 a 99-mile (159-kilometer) section of the Ice Shelf broke off.

The parts of the puzzle in loose pack have floated slightly apart and become disarranged; at numerous places they have pressed together again; as the pack gets closer the congested areas grow larger and the parts are jammed harder till finally it becomes "close pack," when the whole of the jigsaw-puzzle becomes jammed to such an extent that with care and labour it can be traversed in every direction on foot. Where the parts do not fit closely there is, of course, open water, which freezes over in a few hours after giving off volumes of "frost smoke."[2]

You do have to watch carefully where you're going, because even this new ice is soon covered with falling snow or is buried in drifting snow. With continued drifting, this new ice breaks and then slides over other pieces and forms brash ice, which is several times thicker. The edges of the largest floes are then rammed forcefully against the others, the sides buckle, and on each puzzle piece, edges of broken ice form. Where the floes are crushed together with great force, chaotic groups of blocks pile up wildly.

Sometimes it happens that piles form many meters high, made of such precisely even-sized blocks, and with such consistency, that it seems impossible that they could have been formed that way by nature alone. At other times a crooked channel forms between walls of ice six or ten feet high, or an arched cupola rises up, which under even greater pressure explodes upward like a volcano. Through it all, the pack keeps changing its appearance: it grows as frost accumulates, gets thicker from the shoving of the floes against each other, and is pushed together by drifting. If, driven farther by currents and wind, it hauls up against a coast somewhere — as, for example, in the Ross Sea on the coast of South Victoria Land — then a tremendous crumpling occurs, which forms a chaos of blocks, ridges, and ramparts of ice, a wilderness of ice, broken and shoved around, which can stretch out to perhaps 150 or 200 miles off the coast. Broken pieces of this ice drift away and then freeze solid again in newer ice. So one can encounter all sorts of ice, from pack ice to one huge mass solidly frozen together, from enormous, completely flat floes to the wildest heaped-up drift ice.

2. The quotation that Van der Does cites is from the first chapter (entitled "Into the Weddell Sea") of Sir Ernest Shackleton's *South* (London, 1919), his own account of the ill-fated Imperial Trans-Antarctic Expedition (aboard the *Endurance*) of 1914-1916. Shackleton's book is now available in a modern edition: *South: The Last Antarctic Expedition of Shackleton and the* Endurance (New York: Lyons Press, 1998).

The snow, which fills up all the unevenness of the masses of ice, contributes its share to changing the appearance of the pack, as does the sea, which not only breaks the ice but also sprays huge amounts of water over it, which goes on to freeze and further enlarge the quantity of the ice. Even the icebergs play a part in the formation of the pack. The old, decayed bergs begin to crumble and finally collapse completely, forming great fields of raw, broken ice, easily recognized by their bluish color.

In this way the sea is constantly busy grinding up the ice, and the frost always makes it grow again. It's a matter of which is stronger. In the polar winter, when it freezes tremendously hard, the pack always grows and covers an ever-greater surface area of the sea. Even during the short polar summer, the temperature is nearly always below freezing, but then the ice doesn't grow so fast that the restless waves aren't in a position to destroy a great deal of it. But the Antarctic is never wholly free of ice; one always finds extended fields of pack ice, hundreds of miles wide.

As one would expect, it is unusually taxing work to navigate a ship through such ice. It demands unbroken concentration, and along with that, of course, a thorough knowledge of ice conditions.

Captain Larsen and second mate Gjertsen, our ice pilots, were responsible for navigating through the ice. As long as their special attention was needed, they took turns keeping watch in the lookout. The steersman on duty then stood on the bridge by the telegraph.

In difficult ice, the maneuvers were endless, and commands constantly

Iceberg in the pack ice

filled the air: "A little to portside!" "Come . . . up . . . slowly!" "Stea . . . dy . . . !" "Stop!" "Hard to starboard!" "Turn it, will you, man!" "Prop it up!" "Just like that!" "Harder to starboard!" "Full rudder!" "Stop!" "Full speed astern!" So rang the commands without stopping from the lookout, usually through a bullhorn.

In thick, heavy ice, when it rained orders like that, everyone who could afford to leave his work for a moment came up to see how the ship wrestled its way through the ice. The best view was to be had standing on deck. You could stand there for hours at a time looking at the fascinating struggle between the ship and the ice, in which the *Ross* steadily had the upper hand, although the victory wasn't always easily gained. After a hard-won success over an unusually firmly-stuck piece, the men looked at each other triumphantly and said with unmistakable pride, "She did it again, didn't she?" — meaning the ship, for which they had respect, because against their expectations it was evidently holding up very well under this unusual test of strength.

It was beautiful to see how gallantly the ship worked its way through the ice. As the bow rammed a floe a few hundred meters large, such a shock went through the ship that it groaned and creaked down to its last seam. Several times the shock hit so heavily that the men were nearly knocked off their feet, and we began to fear that the mast might snap off. When we rammed a floe so large that sometimes we couldn't see the end of it, we did it with the engines stopped, to lessen the shock, and the ice mass would usually split right at the point of contact. Then a crack would appear, steadily running and twisting, extending out from the ship. The violence of the collision stopped the ship's motion entirely; it would even shoot backward a bit.

When the ship advanced again, the bow wriggled its way into the newly opened fissure, which then grew longer and wider. Banging and cracking, great chunks broke off, which toppled over or were forced under the solid ice. The wrestling went on without stopping. One after another, floes of all sizes came up against the armored bow, and one after another they were rammed, shattered, and shoved to the side, only to close together again immediately behind the ship, leaving a narrow channel of broken ice.

By shifting the coal and moving the fresh water stored in the double hull from one compartment to another, we took care that the screw always stayed so deep underwater that it couldn't get stuck in the ice. Still, we often worried about the screw, especially in rugged drift ice whose thickness was difficult to estimate. If an unusually heavy ice mass passed by the stern, we would stop the engine in order to avoid damaging the screw.

There were more icebergs in the pack ice than outside it. There were always large and small ones nearby, in all sorts of shapes. There were true tabular icebergs and older ones, which in their wanderings had sometimes developed the most whimsical forms. One of the tabular icebergs was a good 600 meters [2,000 feet] long, by far the largest we had yet seen.

Larger icebergs than that occur in the Antarctic. The Australian South Pole Expedition came across one that was thirty miles long — so long that Sir Douglas Mawson figured he was seeing a portion of the Great Ice Barrier. It was in sailing alongside it that he first realized it was a loose-floating iceberg; this was an exception, naturally.

The tabular icebergs with their straight lines and rigid forms made a powerful impression on the observer, especially with the opportunity to see one up close. Such an immense ice-monster inspired respect when, from a short distance away, one looked up at the high sides, carved as if from marble. "What a dreadful place Antarctica must be," one thought, unbidden. "It has lain buried forever under such an enormous layer of ice. Dead, without any trace of life, the absolute end of the earth, hopeless, empty, and deserted."

The old icebergs didn't have that same mighty, stately appearance, but they often had very strange and very amusing shapes. Imagination was given

In heavy ice

free rein here, assisted by refraction, reflection, cloud shadows, and the sun, which all worked together to distort the shapes.

Sometimes men would swear they saw an island rising out of the endless ice layer, or a whole chain of mountains. The more distorted the icebergs were, the more capricious their shapes became. Somebody would see a knight's medieval castle, with towers and battlements, sally ports and bastions. In fact, it really didn't require an above-average imagination to see such things in the exceptional ice creations.

One iceberg made me think vividly of a large Indies-style house with high, sweeping roof ridges. Another one was exactly like a mastless, disabled, ice-covered ship, rolling with flooded decks on the scarcely perceptible swell. That ice mass must have been fairly top-heavy. It was immediately nicknamed "The Reeling Derelict."

One time out of the mists that slithered over the ice there loomed an iceberg that, if we hadn't known better, we would have taken for a tall, slender lighthouse. Even the lighthouse-keeper's house and the magazine were there. But the last real lighthouse we had seen had stood outlined white against the green slopes of Tasmania's mountains, more than a thousand miles northward. Another time a cheerful conglomeration of icebergs looked like a row of mighty skyscrapers from the land of the dollar.

Often the older icebergs got so crumbled and decayed and their volume so diminished that they lost their balance and capsized. In such cases, moraine layers became visible as dark bands that ran sideways through the ice.

In the pack ice the weather was rather quiet, and the icebergs glided by as soundlessly as silent white ghosts. In misty weather, which developed rather often, the sight of these pale, enormous leviathans gliding by in mysterious silence could send shivers through a man, but the icebergs always formed picturesque and very fitting subjects in the stark, wild, natural scene.

They were at their prettiest when the sun shone; then there was a glittering and glistening, a shining and shimmering such as you cannot imagine. When the light shone favorably, an iceberg looked like a tremendous work of art made of lightly polished crystal. While the giant rocked softly, almost imperceptibly, on the swell, countless facets reflected the white light, and thousands upon thousands of little sparkles went dancing and springing over the whole iceberg.

The icebergs displayed a wholly other sort of beauty if on a clear day the low-lying sun dipped below a cloudless horizon. Then the great masses of ice were flooded with a gush of glowing orange- and salmon-colored light, while the shadows darkened in every shade of deep blue, purple, violet, and brown. Then a wealth of rich, glorious colors poured over the otherwise-so-comfortless gray and white heaps of ice.

No, the polar world isn't always a bleak and dismal wasteland of ice and snow without end. This same wide, white, seemingly dead world can be movingly and enchantingly gorgeous. Indeed, the ethereal beauty that can adorn the polar regions is to be found nowhere else in the world.

WHEN THE pack ice got heavier and heavier, the chase boats had to be towed again because their screws wouldn't turn. They didn't reach deep enough because they were too small. And even though their propellers were protected with a sort of grille, in the ice it quickly became too dangerous to let the engine run.

All five were taken on towropes. That didn't always go easily; the towropes broke from time to time. It was hard enough for the boats to avoid the heavy floes. Sometimes they couldn't be avoided, and a boat would crash against solid ice. Then the rope would break, and a new one would have to be brought out or the old one repaired.

The first time that the rope broke was during my watch below. The *Ross* stopped, which woke me up. Curious to know what had happened, I went up on deck in slippers and pajamas. I jumped right into the situation, and a minute later I was running in my airy clothing on the sea ice to bring a towrope to the chase boat. The whole job lasted quite a while, and I believe that never on the whole trip was I so cold as then, even though it wasn't below -10° C [14° F]. After that I took care to appear on deck with more clothes on.

The ice breaking in front of the bow made such a thundering noise that sleeping was out of the question the first night in the pack. But we quickly became accustomed to it, and later on, when the ship was out in open water again, we actually missed the groaning, crashing, and thumping. It made me think of one of my first sea voyages, when as a ship's boy I had to settle for the least desirable bunk in the cabins. The hawse-hole ran through it, so I had to twist myself into a graceful but uncomfortable curve around it in order to be able to sleep. But the sleep of youth is healthy and sound. I don't remember anymore whether they had any trouble waking me up. But they must have, because even the dropping of the anchor wasn't enough to recall me from the

Curious Adélie penguins

land of dreams. And you know what a deafening noise accompanies the dropping of the anchor!

The ice got steadily thicker and heavier, until there was scarcely a single square foot of open water to be seen anywhere. It froze hard, and all the openings that might have developed between the moving floes immediately froze shut again. In addition, freshly fallen snow made the channels completely invisible. In the thick, close pack we saw for the first time the true polar penguins, the Adélies. In the heavier ice, the ship sailed steadily slower and finally proceeded so slowly that the curious penguins, running over the ice, could keep up with the ship.

The sound that these penguins made sounded something like "kraak" or "clark." Were they angrily scolding the good *Ross* as if it were an old burglar[3] invading their territory? One old wag onboard claimed that they were calling for our secretary (who was the ship's clerk) and went to tell him that he was being summoned. When the clerk came and saw that he was being called by penguins, he pelted them with lumps of coal. Luckily, he was a bad shot, and the penguins only chattered louder.

A solitary seal that lay sleeping splendidly on a floe looked around with big, round calf's-eyes when the cracking and breaking of the ice against the bow startled him out of his sweet sleep. He must have been stunned with surprise at the sight of the enormous ship, which he probably took for some frightful, unknown sea monster.

In his stupefaction he forgot to flee, and only when the ship had already gone by did he remember that it's always good to let everyone see that you're

3. *Kraak* is Dutch slang for a burglary job.

not frightened. Then he opened up his muzzle tremendously wide. At the same time, he seemed to realize that his heroic demonstration had actually come a little late, or maybe he even thought that the monster, afraid of his distended jaws, was taking flight. So he stretched himself comfortably out on the ice again, rolled over on one side, grunting with satisfaction, rolled over on his other side, scratched around lazily over his round head, and resumed his *dolce far niente*. They're stoics, these seals, and incomparable sleepyheads besides.

A very few times — because they're rare — some stately emperor penguins drifted by, sitting completely alone on a floe. The emperor penguins are the largest representatives of their species, and are about a meter [3 feet] tall. The throat is orange, running to yellow and white on the breast. The distinguished emperor penguins always carried themselves with more dignity and self-awareness than the boisterous little Adélie penguins. The Adélies are the street urchins of the South Polar area, while the large emperors with their dignified behavior tend toward the indisputably aristocratic. Cool and imperturbable, an emperor would sit stiffly on his ice floe as the ship sailed past. Despite his name, however, he usually didn't seem unreceptive to friendly treatment. When the sailors noisily greeted him, he made a formal bow as a sign that he had graciously accepted their homage. One of these grand *seigneurs* remained unperturbed on his throne of ice even when the ship came so close by that the floe broke, and the piece on which he was standing began to totter alarmingly. But when it partially sank, he did finally get mad. He was most offended at such improper treatment, and he muttered and grumbled under his breath. But that this stately gentleman swore, as Tofte [another shipmate] kept insisting — that I simply don't believe.

AFTER WE crossed the Antarctic Circle, the pack became one endless layer of ice, although the one wasn't the consequence of the other. The sea had completely lost her normal appearance, and there wasn't a trace of swell to be detected. The sea was covered with an immense garment of ice, and with the fresh snow that lay over it, it looked like a shroud.

In the uniform ice we couldn't search for open channels or sections of thinner ice; there simply weren't any. And so we sailed straight by the compass: due south.

The weather wasn't clear and open anymore, either, as it had been during the first few days we had spent in the ice. There was also no difference whatsoever between day and night: a pale, diffuse light seeped out of the cheerless gray sky twenty-four hours a day. Neither sun nor stars showed themselves, and the *Ross* sailed day after day on dead reckoning. It snowed often, and when it did, the visibility was so poor in the deceptive, colorless light that the engine had to be stopped for safety reasons. In these conditions the ship might run into an iceberg or an unknown island. The maps of the polar region are far from complete and anything but precise.

The icebergs became rarer, and farther on they disappeared entirely, but with poor visibility during a heavy snowfall, it was still irresponsible to go on sailing blindly.

It was a very strange sensation to stand on a ship in the open ocean and still not see any sea. I would never have believed that I wouldn't be able to recognize the sea with which I was so intimately familiar. I had sailed nearly all the oceans of the globe for so long, and I knew the sea in all her ever-changing moods so well. How often I had fallen under the enchanted spell of the mystical clarity of a moonlit night in tropical seas, when the moon filled the whole dome of heaven from horizon to horizon with her glimmering white peace, and the black ocean in unruffled quiet lay dreaming while the long, low swell waved a limpid reflection.

I recognized the sea in the temperate climates when the storms celebrated high tide, and the growling water swept up angrily until the wild, roaring waves galloped over the dark depths like a herd of frightened mustangs fleeing from a prairie fire, their white manes flying, until with thundering force they pounded onto some far coast, rumbling and smashing their heads to pieces.

I had sailed the bleak northern seas, where the greedy waves spring over the shuddering ships and try to bury them under masses of chill green water. Not long ago my shipmates and I had been in the "Roaring Forties," where the kingly albatross proudly ignored the storm, where the house-high waves blindly chased their way around the globe.

Well might I thus assume that I knew her, the sea. But in the Antarctic pack ice she made me stand still for a moment, bewildered. I did not recognize her.

No matter where and under what guise she might earlier have appeared to my eyes, she had always been grand, mighty and free, not to be confined within bounds, but powerful through and through, a symbol of life itself, carrying a vigorous and ever-renewed life within herself. That is, until I saw her lying motionless in the pack ice, lifeless, squeezed into an icy coat of armor, covered with a chill layer of snow like a death-shroud.

In no way did she still resemble her untamable self. Had I not been standing on the deck of a sailing ship, I would have had no way of knowing that the full depths of the ocean stretched away under my feet. No waves burbled or battered roughly along the sides of the ship; there was nothing but the dull, grinding sound of crushed ice. It looked more like the ship was creeping forward over an immense, empty layer of snow. The only sign of life was the laborious, toiling support of the engine, which with her four thousand horsepower pushed the ship slowly, foot by foot, through the ice.

There wasn't a trace of water anywhere around. Even along the sides of the ship there wasn't a centimeter of water to be seen between the ship's hull and the ice, neither in front of the bow nor behind it. Nothing other than snow and more snow everywhere, as far as the eye could see and farther still.

Hummocky ice

It made me feel quite strange as the ship crept so slowly over the snowy shroud. No, that can't possibly be the ocean, I thought to myself — not that motionless, empty, dead surface. I felt deserted, as if I were at the deathbed of a friend whom I had always known as hearty and happy but now saw lying still, with a face as white as a sheet. How could this be the ocean stretched out all around me, motionless in the pack ice, stripped of all life, unmoving, silent and white? There was no sign of movement, of life, nothing to keep me from just stepping off the ship onto the ice if I wanted to.

No birds hovered over the *Ross* anymore, a sign that open water was a long ways away. And there wasn't a single iceberg in this thick ice to break the monotony. The reason was that icebergs stick up high above the water, offering a large surface to the wind, and thus drift to the north far faster than the flat pack ice, which is driven by the southeast wind that usually blows in this area.

MORE AND MORE slowly and laboriously the *Ross* writhed its way through the steadily thicker and heavier ice. We went at a snail's pace, no matter how hard the engine turned and toiled. The heavy ice layer surrendered nothing. No more cracks formed in front of the bow through which the ship could push. The ice had to be conquered foot by foot by the propulsion power of the screw. As long as the *Ross* was still moving somewhat, the ship added to the force with which the ice was rammed. But now, as the speed steadily dropped, the power steadily ebbed.

Precisely a week after we entered the pack ice, the ship got stuck at the 69th parallel. We tried to get the ship in motion again by running the engine forward and backward for a long time, but that didn't work; there was nothing more to be done. So we stopped the engine to keep from wasting coal pointlessly.

"Lasciate ogni speranza!" ("Abandon all hope!"), quoted the doctor in a melancholy voice. We smiled at his somber face.

Give up courage already? Surely that was preposterous!

But our situation had certainly become precarious. One way or another, the ship had to be put in motion again. It was unthinkable to wait for a storm to come to break up the ice. The ship would be rammed full of leaks in the shifting ice, and the men would have to flee onto the ice. A voyage of drifting like Shackleton's would be the unavoidable result. But it was doubtful whether our crew, which was much larger than his had been, would get through it as well. Not an attractive prospect.

The ice, which looked so innocent and flat now, could also start drifting. That was the second, more serious possibility if the *Ross* stayed hopelessly stuck. If the ice began to drift, the ship would be squashed flat in no time, just like an empty gas can under a truck, with the same voyage of drifting for us as a result.

Luckily, most of the men weren't aware of the seriousness of our situation. Everything looked quiet and peaceful. There wasn't a breath of wind, and the ice lay motionless, flat and white on the invisible sea. Nature seemed to be sleeping in, as one saw complete peace all around; indeed, it seemed absurd to be thinking about danger.

Most of the men were in fact happy with the change that this unexpected delay provided. The dead, oppressive silence that enveloped the pack, the endless emptiness, and the dreary view of the wide white shoals that hid the ocean from sight — these preyed on people's nerves. During this time many men went to the doctor with all sorts of vague complaints. The doctor, who understood the cause, set the minds of such patients at rest with the assurance that we would soon reach open water again, and he gave them a good swig of firewater to cheer them up.

When the ship was really well and truly imprisoned in the ice, those who were off duty immediately took the opportunity to stretch their legs. They let themselves down to the ice with loose lengths of rope. Nowhere could you get even so much as a finger between the ship and the ice. Skis were brought out, and some of the men threw snowballs, and soon there was a Norway vs. Tasmania soccer match in full swing. But the game didn't get finished. A couple of Adélie penguins popped up out of who-knows-where and came, full of curiosity, to look at the ship and at the strange beings who walked on two legs, just like they did.

Everyone's attention went immediately from the soccer ball to the penguins. Those who had never been in the South Polar area before were the most interested in the funny birds. They looked so serious, but their white-rimmed eyes and their motions were so comical. We were happy that the

Stuck in the ice

penguins showed up, not so much because of the birds themselves but because their presence indicated that open water, or at least looser ice, wasn't far away, because these creatures can't under any circumstances do without water: it's where they find their food.

Ice saws, jimmies, and pickaxes were hauled out of the *Ross*, and the smiths quickly made a couple of crowbars. Armed with these tools, a crew of men set to work to create some open water in front of the ship. They sawed channels in the ice from twenty meters [65 feet] in front of the bow and just as far behind, at a little distance from the sides of the ship, breaking up the pieces with the crowbars. Next they worked the loose pieces underneath the solid ice as much as possible, and then they broke up the whole piece, so that no more ice enclosed the prow.

The ice layer in which we were stuck was no more than about four feet thick, but after you labored at breaking it up for hours at a time, you were tenderly reminded that you had a back. Amazingly, the eight-foot-long ice saws, which have very large teeth, were managed by one man.

It took longer than one watch before the channel was ready. The engine was started and run forward, then backward. Then the ice was rammed under full steam. After this maneuver was repeated several times, the ice cracked in front of the bow. Hooray! The *Ross* was moving again! The ice had been conquered. Slowly the ship wriggled farther into the opened crack, fathom by fathom, but it kept advancing. For the next few hours it often looked as if the *Ross* might have to give up again, but luckily, it could manage to keep sailing under full power, even though a snail would have had a good chance of beating us in a race. Sometimes a few men walked calmly beside the ship over the ice. A couple of them even wondered whether we might haul them along with a towrope. Lots of jokes were made about our sailing, which was so slow it would have embarrassed a tortoise, but everyone was relieved that the ship was at least moving again.

Curious Adélie penguins often jogged for quite a ways alongside the ship, heavily in discussion among themselves over this strange sight. We could see them come running out of the distance. They were in such a hurry to see this unusual monster closer up that their short little feet couldn't help them forward fast enough. So they let themselves fall face forward in the snow and used their wings as oars; that went faster. Two birds were sacrificed to science, and many others paid for their curiosity with death: they landed in the cook's frying pan.

The doctor was so busy preparing animal specimens, classifying and identifying and whatnot, that he got the mocking nickname of "The Penguin Doctor." He was otherwise not busy during his office hours. Only a few influenza patients showed up; there was only the occasional wound or broken arm. Sometimes teeth had to be pulled — the only time he needed assistance. Then I put palette and pencils aside in order to hold the victim down and to watch out that the doctor didn't get a punch in the face by accident as thanks for his dental help.

WE WERE NOW within the Antarctic Circle, and it was the second half of December, so it was getting close to the longest day. It's quite strange to see nothing but snow and ice around you in the middle of the summer. The sun no longer vanished below the horizon but stood several degrees above it and filled the sky with soft sunset colors all night long. Often the nearly horizontal rays of the sun were orange; they made a remarkable, wonderfully beautiful color combination with the long blue and violet shadows next to them.

The midnight sun.

It feels very strange when there's no difference anymore between day and night, but you quickly get used to it. Still, if you don't watch the clock carefully, you quickly lose track of time and get hopelessly confused. During the months-long polar summer or polar day, when neither mornings nor evenings measure the days, the course of the day is almost impossible to keep track of.

I could write much more about the wonder of the midnight sun. The principal response one has isn't due to any special natural phenomenon but rather to the idea that the sun seems to have totally forgotten that it is supposed to rise and set every day as befits a respectable heavenly body.

A few watches after the *Ross* was freed from the ice, the ice grew noticeably thinner. The penguins hadn't deceived us. Now and then water was visible, and the ice wash was melting along with the snow that lay on it. Rot ice, that's called in polar terminology; it was dirty and greenish-colored. Another sign that open water was near also appeared: a faint water horizon seemed visible in the south, whereas before this time only iceblink had been visible.

But whether or not that was really a water horizon — of that we were by no means certain. All too often our hopes on this point were dashed. Refraction had played tricks on us so many times already that we were inclined

Drift ice

not to believe there was open water until we actually saw it. The swell, also a herald of the open sea, had also betrayed us just as often. The previous day the ice pilot had already determined that there was a swell out of the south. That we didn't yet see it we attributed to our untrained eyes, but later on even those with more practice couldn't discover it.

The immense ice layer stretched itself out around the ship in complete stillness. Now nobody believed in that swell anymore — not when the pack ice didn't show the least inclination to open up. In fact, it got heavier and more rugged, so that we were lucky to be able to maintain a speed of five knots. Remains of icebergs, made of ice as hard as glass, were frozen in the ice, and that made for a very anxious day. That calved-off ice was indistinguishable from the rest of the pack ice, and many times the ship pounded against it with such force that the crew couldn't stay on their feet, so great was the unexpected shock.

It was certainly a wild and adventurous trip. Originally it was the desire for adventure, the hope of experiencing out-of-the-ordinary things, that inspired all these men. And along with that, as with the old Vikings, came the prospect of profitable booty. But some authentic pirate blood must have coursed through their veins.

The day ended with an orgy of colors that simultaneously led in the new day, since the one day flowed into the next with no transition. The midnight sun hid itself, but all along the horizon a fiery glow brooded, fantastically lighting up the rough, curiously wrought formations of drift ice.

In the red fire lay a huge crab-eater seal stretched out motionless on a floe. A skua gull sat nearby on another chunk of ice, waiting calmly. The seal was probably awaiting its death, and the bird, an abundant meal.

FOR MORE than a week now our weary eyes had searched for something other than the endless, deathly pack ice, which held prisoner in its chilly shackles not only the sea but our souls as well. As convicts long for freedom, so we all hankered after open water, for life. Over and over again we asked the southern skies whether they indicated open water. They were lead-gray, but we had been betrayed so many times already.

Refraction in the ice played a deceptive role, and the light and dark parts above the horizon that we were used to calling ice-sky and water-sky didn't necessarily predict ice or open water. Even the much-discussed Ross Sea swell, with a ten-shilling reward offered to the one who discovered it, seemed to remain a delusion. The longing to reach the open Ross Sea quickly might well have led the ice pilot to think that he "clearly" saw it. Perhaps he had really seen it, but then its origin must have lain in a large blowhole.

A great oppression arises from the pack ice, which in its deathly silence is reminiscent of a cemetery, where the living dare not speak above whispers. The ice floes pushed end over end by drifting are the marble gravestones in nature's endless churchyard.

But finally there came a clear sign! The seabirds had left us long ago, and thus the appearance of an ice bird — the snow petrel, with its black beak and feet — was an irrefutable herald of open sea, the revival of sunken hope. Shortly thereafter a very clear, unmistakable water-sky gave us even greater assurance. So, as we approached the 70th parallel, we believed even without visible swell that open water lay nearby.

And a ten-shilling reward had been promised for the first glimpse of open water. When toward midnight I went up on deck to enjoy the beautiful colors of the midnight sun, I saw a sailor on lookout up in the *tönne*. He neither sat nor stood in the crow's nest but hovered atop its edge. He was searching the horizon for ten shillings. The other sailors on watch stood stiff as boards on deck and peered straight out in front of them at the horizon to see if by any chance they could see that half-pound swelling.

We stayed on deck a long time, although it wasn't the hope of reward that kept us from returning to our bunks. The beautiful, brightly colored light kept our eyes open, as did the thought that the ship, having come out of the high north, was now the only living, moving speck in the far southern ice, as solitary as the petrel that skimmed over the ship in wide arcs.

Only after ten days' sailing in the pack ice did the ice finally thin out. In the east, the first open channels revealed themselves, while in the west, thick ice continued to stretch out. The sky, which up till now had been hidden, drab and colorless, took on a pale blue color. The channels grew larger and wider. The water in them looked darker and deeper under the ever-deepening blue of the sky. Thereafter the long-awaited swell began ever so slightly to rock the farthest lanes of ice. The open water made for a happy mood all around. It was a relief to finally see open water that moved and lived, after having been imprisoned in the silent, dead pack ice for so long, and the burbling waves brought rest to strained nerves faster than the bromides that the doctor had been serving up lately.

The open Ross Sea stretched out before us, free of ice as far as the eye could see. We made grateful use of the favorable weather conditions to furnish the chase boats with provisions and coal. It took a few hours, but then we could go happily south again, with the chase boats following the ship under their own power, without towropes. Southward, full steam ahead!

WE WERE happy to turn our backs on the dismal wilderness of the pack ice. Even the ship and the chase boats seemed to be happy to bore their noses into rushing, ice-free waves and to dance on the swell again to their hearts' content.

The pack ice swiftly disappeared beyond the horizon; not a single iceberg interrupted the straight line that separated air and water. It seemed almost like a dream to so suddenly see not a single piece of ice after having wrestled with it day after day without stopping and with such difficulty. Strange, that the ice not only diminished but completely disappeared, while we were in fact steadily nearing Antarctica, the land of the South Pole, the cradle of all the cold and ice.

The presence of the pack ice between the 60th and 70th parallels and the open water in the Ross Sea are caused by the geographic position of the Ross Sea, which is a very large bay that indents into the southern continent. In the Ross Sea the prevailing wind comes out of the southwest and drives all the ice forward out to the pack, which at about 60° comes up against the northwest wind that prevails in the open ocean. Between these two wind currents that drive the ice out before them is a windless zone where the ice piles up.

The way to the Bay of Whales seemed to be free, and the nightmare of the somber pack ice was forgotten as soon as open water again surrounded the ship.

It was only natural that our thoughts turned again to sober, essential matters: the whales, which awaited us impatiently there in the south, ready to give us their oil. Opinions were divided. Some predicted unimaginably large schools of whales; others thought that the whales would be scarce, while the hunting season could only be short. The men were as changeable and restless as the ice pack, but still, the mood hadn't been this good since we left Tasmania. Happy voices and songs rang in the cabins; a decidedly cheerful and pleasant spirit reigned.

Southward! To the Bay of Whales!

Swell?

CHAPTER ELEVEN

Through the Ice-Free Ross Sea

Fantastic ice formation

I f everything went well, as we hoped but didn't actually expect, we would reach our destination, the Great Ice Barrier, by Christmas. We would then be able to celebrate Christmas lying at anchor in the Bay of Whales. For us, snow and ice are the things that really create the most characteristic mood for the ancient midwinter festival, and they would certainly not be lacking there.

The approaching Christmas celebration was already becoming evident in a number of ways. The cabins had gotten an extra cleaning and, where necessary, a coat of paint. The washing and repairing of clothes was done diligently, so that the hatches hung full of laundry, all frozen stiff. All sorts of Christmas surprises were prepared, and the ship's clerk was busy wrapping presents; each man would find one under the Christmas tree.

For the occasion I drew a caricature of the ice pilot that greatly amused Captain Larsen. He had the carpenter make a frame for it, and the print was to be hung up in the victim's cabin as a surprise on Christmas. I would have loved to have seen his face when he found the surprise. The ice pilot, a Norwegian navy captain, wasn't usually taken all that seriously by most people; as a navy man, he lacked the great simplicity that is so characteristic of the Norwegian sailor. So, for instance, when the Ross was stuck in the ice, he sent momentous wireless telegrams about it to Norway. (When we got back to Europe, we heard that those radiograms had caused great consternation. People thought that the whole fleet had perished in the ice.) For this ostentation of his, Captain Gjertsen was teased and mocked more than he liked. We thought him a little unbalanced, so in my cartoon I portrayed him as an ice pilot, on watch on the mast, in a condition of exceeding instability. You can well imagine that the portrait met with general approval from everyone except the subject himself.

It was December 21, Midsummer's Day, when we came out of the pack ice into open water. The weather was excellent, and it froze hard in cheerful sunshine. It seemed very odd that here, in the middle of the summer, there were temperatures that would make the directors of ice clubs back in the home country snicker. For us it was really mid-summer. (Midsummer's Day in the Southern Hemisphere happens on the same day as Midwinter's Day in the Northern Hemisphere.)

There was a northwesterly breeze with rising seas, just enough to give the big ship a light rolling movement. This did us good after the rigid motionlessness of the silent pack ice.

The water in the Ross Sea seemed to be markedly saltier than the waters in the open ocean. This was because no rivers added fresh water to it, as is the case with other seas. The layer of ice that covers the land does slowly glide into the sea, but that ice doesn't lower the salt content, because it doesn't melt until it's driven toward the warmer, open ocean, where the pack ice also melts. It thus removes water but almost no salt from the Ross Sea, since sea ice contains much less salt than the water from which it develops.

Other than the low temperature, it was actually especially nice summer weather. The sun shone cheerfully on the deep blue water. Puffy white clouds sailed along in the sky. And crowds of birds accompanied the ship, their wings shining in the light. At lunchtime the men lay on the hatches basking in the sun, so that you might think it was a nice fall day in the North Sea. The snow goggles that had been necessary in the pack ice could be stowed away again for the time being.

So happy and innocent it looked, the Ross Sea did, that if you didn't know better, you might think that it was always this peaceful. But it's only during the short Antarctic summer that it shows such a smiling face. That at least it can do. But during the long winter, as the snowstorms beat down, howling, from the icy polar plateau, the great inland sea is nastier and more dangerous than any ocean in the world. Then it is for the most part covered with ice, piled up high and wildly by the biting storm and the turbulent waves.

Woe to the ship that is then jammed in the ice; only Providence can save both ship and crew from certain destruction. In ninety-nine out of a hundred cases, that vessel will be splintered into a helpless piece of wreckage by the drifting ice, in which powerful forces are at work, while the crew, who have to try to save their ill-starred lives on the untrustworthy, shifting ice, await endless hardships.

A ship held up for the winter in the Ross Sea that's been lucky enough not to be trapped in the ice isn't really much better off. The ceaseless bliz-

The ice pilot

zards, obstructing all visibility, make navigation very dangerous, and the polar winter is one months-long night, so darkness doubles the dangers. At any moment such a ship can run into an iceberg or spring leaks after being rammed by ice floes that are flung around by the seething waves. The ship wouldn't hold out long in the open sea; it would be constantly inundated with ice-cold spray that would soon cover everything with a thick layer of ice, making all work on deck impossible. We found this to be true on the *Ross* even in the summertime; sometimes the chase boats came back covered with ice, every bow one formless mass of ice, as if they had gone through a snowstorm. Only if a ship can get itself frozen in a patch of still water, like a protected inlet, does it have any chance of surviving the harsh polar winter.

We would most likely not have to experience such things. It was in any case not our intention to overwinter and brave the grim god of winter, who tolerates no life in his domain. But the weather was too favorable for us to harbor such gloomy thoughts, although we knew the sea too well to be misled by its chance friendliness. At sea one is used to accepting things as they are, most of all the sea itself. There's no other choice, in any case. Much could be written on this interesting subject. And that has been done by many authors, including Joseph Conrad in his *Mirror of the Sea,* a book for seamen, written by a seaman with a great and tender heart.

To OUR amazement, we sailed southward in the Ross Sea for nearly two days without seeing ice. That was almost unbelievable, since it was well below freezing, and the temperature of the seawater was also several degrees below zero [Celsius]. The water was too much in motion for the whole sea to freeze, but the fact that we saw no pack ice at all we could only ascribe to the northwesterly wind that we encountered in the mouth of the Ross Sea. This air current had undoubtedly blown all the ice to the south. (We figured that we would come across a great deal of sea ice before reaching the Great Ice Barrier.) Nowhere else in the South Polar area is it possible to find open, navigable water at such a high latitude. Only the Ross Sea with its 200,000 square-mile surface is large enough to stay more or less ice-free. The wind keeps the water's surface constantly in motion so that it can't form ice quickly.

The *Ross* was sailing under less-than-full power, so as not to leave the slower chase boats behind. In these unknown waters, it was more important than ever to stay together. But after two days, the fastest chase boat, the *Star 1,* was sent ahead on a reconnaissance mission.

Captain Larsen suspected that we wouldn't encounter ice, that the sea ice at the foot of the Great Ice Barrier hadn't broken up yet. Plans had already been made to wait for the break-up of the sea ice around the edges, and to anchor there or to moor off the permanent ice, and meanwhile use the time for the whale hunt.

Toward midnight one of the officers measured the meridian altitude of the sun, and it appeared that the *Ross* had already reached the parallel 77° 30′ S; now the Great Ice Barrier couldn't be much farther. (Taking the sun's altitude at midnight struck me as being no everyday nautical curiosity.) It was remarkable how there was no ice to be seen at this high latitude in the heart of the South Polar Region. We were curious to find out what news the *Star 1* would bring back with it. A pale iceblink showed itself above the horizon in the south. Was it the reflection of the sunlight on the Great Ice Barrier, or was there more sea ice waiting for us to wrestle through?

The *Star 1* returned with the report that heavy, impenetrable ice blocked the way. Such long faces the crew had! But they brightened right up when the chase-boat captain said that he had seen plenty of whales held up at the edge of the ice, and blue whales at that, the largest species of all, and the one that whalers like best.

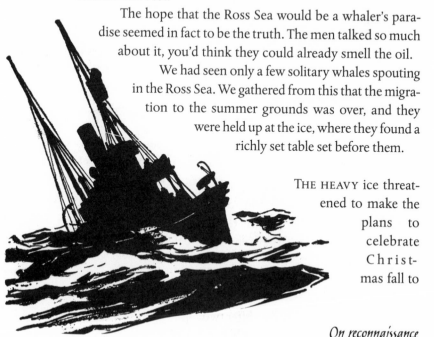

The hope that the Ross Sea would be a whaler's paradise seemed in fact to be the truth. The men talked so much about it, you'd think they could already smell the oil.

We had seen only a few solitary whales spouting in the Ross Sea. We gathered from this that the migration to the summer grounds was over, and they were held up at the ice, where they found a richly set table set before them.

THE HEAVY ice threatened to make the plans to celebrate Christmas fall to

On reconnaissance

pieces. The men had counted on celebrating Christmas Eve safely in the shelter of the Bay of Whales, but the chance of that seemed to be lost, and the mood grew dejected. On top of that, we were concerned about the *Star 2*, which had been out of sight for more than a day.

We had understood that the jealous urge to bring in the first whale had moved the stalwart Iversen, the captain, to go on ahead alone, against orders. But now that we had come up against the impenetrable ice but still didn't see any sign of the boat, not even smoke from its stack, we feared that something had gone wrong. That thought drove the happy Christmas notions almost completely from our minds. Of course, it was also possible that Captain Iversen had managed to clear a path through the ice, because he was the most undaunted and capable of our gunners, who were all intrepid sea-types of the best sort.

As far as we could see, the way to the Bay of Whales was blocked by heavy ice. First came loose, drifting clumps covered with fresh, glistening snow; after that there was ice that was piled up thickly, but of a completely different sort than we had seen before. The pack-ice barrier was made up mostly of flat floes, but this icebank was formed by coastal ice and broken ice debris from the Great Ice Barrier — and it had all frozen solid together. It made for a fantastic, bizarre sight; we could see a whole world of wonders in it. Without much imagination we saw all sorts of marble sculptures, whole groups of animals, charging bands of knights, camels, odd and enormous sarcophagi, gardens full of pure white flowers, native sailing vessels, a fishing village. On one block, icicles hung on a thin, horizontal bar, which looked like a shining silver comb from a fairy tale. Such strange ice formations are much like certain cloud formations: people discover all sorts of strange figures in them if they look at them for awhile.

We followed the edge of the ice in the southeasterly direction to look for an entrance, but there wasn't a single weak spot to be found anywhere in the ice field. So we sent chase boats to the east and west on reconnaissance, to look for the *Star 2* and at the same time to look for a passage. After a few hours they turned back without success. There was no sign of the *Star 2*, and the ice was shut tight everywhere. We still hoped that Captain Iversen had managed to find a weak point in the ice field, but we still saw no sign, not even a plume of smoke, so we began to get seriously uneasy about the stray boat.

While we were waiting for the return of the search party, we took a sounding that gave a depth of about 500 meters [about 1,600 feet].

The city of ice

Naturally we kept a keen lookout, and more than once someone hailed down from the crow's nest that the missing chase boat was in sight. That announcement brought great joy all around; but time and again what was sighted turned out to be a peculiar formation of ice, and the "clearly" seen smoke turned out to be a distorted shadow, raised and extended by a mirage on the ice.

It was a strange and wonderful world that stretched out around the ship when the sun skimmed low along the horizon that night. With the dimming of the light, the ice masses seemed to grow higher. In the east a whole city seemed to expand, with towers and monumental buildings. The solitary icebergs that we saw rose up entirely above the horizon and seemed to float in the air, separate from the rest of the ice. The invisible ice-field gave the impression of an insurmountably high wall.

Mostly to reach some certainty about the fate of the missing chase boat and her crew of twelve, Captain Larsen decided not to wait any longer that night but to try to force a way through the ice.

Anxiously the weather signs were studied: the wind, the movement of the clouds, and the barometer. If this heavy ice started to move while the ship was in the middle of it, then everything would go straight to the dogs. Luckily, everything pointed to good weather.

Carefully we steered into the ice, sailing slowly while searching for the thinnest places and making use of each channel, no matter how small. Strings of mist that hovered low over the ice forced us to stop for hours at a time until visibility improved. From time to time the ship shuddered and trembled in its every seam when it crashed into a heavy piece of ice that couldn't be completely avoided.

The following day the ice thinned; now we could see large, open channels. Large, flat floes, meters thick and sometimes hundreds of meters long, alternated with clumsy, formless blocks, which often showed clear layer formation. That was calf-ice. At the waterline such pieces of glacier ice were often colored brown by gravel algae. The flat floes carried seal and penguin tracks in the snow that lay on them, and sometimes the white covering of snow was as trampled as if a pack of children had romped on it.

The ice field as a whole was reminiscent of a hilly winter landscape with dark woods (suggested by the winding waterways) and coasts and houses (formed by blocks of ice and their shadows). It looked like a typical Norwegian winter landscape. Indeed, the thoughts of many flew far away to the north, where wives and children lived in a similar landscape and were now of course busy preparing their Christmas celebrations.

Already for some time now a hazy white line had been visible above the horizon in the south, but mirages had deceived us so often already that we weren't certain what the thin, light strip really was. We really didn't know what we were seeing until we came close by, so much did the mirage distort the image.

Icebergs, which from a distance we saw towering high above the sea ice, turned out not to exist once we got closer. Whole formations of ice appeared to float in the air. Things would change even as we stood looking at them: icebergs would turn into clouds and pack ice into open water, or heavy masses of ice would turn out to be completely blocking the way where a channel had seemed to be.

We did expect that the Great Ice Barrier would soon be visible, but the white strip above the ice was rendered so uncertain and changeable by the shifting movement of light that we never dared identify it as the Ice Barrier with any certainty. But toward midday, Captain Larsen, who stood watch in the lookout, announced that he did indeed see the Great Ice Barrier!

The white band in the south came steadily nearer and grew higher and higher. It shone in the sun, in stark contrast with the dark, almost black water-sky that stood in the east.

CHAPTER TWELVE

Christmas on the Sea Ice at the Foot of the Great Ice Barrier

At the foot of the Great Ice Barrier

———❧———

After noon the *Ross* reached the open water that stretched out a mile wide along the Great Ice Barrier. Keeping the wall at a distance of a half-mile, we steered the ship to the southeast, where the Bay of Whales was to be found. We hoped that the missing chase boat would already have arrived there. But the heavy ice-field that we had just left behind us made us doubt whether we would meet the *Star 2* and its crew there.

The Ice Barrier made an overwhelming impression. It rose straight up out of the sea, about 35 meters [100 feet] high, while its upper surface, which is perfectly horizontal, lost itself in the immense distance. In one place the plumb-straight wall showed an angular break, as if an enormous square block had been carved out with a giant knife. An iceberg had probably gotten loose from the body of the glacier at that spot. There was an overhanging edge almost everywhere along the top of the wall. All such details were of purely scientific interest, but the powerful whole of this, the largest glacier in the world, held us captive in the thrall of its grandeur. From Cape Crozier to King Edward VII Land, it bounded the Ross Sea to the south along a front of about 400 nautical miles. The observer of this mighty masterpiece of creation stands thunderstruck. He knows that this is the end of the world, the barrier before which all life stands still.

Behind this forbidding wall of ice, no organic life is possible. In the entire immense ice wilderness of Antarctica, there isn't a trace of either plant or animal life to be found.[1] Immediately behind the ice wall that rises straight up out of the waves begins the bleak, deserted kingdom of the dead. The name "Great Ice Barrier," which its discoverer Sir James Clark Ross gave to this imposing ice formation, was very well chosen indeed.

There on the boundary between life and death, one grows quiet and feels oh-so-small. The silent, grim wall of ice seems to stare at mankind out of the dark ice caves. They are the empty, fixed eyes of the dead, whose ice-cold gaze bores through to the soul and makes man conscious of his complete insignificance.

The Ice Barrier is frightening and forbidding, yet indescribably great and beautiful. It is powerful in its cold, silent impassivity. But dead it is not. A hard life, forbidding and cruel, seems to quiver within it, one that makes men shudder. It is a powerfully strong and mighty life, but of a horrible kind, one that tolerates no other life beside it.

Despite its forbidding nature, the Ice Barrier makes one feel a great and lasting sense of having grown richer from encountering it. Although the Barrier cuts off the clear view to the south, one gets a better idea of endlessness here than anywhere else in the world. Anything that a man has preserved in his innermost being as his most powerful impression of nature sinks to nothing before the majesty of the Ice Barrier. The proud glory of the mountain peaks, the wide emptiness of the wilderness, the swelling expanse of the ocean — all lose their glory beside the overwhelming, deadly severity of this endless wall of ice, which shuts off a whole continent of nameless desolation, emptiness, and cold from the living world around it.

1. So it was mistakenly thought at the time.

Protruding corner of the Ice Barrier

Roughly indicated, the edge of the Ice Barrier runs east-west, from 171° E to 158° W, and it lies around 78° 30′ S, only 11° 30′ away from the South Pole. What is most remarkable is that it floats on the sea, extending hundreds of miles farther toward the south, where it turns into the ice layer that covers the land where the South Pole lies buried. It is one enormous, floating glacier, so large that it appears to be land. Near the plumb-vertical wall of ice we took a sounding of 300 fathoms of water.

Even though it was summer as we sailed along the Barrier, there was still fresh, hard snow on it, and rough masses of snow were frozen solid against the rising wall. This made the Ice Barrier look a lot like a steep chalk-cliff coast, the kind one sees in the [English] Channel and on Rügen.[2]

The Barrier is the most characteristic ice formation in the far south, typical of the Antarctic environment. On this eternal wall of ice, death reigns supreme. But life teems in the water that swirls around the foot of the ice.

Life and death border each other immediately there. In the sea, we saw seals and penguins frolicking; a few small whales swam on the surface with open mouths, sifting through their baleen the countless, tiny shrimplike creatures that serve as their food. All sorts of Antarctic birds fluttered around the great mammals. All that animal life and the genial, open sunlight cheered the bare, starkly drawn picture of nature. But during the long, dark polar night there isn't a trace of life to be found. Then an endless silence reigns, and darkness, as on an extinguished planet at the outermost boundaries of the universe.

2. This is a large island mass on the north coast of Germany in the Baltic Sea.

THE WHOLE fleet steamed slowly along the Ice Barrier, which continued until the steep wall suddenly seemed to be interrupted. Behind it stretched a low layer of sea ice, and about ten miles farther on a steep wall of ice shone again, bending toward the south. It only looked as if the Barrier stopped there; sailing farther, we saw that it receded at a right angle to the south, forming a wide bay, the Bay of Whales. Finally we had reached our destination — but what a disappointment it was!

The entire bay was one white layer of snow. The sea ice hadn't yet broken up, and the safe harbor that we had thought we would find was completely shut off by solid bay ice, which was meters thick.

Was it still too early in the summer, or had we come during a heavy ice year? Who could say? The wide, thick circle of pack ice that we had come across outside the Ross Sea seemed to argue for the latter view. And the few whales that we saw spouting along the trip southward pointed in the same direction. The whales couldn't get through a thick belt of ice. There must always be a sufficient number of blow holes for the creatures to be able to come to the surface to breathe. No, we didn't see the countless whales that we had expected. But what struck us as much more important was that the missing chase boat wasn't there. Not even an encouraging plume of smoke was to be seen on the horizon.

We were all deeply touched by the thought that the brave crew of the *Star* 2 wouldn't be able to celebrate the happy Christmastime with us now, and we made increasingly somber assumptions.

Undoubtedly the little vessel lay trapped in the ice somewhere, unless something even worse had happened to it. Would that paltry little ship have been able to wrestle through that last, heavy ice-field? Did it have a sufficient supply of coal? Had it perhaps lost its propeller in the ice? These and other questions were thrown out, but no one could answer them. We just hoped that the good weather would hold out. A blizzard would mean a disaster in any case. Naturally, under these circumstances there could be no talk of a cheerful Christmas celebration. And the general opinion was that something had to be done.

Luckily, the weather left nothing to be desired, and we stopped a half-mile outside the solid bay-ice. The *Ross* and the chase boats could keep sailing there without danger — under steam, of course — so that we could be prepared for anything. And anything could happen in the vicinity of the solid ice. A wind coming up could put the ice field in motion; the bay ice could break up at any moment and force the *Ross* to flee; the Ice Barrier could start calving, letting loose some icebergs, from which we would prefer to keep a respectable distance.

On the bay ice we saw a black speck moving. Some thought that it must be one of the dogs that ran off from one of Roald Amundsen's teams when he was on his way to the geographic South Pole. At that time the great polar explorer had his headquarters, "Framhjem," here in the Bay of Whales. It was really difficult to believe that a dog could survive so long all alone in this barren world, destitute of everything. And indeed, the binoculars proved that the solitary, moving speck was not a dog but rather an emperor penguin.

It may seem strange that the men were so interested in a little speck in the distance. But in a world from which all life is banished, every token of living beings necessarily attracts attention. In addition, the Bay of Whales was for the Norwegians a truly legendary place, more or less. It was, after all, the place from which the great national hero Amundsen began the journey in which he stormed and conquered the South Pole, which had been thought unreachable. At the time of our voyage, Amundsen was still alive and kicking; he was in Alaska, preparing his flight over the North Pole. But his famous South Pole victory had already lent him a hero's halo, and everything that was connected to his name was regarded with a certain reverence. And so there was unusual interest in the frozen-shut bay, where "Framhjem" had stood and probably still stood, although now, after more than thirteen polar years, buried meters deep under the snow layer.

A few miles southward, on the western shore of the bay, a few hilly elevations stuck up above the otherwise flat snow layer. Probably Amundsen's quarters lay there, sleeping under the eternal snow. We asked Gjertsen, the ice pilot, who had been helmsman on the *Fram* at the time, what he thought. But at that distance he couldn't determine the position of "Framhjem" with certainty. And the appearance and the form of the bay had been greatly altered over the course of the years. The shores of the bay were, after all, not solid ground but moving, floating ice, from which huge pieces, in the form of icebergs, broke off. Meanwhile, all thoughts were still occupied with the missing chase boat and her crew; there could be no talk of cheerful Christmas spirits under such circumstances. The other chase boats searched the edge of the ice field from east to west, but without any result.

Now THAT the Bay of Whales was shut and unusable as a harbor, Captain Larsen decided to look for another anchorage. He wanted to find another break in the Ice Barrier more to the west: Discovery Inlet, which might offer a usable harbor. A more or less tranquil spot was necessary to process the whales that we still hoped to catch.

Captain Larsen himself was convinced that the chase boat hadn't disappeared but had only had trouble getting through the ice, or that Iversen was sailing eastward or westward to get around the heavy ice. He stood nearly alone in this opinion, but he knew Iversen very well and didn't doubt for a moment the correctness of his view.

We were going to set up a depot on the sea ice and leave behind in it a letter with instructions for Iversen. If the missing crew reached the Bay of Whales, then they would be able to rescue themselves. The second mate and I received instructions to lay out the depot. The necessary sacks of coal were loaded onto a chase boat, along with boxes and barrels of provisions: hardtack, salted meat, dried vegetables, butter, sugar, and coffee.

We were also taking along two sledges and a flag and the letter with instructions in a firmly stoppered bottle. Volunteers to help with the work reported in great numbers, Norwegians as well as Tasmanians. They would miss the Christmas celebrations onboard, but all of them were eager to do something for their missing shipmates. And the Tasmanians especially hankered to set foot on the Antarctic ice for the first time.

After we were served an abundant Christmas feast, the chase boat sailed off from the *Ross*. After a short trip we moored the boat along the solid

Securing the ice anchors

bay-ice, which seemed to be fifteen to twenty feet thick. To use the ice anchors, we first had to chop holes in the ice for the anchor flukes.

We unloaded the cargo at a distance of three hundred yards from the edge of the ice. If the depot stood too close to the water, it might float away when the ice broke up. It was well below freezing, but dragging the heavy sledges through the thick snow was strenuous, and we got so warm doing it that we took off our jackets.

In the middle of the depot we set up the flag on a long bamboo pole. We piled boxes and sacks high around it to secure the long flagpole. Several stays, held fast by a pile of sacks, made it even more secure. Then we fastened the bottle with the letter of instructions to the flagpole.

The depot was visible from a great distance. The sacks of coal piled up made a big black spot on the wide white surface, and the red-and-blue Norwegian flag, the only color in the white emptiness all around, was clearly visible. It would have been impossible to sail past the depot without noticing it.

It was a still, clear, sunny evening. At midnight, when the sun stood directly in the south and we had already been working hard for about four hours, we took a rest and stuffed our pipes.

At that point all our thoughts flew northward, toward Norway, Tasmania, and Holland, toward family and friends, who undoubtedly were also thinking of us while they sat together in warm, cozy living rooms around their Christmas trees, cheerfully lit and decorated, while outside it was snowing or freezing, and there was truly wintry darkness. We imagined how people in Norway or Holland might look outside in the dark night, where the stars would sparkle in the black heavens, or the snowflakes whirl down silently in the serene, velvety darkness.

How different it was for us outside on the sea ice. At midnight we sat there on the sledges in the clear sunshine; the long, sharp shadows on the snow made it difficult to realize that it was actually the middle of the night.

Our thoughts kept turning to the missing chase boat and its crew, but we could scarcely guess what had become of it and where it now found itself. The atmosphere was completely still, and the sea was so calm that a thick layer of ice quickly formed around our chase boat. The sacks of coal also quickly froze into hard clumps that were difficult to handle.

While we were pulling the sledges, a number of curious penguins came closer to investigate. A couple of large, stately emperor penguins kept themselves at a dignified distance, but the less distinguished Adélie penguins

apparently didn't have
to preserve any deco-
rum. Just like mis-
chievous little
boys, they came
running and fol-
lowed the sledges
while they yelled
excitedly to each
other, apparently
making all sorts of observations and remarks.

What could that be?

They were nervously ex-
cited about the unusual activity and all the strange things appearing in their
otherwise-so-peaceful world. They probably took humans to be an unusually large species of penguin. The things that we left behind in the snow attracted unusual attention. For a long time they stood inspecting with the
greatest of interest our empty jam and cigarette tins, looking at them from all
angles. No, they didn't understand them one bit.

The lovely emperor penguins, the distinguished patricians, remained
unruffled and dignified. They walked up to us in a calm, stately fashion, but
even so, they couldn't completely control their curiosity. Coming close, they
sat quietly in the snow, their heads held proudly high, waiting calmly to see
what might happen next.

Alas, their first acquaintance with man was to be less than pleasant.
The doctor had asked me if at all possible to bring a couple of emperors back
for scientific research. But as we watched the regal birds sitting there, meaning no harm, it wasn't easy to offer them up to science. Still, it had to be done,
and we tried to catch two of them.

The birds protested vehemently when we tried to drive them toward
the chase boat. The one firmly resisted, dealing out hefty blows with his
strong wings while screeching loudly. With his beak and wings he bravely resisted and let no one come closer. But when a jacket was thrown over him, he
let himself be dragged away without protest. Evidently he was so surprised
by this bizarre sort of treatment that he forgot to resist.

The other penguin resisted the attack on her freedom. She didn't let
herself be caught under the jacket, and she skillfully evaded us when we

chased her. She didn't go one step in the desired direction until we succeeded in driving her along by using snowballs.

Throwing snowballs seemed to be a strategy that greatly annoyed her. Already with the first ball that hit her, she fell over and tried to get away by rowing with her wings through the snow, but with well-aimed projectiles we kept her going steadily in the right direction. Rowing through the snow like that, she worked up a respectably high speed, and it took real work to keep up with her. It is truly a comic sight to see a bird sliding on its belly like that, as if it were on a sled.

When penguins want to move fast, this rowing over the snow seems to be their usual mode of travel. We saw evidence of this: there were more of these sled-tracks in the snow. For them, sledding is much faster and easier than walking, since their feet are so awfully short.

When we arrived at the chase boat with our booty, a couple of Norwegians onboard who had looked a little too deep into their glasses because of the Christmas holiday got into a fight on account of the penguins. Especially on Christmas night a fight seemed out of place, and as a result the penguins got their freedom back. In any case, it would have been really hard for me personally to let these beautiful animals be killed. The doctor would surely be able to get hold of a couple of other emperors later on for his collection.

After this intermezzo we worked diligently on the depot, until everything lay piled up around the flag: sacks of coal and boxes of butter, coffee, tea, hardtack, fishballs, salted cod,[3] and blankets. We also left one of the sledges behind at the depot fastening it between boxes and bags, so that it couldn't slide away if the wind began to blow. The *Star 2* would need a sledge to transport everything if it found the depot.

When the depot was finally ready, it was time for the cameras. Everyone was very interested in being photographed on top of the depot. That kind of picture in an authentic Antarctic entourage is something all the men would love to bring home later. One always hears about them in all the travel descriptions of true polar expeditions. So everyone stood in the appropriate posture on or near the depot, put on the proper face for the occasion, and was very happy when the camera clicked a couple of times. (Meanwhile, I made a drawing as a souvenir of the event.) The fellows would later proudly

3. Van der Does uses the Norwegian words *fiskeboller* and *salt kjödt*.

The depot

show their friends and family these photos of a real polar depot atop which they were immortalized as authentic polar travelers.

SETTING UP the depot had taken most of the night, so we figured we had missed the Christmas party on the *Ross*. Still, we had gotten the satisfaction of doing something for our missing shipmates. But when we completed our task and got back onboard, we heard that there hadn't been a Christmas party on the *Ross* after all. They did burn candles on the paper Christmas trees in the salon and in the cabins, but there was no trace of high spirits. Not much justice had been done to the abundant Christmas meal, and nobody felt like playing the gramophone.

On the second day of Christmas, when the *Star 2* still hadn't turned up and her smoke-plume appeared nowhere on the horizon, the men began to get impatient. They asked Captain Larsen if it wouldn't be better to send out a proper rescue expedition to look for the missing. But Larsen, as sure of his business as always, wanted to wait until the following day. According to his reckoning, the chase boat might still come back that night; he was sure that it was only delayed by having to make a long detour through the thick, rough ice. The whole day the other chase boats patrolled along the edge of the ice field, and on the *Ross* there were constantly men on lookout.

Captain Larsen turned out to be right.

Not long after midnight the watch in the lookout reported that he saw smoke rising up out of the west. Immediately the happy news spread around the ship like a racing fire. There was general rejoicing, for we couldn't have wished for a nicer Christmas present. When the disobedient gunner moored his chase boat alongside the mother ship, our big family was complete again.

Iversen had been very ambitious in wanting to be the first in the Bay of

Whales and the first to harpoon a whale, but the heavy ice had foiled his plans and had caused the whole expedition several days of anxious tension. At the same time, we were far too happy that the prodigal sons had returned to reproach Iversen for his stubbornness. The happiness of seeing them again even made for a festive mood, but the celebration couldn't last for long; work awaited us.

We had to find whales. We had come from the far Norwegian coasts over the oceans and through the pack ice to the uttermost ends of the earth for that purpose. But where were they? The whales, which all earlier expeditions had encountered here in such great numbers that the bay had been named for them, simply didn't appear.

Some thought that we had come too early and that the great whale migration hadn't yet reached the Ice Barrier. Others thought that it was a heavy ice year, and that the development of plankton, the whales' food, had been hindered and consequently also the arrival of the animals themselves. Or perhaps the members of the previous expeditions, not a one of them whalers themselves, supposed a wealth of whales with every spout they saw, when in fact there was no such thing? Maybe they really had seen many whales blowing, but they could also have seen orcas or minke whales, the smaller species, which aren't considered for the great hunt because they aren't worth the trouble.

Animal life in the vicinity of the Bay of Whales was definitely scarce. We did encounter all the kinds of animals that earlier expeditions had reported, but their numbers were very small. When we had put up the depot, we had seen just a few penguins and seals. Our ice pilot was astonished at the poverty of the fauna. When he had been in the Bay of Whales in 1911 aboard Amundsen's ship, the place was teeming with animals; in fact, Amundsen had been able to set up numerous meat depots for his trip to the Pole. When our attention was attracted by movement in the water, it was usually a penguin or a Weddell seal, which came up full of curiosity to check out the ship. Sometimes it was a school of killer whales (*Orca gladiator*), which occur frequently in the southern seas. And we had seen very few birds: just a few Antarctic petrels, a skua gull, and a pair of snow petrels had followed us to the frozen bay.

We had to go search for the great whales somewhere else.

Now that worry over the runaway chase boat no longer occupied our thoughts, we could again fully appreciate the grandeur of the polar environment and its severe beauty. Over and over again our gaze was captured by the Ice Barrier, which stretched from east to west as far as the eye could see. The tremendous glacier was wondrously beautiful whenever the sun sparkled on it. It seemed to change shape constantly. At midday, when the sun stood in the north and its rays fell directly on the Barrier, it seemed to be one long, flat chalk-cliff. At night, when the sun stood above the horizon in the south, the wall was entirely clothed in dark blue shadows and stood sharply profiled against the luminous tints of the midnight sun. But the Ice Barrier was at its most beautiful in the morning and afternoon hours. Then the slipping shadows constantly altered and delineated, clearly and sharply, all the relief details of the steep wall. Every indentation, every protruding corner, every peculiarity of the complexly fractured surfaces became cleanly and clearly visible. And the changing combination of light and shadow kept pace with the changing position of the sun.

It was a constantly transforming play of light and shadow that was so confusing that one was never really sure of the shape of any particular section of the wall until one had carefully observed it at all hours of the day. Only in diffuse light could one be certain of the forms of the imposing ice massif.

We were used to making rough estimates of the time from the position of the sun, making use of the compass. Here this caused many difficulties because the directions of the compass were rather uncertain. The horizontal component of the earth's magnetic field was slight, and the inclination of the compass needle, so close to the magnetic pole, was very great. And the variation of the compass was unbelievably great, almost 150°, because the magnetic South Pole lay not to the south of us but in the northwest, in South Victoria Land.

But we quickly learned to estimate the time from the position of the sun, as the Javanese do. It was convenient that here the sun was available as a "time meter" at night as well.

THE MORNING after the lost *Star 2* had returned safely, we saw that the depot that we had set up on the sea ice with so much effort had drifted in a westerly direction. It seemed almost as if it was offended at not having been used. Part of the bay's winter ice had come loose in large pieces, and it was floating westward with the current; the depot was sailing safely away in the middle of a large floe. Of course we had no intention of losing those supplies. The *Star 2*, for which this was all originally intended, was sent over to rescue the depot.

Amazingly enough, the bay ice had broken up into almost perfectly square pieces. The chase boat had to make her way very carefully among the big twenty-foot-thick floes, which had only a little open water between them, in order to board the floe that was floating away.

Dismantling the depot proved much easier than setting it up. It lay no more than twenty meters from the edge of the floe, and in a short time the supply of coal was poured into the chase boat's bunkers and the provisions were packed up in storage.

Meanwhile, the other four chase boats were also provisioned with coal. Then the *Ross* put up steam again, heading northward into the ice. The frozen Bay of Whales was unusable as a harbor, and there weren't any whales there, either. We would thus have to seek our fortunes elsewhere.

CHAPTER THIRTEEN

Looking for a Harbor and Some Whales

Harpooned whale

⟨◦/◦/◦⟩

The *Ross* had to do battle with the ice again immediately. Captain Larsen again led the navigation from the *tönne*. The ice wasn't especially thick, and there were enough open, winding waterways. Still, navigation was unusually difficult. The ice field consisted almost entirely of coastal ice, meters thick, and pieces of debris from the Ice Barrier, irregular masses of ice, very diverse in weight, here and there frozen together into a solid whole.

Cautiously we sailed along the whimsical, meandering paths of the ice maze, but with the huge ship it wasn't possible to avoid all collisions. If a heavy chunk of ice couldn't be avoided, we stopped the engine so as not to approach the shock too violently. Even so, during the journey through that old ice-field, the *Ross* suffered many dents along the waterline, even though the prow was still well-protected by the heavy oaken reinforcement, which absorbed the impact for the most part. Without that ice hull, things would have looked bad for the *Ross*, and we thanked heaven that it was windless, with the ice at complete rest. Still, massive collisions with the ice that made the whole ship shudder and the ice crack happened again and again — so often, in fact, that many of the men grew agitated.

Often with unusually heavy shocks we also feared that the bow plates would give way. While there wasn't much chance that the ship would rapidly sink, because it was divided into a number of watertight compartments, it's still far from safe to wander around all alone in the ice on an unknown sea with a leaking ship. So we checked the pumps constantly. And with water seeping from countless buckled rivets, we posted a watch in the forepeak to find and repair leaks immediately.

Going through a homogenous pack of ice is something one quickly gets used to, although the noise of the cracking ice is very bothersome if one has to sleep nearby. But in this ice field the shocks were often so heavy and unexpected that it seemed as if the ship was stumbling over a reef. It got on our nerves, that constant ramming.

A little after noon the ship collided against the ice with such force that all of us were knocked off our feet. We had never experienced such a heavy shock before, and even before the watch on the forepeak came to report it, we knew that the *Ross* had now definitely sprung a major leak. That turned out pretty well: with rubber and a lot of cement we were able to repair the leak. We had more trouble with the leaks in the forward compartments. Numerous buckled rivets and seams lay underneath the coal that filled these compartments. The water that had streamed in had frozen the mass of coal into one solid whole, and pickaxes had to be used on it. Meanwhile, it appeared that not only all the bow plates on the waterline but also several timber frames had suffered nasty dents. Luckily, the oaken ice-hull had protected the ship's steel skin; otherwise, we wouldn't have been in the relatively good shape that we were. Still, the ice hull was damaged and ripped away in several places, and it was clear that the *Ross* couldn't survive long in such heavy ice. So we felt very relieved when it appeared that the ice field wasn't wide. And it wasn't: by evening we had reached open water again.

Along the edge of the ice we saw many whale spouts, and the gunners on the chase boats didn't need to be told twice to go find out what sort of whales they were, nor was it necessary to urge them to go hunt them. With a loud cry of "Hurrah!" they went after them at full speed. The whales were so numerous that the men thought that we had finally reached the whalers' Promised Land.

One of the chase boats, "Bulken" ("The Bruise"), which had its unsightly appearance to thank for its nickname, came back quickly with the report that they were only minke whales. What were those? As had so often been the case already, Captain Larsen here too had to educate us novices and explain what "minke" meant.

Meincke was the name of a sailor who had been in service to the pioneer of the whaling industry, Svend Föyn, in the Arctic Ocean. Meincke had the unfortunate distinction of coming alongside the ship with mostly small whales. They belong to the baleen type of whales, called dwarf or beaked whales, which have only a small amount of blubber and so provide little oil. Consequently, whalers in the southern seas disdained it. And since the time of Svend Föyn, these unusable whales have been disparagingly called minke whales.

The other chasers came back with the same bad news.[1] The gunners looked gruff and were in no mood to be spoken to, while the crew reacted childishly to the news and went about with long faces.

During the past few days, which had brought so many sorts of ill fortune, we learned to be in awe of Captain Larsen, who, trusting in his lucky stars, overcame all dangers and difficulties, smiling all the while: the heavy ice-pack, the frozen-shut, whale-free Bay of Whales, the leaky ship. His ever-ready humor, which was worth more than gold during an uncertain enterprise such as ours, almost never missed its mark. With his unshakable confidence, Larsen gave heart to anyone who needed it. Our leader was one of those uncommon men who only grows stronger through misfortune, and whose trust in the future only builds as the difficulties mount — in short, a splendid fellow.

Nevertheless, the absence of whales depressed the general mood.

AFTER A QUIET, ice-free night, Fortune had pity on the discouraged whalers. Already very early the next morning the men rejoiced in the many a heavy whale *blååst* from several directions, and the chasers were charged to go hunt-

---

1. In Dutch the charming word is *jobstijding*, "Job's news."

ing in earnest immediately. Of course, every gunner hoped that he would shoot the first whale. That was considered a real honor, so a great sporting contest arose. Like dogs who'd smelled the scent, the boats steamed off.

Finally, the long-awaited hunting season had begun. The air was mild, a light breeze blew out of the west in veiled light, and the sea was calm — ideal weather for hunting.

Everyone wanted to witness the first shot. Everywhere on deck stood groups of men wanting to follow the interesting and exciting drama.

The chasers had spread themselves out while the *Ross* steamed slowly after them. The *Star* 2 came across our bow about a mile distant. We couldn't follow what it did, but it lay maneuvering, and we saw it now from behind and then again from the side. Coming closer, we saw not far from the chase boat the *blååst* of a whale rise up — always three times in a row, with short pauses in between. Then the animal dove down only to surface again a little later, now right in front of the chase boat's bow, but still too far away for a certain shot. Three *blååsten* and the whale disappeared again. Now it was the task of the captain — who was also the gunner — to guess where the fish would resurface.

It required much patience and maneuvering, which had to be done as silently as possible in order not to frighten the whale. So the engine had to be used as sparingly as possible, since water is an excellent transmitter of sound.

After a few minutes the whale appeared on the surface again, but it was another half an hour before the shot fell.

Was it a hit?

The whale immediately dove under again, and when we looked closely, we could see the harpoon rope stretched out in front of the gunner.

"*Fast fisk!!*"[2] rejoiced the enthusiastic onlookers. The first wounded whale dragged the chase boat after itself. Now the long faces of the previous day were gone. Everyone smiled, and laughter and happy shouts resounded over the whole ship.

A few minutes later the wounded animal came to the surface again to breathe, the water whipping from its tremendous tail. It thrashed around wildly in a pool of foam that began to turn red.

The first harpoon hadn't been enough to kill the colossal animal; evidently no vital organs had been hit. So a second harpoon was shot at close

2. This is Norwegian for "fish fast" — that is, "We're fastened to a whale," as in "We've got one!"

The gunner

range. We clearly saw the explosion of the grenade that was screwed on to the point of the harpoon. Now the animal was mortally wounded. It took another couple of breaths, but now it was streams of blood that spouted up out of its nostrils. Soon the great tail stopped churning the water into foam. The whale was dead.

With the harpoon rope the cadaver was hauled alongside the chase boat and fastened to the bollards with a chain around the base of its tail. A hollow tube was driven into the smooth, round body so that steam could be blown into it to keep it afloat.

The first whale was pulled in triumph to the *Ross* and fastened firmly alongside with a chain around the tail. This first catch was inspected with unusually high interest and expertly categorized. It was a so-called blue whale, 90 feet long and weighing an estimated 90 tons. (With the large whales, one figures on about a ton of weight for every foot of length.) Men stand amazed when they see an animal of prehistoric proportions close up for the first time. This whale was every bit as long as the chase boat that had caught it.

It was Captain Iversen with the *Star 2* to whom went the honor of having brought in the first whale. In his earlier attempt to claim this reward for himself and to scoop up the associated bounty of a hundred kroner, he had provided us with days of unrest and anxiety when he tried to reach the Bay of Whales on his own. Now he had the satisfaction of his ambitious striving being crowned with success.

The whole day the chase boats kept hunting whales, while the mother ship followed slowly. The seawater was a cloudy green color from the plankton in the upper layer. The Norwegians nodded in satisfaction when they saw the green, cloudy water. The more plankton, the more *hval* [whale(s)].

That evening a second whale was brought alongside: a blue whale again, this time a female, 85 feet long.

On the big board on the bridge deck, where from now on the total catch would be written, four whales were notated that evening, the hunting booty of the first day. Involuntarily that blackboard made me think of prize races, where the names and times of the horses are emblazoned on big blackboards such as this. The only thing missing here was the betting machine. Things hadn't gone quite that far with the oilmakers; the work was too hard and also too serious.

THAT DAY it was unusually mild. It was even a few degrees above freezing, a rarity at this high latitude of about 78° S. Still, about midday the gray clouds descended all the way to the water; it looked a lot like a dark November day in Holland. Then it began to snow, and the barometer fell. Everything pointed to an approaching change in the weather, and now a light swell rose up that prevented us from processing the captured fish immediately. That was really a shame, because everyone burned with the desire to work; the men wanted nothing more than to get on the job right away. Everything was ready onboard: the machinery awaited the first blubber to produce oil.

To accommodate the flensing of the whales — that is, the cutting off of the blubber layer — the ship needs to lie in still water, because the flensing is done overboard by men who stand on flat-bottomed platforms, cutting the blubber into long strips with huge flensing-knives. The colossal sides of blubber are then pulled loose with steam winches and hauled on deck to be processed further.

If the water isn't completely calm, then this flensing overboard is very dangerous, because everything is in motion: the ship, the loading boom, the whale, and the sliced blubber. The danger is intensified because these things of course don't all move equally, and that means that sometimes, very suddenly, the loading rope will be put under tremendous tension, with the full weight of a whale — 80 to 100 tons — suddenly hanging on it all at once. Later on it did happen several times that a boom hanger or a cargo rope broke, putting the men who were at work underneath it in great danger.

So it was out of the question to start up the oil factory right away, and this brought with it a new problem: Where on this grim ice barrier could we find something that looked like a harbor, a place where we could be protected from sea and swell and could work without too much difficulty?

All our hope lay in a break in the Ice Barrier, one that on the English Admiralty charts was the only interruption indicated in the barrier other than the Bay of Whales. This bend carried the name of Discovery Inlet, after the expedition of Scott, who discovered this dubitable harbor in 1902.

The *Star 1*, the strongest and most capable of our chasers, was sent out ahead to see whether the "Ice Cellar," as we called Discovery Inlet among ourselves, was free of ice and offered a useful anchorage.

The other chase boats kept chasing whales with unflagging energy, and on the second day three more blue whales were notated on the board. We always rejoiced to receive these special-interest bulletins. It looked like announcements on the stock exchange, where the lucky shareholders eagerly throng together. And actually the captured fish were in a sense shares for the voyagers. Every man mustered aboard received, above and beyond his wages, a share of the profit in proportion to his salary. Not surprisingly, a lot of fervent calculating went on in front of that famous board.

Since the *Ross* lay floating the whole day with its engines idle, the scientists had a fine opportunity to make a series of hydrographic measurements. Soundings were taken, and seafloor samples were hauled up; the water temperature and the salinity were also measured at various depths. The scientists got sore arms and blistered hands from repeatedly drawing up the steel sounding-line, but fortunately they were very satisfied with the results they got. There wasn't often an opportunity to make a whole series of measurements, and all the data that could be collected were of great scientific interest, since no decent hydrographic observations had yet been made in the Ross Sea.

The *Star 1* returned with a triply good report: both Discovery Inlet and the route to it were ice-free, and it had encountered plenty of whales on the way. With this favorable news the *Ross* immediately headed for the unexpected harbor. It appeared that our fortunes had turned. Nobody bothered too much now about the leak in the bow. For the time being, we preferred to set aside somber thoughts about the trip home through the pack ice and over the stormy ocean in a leaky ship. Like the Vikings centuries before, choosing a harbor from which to plunder and despoil, we also sought a safe place from which to gather our precious booty.

We knew very little about Discovery Inlet, however — not much more than what Scott wrote about it in his work entitled *The Voyage of the "Discovery."* On January 26 he reported, "It was very misty and thick; we could not see the end of our channel, even when we came close by. We could do nothing else than turn back and go outside again."

We weren't a great deal wiser on account of that; we would in fact have to discover Discovery Inlet all over again. But we were just happy that, after eleven years, the bay still existed. With the ever-changing shape of the Ice Barrier, it could just as easily not have been there anymore.

The seven whales alongside the *Ross* forced it to sail at a moderate pace. Under full steam the cadavers, which were steadily expanding from the accumulating gases of decomposition, might shear off and drift away. In addition, thick snow squalls made cautious navigation imperative, especially since the Barrier couldn't be far away.

Fog alternated with the snow. The mist was sometimes so thick that the men on the command bridge couldn't see the anchor winch. Then it was safer to stop, keeping the steam whistle sounding continually, and listen very closely to see if an echo betrayed the proximity of the Ice Barrier or icebergs. It was a ghastly trip through the snow squalls and fogbanks over an unknown sea, where the silent ice giants might at any moment come looming up out of the layers of mist. The thick, clammy fog layer dampened sound so thoroughly that it seemed as if the dull drone of the whistle reached no farther than the immediate surroundings of the ship. In order to hear better, we stopped the engine, while many pairs of ears listened intently to see if a weak echo or the gurgling of the swell indicated that solid ice lay nearby.

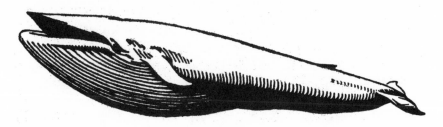

Blue whale

CHAPTER FOURTEEN

Giants of the Sea

Humpback whale

—⟨◎◎◎⟩—

Whales are true giants, at least the larger species, compared to which even the African elephant is only the size of a child. In earlier geologic eras, even larger animals lived on our earth, but in modern times the whale is without rival the largest species of animal found on the planet. Many of them weigh over a hundred tons, a staggering weight, roughly comparable to that of thirty elephants.

Its name of "whale-fish"[1] notwithstanding, the whale is classified as a mammal because it bears live young. (The mother suckles her young with milk glands that lie hidden in deep, bowl-shaped hollows, thus preventing the milk from getting mixed with seawater. To drink, the young whale presses its snout into one of these hollows.) That the whale uses lungs to breathe also marks it as a mammal. (In order to breathe, the animal must surface above water about every fifteen minutes. When chased, it can actually stay underwater longer, but if it stays under too long, it inevitably drowns, like every other mammal.)

1. The Dutch word the author uses for whale is *walvisch* (literally, "whale-fish"; now spelled *walvis*).

Whales have only front limbs, which is unique among mammals. When processing these colossal bodies, we did find rudiments of the rear limbs, but from the outside not a trace of them was visible. But the lack of hind feet is more than compensated for by the powerful tail fin, which isn't oriented vertically, like that of fishes, but rather horizontally. The animals use this tremendous tail as a propeller to move forward. They use their front limbs not so much for forward movement as for making turns. These limbs are usually called fins, but in reality they most certainly are not: the skeleton of a whale clearly shows five fingers and the remains of arm bones. Yet these "hands" have grown to become very useful rowing-fins — hence the common name.

The whale is, of course, a very unusual mammal. It lives exclusively on other animals, and one might think that it could swallow up the largest animals with hide and hair; the enormous maw is large enough for that. But the tremendous giant is destined to satisfy itself with just the smallest of sea creatures because, behind its immovable tongue, its gullet narrows so sharply that a mackerel could scarcely fit through it. Despite this seeming drawback, this Goliath doesn't have to suffer from hunger. On the contrary, it fills itself up nicely by swallowing literally tons of plankton. It's a real glutton, focused completely on eating, so much so that it has an accordion-style belly that it can unfold as needed. This is why its entire underside is filled with grooves from the chin to the anus and looks like a corrugated tin roof.

The lower jaw of a whale is tremendously large and heavy — so heavy, in fact, that closing the mouth sometimes seems to cause difficulties. When the animal has collected food with its open maw and the "fishing net" is full, it frequently rolls over on its side in order to be able to close its mouth more easily.

So that the whale doesn't swallow a mass of seawater with every bite it takes, the maw is furnished with a very efficient fishing-net. On the palate, square, horny plates, about half a centimeter thick, are fastened crosswise, a finger's-breadth apart: this is the baleen, which runs out into rough, beard-like filaments, the fringes. Toward the front of the maw the baleen grows smaller. It all looks like a rough coconut mat. When the whale closes its mouth, the baleen works like a sieve through which the seawater can flow away while the fishes, shrimp, jellyfish, and other small sea-creatures remain captured, ready to be sent coursing over the thick tongue and swallowed.

The nostrils open up on the top of the head on a slight elevation, which is above water when the whale breathes. These nostrils, which can be shut watertight, open up directly into the pharynx.

Not much is yet known about the reproduction of whales. That's a very difficult subject to study, given that the animals live in the water and move from one ocean to another. It appears that the females carry their young for ten months to a year. The young blue and fin whales are 18 to 20 feet long at birth — a respectable size for suckling infants.

There are many types of baleen whales, not all of which come into consideration in modern whaling; only the largest species are worth the trouble. In modern times the blue whale, the fin whale, the sei whale, the roundback or humpback whale, the North Cape whale, and the gray whale are hunted — and exclusively for the oil they furnish. In the time when Hollanders were the leading whalers and every year a whole fleet was sent to Spitsbergen, it was primarily the Greenland whale that suffered for it. This species is now nearly wiped out.

In earlier times the hunt was for the baleen, but since modern technology has enabled us to manufacture materials that replace baleen and are cheaper, the baleen is left alone, and more attention is paid to the blubber layer that protects the giants against the cold seawater. Oil cooked from the blubber is processed into all sorts of industrial lubricants and edible fats, soap, glycerin, and much more. If you use a piece of Sunlight soap or put a pat of Blue Band in the pan to fry a steak, you wouldn't guess that the basic materials for these useful consumer goods come from whales, which once frolicked happy and free in the far south. In fact, the Sunlight factories have their own whaling stations on South Georgia Island. They also have their own tankers, which bring the oil to Port Sunlight and Vlaardingen. Many cargoes of oil are also sold to the great margarine factories of Europe. But I must reassure you that whale oil is something completely different from cod-liver oil, that awful, foul-smelling oil that we as children would swallow only if something yummy was added to it. Whale oil is a pure, tasteless, and unscented animal fat. The [Dutch] name is not correct;[2] the Norwegians and the English call it *hvalolje* and "whale oil."

Although in earlier years it was Basques, Hollanders, the English, and the Americans who practiced whaling, today it is the Norwegians who control nearly the entire whaling business wherever these giants of the sea are

2. The Dutch name for whale oil is *traan* (literally, "tears").

hunted: in the Arctic and Antarctic Oceans; along the coasts of South America, South Africa, and Australia; in Californian and Japanese waters; around the Shetland Islands and Alaska; and in the fjords of the Finnmark.[3]

The blue whale is the largest of all and thus the most sought after. It is, on average, 70 to 75 feet long, but individual whales more than a hundred feet long have been caught. The largest that we ever heard of measured 107 feet. The body of the blue whale is rather slim, torpedo-shaped; the color is a dark blue-gray, with lighter patches on the underside. The underside of the fins is mostly white. The baleen and fringes are black.

The blue whale seems to prefer to stay in the vicinity of ice; almost all of the whales that we found in the Ross Sea along the Great Ice Barrier were blue whales. In the summer, blue whales are found in the Arctic as well as in the Antarctic Oceans, while they spend the winter in warmer water, near the Azores, the Falkland Islands, and the islands around Australia, although they are also seen along the coasts of Chile and South Africa, as well as in the Gulf of Mexico, off Japan, and in the Bering Sea.

In contrast to other whale species, which like to live together in schools, the mighty blue whale lives alone. It is extremely strong, and a wounded animal can sometimes pull a chase boat along behind itself for more than twenty-four hours before it's exhausted.

The fin whale isn't as large as the blue whale; on average it grows from 60 to 65 feet long, although a single one may reach a length of more than 80 feet, and it's slimmer and more elegant in body shape than its larger brother. It's also lighter in color: on the back side it's dark gray, on the belly side, white. The baleen are also lighter, gray in color, and the fringes are white. The fin whale is a fish-eater and likes to follow the migration of herring, mackerel, and other fishes, which always assure him a well-set table.

As befits its slender build, the fin whale is lively in its movements, in contrast to the other baleen whales, which are dull and defenseless. The fin whale also possesses a lively temperament, which sometimes makes it dangerous. Often a wounded one decides to attack a chase boat. The fin whale is found in the same oceans as the blue whale, mostly in the waters of the high north and south, not in warm seas.

3. The Finnmark is the northern area of Norway, above the Arctic Circle, home to the Lapps.

WHALES ARE often caught in the waters off Japan. There they are prized not for the oil but for the meat. Whale meat is also very popular in Norway. As is well-known, Eskimos are partial to blubber and whale meat, and for them a whale supplies a complete cache of provisions. I know from experience that the meat is very tasty; on the *Ross* we savored many a whale steak. The meat is fairly rough in texture and looks dark, like the meat of a water buffalo, but it tastes much like beef. In the Antarctic it was often featured on our menu, in the form of roasts, ground meat, or steak.

Fin whale

If a young whale was caught and the blubber layer removed, then a nice piece of meat, sometimes weighing half a ton, was cut off the flensed carcass and hung up in the rigging, where it froze almost immediately and thus was kept free of spoilage. The cooks made grateful use of this supply of meat, without which we would have had to subsist on preserved food. But all of us onboard were welcome to cut off a piece whenever we liked and cook it up however we liked. Especially at night, when the cooks weren't in the galleys, one could find men in there industriously baking, broiling, and frying whale delicacies.

Captain Larsen purposely encouraged the use of whale meat as food. The supplies that we had taken with us from Tasmania were quickly used up or spoiled, so that we would have had to rely for a long time on preserved food, which contains little or no vitamins and causes scurvy and beri-beri, the greatest plagues of long sea-journeys in the olden days. The use of fresh food completely prevents the occurrence of these diseases.

There were those among us on the *Ross* who in their stupidity thought that whale meat wasn't fit for human consumption. It was striking that almost all those who stubbornly refused to eat whale meat showed symptoms of scurvy sooner or later and got more or less seriously ill, while not a single eater of whale meat had even the slightest trouble with this.

A THIRD whale species that in all respects corresponds to the above-named types is the sei whale, which is actually much smaller, but still reaches 40 to 48 feet in length.

Its features are much like those of the blue and fin whales except that its dorsal fin is larger and placed farther forward on its body than is the case with other species. In southern whale-hunting, the sei whale is found only sporadically.

The roundback or humpback whale looks completely different. Compared to the slender, graceful fin whale, which has an aristocratic appearance, it is a thick, clumsy bourgeois. The large, warty growths on its head and fins don't enhance its external beauty, even less the impossibly large fins, which earlier gave it the name of "long-armed whale." Among the Norwegian whalers, it is called *knölhval,* or knobby whale. It is a cheerful bag of fat, which is easily caught and provides lots of oil; it is therefore regarded highly, even though it is so very ugly. So much hunting has been done of this peaceful source of oil that in the Arctic Ocean it is threatened with extinction.

Another whale that can boast even less of outward beauty is the well-known North Cape whale, which every sailor knows. In every season North Capers can be seen blowing in every part of the Atlantic Ocean. The head, which makes up a quarter of the total body length, is especially ugly, with the mouth bent downward in an S-form. The eyes, remarkably enough, lie under the corners of the mouth. It is a plump, unsightly monster, although the Greenland whale, with a head a third the size of its body, still betters the North Caper in this respect. A full-grown North Caper is about 15 meters [about 50 feet] long; its color is mostly an even black. It has no dorsal fin, as is the case with its Greenland relative, and for this reason is called the *rethval,* or smooth whale.

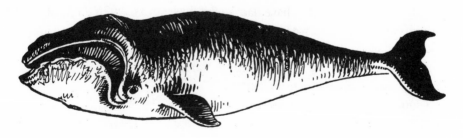

North Cape whale

In the northern part of the Pacific Ocean there lives yet another species of whale without a back fin, the Californian gray whale, what the Japanese call the "devilfish."

All the whale species mentioned so far belong to the large group of baleen whales.

ANOTHER LARGE group are the toothed whales, to which, among others, the porpoises and dolphins belong. The dolphin is a gluttonous thief and also has a mouth full of sharp teeth. Apart from that, it is a fast and cheerful animal. A pretty sight it is when a school of these frolicking fish, with their leader in front, swim springing and snorting in front of the ship, as if they're pulling it. One is reminded of the fable in which Venus, born from the seafoam, is pulled forth in a shell drawn like a wagon by dolphins. Perhaps the myth has this to thank for its origin. It is known that the coastal dwellers in old Hellas knew how to tame these creatures.

The narwhal is also a toothed whale, from four to five meters [about 12 to 15 feet] long. What is most remarkable about this animal is its huge, spiral-wound stabbing tooth, which can sometimes grow to two meters [over six feet] long. It's the only tooth that this creature possesses, but what a sizable one!

In earlier times men ascribed great medicinal powers to the narwhal tusk. They thought that the horn was that of the mythical unicorn. (In Dutch this animal is also called the "unicorn fish.") No self-respecting pharmacy could be without such a horn.

The killer whale, the *Orca gladiator*, is also a toothed whale, which grows to nine meters in length [about 30 feet]. It is a tremendously rapacious animal that kills seals, even elephant seals, and, as my shipmates and I witnessed, doesn't even shrink from attacking the great whales.

In the Antarctic Ocean we saw many of these orcas. Often they pulled the strips of blubber off a whale that we were flensing, and it happened a few times that they bit at the men who were at work on a dead whale alongside the *Ross*. The flensers had to force them to retreat by beating them off with the long handles of their flensing knives.

Orcas are much more dangerous than sharks. The Norwegian whalers thoroughly hated them and called them *mörderhval*. The English term "killer whale" also indicates no great sympathy for them.

Near New Zealand we witnessed an unusual hunt in the water. A school of at least twenty killer whales was hunting an enormous sperm whale, like a pack of wolves on a deer. The whale put up a good fight against many of its attackers, but in the end, outnumbered, it still got the worst of it.

The bottlenose or snout whale also belongs to a subspecies of toothed whales. As its name implies, it has a long, flat snout, like the dolphin. It grows from six to ten meters [20 to 33 feet] long.

In earlier days it was often caught along the coast of the North Atlantic Ocean — in fact, it was caught very often, because the bottlenose's great curiosity simplifies the hunt in no small measure. They are companionable creatures, and if one is wounded, its comrades don't race off but, full of curiosity, keep swimming around the chase boat, so that they can usually be harpooned one after the other. We saw them in the Ross Sea, but we left them alone; for our purposes they were too small.

The potfish, also called the cachalot or sperm whale, is by far the largest of the toothed whales. It can grow as large as 20 meters [65 feet] long, and its enormous tail fin is five meters [16 feet] wide. It is actually the only toothed whale that is considered in the modern hunt and presents a true challenge, since it is a master of fighting readiness.

The sperm whale has a gullet large enough to let more than plankton and small fish through it. The food it enjoys most is squid, and it seems to dare to attack even the horrid, eight-armed squid, the octopus. Great pieces of the long sucker-arms are frequently found in the bellies of sperm whales.

The sperm whale has a long, narrow lower jaw containing a great number of sharp, rootless teeth that fit into hollows in the upper jaw. The nearly square head, which from the front looks almost horizontally truncated, is unusually large, making up at least a third of the whole body. In the powerful skullbones there is a large cavity that is filled with a liquid fat, the spermaceti, for which this species of whale used to be relentlessly hunted. One sperm whale produces at least a dozen barrels of spermaceti, which becomes hard and white outside its body. Fine candles and salves are made from it.

In the intestines of a sperm whale a curious secretion is sometimes found: ambergris. It is used in perfume production and is very precious. Pieces of ambergris sometimes wash up on the beaches of the South Sea islands, and for the Kanaka people who find them, they signify good fortune.

The blowhole of the sperm whale is directed sideways, so it can be immediately identified by its *blååst*. This animal is found in all warm oceans, especially the Pacific. It is more defensive and willing to fight than the good-natured baleen whales.

When wounded, sperm whales quickly go on the attack. Especially females whose young have been killed or wounded vehemently defend themselves. There is even a known case in which a mother sperm whale whose young had been killed rammed a schooner by blindly dashing at it, keeping at it until the vessel sprang leaks and sank. And many a chase boat has been smashed to splinters by the whale's dangerous tail. In earlier times, when whaling was still done with hand-held harpoons and open whaleboats, the catching of sperm whales was an unusually dangerous and risky business that required a large dose of cold-bloodedness. This hunt also provided many a subject for exciting adventure novels.

CHAPTER FIFTEEN

In Discovery Inlet

Ice-covered chase boat with whales

Mists and snow showers prevented us from scouting out the Ice Barrier. Only around midnight, between two showers, did it first become just slightly visible. This required us to take even greater care with navigation. But when it cleared up in the early morning and the Barrier was plainly visible, things went easier. Following along the Ice Barrier, we reached Discovery Inlet shortly thereafter.

It appeared to be a narrow bay, scarcely a mile wide at the entrance.

The *Ross* carefully steamed into the bay, which ran very nearly west to east. It wasn't advisable to go in very far, since deep in the inlet the ice still appeared to be solid. The ship anchored in the mouth of the bay in 360 fathoms of water. Of course, we didn't use a bow anchor; we dropped a heavy drag anchor on 450 fathoms of three-inch cable. A bow anchor on that much chain couldn't be raised quickly enough in an emergency.

Insofar as the floating mist and the deflection of light allowed us to judge, Discovery Bay seemed to be a long, narrow, tapering arm of the sea, extending inward about fifteen miles deep. Farther inside, the ice walls that formed the borders of the bay in the north and south grew gradually lower, and in the farthest section even approached sea level with a slight slope.

The whales alongside the ship had already begun to decompose. The upright, grooved bellies stuck up above the water like inflated balloons. An incision was made in the soft underbellies to allow the gasses to escape. And that they did, with the sound of a whistling steam-kettle. The entrails were pushed outward under the pressure, and awful-smelling gasses bubbled up from the masses of intestines.

All those decaying cadavers alongside formed a lugubrious sight and spread a pestilential odor. Luckily, we were able to adapt to the foul smell. The first few days we were terribly nauseated from the appalling air, but already a few days later we hardly noticed it anymore. And later, when the whole ship had been steeped in those smells for months, our olfactory organs didn't even react at all. A fresh whale body spreads a penetrating, sickeningly sweet smell that stings the nose most unpleasantly. But what the cadavers achieved on that score was almost overwhelming; without the human ability to adjust, we would have died from the stench.

THERE WAS little wind, and the water was calm, so the processing of the whales could begin immediately. Already after lunch, by way of dessert, the first oil was running.

It was approved by the experts and carefully tasted by spoonfuls as a drink. One enthusiast even put the whole bottle to his mouth without a second thought, but most of us didn't possess such inclinations. In any case, this first and first-rate oil was almost as clear as water, and completely tasteless and scent-free.

Around midday, two more chase boats came in with catches. Already from a great distance we could see from their slanting masts that they were loaded.

As an anchorage, Discovery Bay couldn't exactly have been called safe, because when the wind turned more to the southeast, it not only brought great cold with it but also drove out huge pieces of heavy sea ice from the deeper part of the bay. It was four-year-old sea ice, as could clearly be seen from the four thick snow layers on top. Huge floes of more than a hundred meters [over 325 feet] long, they protruded several meters above the water. By constant maneuvering with propeller and rudder, we ensured that the ship stayed free of the ice.

As long as the *Ross* lay at anchor in Discovery Inlet, we maintained steam at all times in order to be able to maneuver if necessary. And it was necessary almost every day. Now some bay ice would come drifting out; then another piece of the Ice Barrier would calve off and cover the bay with large fields of ice debris. Sometimes whole icebergs were even dislodged. Blizzards lasting several days also required us to keep the engines at half power, and sometimes even to let them run at full power in order to offer resistance to the storm. Otherwise, despite the anchor, which at times like this dragged merrily along, the *Ross* would have been driven into the Ice Barrier.

Farther up the bay there appeared to be a colony of Adélie penguins. Many of these birds came floating out on the loosened floes, and naturally the curious creatures came to get a close look at the strange monster that had disturbed the peace of their quiet bay. This penguin has the strange habit, like a little devil-in-a-bottle, of suddenly diving into the water and then immediately springing up again somewhere else.

Now and then one of these penguins would sud-

A little slice of bacon

denly hop up onto a flensing platform where the men were busy cutting slabs of blubber loose from the whales. Greatly frightened and cackling loudly, it would quickly plop back into the water. Sometimes one would jump onto a whale carcass and then scamper about, gesticulating wildly. If the men onboard whistled at the penguins, they would stand with their necks craned upward, listening with full attention. It looked as if they really wanted to come aboard to satisfy their curiosity, but the ship was too tall for them to reach.

Aboard ship there was hard work going on. The flensing platforms, each with three men on it, were all in the water. Colossal slabs of blubber — fifteen meters [50 feet] long, two meters [6 feet] wide, and sometimes more than a foot thick — were hauled onboard. All that blubber was delivered to the flensing deck, where it was divided into manageable pieces and brought to the chopping machine, which cut it into slices so that all the fat could more easily be cooked out of it.

Soon the whole ship was transformed into a giant abattoir. The forward and rear holds were filled to the bulwarks with mountains of quivering, bloody blubber. Men waded up to their knees in the slithery mounds of fat; seaboots were indispensable for this work. Boots with sharp iron cleats in the soles were absolutely necessary for work on deck and even more so for the outboard work, because the whales were slick with fat and ice. Nobody wanted to slip off a carcass: a dunking into the ice-cold water wasn't attractive to anyone, and all too often there were orcas in the vicinity. These brigands would have made short work of anyone who ended up in the drink.

The stiff southeasterly wind that steadily blew here not only drove the ice out of the bay but also made the water so choppy that the outboard work had to be halted. The whales, which were covered with an armored layer of ice, lay jostling so heavily alongside that it was irresponsible to continue working. There was nothing to be done but to proceed deeper into the inlet. The sea must surely be calmer there.

On Old Year's Day the anchor was weighed, and we steamed farther into the bay, where we set to the work of tethering the *Ross* with two anchors spread far apart from each other. By hauling one anchor up and letting the cable of the other one out at the same time, we would easily be able to shift the ship a bit to port or starboard to avoid the ice coming out of the inlet. It was hours before that setup was ready. It was difficult to clear all those hundreds of fathoms of cable. Meanwhile, the temperature dropped to -20° C [-4° F] — not exactly a summer temperature! And a hard southeast wind, which brought with it icy cold and blowing snows from the Barrier, made the endless steel cables almost unmanageable because of the ice crust that formed on them.

It froze "to a harpoon's hook," as the Norwegians put it, and the bay would have frozen solid too, had it not been so stormy. The ice crystals that floated in the air shimmered like diamond dust in the sunlight, while the sharp, biting wind drove out before it a thick mist of frost smoke, formed from the thickening atmosphere.

It was soon clear that the new anchorage was almost as bad as the first. When it stormed, as was often the case, the anchors didn't keep hold of the soft, oozy seafloor, and they began to drag, so that the ship slowly but surely drifted leeward, where the Ice Barrier rose up steeply out of the sea. Now and then we had to steam away if we came too close to the Barrier. It wasn't necessary to raise the anchors; we simply dragged them along over the seafloor until we reached the new anchorage. We had to shift position so often that to simplify things we kept just one anchor on the bottom.

No, Discovery Inlet was most certainly not an ideal anchorage.

Stormy weather accompanied the waning old year, and the choppy seas made the outboard work impossible. The whales, which lay riding alongside the ship like stiffly inflated balloons, weren't getting any fresher. As the belly interiors decomposed, the cadavers swelled up horribly, and the intestines were pushed outward. Needless to say, this didn't improve the smell of the old whales. It is truly unbelievable what a stench such enormous, decaying mounds of flesh spread.

As soon as the atmosphere calmed down a little and the condition of the sea offered no hindrance to the work, the old carcasses were processed as quickly as possible.

On a whaler one can't be all that squeamish, because an unbelievably intense filth develops on a *flytende kokeri*, a "floating boiler." On the *Ross* we waded knee-deep in the bloody, greasy blubber. Enormous sides of blubber were thrown down on deck. With the ship's heaving, the enormous slices of quivering fat slammed into everything, so that blubber, blood, and filth spattered everywhere. From stem to stern the decks were almost full of chunks and strips of bloody blubber. Fat and filth dripped from everything, while the frost also lent a hand to make the ghastly mess even worse, until everything was so slippery that we couldn't take a step without sliding. To get to our cabins, we had to slither over mountains of blubber. The whole ship from prow to poop deck was covered with a thick, nasty layer of fatty filth.

The blubber- and meat-cutters, who stood on the grubby carcasses, slicing and hacking, were the most loathsome creatures you could possibly imagine. Often they had to crawl around on their hands and feet over the disgusting, decomposing monsters; they literally dripped with unspeakable filth. Just looking at them was enough to make a person sick.

The worst thing was mealtimes amid such a mess that stank to high heaven. Luckily, the extreme cold made the men so hungry that they could easily surmount such hindrances. In any case, it would have been unfair of me to hold my nose in front of my shipmates. Fat and filth stuck tight to everyone impartially; like everyone else, I looked like someone you wouldn't want to touch with a ten-foot pole.

There was absolutely no time to clean the ship. We worked without stopping, day and night; the short summer season had to be used to the fullest. We knew that under the most favorable circumstances we would be able to hunt and produce oil for two months. Then the short, icy summer would be over, and the grim prince of winter would inevitably drive us out of his realm, and we didn't want to sacrifice either the ship or ourselves. The point was to catch as many whales and make as much oil as possible in those two months.

With all that filth around us, it did us good to marvel at the pretty snow crystals, which seemed to do their best to cover the intense squalor. The snow whirled down in unusually large and

A whale is hauled alongside

beautiful six-sided crystal stars with many-branched arms. This was truly fresh snow, whirling out of the sky, whereas at other times the ship had been covered with drifting snow — snow powder — that the wind brought along from the Barrier.

NEW YEAR'S DAY, 1924.

This was a day of quiet calm — not only on the ship but also in nature. We didn't work that day; we had the day off. The atmosphere was completely in balance, and a layer of new sea ice formed on the ship. In honor of the holiday, the frost celebrated superabundantly in rime: ropes and hawsers, bridge and boats, everything on deck was enveloped in glittering white winter beauty. Even the fundamentally unaesthetic whale corpses were covered with a thick layer of shining white crystals, which tempered their unsightliness a bit and made them do a little less violence to one's nasal passages.

Not many agreed with the steward, who, when the chaos of blood, filth, and fat had reached its peak, had roundly declared that he was now really back in his element.

Never had I celebrated the New Year with such overwhelming solitude around me. Nowhere else in the world can one so deeply comprehend the meaning of endlessness as in the desolation of the Pole: and nowhere else in the world does one believe so strongly that our planet rushes alone through the universe, and all the life on her surface is nothing more than brief, unimportant phenomena.

On three sides the Ice Barrier shut us in, and the bay too was covered with a layer of ice. Only in the west was there a bit of water visible: the open sea. The sky and the water were gray; the ice was white with a gray hue. Only in the southeast, at the end of the bay, was there a sun-strewn surface that shone and sparkled like a large, luminous diamond.

If a writer wanted to reproduce the impressions that besieged him here, an oppressive anxiety would have to emanate from his work. A poet would receive inspiration for a heroic ode of unbridled power and demonic force. A master artist would have to use dark, heavy pencil on the canvas, and only if the sun lightened this desolate, somber wilderness would he need to mix some wonderful, delicate colors on his palette.

The Antarctic landscape is hard and repellent, and yet at the same time it exercises great powers of attraction, just as men with a hard, sharp way

about them don't incite any inclination to closer acquaintance and yet still
awaken interest.

The polar environment is hard, stern, and empty, and not everyone can
tolerate such an atmosphere. That was apparent from the tense, prickly
mood that often developed among some of us. On the other hand, the avian
world had adapted itself completely to the somber landscape. Skua gulls,
brown with white wingtips, wandered curiously around the ship, longing for
booty. There were no other birds, except a few penguins that played on the
floes that drifted by, and one solitary, slender snowbird.

AFTER OUR day of rest, we went at the new year with renewed zeal. The numbers on the blackboard, which indicated the number of captured whales and
the extracted barrels of oil, grew ever greater, and the improvement in the
general mood onboard kept pace right along with them — especially during
the few times that the sun softened the pitiless hardness of the natural world
around us.

In fact, however, not many whales were being caught; the chase boats
stayed out for days before they came back alongside with new prizes.

Discovery Inlet also appeared to be a very unsafe harbor.

Much ice was driven outward from the innermost part of the bay, sea
ice as well as glacial debris, and unflagging alertness was absolutely necessary to prevent the floating masses of ice from damaging the ship or shearing
away the whales lying alongside.

There were also great forces at work in the glacier itself. Dull droning,
like the distant thunder of cannons, echoed constantly in the enormous ice-
massif. Soon the Barrier would calve. That gave us an unsafe feeling in the
narrow bay where we lay. In other places the Ice Barrier had already clearly
begun to move. Along the entrance to Discovery Inlet, huge fields of heavy

A procession of icebergs

ice floated by on the ocean currents, as well as whole processions of fresh, newly calved icebergs of the tabular variety.

So one of the chase boats was sent westward to look for a safer anchorage behind Ross Island in McMurdo Sound, where, near Cape Evans, Scott had had his winter quarters. When the boat returned from its reconnaissance mission, the whole prow was covered with ice, and the captain's report didn't sound hopeful. Everywhere along the Ice Barrier the sea was covered with thick ice-fields. The ice in the vicinity of Ross Island wasn't especially heavy, and there was a usable anchorage in forty fathoms of water, but the whole way there, four hundred nautical miles long, the captain and his crew had counted only four whales — pitifully few.

Moreover, ice fields driven into Discovery Inlet from the sea threatened time and time again to block the entrance to the bay, and where the *Ross* lay at anchor, local currents were dominant and appeared to be so strong that they would carry the ship along, anchors and all.

So a chase boat was sent deep into the bay to take a sounding to see whether there might be a place there where the ship could lie safely behind its bow anchors. But everywhere the sounding line reached the bottom only after about 300 fathoms. In such a relatively narrow bay, that was much too much water to offer a good anchorage, and we were forced to let the *Ross* lie in the same spot.

When the flensed, bloody whale carcasses had been relieved of blubber, head, and tail, they were let loose and driven away as prey for the greedy orcas. Then the carpenter, who had also been hired as a diver, went to inspect the leaks in the *Ross* under the waterline. The air pump and the oxygen tanks were put in a boat in which several men armed with razor-sharp flensing knives took their posts to keep threatening killer whales at a distance. It was no wonder that on this occasion the courageous carpenter was done with his investigation in an amazingly short time. He couldn't have felt too terribly comfortable there underwater, in the stiff, unwieldy diver's outfit, with rapacious orcas nearby.

When the worst pressure was behind us, we could devote more attention to our surroundings. Where the *Ross* lay at anchor, the Barrier, which on average is 90 to 100 feet high, was rather low, about 15 meters [about 50 feet] and slanted with a slight slope toward the water, so that its surface was visible. The snow on top wasn't bright white, as one might expect, but had a weak red color, which was caused, the scientists assured us, by microscopically small algae.

With a new whale lying alongside the ship, the killer whales also kept popping up, and when a few seals floated by on the ice, we could see how those pirates stalk their prey. As a harmless seal lay sleeping close to the edge of a floe, an orca would go directly at it. Its teeth flashing in its open maw, the thief would shoot as far as possible over the ice, sometimes coming almost completely up out of the water. The seal, frightened to death, would then plunk into the water on the opposite side of the floe, to be captured by the other gluttons who lay there in wait. Then they would go systematically to work.

Before they shot after their prey lightning-fast, we saw them first raise their heads completely above water a few times to determine the precise place where the unsuspecting seal lay sleeping. The whalers explained that they had often seen the orcas even manage to catch seals that lay in the middle of a large ice-field. As a seal reached a place where the ice was thin, the killer whales dove under it quick as arrows and rammed through the ice under the animal with their powerful heads, so that the defenseless prey fell into the water and became their next meal.

AFTER SEVERAL quiet days during which not a single whale was shot, we took it as a good sign that in general more animal life was evident all over the bay. Seals and penguins became more numerous, and there were also the skua gulls, which seemed to follow them. We expected that the number of whales would also increase, although they still didn't show themselves in the vicinity of the inlet.

The weather was a hopeless story; it never stayed manageable for very long. Soon a stiff southeaster came up again, which swept the sea up into peaks and made the outboard work impossible, so that we were forced to remain idle once more.

CHAPTER SIXTEEN

Snowstorms and Icebergs Run Amok

In the blizzard

A snowstorm out of the southeast, lasting for days and bringing with it
the icy breath of Antarctica, condemned us to an idleness nobody
wanted. Every day that went by shortened the already limited hunting season
by a precious twenty-four hours. The blizzard inundated the ship with heaps
of fine, powdery snow that penetrated everywhere, like dust. The snow piled
up high on everything, especially on the leeside.

But what was worse was that the ship's two anchors simply weren't
holding anymore. The storm had built up such force that the anchors began
to scrabble; they were just dragged along the seafloor by the mighty power
that the storm brought to bear on the ship. This put the *Ross* in an extremely
dangerous situation. The Ice Barrier threatened, rising high above the ship,
both before and behind, and crashing into such a massif would be as dangerous as crashing into rocks.

181

The howling whirl of snow so impaired visibility that sometimes neither bow nor stern could be seen from the bridge. That made things even
more precarious.

It goes without saying that a sharp lookout was kept from all sides.
Many eyes strained to the utmost, trying to pierce through the thick curtain
of driving, lashing snow. Of course, this would probably make precious little
difference if we were crushed against the hard wall of ice.

Then we suddenly saw, between the sweeping snowdrifts, a threatening
white mass rise up vaguely above the stern. It was the gray-white, perpendicular wall of the Barrier, lost in the whirl of swirling ice crystals, shadowy and
indeterminate, but all the more terrifying because of that.

Although we saw it only as a hazy, fleeting ghost, we knew that this rarefied, unreal form was the dependably solid Ice Barrier, hard and immovable.
A collision would be our undoing. It wasn't a happy thought to consider that
the *Ross* was just an ordinary steel freighter, not built to withstand the dangers of ice. The sight of that threatening, ghostly white wall of forbidding ice,
from which a bleak polar death grinned at us, awakened memories of
Dante's Inferno. But don't think that there on the *Ross* we occupied ourselves
with such musings. We just dealt with it. Short, sharp orders cut through the
howl of the snowstorm; hasty, heavy footsteps thumped hollow over the
frozen decks; heavy chains thudded and rattled; and men with clothes thick
with white powder were at work on the prow, scarcely visible in the blinding
snow.

Over and over again, by firm and expert maneuvering, we managed to
swing the ship free of the threatening ice.

The ship's telegraph jingled impatiently, answered by the groaning and
grinding of the engines, which began to turn, heavily and with difficulty, so
that the ship shuddered and creaked in every seam. Then the men stood at
anxious attention, watching how the ship oh-so-slowly — so exasperatingly
slowly — began to swing. The somber, bleak wall of death disappeared again
like a ghost behind the howling curtain of snow, as if dissolving into nothingness.

Nothing remained to show that we had once again narrowly escaped a
miserable death. Still, the storm kept roaring and howling ominously
through the rigging, the snow streaming in horizontal flashes through the
sky, the fierce wind whistling and bellowing and sighing as it screamed
around the protruding corners of the Ice Barrier or sought passage through

the cold blue ice caves. Despite the seeming absence of immediate danger, none of us let ourselves be tempted to lesser vigilance. We knew all too well that the same wall of ice — or perhaps the one lying on the other side — could threaten the ship in the same way at any moment. In fact, we were more or less feeling our way, wandering around Discovery Inlet, which, since it was less than a mile wide, held the ship prisoner between its two banks — two high, steep, threatening walls of cruel ice. *If we could only ride out this blizzard on the high seas,* many were thinking. But there were very serious objections to that too. Outside the inlet a storm like this would make for a nasty sea filled with drifting icefields and icebergs, heavy and dangerous. So it was unthinkable to abandon the "Ice Cellar," as we called the inlet amongst ourselves.

We didn't feel safe by a long shot there in the narrow bay, behind dragging anchors. But as we thought about the long procession of icebergs that we had seen marching by on the open sea, we were happy to be in the more or less protected bay, where we had only the solid walls of ice to fear. The blizzard kicked loose tremendous quantities of powdered snow from the Barrier, and every sharp gust of wind drove thick clouds of it forward. Around the ship we could see nothing but snow flying by horizontally, blocking all visibility. To us the entire universe seemed to be filled with thick, driving clouds of snow.

We didn't have the faintest idea what part of the inlet we were in; luckily, there were no shallows in the bay. But the ice walls seemed to be closing in on us. First the storm would drive us toward the threatening wall that rose up behind us; then we would be in danger again, because with the engines running at full power to avoid that obstacle, we were in danger of colliding with the equally frightful wall that must have been rising up not far in front of us. But the snow was so thick that we never really saw that wall; we only sensed that it was close from the irregularity of the wind that blew on the leeside of it.

So we drifted around the bay, groping blindly, constantly dragging the anchors along with us through the slime on the seafloor, going from the one wall of ice to the other, avoiding the one only to see the other one loom up, grim and threatening, out of the ice-laden storm. The direction of the wind was the only handhold, however unsteady, that we had in this unusual game of drifting. We knew that in these parts a snowstorm always blows its biting, benumbing breath from out of the southeast, from the South Polar Plateau.

In order to offer the wind as small a surface area as possible and to stay in the same place as much as possible, we kept the *Ross* with its head to the wind.

Not only did we have to keep an unusually close eye on the Barrier, but we also had to pay equally close attention to the ice that was now floating in the bay. The fierce storm churned the sea turbulently and hurled the waves into the cold white ice wall with such force that it began to be undermined and started to calve. Both large and small pieces broke loose from the glacier, and we had to keep a close watch on all of them; there were some good-sized icebergs among the pieces.

Some of these newborn icebergs came sailing right up to the *Ross*. These were anxious moments, when out of the thick veil of flying snow, a huge monster would loom up and come right toward us. A vague wall of ice would grow higher and mightier as it came closer and would differentiate itself from the blinding snow. At first we were sometimes unsure whether it was the Ice Barrier that we were approaching or an iceberg that was coming toward us. But we soon recognized the icebergs because they came closer to us faster than the Barrier did. The storm pushed these drifting giants out forward, ahead of us. We never approached the solid glacier with great speed, because we estimated the wind's force and regulated the engine speed to match it as well as possible.

The icebergs that threatened the ship as if driven forth by a mysterious power were much more frightening than the huge, solid walls of ice. With fearful hearts the men stared at these bleak, hazy-edged apparitions when they were briefly visible between the sweeping showers of snow.

These were moments of great tension for the men on the command bridge, for in no small measure it was their cool heads and and quick actions that determined whether the danger could be averted.

On deck

Avoiding an iceberg produced moments of great and instant activity on deck. The anchorline on the side that the iceberg had to pass was let out a good ways, more and more, so that it lay loose below. If the underwater portion of the berg hit the rope, the ship would unavoidably swing against the berg, with incalculable consequences. Meanwhile, on the bridge they maneuvered with propeller and engine to remain clear of the iceberg.

Once during my turn at the helm, at least ten men simultaneously saw a vague, pale spot in front of the ship, looming high up over the water out of the whirling snow, and ten hoarse voices called out together, *"Is forever!"*[1] At the same moment those of us up on the bridge also saw the approaching iceberg, and instantly, almost instinctively, I turned the wheel with all my might to starboard as the command "Hard starboard!" was called out. The iceberg — actually the vague shadow of the iceberg — was just visible on the port bow. I really stayed focused on the vague, whitish spot, which suddenly dissolved into the flying snow.

For a second my eyes flew to the officers who stood on the bridge, but they were also peering as far as they could toward the point where the pale shadow had shown itself for a fleeting moment, the blink of an eye. It was nowhere to be seen. Had it been a hallucination? No, there it was again! The same vague, greenish-white spot that might determine the fate of us all.

In those moments, without a doubt, nobody onboard saw anything other than that mass, only vaguely distinguishable and yet hugely threatening.

It seemed to take ages before the ship obeyed her wheel. Thinking back on it now, after so many years, I can still feel the great tension that came over me as the ship slowly, almost imperceptibly at first, turned to starboard, away from the danger. And I can still feel how the cold stream of air felt like ice in my lungs when, in my relief, I took a deep breath. The intense tension had apparently made me hold my breath for a long time.

The danger had been averted for the moment but was not by any means over. The iceberg was no longer right in front of us, but was safely to the port bow. But in no time it came quickly closer again, pushed forward forcefully by the storm, and the ship, which couldn't build up speed quickly enough because it was no longer headed into the wind, was driven increasingly sideways by the great force of the wind. At the same time, it was also driven

1. This is Norwegian for "Ice ahead!"

steadily backward, into the path that the iceberg would follow, by the fierce wind coming in frontwards at a slant.

The engine hit full speed ahead, but it did no good; the storm was stronger. A collision with the deadly danger seemed almost unavoidable. When that became clear, the ship was made to head into the wind as much as possible with the help of engine and wheel. That might reduce the collision to a less serious, glancing blow.

Again it was excruciating to see how slowly the ship reacted to wheel and screw. The violent wind also sharply hindered our ship's ability to move. Meanwhile, the iceberg came visibly closer, while the ship seemed to be frozen in place. More and more clearly the gloomy colossus took shape out of the whirling, icy haze of snow, growing higher and higher. Within moments its dangerously overhanging top was visible, thirty meters [100 feet] high, sinister and threatening, as if it were a vengeful living being that awaited a favorable moment to dash its thousands of tons of heavy weight against the defenseless ship. On the starboard side the lifeboats were hastily turned outward, ready to be launched in an instant, and the doors of the watertight compartments were quickly closed.

But in the end, after much fruitless maneuvering, to which the ship reacted wrongly or not at all, the bow eventually swerved free of the danger on its own. We probably had a very local current or wind change to thank for this, caused by the iceberg itself in its immediate surroundings. The tremendous block of ice glided past the ship at a distance of several meters.

Underwater a wide appendage of ice stuck out from the berg. It barely grazed the ship as it went by, but in passing it snagged a thirty-meters-long [hundred-foot-long] whale that was lying fastened alongside the ship. For a moment the huge carcass remained hanging on the ice foot; then it got jammed between the ship and the ice. The whole tremendous body slammed over headfirst; it looked as if the corpse had suddenly come back to life. While the enormous tail waved high in the air, the chain by which the whale was fastened snapped like a piece of yarn. Then the huge tail fin smashed the front end of a lifeboat to splinters and dented the railing to which the boat had been firmly lashed. An air shaft next to it was smashed totally flat against the deck. Falling back down, the heavy mass of flesh, bone, and blubber was pulverized into an unrecognizable pulp between the ship and the ice.

The thick steel hull of the ship did pick up a couple of deep dents on this occasion but luckily didn't spring any leaks.

The flailing tail

While the high-rise ice monster glided past, I felt for a moment as if this tremendous hunk of glacier was a conscious, living being, malevolent and eager to make mischief. You could imagine, as it moved past ever so slowly, that it was thinking to itself what a shame it was to let a ship go by unmolested, when this situation offered such an inviting opportunity to totally annihilate both ship and crew with one blow. But the iceberg pushed on farther behind us, majestic and silent.

Then we were suddenly overcome with paralyzing anxiety when the grim, high wall of ice reappeared right in front of our eyes, pale green and ragged. The surface of this ice leviathan was as hard and grainy as a fissure in a block of marble. The protruding top of the iceberg hung threateningly in the air over the ship.

Our breath caught in our throats when suddenly a rain of ice chunks broke off the overhanging piece and poured down on the ship. I was at the steering wheel, so I couldn't look behind me to see what was happening, but I heard the dull sound of ice thudding down and the hasty footsteps of men looking for a good escape; through it all was mingled the sound of breaking woodwork and tearing canvas. When it was over, two boats lay ripped out of their davits and splintered against the deck, buried under ice debris, and the roof of the radio hut was smashed to pieces. (Luckily, the radio operator wasn't in the hut at the time, and apparently nobody was hit by the plummeting ice.) After this first bombardment we waited, fearful that even greater masses of ice would follow, but the berg left us further untroubled, glided past, and soon disappeared again, dissolved in the howling storm and the flying haze of snow.

As soon as the immediate danger had passed, the great tension that had enveloped us was followed by a strong reaction, which, remarkably enough, manifested itself in a feeling of great exhaustion. At least that's how it affected me personally. The threat of the iceberg had so completely commanded my attention that it was only afterward that I realized that I had turned into an ice statue at the wheel. I was completely covered by a thick crust of ice, and all my stiffly frozen clothes greatly hindered my movements. In fact, everyone had been exposed to the wind and frost for hours on end, and the men walked around like stiff snow-puppets. Their faces were unrecognizable because of the clods of ice that clung to their mustaches, beards, and eyebrows.

After standing for a long time behind the wheel in the piercing cold, it did me good when the second mate, as he took over the wheel from me, winked to me that there was some whiskey waiting in his cabin.

A swig out of that bottle and a cup of red-

Ice mask of a kjodtkjaerer
(blubber cutter)

hot coffee did their part to drive off the cold inside me. Low temperatures make a man unbelievably hungry, and on the way to the galley I hacked off a respectable hunk of whale meat from the supply that hung in the rigging. When the whale steak was sizzling in the pan and the hot coffee was warming up the inner man, then blizzards and icebergs run amok were for a moment forgotten.

The benevolent warmth of the galley, which thawed the icy suit of armor that my clothes had become and removed the icicles from my mustache and beard, gave me a pleasant feeling of peace and safety. But I must admit that this feeling of safety came first of all from knowing that every man onboard, from the captain to the cabin boy,[2] was a solid fellow and a sailor you could depend on.

As THE BLIZZARDS blew over the ship, I liked to be on deck to enjoy the thundering power of the wind, which came storming with unbridled force over the endless snow and ice wastelands of the mysterious land of the Pole. Where did the blustery gusts of wind come from, and over what strange landscapes had they flown during their precipitous run toward Discovery Inlet?

There wasn't much to see on deck, no great natural tableaux or wonderful colors. Nothing but smoking, churning water, gray and dismal, as far as the severely limited horizon stretched out, and beyond that nothing but the flying snow and the force of the icy blizzard, which howled and whistled through the rigging and wildly shook and wrenched everything that was not securely fastened.

But it was a pleasure to stand in the middle of the rebellious elements and take in the power of their mighty wrath with all the senses. At the same time, I got a good dose of the unlimited energy that fills the whole atmosphere.

THE SNOWSTORM kept blowing with undiminished fury and more than once threatened us with a collision with the Ice Barrier or with an iceberg. We also still had to avoid fields of bay ice and glacial debris, although they didn't represent as much danger as the tall masses of ice. Luckily, the big, vulnerable ship always swung out of the way just in time.

---

2. The author here uses the Norwegian "[from the] *bestyrer* [to the] *daeksgütte*."

The chase boats all stayed nearby during the storm, like chicks around the mother hen. One of the less fortunate ones narrowly escaped colliding with the Ice Barrier. During a temporary clearing, when the dashing snow wasn't raging quite so heavily, we saw to our horror that it was sailing without a mast, its bridge dented and splintered. It had actually been pushed up against the Barrier. The snow swirl had been so thick that the men hadn't seen the enormous ice wall until the boat had practically collided with it. By whirling the wheel lightning-fast, the crew got the ship itself to swerve just free of the wall, but they couldn't prevent the mast and the bridge from smashing against the immovable wall of ice, which snapped off the mast like a match and partially splintered the bridge.

The men in the chase boat must have been terribly anxious when they suddenly saw the tremendous wall of ice looming up right in front of them and rising high above the mast. At the spot where the boat had its accident, the Ice Barrier slanted with a sharp overhang, and during the collision the men must have thought that a piece of the wall would thud down on top of them and bury them, ship and all, underwater. We could thank our lucky stars that the accident caused only material damage and that nobody was injured.

AFTER RAGING for three days without stopping, the snowstorm was finally spent. Soon the Ice Barrier, the ship, the chase boats, and the whales bathed in clear sunshine, even if the sun's rays didn't spread much warmth.

It was still fifteen degrees below zero Celsius [5° F], but the temperature felt good after the biting cold of the storm, even though then the temperature had risen to five degrees below zero [23° F]. Wind strongly increases the effect of a low temperature. When there is no wind, you don't feel the cold so much, even if it's well below freezing.

The two sheer walls of ice that framed Discovery Inlet now looked almost friendly and innocent in the happy sunlight.

The storm had broken the solid sea ice that was deep in the bay. Already during the blizzard some of it had sailed outside the bay with the wind, and the rest now drifted calmly and peacefully toward the open sea, in huge, almost square floes. It would still be another few days before the whole bay was free of ice.

As long as so much ice was still floating about, we couldn't think of sailing up the inlet to look for a suitable place to land on the Ice Barrier. Deep in the bay that had seemed possible. But now, though we thought we could see that the Barrier in some places there didn't rise straight up out of the sea but came down with a long sloping of its upper edge almost to the water, we weren't sure of it.

That far into the bay, the Barrier certainly didn't look like its normal self. We knew the Barrier pretty well already, as it rose, steep and unclimbable, out of the sea, sown with chunks of glacier and drifting ice. But here in the bay we weren't entirely sure what we were seeing, because light reflections distorted the images in a deceptive way. So sometimes it looked as if the Barrier hovered in the air above the horizon, but as the sun changed position, the look of things changed with it. One minute it looked as if a steep wall of ice shut off the end of the bay, the next minute as if that wall was pierced and honeycombed with countless clefts and fissures; then a moment later, we thought again that a layer of sea ice stopped up the innermost part of the bay. Sometimes we would see an enormous iceberg coming toward us. But, once it came closer, it appeared to be nothing more than a floe of bay ice, sticking up out of the water no more than a couple of feet.

CHAPTER SEVENTEEN

On the Ice Barrier

On skis

On a pleasant, peaceful night, after the snowstorms had blown themselves out, the ship's motorboat sailed into the bay with a hunting party aboard on a mission to catch penguins and seals in order to replenish our markedly reduced stock of fresh meat.

The doctor and I were included in the party. With both hands we eagerly grasped this opportunity to get to know the Barrier better. Our idea was to do some reconnaissance by attempting a landing. If the right opportunity arose later, we would perhaps make more extensive trips in order to try to get to know more about this gigantic glacier.

A chill layer of frost smoke floated over the calm sea, covered with pancake ice, when the motorboat pushed off. On our low-lying boat, we had almost no visibility in this frozen fog, and we were beginning to fear that there would be precious little to see. But then a breeze blew up out of the south and drove the mists away so that the contours of the Ice Barrier were clearly distinguishable again.

With the little motorboat we could risk coming close to the solid ice, although the danger involved was still extremely great. The last few days we had repeatedly seen and heard how the Barrier could calve with a thunderous crash, freeing new icebergs from the mother glacier, or how a section of wall could collapse, flinging thick clouds of ice dust into the air. We had also had plenty of trouble from the icebergs and ice fields that the blizzard had chased out of the bay. So we took care not to get all that close to the Ice Barrier.

Thin fields of ice debris sometimes forced us to detour, but usually we could sail along parallel to the ice. So our attention was piqued at the point where our launch came alongside a portion of the Ice Barrier that protruded from the otherwise mostly straight wall over a distance of several hundred meters.

While we were discussing how this piece would probably break off soon, we heard a dull rumbling and thundering. We knew those sounds all too well; they go along with calving. With the secure feeling of knowing we were outside the danger zone, we watched the great drama play out in front of our eyes. A cloud of ice dust enveloped the newborn iceberg. The ice debris plunking into the sea whipped the whitecaps high and caused a short, angry swell that rapidly spread over the whole bay. When the wind blew

The newborn iceberg

away the cloud of ice dust, we saw the infant iceberg. It wasn't a tall, imposing berg, but we were still happy to have been such close witnesses to its birth.

The baby didn't have to be registered with the civil authorities, and it floated away in a calm and stately fashion to meet the open sea.

Where would it end its wandering life, as it was carried along willy-nilly by wind and tide? We felt more or less like its godparents, and we agreed to keep an eye out for it once we left the polar currents behind us again, searching our way among icebergs and pack ice. It was easily recognizable from the two parallel horizontal bands on its sides; these were moraine stripes, thin layers of stony grit probably hailing from the far-off South Polar Plateau.

The motorboat puttered farther on. We passed by beautiful, improbably blue ice-caves where the playful waves skipped in and out. We saw all sorts of glacial fissures, large and small, where the many grottoes and caves develop as the slap of the waves washes away the ice wall.

It is a lovely adventure to sail in waters that have not yet been cloven by a keel. The alluring siren-song of the unknown then sounds loud and clear in one's innermost being.

Never before had a human being been in Discovery Inlet. Sir James Clark Ross had seen the inlet as he sailed by, but he hadn't explored it further, although he later named it Discovery Inlet after his ship, the *Discovery*.

There wasn't much animal life in the bay; only the occasional bird represented the fauna. Our trusty old daily companion, that bold thief and freebooter and street urchin besides — the skua gull — was more audacious than ever and completely unafraid, even though it could never before in its whole sinful life have heard the droning of a motor. One of these skuas, assuming it held sovereign sway over the bay, seemed offended by our invasion of this area and adopted a threatening posture. Screeching loudly, it circled over the boat and several times let itself fall from a great height to just above our heads, like a hawk shooting after its prey. When its violent wing-flapping and furious shrieking didn't scare us off — when, on the contrary, we drove it off with a boat hook — it gave up its hostile attitude, but still stayed close by, keeping an eye on us.

Then a snow petrel followed us, the small, totally white dweller on the ice-covered seas of the far south. The snow petrel has the restless, wandering flight of the swallow. It is an elegant *femme du monde* alongside the larger, heavier birds of this region. It is a fluttering shadow that you keep losing sight of; it is so well camouflaged in its outfit of white feathers that it provides not the slightest contrast with all the whiteness of the snow and ice in its domain. Next to the fragile little snow petrel, the large, dark storm petrel, which crossed our wake a few times with its slow, heavy wingbeats, was a clumsy oaf.

In places where no calving threatened, our voyage took us right under the Ice Barrier. The wall rose fifteen to twenty meters [50 to 60 feet] straight up out of the sea. On the top portion, different annual layers could clearly be seen: the well-separated snow layers that were left on the glacier each year. Farther down, the boundaries between the layers grew steadily fainter, and the bottom portion of the ice was crushed into a homogenous mass by the weight of the layers above it. On the surface of the water the ice was brown. The doctor told us that this discoloration was caused by algae.

Deeper in the inlet, the height of the wall gradually decreased. The overhanging edge dipped steadily nearer to the water, while the bay itself grew much narrower. After two hours we reached the farthest end of the inlet. Pancake ice had already formed on this sheltered water, and the ripening frost smoke had brought pretty white blossoms enchantingly to life in high relief on the ice. It looked wonderfully fairy-tale-like.

The pancake ice, rising gently with the swell on the nearly still water, exhibited a richness of color that was unexpected in these barren regions. It was about midnight, and the sun stood low above the horizon. Her golden rays were almost orange, and alongside all that golden light the shadow darkened into a welter of blue, violet, and brown. The ice underwater looked bright emerald, while over the deep indigo blue and gray water glided violet, green, blue, and red reflections, mirrorings of all the colors that shone in the midnight sky. Snow and ice are white, they say, although a painter knows better; but here there wasn't a scrap of white to be seen. Sky, ice, and water displayed all the colors of the rainbow in an exuberant wealth of the finest, most delicate hues. Probably nobody but Bill[1] observed these things; all attention was focused on the steadily narrowing cove whose sides suddenly rose to the south when we thought we had nearly reached the end of it. Visibility was poor there; fog and frost smoke hung about. With anxious expec-

---

1. Van der Does is referring to himself, since he answered to the name "Bill" onboard.

tation we carefully sailed farther along the opposite bank where the water was free of ice.

GRADUALLY THE ICE descended at the end of the narrow arm of the sea with an edge much broken up toward the water, so low that it was possible to walk directly onto the ice.

At the end of the bay, we stopped the motorboat and prudently secured it. The outer edge of the ice leaned over precipitously, but beyond that the snow layer rose slowly higher at a manageable ten degrees. The edge of the ice had been seriously undermined by the water, so the doctor, an experienced alpinist, first tested it with his ice axe to see if it could support his weight. It appeared to be sturdy enough to hold a man, so he soon sprang onto the wall with a line and moored the boat to one of the oars stuck in the snow. He advised us not to jump onto the weak edge of the ice all at once, or it would break.

Right after we landed, we were frightened by a dull "boom" under our feet. The upper layer of snow had come loose from the sturdier underlying ice under the great strain, but it stayed in place.

Our equipment was simple: skis, an alpine rope, a compass, crampons, binoculars, a camera, and a sketchbook. While the others committed a massacre among the penguins, who stood peacefully in the snow, watching us,

Landing on the Ice Barrier

the doctor and I wanted to use the brief time available to us to make a short march southward. We wanted to see what things looked like up on the Ice Barrier and to see whether we could discover any trace of actual land. Although the Ice Barrier looked deceptively like solid ground, it most certainly was not. It floated on the water, even if that was hard to believe when, like now, we stood high up on the ice, thirty meters [a hundred feet] above sea level,[2] with an unbroken layer of snow all around. But a series of soundings in Discovery Inlet had proved to us that there was water under the Ice Barrier.

Beyond the roughly drawn line of the Ice Barrier there is on maps a large, empty white spot that stretches out over the Pole all the way to the other side of Antarctica, where no more than a few isolated fragments of coastline are known. Almost the entire land of the South Pole is still *terra incognita*. It is almost unapproachable because the ring of ice that surrounds it is so difficult to penetrate. And since the whole continent lies buried under a permanent layer of ice, it's often hard to say whether the ice one is standing on rests on solid ground or is just floating on the sea. We were so close to uncharted territory: everything beyond the Barrier was still completely unknown.[3]

The Ice Barrier in general ran very evenly except for the curious interruption at the spot where Discovery Inlet was located, which led us to surmise that the driving glacier, pushing forward, had run up against an obstacle here. Was it an island, the crest of a hill, or nothing more than a rise in the seafloor that disturbed the uniform movement of the ice layer?

On our skiing trip we hoped to be able to find the answer to that question and perhaps even to see "new" land. No man had ever been here before, and geographic knowledge came to a halt here at the edge of the Barrier. There wasn't much time, and we were burning with curiosity to see what things were like on top of the wall of ice. So we didn't dawdle; we strapped on our skis and zig-zagged up the slope. We were in a boisterous mood; we were heading into the unknown, after all, which holds such a great fascination for

2. This was perhaps especially impressive to a Dutchman. Fully a third of the Netherlands lies *below* sea level; the average elevation of the entire country is only 11 meters above sea level.

3. Van der Does presumably means that nothing was known beyond the Barrier at this particular spot, Discovery Inlet. The routes that Amundsen and Scott had taken to the Pole in 1911 both began from the Barrier, but from points far to the east and west of this inlet.

us all. Every ski-length we advanced was "new," totally virgin territory. A pure and free environment that has never before been troubled by a human being exercises a powerful attraction on anyone who really loves nature.

It is a rare, hard-to-define sensation that a man experiences when treading on wholly uncharted territory. For the most part it is joy, inner happiness, that makes the blood course faster through the arteries and makes the eyes shine as they look over this new world that has never before been seen by the human eye. At least that's what I saw on the doctor's face. While we quickly glided forward over the wide white surface, we talked about how we felt like the only living beings on an uninhabited planet, and what a great feeling of freedom it gave us to be absolutely alone in this unbounded space. The whole land of the South Pole spread out before us — empty, barren, and completely deserted. We knew that we were the only people on the entire vast expanse of the sixth continent, the only living beings on the measureless ice layer that makes Antarctica a "dead" land, the only flecks of life in the endless white emptiness. Knowing this aroused a very unusual sensation in us, and it came with a slight shiver.

The darker water of the bay quickly disappeared from sight, and both ice walls flowed together. If we hadn't seen the lead-gray atmosphere above the Ross Sea behind us, then the overwhelming impression of the white wilderness around us would certainly have grown oppressive.

A pale and complete emptiness stretched all around us. Not a single bird hovered under the high, wide arch of heaven, and not a single animal moved over the endless snow surface — nor did we expect that. There is neither animal nor plant life in the land of the South Pole; life isn't possible because the whole continent lies eternally buried under a monumental layer of ice. Not even so much as one of the undemanding mosses can make a life for itself on the icebound land. This is in contrast to the North Polar Region, where even on the northernmost groups of islands both animal life and plant life are still possible, where even reindeer and musk oxen can live, thanks to the sparse vegetation. But in the South Polar Region, where lower temperatures prevail, all life is limited to the water; outside of it, there is no nourishment to be found, not for a single animal.

We sped forward, headed straight south, over the wide, empty surface. The temperature was well below zero, and the snow was excellent. There were no snow ridges to impede us, and the waves of powder snow that the wind had formed into ripples like those on a dry, sandy beach didn't cause us much difficulty. As far as the eye could see, the ice was completely flat, showing not even a trace of crevasses or fissures, which usually constitute the greatest danger on a glacier.

An endless white surface spread itself out before us, an absolute emptiness, ominous in its silent, deadly loneliness. Nothing interrupted the wide, even circle of the horizon. No line, not a scrap of color, not a trace of life, not a single movement, not even a single sound interrupted the lifeless emptiness all around us.

There is nothing more comfortless and oppressive imaginable than this silent, wholly dead polar environment. One feels namelessly small and lonely in this stark, still kingdom of death, in which the white-gray emptiness of sky and snow flow together into an appalling and palpable nothingness. And so it was a relief for us when we saw a couple of dark dots far in the distance on the endless white shroud. There was "something" in the measureless, sense-stunning nothingness. Immediately we no longer felt like lonely wanderers in the vast universe. Once we got closer, the dark spots turned out to be a couple of skua feathers. We went on our way in silence.

Up until now it had been more or less hazy in the vicinity of the water, but after an hour the visibility improved, and we noticed that the ice rose gradually toward the south, but so gently that skiing was just as easy as on completely level terrain.

Shortly afterward we came alongside a place where the glacier showed a clear upward bulge. Next to it in the ice there were two fissures, from ten to fifteen meters [thirty to fifty feet] long and a meter and a half [five feet] wide, typical glacial crevasses. From time to time we heard the ice shifting, which sounded like the distant rumbling of thunder.

Investigating a glacial crevasse

Dull, muffled sounds under the snow made us a little uneasy. These sounds were caused by differences in tension in the ice as the glacier glided over an unevenness in its bed. We were undoubtedly at a place where the glacier, pressing forward, moved over a rise in the seafloor. Now things were really getting interesting! So we were all the more disappointed that we couldn't go farther.

If only we had more time! But we needed to get back to the motorboat, where the crewmen were probably already getting uneasy about us. We couldn't make them wait for us any longer in the cold; no doubt they had already gathered the store of provisions they had been sent out for.

Still, it wasn't easy for us to turn our backs on this dreary and desolate emptiness; the lust for adventure had utterly overpowered us.

With the binoculars we looked just once more at the wide, white surface and the stark circle of the empty horizon. The mysterious dead land stretched out around us on all sides, white — hopelessly white — and deserted. This was the land of the South Pole, which had already irresistibly attracted so many, and where so many a brave man had already found a long-forgotten, unknown grave.

We too heard just as clearly the alluring voice of the unknown calling to us, and the drive to go further, ever further out toward the wide expanse of the horizon revealed itself powerfully — the drive to discover and see things that no one had ever seen before us. Somewhere, far across the wide, deadly surface, lay the imaginary point around which our earth turned, with her mountains and seas, with her hundreds of millions,[4] with the whole immeasurable burden of all her joy and sorrow, where she revolved restlessly on that one point, the Pole.

The South Pole!

Two men have reached it: Roald Amundsen, on 16 December 1911, and Robert Falcon Scott, on 18 January 1912. Fate smiled happily on the first, giving him fame and honor when he had reached his goal; the other man it embraced with an inexorable polar death.

Out there in the southwest, on the very same cruel, deathly surface, far beyond the thin, shadowy horizon, lay Scott and his brave companions, resting deep under an eternal white shroud.

We gazed a long time over the silent, eternal ice and stared in the icy,

4. In 1924 the global population was under two billion.

blank sphinx-face of Antarctica. It chilled our hearts, and we shuddered. Then we turned back, without speaking, but with heads full of fitful and somber thoughts.

THE TRIP BACK was easy; the trail we ourselves had made led the way. We glided forward for a while in silence, with only the regular hissing of the skis over the snow irreverently breaking the eternal silence of the polar land. And yet we couldn't be content to keep our varied unspoken thoughts to ourselves, and soon we were talking about the men who had been on the Ice Barrier before us and the grim battle they had waged for and with the Pole. We could sympathize so well with what these brave men had experienced, well-acquainted as we were with the history of South Polar exploration.

We compared the expeditions of Amundsen and Scott, undertaken almost simultaneously and under similar circumstances, beginning from equally distant points on the Ice Barrier. Fortune hadn't abandoned Amundsen for a moment, but we also knew that this fortune was largely due to Amundsen's unequaled polar experience and his superbly skillful and goal-oriented preparation. The Norwegian had carefully laid out his plans step by step, and as a consequence his expedition had looked a lot like a simple stroll to the South Pole.

How differently things went for the courageous Scott and his comrades! Certainly they didn't have the great polar experience of the Norwegians, and probably they had somewhat greater difficulties to overcome. But what a bitter disappointment those brave men experienced when they, having at long last reached the Pole, realized that they had come too late. There it stood, the little tent that Amundsen had left behind, with the Norwegian flag planted on top. That must have been an insurmountable blow, one that struck their morale at its core.

None of the members of Scott's expedition left behind a single word about this disappointment, and that silence is perfectly characteristic of such explorers. We were completely convinced that this blow to their morale was the indirect cause of the death of Scott and his companions.

We knew the history of South Polar exploration so well; it was an inexhaustible source of conversation on the *Ross*. There were a number of old pole-rats among us with experience in both the North Polar Region and the South Polar Region. First of all, there was Captain Larsen; in addition, two of our men had taken part in Amundsen's expedition. This being the case, we knew much about the internal history of polar exploration, more than can ever be learned from travel descriptions.

We considered the five heroes of Scott's expedition one by one. How they had striven to the bitter end, these brave souls, who in their failure certainly achieved and deserved as great a fame as that of the celebrated Amundsen in attaining the South Pole!

On the trip back, the miseries quickly began for Scott's men: one misfortune followed another and sapped their low morale even further. Evans was the first whose powers gave way; he lost his mind and died wretchedly. The second who fell was Captain Oates. He gave the world an undying example of self-sacrifice by freely seeking death in order not to continue to burden the other three and to increase their chance of survival. Yet he made his noble offering in vain. Scott, Wilson, and Bowers died shortly thereafter from indescribable misery and exertion. They died the grisly death of the Pole, without knowing that rescue had been within reach.

No doubt the memory of these brave men will seldom be so sincerely honored as it was by the doctor and me as we glided quickly forward on our skis over the surface of that same Ice Barrier on which they had lost their lives. The cruel, merciless atmosphere of the Pole that had driven their souls from their haggard bodies enveloped us also, threatening and silent, even though we had the certainty that we could return to our ship and the safety that it embodied. We hadn't taken provisions along — only our pipes. The weather was calm; we didn't have to fear being overtaken by a blizzard that could wipe out our ski-trail. Safe and sure as a highway it led us back to Discovery Inlet and the motorboat.

So, were we frightened? "Frightened" isn't the right word. Nevertheless, we made the trip back faster than we had made the trip out, and I was personally convinced that this was partly because we felt a vague, undefinable threat in the grim, silent emptiness behind us. That was where many dangers lurked; that was where the chill, cruel white death lay in wait. But anxiety wasn't what we felt, either — it certainly wasn't the primary feeling we had. Indeed, it was on this very trip back that, accompanied by the hissing of our skis, we sketched out a serious, enthusiastic plan for our own scientific expedition to the Great Ice Barrier. We decided that the doctor would concentrate on scientific matters, and I would take care of the practical matters.

It remained just a plan; our lives ended up taking other routes. But it was characteristic of the fascinating effect that the threatening, somber polar region had on a lively, adventurous spirit. The completely inhospitable, barren environment certainly doesn't attract men, but for those with a romantic inclination, the unknown possesses a powerful enchantment, a psychic attraction that is far greater than the simple physical repulsion it produces.

It is ambition, one of the best manly characteristics, that drove several truly remarkable men to take up the struggle with the polar environment, even though they knew that their opponent was forever stronger than they themselves were. It isn't arrogance but an unconscious realization of one's own latent powers that with irresistible force drives one to confront the dangers and the hardships.

These polar explorers are men with a great, strong spirit — all of them are, without exception. It can't be otherwise. I can't help but think now, years later, of Amundsen, who in his dying gave abundant proof that he was a man with a great spirit and a noble heart. Disappointed, despondent, and deceived as he was, he died a hero's death in a great and honorable attempt to save Nobile — whom he certainly didn't regard as a friend — from the grip of a polar death, when the *Italia* was wrecked near Spitsbergen.

These things lay hidden in the future as the doctor and I glided over the Ice Barrier, although we did speak frequently of Amundsen, who at the time was sailing around in the Arctic Ocean on the *Maud*.

Talking shortened the lonely trip back over the bleak, empty snow surface of the Barrier. During the hours that the doctor and I were away, the men had long since finished their ruthless slaughtering. Of the peaceful penguin colony that had been there at our landing spot, only a few scattered groups remained. The decimated settlement was a sorry sight, which wasn't totally

A wide emptiness

redeemed by the prospect of soon seeing roast penguin breast steaming on the table.

They are such attractive, cute animals, the penguins; in many respects they are so like humans, so unusually trustworthy and free of all shyness. They were always a source of pleasure for us with their clever curiosity as well as their comical movements and gestures. In the dreary desolation of the wide snow barrens, the friendly birds became comrades of sorts, the only living beings besides humans that we could get on with. It made us sad to see them lying in rows in the motorboat, with their short feet and their featherless wings, which they could use to gesture so humorously, now stiff and lifeless. Onboard the men would doubtless view the dead birds with less sentimental feelings.

We had to get back to the *Ross*; our shipmates, who had waited for us in bone-chilling weather — it was twenty below zero [-4° F] — were more interested in the warm mess-room onboard than in melancholy reflections. As we sailed the inlet, the Barrier's formation immediately commanded our attention again. We steeped ourselves in theories. What accounted for the deep cuts in the straight walls of the Ice Barrier? The most popular theory was that somewhere in the lengthening of the inlet the glacier had slid over a bulge in the seafloor that was high enough to break the cohesion of the ice, so that the glacial mass split in two. Our own observations supported this conclusion.

We remarked that the side of the Ice Barrier which formed the northern boundary of the inlet displayed the most holes and caves. This wall was the one most exposed to the wind, and thus also to the pounding of the waves, which washed out the deep blue grottoes in the ice everywhere that the whirling water found a weak spot.

During our ski trip the sea hadn't stopped its advance on the ice walls, as we could see from the great masses of glacial debris that covered the surface of the inlet and markedly hindered our return trip. These masses froze hard, and frost smoke impaired visibility, so that it was quite some time before we saw the ship again. When we did, its whole distorted form seemed to float high in the air. This was caused by a mirage, and only when we were within several hundred meters of the ship did it resume its normal shape.

It was in clambering up the boarding ladder against the hull that we first noticed how numb our hands were. And as always after such trips, we appreciated more than ever the comfort that a large, well-equipped ship offered.

CHAPTER EIGHTEEN

Snow, Ice, and Blubber

Marked whale

The weather we experienced in Discovery Inlet didn't continue to give us cause for unbridled joy. The inlet turned out to be a real chimney-spout for weather; after a single lovely day that made outboard work possible, there followed days on end where the sea was so turbulent that the whales had to continue to lie untouched alongside the *Ross*.

When the chase-boat captains returned from their forays, they usually reported that weather conditions were generally much better in the open Ross Sea. So Captain Larsen decided to leave the inhospitable harbor and try his luck a hundred miles northward on the high seas. With a great amount of difficulty and at the cost of several frozen fingers — it was fifteen degrees below zero during this soggy business — the anchors and the hundreds of fathoms' worth of dripping and frozen steel chain were hauled back on deck. But just when the *Ross* was ready to steam out of the inlet, up came one of the chase boats with a whale, and while the ship stopped and drifted, the work of slicing blubber began immediately.

That same night three more whales were brought alongside, and they were also taken in hand immediately. Meanwhile, wind and current drove the ship out of the bay, but once it was out, the sea was so high that work had to be stopped. So, with the cadavers alongside, we steamed slowly northward.

We didn't come up against much ice, at least no thick pack-ice; with the whales alongside we would only have been able to go through very light drift-ice. We navigated around a string of old, heavy chunks of sea ice that blocked our way. Farther on the sea appeared to be totally ice-free, and a pronounced dark sky over the water in the distance indicated that there couldn't be much ice in the north, either.

Trying not to lose the whales, we steamed ahead very slowly. But even then we couldn't prevent the chains that were holding the whales from fraying to pieces. When one of the cadavers floated away, the ship steamed around until the gigantic body was floating alongside again. It didn't work to try to put a new chain around the whale from the deck, since the heavy, broken chain was still tied around the base of the tail and pulled the whole hind end completely underwater with its weight — so the monster naturally floated away again. This time a couple of men and I attempted to secure the carcass from a flensing platform. There was a strong swell that lashed the enormous tail to and fro so much that it looked as if the whale was still alive and was lashing out to prevent being tied up. Over and over the swaying whale threatened to capsize the little platform, but still we had to try to hold on in order to slip the cable around it. We finally managed to slip a steel cable around the tail and attach the whale securely to the *Ross*, but only after two hours of drudgery did we stand on deck again, dripping wet and covered with unspeakable filth.

An hour later another whale carcass bolted, and the same ordeal started all over again. This unpleasant business happened several more times.

About a hundred miles north of Discovery Inlet, we anchored in 330 fathoms of water. It was certainly the most unusual place a ship had ever anchored — several hundred miles distant from all land, on the high seas, and at such a depth!

Discovery Inlet wasn't really an ideal anchorage spot for a *flytende kokeri*, but here it was even worse. On our first day the weather was excellent, but the sea was much too high, so work was out of the question. We tried to make a lee so that we could flense on at least one side of the ship: with full rudder we turned slowly after the anchor until the ship lay more crosswise against the wind. Doing this did make for some leeside water where the whales could lie fairly calmly, but at the same time the ship swung about so hard that we quickly had to give up the attempt to cut blubber. We would have broken our rigging and probably have risked a few lives to boot. Meanwhile, the chase boats delivered eight fresh whales. They had to lie alongside the *Ross* untouched; there was nothing else to do.

As we waited for better weather, our supply of fresh water began to dwindle. To replenish this supply, we needed to visit the Ice Barrier again or find another place where we could get fresh ice to melt. To our great amazement, we didn't see a single piece of ice afloat for days on end. We could have melted glacier ice for fresh water. Evaporating seawater would cost us a great deal of coal, although in an emergency we could always fall back on that way of providing fresh water.

On the high seas it wasn't cold. At first it was sunny, and in the sun it was actually pleasantly warm, and the thick layer of ice that had built up over the whole ship in Discovery Inlet gradually began to melt away. In the inlet, bordered on three sides by the tremendous ice masses of the Ice Barrier, it was bitterly cold, so onboard the *Ross* we had christened it "the Ice Cellar," a name the inlet earned honestly.

During this time the chase boats went indefatigably out to sea and eventually came back in towing one or more whales. So that the chasers could easily find the mother ship again, we hoisted a couple of empty coal-baskets into the top; these were clearly visible as beacons from a very great distance.

The hunt went more easily on the open ocean than at the foot of the Ice Barrier; every day the numbers went up higher on the blackboard. But the weather got worse every day. The first few days were clear and sunny; after that it was nearly constantly thick with snow, and the steam whistle had to be sounded continuously so that the chase boats that were out could find the ship again.

It began to snow harder and harder, and soon the whole ship was buried in snow. Since we couldn't do any serious work under these conditions,

The snowman

we killed time with all sorts of winter amusements. We waged huge snowball wars: the air was white with the projectiles while the enemy armies hid behind deckhouses and oil boilers. When the men had had enough of snowball-throwing, they set about industriously making snowmen.

Entire white whales appeared on deck; on the tank stood a giant white gunner behind his snowy harpoon-cannon. And when Captain Larsen opened his door in the morning, he was welcomed by a snowman that kept watch in place of the cabin boy.

Along with the snow a stiff breeze blew up, and the anchor dragged merrily along. Another one was made with flukes enlarged with iron plates riveted to them. That enlarged anchor held a bit better.

Driven by the breeze, the sea mounted up and soon was running so high that the *Ross* lay riding and pitching behind her anchor. The whales danced and pranced up and down next to the ship like grotesque monsters. It looked as if they were trying to jump on deck to be flensed after all. They were already a few days old and hugely inflated from the decomposition that had set in. The deformed, distended bellies stuck up above the railings as the sea tossed the swaying giants upward. Several cadavers had swollen up into enormous balloons, looking as if they wanted to rise into the air and float away with the wind. The stomach walls of some had given way under the great pressure: the enormous corpses had burst open, and now the innards bulged out and drifted behind the whales in disgusting coils — a nasty, wretched spectacle.

When the wind steadily gathered strength and the sea ran higher and higher, it seemed advisable to weigh anchor again; otherwise, we would just waste the good anchor. We wouldn't have any problem at all simply letting the ship drift; the wind wouldn't very quickly blow it so far from its anchorage that the chase boats wouldn't be able to find it again. So we hauled up the custom-made anchor again. Meanwhile, we had our hands full with the whales, which made constant attempts to desert. For days they reared to and fro, jerking frightfully at their chains and steel cables, and over and over again the chains and cables gave way, and the dead whales floated off.

Then the tiresome job of catching the jumping giants and bringing them alongside the ship would begin all over again. In the treacherous seas we often had to tow the fugitives a good long distance. Finally we put the motorboat outboard for this purpose, which saved a good deal of trouble. This period lives on in my memory as a time of torn-up hands. To secure the precious cadavers, we used old cargo balers and other discarded wires, which had prickers sticking out of them everywhere. It wasn't a pretty sight when the cadavers wrenched against these with all their might as they were being secured. The leather gloves that we wore for this work prevented our palms from being ripped open to the bone, but they couldn't prevent our hands from being miserably torn up.

Many whales now lay alongside the *Ross* waiting their turn, but not many new fish were being added; the experienced whalers spoke of a meager hunting season. The thick pack-ice really did seem to have hindered the whales from coming out of the warmer oceans into the Ross Sea in great numbers. The summer seemed to be cold in the entire Southern Hemisphere, as "Sparks" was able to tell us; he listened fairly regularly to various stations such as Point Loma in California and even Frederikstad in far-off Norway.[1] Australia was naturally the station he heard the best, since it was the closest. In Hobart, our last harbor in the inhabited world, they were complaining about the cold; there was even snow on Mount Wellington. The whalers around the South Shetland Islands, south of Tierra del Fuego, were hindered by the ice, just as we were. The *Solstreif*, which lay in Deception Harbor, re-

---

1. "Sparks" was the wireless operator's well-chosen nickname.

ported by wireless that there was so much ice in that area that they had only been able to begin whaling in January. Such news wasn't exactly tailored to put us in a hopeful mood. In general we were convinced the *Ross* wouldn't be bringing back a full cargo of oil.

So it was all the more necessary that we process the whales we had already captured, before the blubber spoiled and became worthless.

We had left Discovery Inlet because the bay offered too little shelter. But the open sea appeared to be equally as unusable for our purposes, and in an angry mood the decision was made to go back to Discovery Inlet again. There at least we could work a few days now and then; in the Ross Sea we couldn't work at all.

After having been away for a week, we were back at the entrance to the "Ice Cellar" again. It was an old acquaintance, and it did us good to see it again. We arrived near midnight, but the sky was clear blue, and the Great Ice Barrier lay there, blinding white in the open sunlight. The entrance to the bay, however, was thick with mist. At first there had just been frost smoke hanging over the water, but it had grown into a thick bank of fog that forced the *Ross* to stop.

In the open sea it had been relatively warm; only at night did it freeze hard. But Discovery Inlet did its best to justify its new name of "Ice Cellar." The walls of ice that shut in the inlet emitted so much cold that the average temperature in the bay was about 10° C lower than outside it. The contact of the cold air with the much warmer water caused frost smoke and mist. Apparently the masses of ice that form the Barrier collect a tremendous amount of cold during the long, icy polar winter, which they slowly release again in the summer. That's why it was so cold in Discovery Inlet between the ice walls.

The heavy mist prevented the *Ross* from going to its old anchorage, and the chase boat that followed us could soon no longer be seen. To let it know our position, we gave a blast of the steam whistle from time to time. Late in the night it cleared up, and during one of the clear periods we steamed deeper into the bay, where we anchored in 280 fathoms of water, a bit farther along than the previous time.

Two chase boats came in, each with two whales, so that now we had a total of seventeen carcasses waiting to be flensed. Since the sea was flat and still, we didn't delay for a single moment: we began flensing immediately. Soon the oil factory was in full steam. The flensers stood hacking merrily away on the swollen cadavers with their long knives. To keep from sliding off the slippery, heaving giants, they notched indentations in the blubber layer to set their feet in for each step; under the circumstances, this wasn't really considered a superfluous safety measure. In a short time whole piles of quivering, bloody blubber lay on the flensing decks.

The ship was now totally transformed into a floating oil factory governed by large-scale activity. The steam winches rattled and sighed; orders, shouts, and curses echoed everywhere, while the colossal strips of blubber were hauled onboard. There they were cut into manageable pieces for the cutting machine. This sheared the thick pieces into thin slices, which were brought by elevators above the cooking kettles, where they were dumped through gutters into the kettles. When the kettles were full, the steam cocks were opened, and under pressure all the fat was cooked out of the blubber. Soon the oil kettles poured out clouds of fatty steam, and the whole ship was enveloped in the grubby, clammy smoke of cooking and scalding blubber.

THE OIL production had now begun in earnest.

We worked without stopping, day and night, with day and night shifts. As long as the weather was favorable and there were still whales lying alongside the ship, no time could be wasted. For the sake of the quality of the oil, it was naturally desirable to work the blubber when it was at its freshest. We also expected that the chase boats would soon be bringing us more whales, since the biologists ascertained that the seawater was getting richer in plankton. That somewhat justified our expectations.

On the flensing deck

On sunny days, when the sky was blue and the cheerful light shone and shimmered on the pure white of the snow and ice, it was a pleasure to keep drinking in the stark, grim beauty of the summer luxuriance of the polar environment. But the image of grand, endless greatness that our surroundings presented us if the sun lent life and color to the eternal ice was driven completely into the background if clouds and mists intercepted the cheery sunlight. Then everything — sky, ice, and water — drowned in a desolate, colorless gray, a somber color that more strongly than ever suggested the threat that emanates from this endless wilderness of eternal ice.

Up to this point, the whales had badly betrayed the trust that the optimists had placed in them. We had caught a small number of them, and luckily these were always the great blue whales of about 90 feet in length, but they wouldn't come anywhere near our anchorage. So the chase boats had to tow the harpooned animals over a great distance to deliver them, and a great deal of valuable hunting time was lost this way. Every chase boat did always try to bring along more than one whale on each trip, but due to the scarcity of the fish, that wasn't always possible. If they had shot a whale, they pumped up the cadaver and fitted it with a sign of ownership, after which they resumed the hunt. The mark consisted chiefly of a flag with the number of the chase boat on it, which was bound to a long lance and planted on the whale.

The animals appeared to gather chiefly near a bank of around six hundred meters [around 2,000 feet] in the middle of the Ross Sea. Because of this, the chasers caught no more than three whales per day, whereas they had counted on catching at least ten.

The weather saw to it, however, that we stayed hard at work. The prevailing wind came out of the southeast, which caused us no problems, but if the wind turned to the north or the west, then the bay lay wide open, and the swell complicated the work to no small degree. It was far from pleasant or easy for the flensers to remain standing on those heaving, slippery whale cadavers, even if they also had sharp iron spikes on the soles of their seaboots and even if they hewed out notches in the blubber layer in order to brace themselves. Still, they had to wield their long flensing knives to cut loose the blubber strips, which were then pulled upward with a cargo rope. If the sea stood high and the carcasses lay restlessly rolling and pitching, the work was even more troublesome and dangerous. Then the men had to be very careful not to slip and fall into the sea. Ending up with wet clothes wasn't the worst thing that could happen — although that isn't exactly pleasant when there's a hard frost. What was worse was the possibility of falling prey to the killer whales that were almost always roving around the cadavers. These audacious thieves sometimes didn't even hesitate to bite off chunks of blubber and flesh from the carcasses right in front of our eyes. The voracious beasts would also no doubt devour any man who fell into the water. Sometimes they even snapped at the men who were working on the whales. Naturally the flensers pummeled the brazen freebooters with their flensing knives and drove them off. But incidents like these made it clear that we had to make sure that nobody fell into the water.

In bad weather, the whales swayed up and down several meters with each wave. The huge pieces of blubber plopped down with a smack on each cadaver — only to be pulled upward with a jerk an instant later, while at the same time the whale partly overturned. This made it very difficult to stay on one's feet. In addition, there was the ever-present danger that the cargo rope on which the blubber hung might snap, or the line that held the whale in position might break. To keep from losing time, we still worked through such awful days — when the ship and the whales were heaving — if it was at all possible. It was then truly dangerous both on deck and on the whales. Sometimes the booms and cables jerked and swayed with such force that the men were afraid that everything would break and come crashing down. Sometimes blocks and tackles really did break, though fortunately without causing accidents, because the men were careful and always kept an eye on the rig above them and tried to keep out from underneath it. Sometimes one of the ropes holding one of the eighty- to ninety-ton carcasses broke, and then the whale immediately floated away and had to be picked up again by a chase boat.

On fair-weather days, the work naturally went better. Then the number rose swiftly on the blackboard where we recorded how many barrels of oil had been processed. When the weather got really bad, of course, the work had to be stopped. Then we had our hands full repairing and organizing the many broken tools.

With everyone working with all his might on oil processing, there was no time to clean the *Ross*, and the layer of filth that covered the entire ship took on disturbing dimensions. Snow, ice, blood, fat, coal dust, and whale refuse all together formed an unbelievably beastly mess that spread everywhere. It was concentrated on the flensing decks and the oil kettles, but we couldn't avoid tracking it all over the ship, since our seaboots and clothes were covered with it. Only the cabins where Captain Larsen lived formed an oasis of cleanliness in the midst of the unspeakable filthiness that covered the rest of the ship. Now and then we would sneak a peek over there just so we wouldn't forget what cleanliness really was, and then we would stare amazed at the clean floors and tables, so accustomed had we become to the ghastly chaos that had transformed our cabins into pigsties.

The chase boats were regularly provided with bunker coal, which was dropped onto their decks with a chute. Especially when it was windy, thick clouds of coal dust rose up, which made the filthy mess even worse. Even the swollen, mutilated whale carcasses were covered with a grisly crust of snow, ice, coal dust, and masses of fat and filth that were spewed out of the oil kettles. Schools of penguins swam by the ship, and if they weren't being pursued by orcas, they came alongside, especially curious to see what unusual activities were going on in Discovery Inlet.

Then with a spring they dove up out of the water, neat as cats, landing with their short little feet on the middle of a whale. Nervously waving their flippers, they tripped about on the cadavers, looking up in amazement at the tall ship, frightened of the unusual noise that was so strange to them. Anxious from the unfamiliar fuss, they called to each other with raw throat sounds.

Once one of them dove up with a bang right through a thick layer of fat and filth that poured out of a refuse pipe from an oil kettle. Totally upset and disgusted with herself, she stood with flayed-out flippers, staring at the filthy fat that had completely fouled her nice black-and-white outfit. The other penguins hooted at her and scattered away, shrieking when their unsightly comrade came closer. That poor animal would have had quite a job getting herself presentable again; it's hard to bathe in ice-cold seawater that's a couple of degrees below freezing.

The Tasmanians, who were included in the night shift along with me because they understood only English, weren't the worst fellows on my shift. They were a group of sturdy young men, all between the ages of twenty and thirty. They had all in fact been carefully selected; in Hobart there were many more young men thirsting for adventure than we needed. The best of the bunch was Paddy, an Irishman and a prize-fighter, who hoped after the hunt to be able to visit his aged mother again on the green island and try to win laurels in the ring. He had brought along his punching ball, on which he practiced faithfully every day. There was also the tall, strapping Curly. It was a mystery how he came by his nickname, because he had completely straight, carrot-colored hair. He had been in the Great War in Flanders and northern France and couldn't say enough about Paris — "the finest place for girls," he claimed. Another of the Tasmanians who was quick as lightning answered to the name of "Bullet." There was also among them a young man who was a newspaper reporter by trade but had mustered on as a laborer in order to write copy about the expedition for his paper.

They all had nicknames — as did most of the men onboard, as a matter of fact. Hardly anyone knew anyone else's real name. The nicknames, which were usually a telling characterization of their bearers, were much easier to remember, even if they weren't always flattering to their owners. For instance, one of the sailors was named Ola. It was his real name, but Ola wasn't especially bright, and when he was called, the men made sure that it sounded like the lowing of a cow. If Ola didn't answer this call immediately, then everyone lowed along as loudly as possible. It appeared to be an effective way to get Ola to come quickly, because he didn't enjoy hearing those cowshed sounds.

They were sturdy lads, these Tasmanians, happy and healthy. But they had a peculiar need to express their excess love of life now and then in a free-for-all fight. We quickly noticed that about once a week a good scuffle was necessary; otherwise, they got bored and had running quarrels with each

Free-for-all

other. When it came time to clear the atmosphere with a fistfight, we did nothing to oppose it. In fact, it became a regular, highly valued sporting pleasure, with a referee who made sure that everything went according to the rules of the game. After such a free-for-all, everything went smoothly for a while, until the situation got tense again and demanded a fresh clearing of the air.

WE USUALLY couldn't be exactly happy about the weather.

The atmospheric conditions were among the leading factors that determined the success of the expedition. But in the meteorological journal, fog and snow and often storms had to be reported daily. In the middle of the day, when the sun was at its highest, it was occasionally clear, but then as soon as the sun stood a bit lower in the sky and the temperature fell again, the fog came driving over the Great Ice Barrier, usually accompanied by snow.

Stormy weather was a hindrance for us on the *Ross* because it stood in the way of our work, but for the chase boats offshore it was even more unpleasant. When it stormed, a chase boat entering the bay with its catch would be covered with a thick crust of ice, especially the foredeck, which caught the most spray. The cannon up front on the prow was then completely buried under a mass of ice that made it unrecognizable, while rigging, decks, and winches were sheathed in a thick coat of icy armor. All that ice was removed with crowbars, pickaxes, and steam. It was especially important to de-ice the harpoon cannon, in order to have it ready to use again. It goes without saying that a chase boat couldn't go anywhere with a completely iced-up cannon, much less with a frozen harpoon line. That always had to be kept flexible. A harpoon rope frozen stiff would inevitably snap as it rapidly uncoiled after a shot went off.

In bad weather the whales lay alongside the ship unprocessed and spread a steadily stronger aroma. This smell, which really did sorely test the stamina of the nose, led the doctor to make all sorts of malicious remarks about the innocent whales. He had no problem with the fact that in prehistoric times the brontosaurus and the ichthyosaurus had perhaps spread a similar stench, but it was decidedly an error in creation that in the era of *Homo sapiens* such things still existed that so stank to high heaven. The incensed academic was afraid that he would lose his sense of smell forever and swore that for the rest of his life he would never again have anything to do with a garbage truck; he yearned for a true dunghill.

ORIGINALLY THE IDEA had been to extract oil only from the whale blubber. But when the whales remained scarce, the enormous lower jawbones, tails, and tongues were used to increase oil production. A special oil-kettle was reserved in the forward hold for the tongues, which produce excellent oil. The huge pieces of lower jawbone and tail were cut up in the rear hold on deck. There the enormous bones were first divided into manageable chunks with electric saws, then with large bone-cutters were chopped into pieces that could fit through the loading hole of the bone kettles. Under high-pressure steam, the bones were completely cooked through — so completely that nothing of the bone tissue remained. In fact, the drain pipes of the bone kettles weren't more than four inches wide. After the oil was piped off, the entire contents — without a single piece of bone — were spewed out through those narrow pipes. It always smelled wonderfully of bouillon when those bone kettles were emptied, and the fragrant meat juice spurted into the sea in a thick stream. Then you could smell that capital was being wasted — seriously. I admit that I've never heard of bouillon produced from whales. But I still think that the enormous masses of flesh that men let float away as worthless from the whale hunt, as prey for the orcas, could be put to good economic use.

On a few land stations in the Finnmark and in South Africa, the whale cadavers are processed into fertilizer. On South Georgia Island, where a great deal of the southern whaling industry is concentrated in a number of oil factories, people have tried to can whale meat in tins just like they can beef in the great Argentinean bouillon factories.

The tests were a great success, but it appeared to be impossible to sell the product. The prejudice that people had against whale meat was just too strong. Nevertheless, it is eminently suitable for consumption, as I know from experience. In Norway and Japan, meanwhile, where it's on the market, it's considered to be as good as beef — and it's much cheaper too.

If no new whales were delivered by the chase boats, then we processed the flensed cadavers even more thoroughly. After all the blubber had been removed, as well as the fat-rich tongue, then the tail was also hacked off and cut up on deck, as well as the enormous head, upper and lower jaws separately. The whole head was too heavy to get up on deck all at once. On the newest whaling ships, that difficulty is taken care of: they're set up so that even the largest specimen can be hauled on deck in its entirety, where men can work much more easily than they could outboard on the bobbing flensing-platforms and on the floating, unstable carcasses themselves. These modern factory-ships are fitted with a tunnel in the bow, which begins at the stem at the waterline and comes out on the flensing deck. This tunnel is wide enough to let any whale through. The animals are immediately hauled with heavy tackle into the boiler onboard.

When on the *Ross* both the upper and the lower jawbones of a whale's head lay together, we could really get a good idea for the first time of the tremendous size of such an animal. The otherworldly dimensions of various bones were truly imposing when we saw them just lying there in front of us. What do you think, for example, of an upper jaw that from the tip of the snout to the hole at the back of the head measures six meters [nearly twenty feet]? That's really enormous.

The long lower jawbones were even bigger, sometimes almost seven meters [23 feet] long. The gigantic size of these bones is illustrated by the fact that these so-called "whale ribs" are often used in Norway as ornamental portals at formal entrances. A haywain would be able to ride underneath one without the slightest difficulty.

TOWARD THE END of January, when the whales were still unwilling to come within firing range in great numbers and bad weather sometimes brought work to a standstill for days at a time, we gave serious thought again to looking for a better anchorage. According to the charts, McMurdo Sound — behind Ross Island, under the smoke of the volcanoes Terror and Erebus — was the only place that could be considered for this purpose.

A chase boat was sent to reconnoiter the whole coast of South Victoria Land, from Ross Island to Cape Adare, and to investigate what the situation was there with the ice and the whales, to assess it as a possible anchorage. But when the scout returned several days later, he couldn't bring much in the way of a good report. The thick ice layer that covered the whole vessel bore witness to the poor weather that it had encountered. A usable harbor couldn't be found along the entire coast; everywhere there was far too much ice, and the whales were just as scarce there as they were elsewhere in the Ross Sea.

Gradually the number of whales that our five chase boats were able to capture also diminished. In the tanks we had seven thousand barrels of oil, but the men estimated that by now they would usually have produced at least thirty thousand barrels.

By the end of January, we would probably have been in the Ross Sea for a longer time than any others before us. On the eleventh of February, the long polar day would end; at night the sun would begin to dive under the horizon again. With the disappearance of the sun would come the Antarctic winter with its inseparable companions: snowstorms and bitter cold. Then we would have to be ready to leave the Antarctic Ocean at a moment's notice. With the arrival of winter, the whales would probably leave too, and it wouldn't make any sense to linger any longer.

It was clear that with our ship, which wasn't built with this in mind, we couldn't risk freezing in and overwintering. We had plenty of provisions and coal on hand, making overwintering possible in that respect, but the ship might not be in good enough shape to withstand it.

But even if the *Ross* could hold out for a while and we could process more oil, we still wouldn't be able to process enough oil to cover the great costs attached to this expedition. Various possibilities for making the trip worthwhile were put under the magnifying glass and examined from every angle. The most obvious solution was to continue the hunt and the oil extraction on another *fangstfelt*[2] — for example, on the west coast of Australia. For years the Norwegian whalers had hunted the humpback whale there and processed it into oil. Another possibility was considered: the *Ross* didn't have to fill all its tanks with oil in order to deliver a favorable balance at the end of its voyage. We could also load coconut oil in the South Seas or in India; even benzine and petroleum weren't completely out of the question.

How things would go we could scarcely guess. The decision about whether the hunt would be continued elsewhere lay with Captain Larsen, who first wanted to wait to see what further results could be had in the polar region. But we were convinced that the ship wouldn't return to Europe with only the oil that the hunt in the Ross Sea had yielded.

GRADUALLY THE tremendous glacier that shut us in on three sides began to show signs of unrest. More and more we heard the heartbeat of Antarctica: dull, rumbling sounds, reminiscent of thunderstorms. When we noticed it for the first time, the weather was rather mild, and we thought it was some kind of electrical discharge in the atmosphere; the phenomenon sounded like long-lasting thunder. But when it kept up for two solid hours, we were suddenly freed from our misconception. In any case, strong discharges of at-

2. This is Norwegian for "hunting grounds."

mospheric electricity weren't really imaginable at such a high latitude. The ominous sounds made us feel as if we were in a witches' cauldron.

For the first few days, the invisible thunderstorm continued, the harbinger of a coming calving of the Ice Barrier. It was in the last days of January that the actual calving process occurred, announced by increasing action in the ice, after which the edge of the Barrier, often over miles of distance, suddenly collapsed. Thick clouds of ice powder and dashing snow then hid the drama from our eyes.

The masses of ice thudding down into the sea sent up a high, steep swell that spread so fast that we had no time to take the necessary precautions.

The result was that in the heavy rolling of the ship the clews of the derricks broke, which inflicted great damage and finally crashed onto the deck. The running rig that was used in flensing broke too, and some of the cables that attached the whales to the *Ross* snapped off, so that the cadavers floated away, while the chase boats that lay alongside were thrown against the big ship and suffered damage. When more calving threatened, we took care not to fasten the chase boats directly alongside; we positioned a whale cadaver like an enormous sack of cork in between mother ship and chase boat.

Huge icebergs didn't calve off into Discovery Inlet; the formation of the Ice Barrier in that location didn't lend itself to that. But incomplete calving did happen there more than once. Great fields of glacial debris floated alongside the ship out to sea and increased the ice fields outside the bay. After several calvings, the balance of tension was restored again in the glacier; no more cannon shots or thunderstorms were heard, and the inlet returned again to quiet.

CHAPTER NINETEEN

Hunting with Harpoon Cannon and Sketchbook

The shot

Without much trouble I received permission several times to work for a while on one of the chase boats. In these cases I replaced the steersman, who as a rule was happy to be able to replace me as bosun on the much more comfortable mother ship, especially if he didn't have to be deprived of the fringe benefits that the hunt offered him. For every whale that was harpooned, the captain of a chase boat received a premium of a hundred kroner, and the rest of the crew also got an extra bonus in proportion to their wages.

It wasn't really official if I took over for a bit the service of one of the chase-boat steersmen, and so their earnings didn't suffer for it. I wanted to do it in order to get to know this side of the interesting business from experience, but most of all to get some impressions as a painter, to have a more multifaceted impression of nature in the polar region. For this reason, sketchbooks were the most important part of the equipment that I took along on these trips.

One night we had sailed out of Discovery Inlet into the open sea on the *Star 3* to hunt for whales. It was thick with fog in the "Ice Cellar" because of the great cold that the enormous ice masses of the Barrier radiated. Outside the bay it was much less cold and the mist less thick; the sun shone happily in the light, open polar night. But a veil of frost smoke, strung out over the ice-cold water in hazy trails by the sharp southeast wind, removed the Ice Barrier from our sight. Thin, feathery clouds wafted very high in the clear azure sky; it was a beautiful, clear night. The fresh southeasterly breeze chased short, sharp waves forward over the ultramarine-blue sea.

Dashing about, they spattered apart against the large, square floes of bay ice, which had probably been driven out of the Bay of Whales. The latest blizzard had left a thick layer of snow on the floes, which lay beaming white in the clear sunshine. The ice under water gleamed green, like clear emerald; it was light emerald just under the surface, but farther down a deep sea-green.

A few Adélie penguins sat on the floes in the loose snow. Turning their heads to the wind, they huddled together quietly, and although it was surely fifteen degrees below zero centigrade [5° F], these extraordinary birds seemed to be enjoying the rather imaginary warmth of the sun. It's hard for people to conceive of it, but for these creatures it must have been a lovely, sultry summer night that they enjoyed in full measure.

They crowed with pleasure as the wind sprayed a rain of salt-water droplets over them. They did shake the water off immediately, but it was so cold that whole clumps of ice still clung to their feathery suits. The water droplets practically froze while they were still flying through the air.

From time to time as the ice grew too heavy and pulled open holes in their feathery coats that allowed the icy wind access to their skin, the birds busily began to pick the ice off their plumage. They did that as quickly and easily as we flick a piece of dust off our jackets.

You might expect that the penguins were wretchedly cold in such low temperatures and kept moving to stay warm. Not in the least! They sat still and resigned, all hunched up, their thick coats of feathers turned up. They looked like old high-society matrons with slick, combed-back hair, black shawls thrown over head and shoulders, and neat white aprons in front. And just as such elderly ladies can sit staring, lost in thought, so these penguins stood still, musing in the snow. Sometimes one screeched with pleasure or spread its stiff fins out to warm them in the chilly sunlight. Just as a pair of ducks can bask gloriously in the cheerful sun on a nice summer day, so these true inhabitants of the South Polar Region enjoyed the scanty sun in their own way, even if they stood with their bare little feet in the snow, and it was cold enough to freeze bricks. (It is incomprehensible to me how the birds manage to keep up their body temperature under such circumstances. The other animals in the polar area — whales and seals — have a thick protective layer of blubber that wards off the cold. True, the penguins are wrapped in warm coats of feathers, but their naked feet are still unavoidably in constant direct contact with the ice.)

The penguins weren't the only living beings enjoying the nice weather. On another floe a crab-eater seal lay quietly sleeping, its fat, sausage-round body stretched out lazily like a cat in front of a roaring hearth. The seal too seemed to find the temperature most pleasant. He grunted and groaned in bliss as he slowly turned to let his other side bask a bit in the benevolent rays of the sun.

It is truly a pleasure to watch seals sleep. The creatures are indescribably lazy and can surrender themselves so completely to their endless *dolce far niente*, hawking and grunting in unequaled sloth, that just seeing the face of such a Morpheus-worshipping bag of blubber could make someone start snoring.

Snow petrels, white as freshly fallen snow, fluttered restlessly over the waves and floes, invisible as they skimmed over the snowy ice but sharply etched against the deep indigo blue of the water. A school of orcas, their large, triangular dorsal fins jutting out above the water, romped like a pack of porpoises among the ice floes. Ribbed jellyfish — mollusks as round as an egg with jelly-like bodies banded by canary-yellow stripes — bobbed on the waves. As the turbulent water tossed them to and fro, soft mother-of-pearl tints shot over the softly glimmering orbs.

But what moved there in the distance on the swelling surface? A living, lead-gray being rose slowly out of the depths until it came partially out of the water, so that the skittish waves broke over it and spilled over it like a boulder on the beach. With a roaring whistle, a stream of white vapor as thick as an arm suddenly rose up from somewhere in the dark mass. Fifteen feet up, the vapor thickened and remained suspended like a little cloud until it was pulled away by the wind and dissolved into the atmosphere. Slowly the gray giant glided forward, rose a little, dipped quietly, then disappeared completely under water to come up again several hundred fathoms farther. It was a whale, lumbering about peacefully and enjoying the nice summer weather just like the penguins and the seal.

Water, ice, sky, and creatures together formed a wonderful natural scene of a purity and beauty that man can find only where nature remains completely untouched. Everything was in complete harmony. There were more than enough subjects to sketch. I was only sorry not to have brought any painting materials with me, since the beauty lay far more in the rich colors than in the forms. The animals and the water, ice, and sky, bathed in a flood of glorious gold-blond light, formed the natural, even essential subject matter of the imposing painting that nature granted us to view: a beautiful summer night in the heart of the South Polar Region, clear and bright, sparkling with sunlight! All of nature appeared to us as it must have been at the beginning of creation.

The inclemency of the climate has long stayed man from stretching out his damaging hand toward this unspoiled world. The notorious industry that man and his civilization always bring with them would cause an especially jarring note in this perfect harmony of nature. But nothing on this earth is safe from man's restlessness; he has penetrated even as far as this solitary, chilly end of the planet that he inhabits, driven by his unquenchable thirst for gain.

A DARK SHAPE loomed up silently out of the suspended frost-smoke, one that did not fit in the harmonious natural scene. It was the *Star 3*. Out of the drifting wisps of mist appeared first the mast, with the swaying basket of its lookout, then the black top of the funnel, until gradually the whole vessel became visible, becoming steadily clearer as it approached.

Superficially the *Star 3* looked somewhat like a tugboat. She was less than a hundred feet long. The bow, which leaned over toward the front to be able to serve as an icebreaker, stood rather high in the water, yet the stern sat low so that the screw would be far enough underwater that it wouldn't easily get stuck against the ice, and so that the propeller wouldn't churn air in heavy seas. An engine that beat continuously would make too much noise and drive the whales away.

Spouting whale

Fixed high in the swaying mast was the small black-and-white *tönne*, or crow's nest. A pair of broad shoulders and a rough, hairy face, with a dark fur cap pulled down to the eyes, stuck out above the edge. They belonged to the man in the lookout, whose glance attentively scoured the seas for any trace of whales. He peered all around, leaning his hands, covered with rough mittens, on the edge of the *tönne*. His sharp eyes, protected by bushy eyebrows, tried to pierce through the ever fainter frost-smoke. Forward on the bow, on a sort of platform, stood a short cannon that could be easily turned around to all sides: the harpoon cannon, with which the heavy harpoons were shot off. Under the barrel on an extended piece of deck lay a fifty-fathom harpoon line, neatly coiled and secured so that the overspilling seas would not wash the rope away. It was six-inch manila rope — nice fishing line, yes? A whole lot more solid than the lines of the fishermen who sit on Sundays along the Schie,[1] patiently staring at their bobbers for hours at a time. But then, a whale is significantly larger than a bream or a roach.[2] The whale that had just now come up to take a breath was eighty feet long, almost as large as the chase boat, and as heavy too — just under a hundred tons.

The uppermost rope-end of the harpoon line was secured with a fastener into the split shaft of the harpoon, which protruded more than a foot out of the mouth of the cannon. The other part of the rope ran over a rotating wheel under the cannon platform and from there upward, to high in the mast, over an iron block that was fitted with coiled springs in such a way that

1. The Schie is a river in the Dutch province of North Holland running through the author's hometown of Schiedam (whose name means simply "the dam on the Schie").

2. These are common European freshwater fishes, the former in the sunfish family, the latter a carp.

it broke the force with which the struck whale tugged on the harpoon line. In this way the line couldn't easily break, no matter how heavily the whale pulled with its hundred-ton weight in its death throes.

From the spring-loaded block on the mast, the harpoon line went back down to the deck, through a heavy jawbone block, and then over the drum of the anchor winch, coming out after that below deck in the cable house, where hundreds of fathoms lay neatly coiled up, ready to run out.

There was a harpoon line on both port and starboard sides, making it possible to shoot two harpoons in rapid succession. The first shot isn't always a deadly hit, and often a second harpoon is necessary to secure the prey and put an end to the death struggle of the wounded leviathan.

The whole bow of the chase boat, cannon and all, was covered with a coating of ice that grew thicker with every wave that washed over it.

AS THE UNNATURALLY light night went on, and the sun climbed slowly in her course, the frost smoke grew thinner and thinner as the temperature gradually rose. Like images that are being developed on a photographic plate, things began to appear out of the mist: fields of drift ice, icebergs, and far away to the south, its base hidden behind the horizon, the Great Ice Barrier, like a straight white line. The captain of the chase boat, who had already been pacing like a polar bear for hours in the narrow command bridge, waiting for the frost smoke to lift, now came tramping down the ladderway in his heavy seaboots and made for the bow. Between two waves that washed over the ship, he opened the door to the cabins and called down below, *"Paa'n igen, gutter!"* ("Get to work, boys!"). Tobacco smoke and the hubbub of voices rose upward out of the stuffy cabins, while a wave forced the captain to slam the door shut again. After a lot of stomping and swearing, the door was opened again, and the sailors, a bunch of raw, bearded fellows, came thumping up on deck, their tall seaboots completely covering their legs. To the eye they looked rather well-fed, but that was just an illusion. Fat they most certainly are not, the leggy whalers; the work is too raw and heavy for that. But they were heavily bundled up, and that was no superfluous luxury, as I know from experience. These rough fellows were anything but effeminate.

It can be intensely cold on the deck of a chase boat in the Antarctic Ocean, even if it is summer, and a temperature of fifteen degrees below zero [5° F] certainly made it necessary to wear a bit of extra clothing.

It can take hours, sometimes half a day, before a hunted whale is killed and secured. Hours on end the sailors wait and work in the biting wind, while spray washes over them constantly, quickly freezing their clothes into icy suits of armor that, like real harnesses, remain moveable only at the joints. They formed a picturesque group, these raw, rugged fellows. Man for man, they could be models for a painter of brute romantic subjects. They provided me with material for a whole series of drawings.

The captain had called his men on deck when the visibility improved; a whale would probably be spotted soon. The color of the seawater led him to expect this. For some time now he had noticed that it had taken on a more or less rosy tint. *"Rödaate!"* ("Red prey!") he had said, looking at the waves racing by, to the man at the helm. The helmsman had simply nodded in agreement without looking up. Every whale hunter knows what the red coloring of seawater means. The phenomenon is caused by a myriad of tiny, shrimplike creatures that float in the upper layers of the water: plankton. And where there is abundant plankton, the whales are usually not far away. These giants of the water always prefer to feed on the tiny organisms, of which they swallow tons! So the skipper immediately had everything made ready so that we could begin the hunt just as soon as the lookout might hail a whale.

First, the ice that covered the cannon, chains, lines, and winches was removed. The roughest ice was hacked away with axes and crowbars; then the rest was melted off with steam. The steam pipes from the capstan and the winches were also thawed out. It took a long time before all the ice and water disappeared from the pipes and the machinery worked decently, but finally the chase boat was declared "fighting ready."

Hartviksen, the skipper-gunner, hauled out of the chart room a carton of powder and loaded the cannon with it, while Einar, who pretty much served as second mate, was already on watch. This Einar was an unusually experienced whale hunter; he had wandered over the whole globe, hunting whales and seals. He had been everywhere that whales were hunted: Iceland, Alaska, the Finnmark, the Sea of Okhotsk, Patagonia, the South Shetlands, South Georgia, and who knows where else. He was a typical old whaler. Hartviksen swore that he had once seen the old tar crying — a claim we took with a huge grain of salt — and that it was drops of pure whale oil that trickled down Einar's weathered cheeks. One could rightfully doubt this assertion, but it was certain that this old sea-dog possessed unusual experience in the area of whaling. The old salt stood by the cannon with a brand-new harpoon to wait for the gunner.

A modern harpoon like this is a completely different thing and much heavier than a hand harpoon
such as was used in earlier times, when men bravely
hunted whales in open boats and whaling
was still an inexhaustible source of adventure, probably the most adventurous work that has ever existed. The
modern harpoon is made of wrought iron.
Cast iron would be cheaper but much less
strong. A cannon harpoon is really quite something; without extremely well-developed biceps,
you couldn't even hoist it onto your shoulder to
carry it off.

A harpoon is about five feet long, while the
shaft, which fits precisely into the barrel of the cannon, has a lengthwise groove for inserting the fastener that secures the harpoon. When the harpoon
flies out of the cannon, the rope is dragged along
with it. The head of the harpoon that has the hooks
on top of it secured, revolving, on the shaft. If, after
the shot, the harpoon penetrates the body of a whale
and is pulled — which happens whenever a struck
fish tries to flee — then the four enormous hooks
spread out automatically, anchoring the harpoon so
firmly in the body of the wounded animal that it is
impossible for it to tear out.

Harpoon

I will spare you further description of the cannon and everything per-
taining to it; it would inspire little interest to know what such a murderous
device looks like and how it is handled according to the rules of the craft.

Before he loads the cannon, the harpooner inspects the harpoon
closely. Only when it passes approval is the sailcloth covering removed and
the harpoon fitted with the spring-loading. Then the harpoon is rammed
into the cannon, and a pointed-edge, bullet-shaped grenade with a timed fuse
is screwed on to the harpoon's tip. Thanks to the timed fuse, the grenade explodes several seconds after the shot goes off. The harpoon strike itself is
usually not enough to kill a whale immediately; the grenade greatly increases
that possibility. Finally, the harpoon line is secured to the harpoon with a fas-

tener. A large quantity of grease in all the joints serves to prevent the gunpowder from getting wet.

Once the cannon was readied for use, its cover was immediately put back on again in order to protect it as much as possible from the water coming across the boat. In truth, it was no weather for hunting. But not many whales would be caught in the Ross Sea if whalers paid much attention to that. The *Star 3* had already been out for three days, but between fog and storm not a single whale had been shot. Now that the weather was getting better and the frost smoke had lifted, the captain was determined to shoot a whale that day if one so much as showed itself. Moreover, the *Ross* had nothing more lying alongside; the oil kettles were cold, and the end of the hunting season was nearing quickly. The annual migration of the whales toward the north had apparently already begun; the animals grew steadily scarcer.

The past few days either the fog had been too thick or it had been stormy. That made navigation in the ice extremely dangerous. Maybe there were actually whales in the area, but the poor weather meant that they weren't spotted. So the gunner hoped to be able to profit from the comparatively better weather conditions and harpoon at least one fish. Judging from the color of the water, he had every right to nurture this hope. The heaving

The cannon is loaded

and pitching of the boat did make it almost impossible to aim the cannon accurately, but a seaman doesn't easily say that something cannot be done.

Every wave dashing up spattered about as the overhanging bow splashed down in it, and again and again a heavy rush of salt water surged over the boat, where it remained as ice, leaving a white layer of salt on the funnels.

As was the custom while the hunt was on, the helmsman was already in the "monkey island," the small open wheel-house above the chart room, while Einar, his hairy face hidden up to his eyes in a thick muffler, had taken his post in the crow's nest, looking out for a pearl-gray *blååst*. Automatically his eyes searched the horizon, scanning the wide expanse of turbulent water and heaving ice. But in spirit he was not in the lookout of the rocking *Star 3* in the Ross Sea, but rather *"langt, langt uit dit gamle Norge"* ("far, far away in old Norway"), with his wife and children on the little homestead in the quiet, friendly valley. He saw his wife bustling in the wash house, looking from time to time with a smile through the open window at the children, who romped with the dog on the tall rock behind the house. Then his thoughts went to Oernölf and Thorsten, his two oldest boys, who that summer were at sea for the first time as deckhands on a whaler headed to South Georgia. He hoped that the lads would get used to the rough life and hard work on a *kokeri* in order to rise eventually to become captains of chase boats, like the intrepid Hartviksen.

For Einar genuinely looked up to the harpooner, the kind of man for whom fear is a totally alien concept. Indeed, the most striking qualities of the captain-harpooner of the *Star 3* were his nonchalant but unbounded daring and his dazzling abilities as a seaman. He was a thoroughbred descendant of the old Norse kings of the sea, the Vikings, who were once the terror of all the oceans. Among the Norwegian seamen you meet that type often: large blond fellows, strong as trees, with friendly blue eyes; men who, despite their rough appearance, look childishly naïve and frequently actually are: cheerful, smiling giants.

While Einar stood dreaming in the swaying crow's nest, a little puff of thin vapor rose up at a distance of two miles, clearly visible against the dark water. Like a miniature cloud it hung in the air for a moment and then floated away on the wind. When it disappeared, a dark, round body popped up out of the waves, its smooth surface glistening in the sunlight. A moment later it sank again without a trace into the deep. Einar's roaming glance had nevertheless caught a glimpse of it. It brought him immediately back to reality.

With a jerk he turned himself in the narrow *tönne,* hollered *"Blååst!"* and nodded to the man at the wheel to indicate how he should steer.

Maybe fifteen seconds later the whale came to the surface again, first just the upper part of the head, which sank away before the round, seemingly finless back became partly visible. Then the giant disappeared again, gliding slowly, as if dissolved in the dancing waves, calmly emerging another fifteen seconds later. This happened several times, at regular intervals, and every time the whale came to the surface, he spouted, calm and sure, suspecting no danger.

After the last *blååst* the gigantic creature sucked his lungs full of air with such power that we could hear it on the chase boat. Then it dove under again. It wouldn't resurface again for another ten minutes or so. But where? Nothing more of the tremendous beast could be seen, and nothing gave away the direction in which it continued to move. But an experienced whaler is so familiar with the habits of whales that he can guess with fairly great accuracy where and approximately when it will resurface.

In warmer waters, seabirds often betray where the hunters will find their prey. They follow the trail that the giants leave behind in the water. Unbeknownst to them, the screeching flocks of birds are a great help to those trying to outwit the leviathan.

We, however, had to figure it out without such feathered hunting dogs. But this presented no problem; it wasn't the first time that the gunner and Einar had hunted in the deserted oceans of the far south. They had estimated where the whale would appear again, and they had told the helmsman where he had to steer the chase boat. Already the *Star 3* flew about through the onrushing seas to make a flanking movement. Waves of spray dashed about.

Everyone was curious to know what sort of whale we were really pursuing. We were still too far away to be able to make out from the *blååst* whether it was a *blaahval* — a blue whale — or another species. The manner of a whale's spouting — the height, shape, and direction of the expelled column of vapor — give an experienced harpooner many sorts of indications about the prey, even from a great distance. In general, the larger the animal, the heavier the *blååst* will be. A full-grown blue whale, for example, spouts much more powerfully than a minke whale (which, because of its small size, isn't worth the trouble to shoot). And the sperm whale has a distinctive spouting: because of the angled position of its nostrils, it doesn't expel its breath vertically, like most other species do.

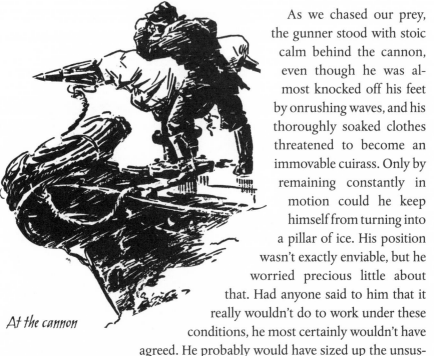

At the cannon

As we chased our prey, the gunner stood with stoic calm behind the cannon, even though he was almost knocked off his feet by onrushing waves, and his thoroughly soaked clothes threatened to become an immovable cuirass. Only by remaining constantly in motion could he keep himself from turning into a pillar of ice. His position wasn't exactly enviable, but he worried precious little about that. Had anyone said to him that it really wouldn't do to work under these conditions, he most certainly wouldn't have agreed. He probably would have sized up the unsuspecting so-and-so with a contemptuous glance and grumbled unkindly in his beard like a growling bear.

The gunner took care that the cannon didn't freeze solid and could easily revolve in all directions. Stubbornly clamped between his teeth was a stump of pipe that quickly contained ice instead of fire; he tried to keep his roughly mittened hands warm with vigorous arm movements. A numb trigger finger at the critical moment could mean losing a whale worth thousands of kroner.

Ha! There came the huge animal back up to blow! Not precisely in the place that the men had expected, but still, the distance from the chase boat was noticeably smaller than it had been the previous time. The whale breathed calmly several times and then dove under again for a little while.

Einar, watching closely from the crow's nest, now had the opportunity to size up the prey better. He knew that the powerful, vertical vapor stream could only come from a blue whale, and so, bending over the edge of the *tönne*, he bellowed, *"Blaahval! En stor hun!"* ("Blue whale! A big male!").

The gunner didn't look up at this shout. He had observed the same thing as Einar, but he wouldn't attempt a shot — the boat was still much too far away. Without seeing the giant of the seas, he felt where it went, as it were. With eyes and cannon he followed the movements of the invisible colossus. It looked as if the barrel was being aimed by a strong magnet.

The steward brought the captain a mug of steaming black coffee. This servantly soul was walking around bareheaded, and he had shoved his shirt-sleeves up above his elbows. Naturally — have you even seen a steward with a cap and a jacket on? Such a thing doesn't even exist, except on passenger ships. Never yet on an ordinary tramp steamer has a steward been spotted with a covered head and clothed arms. Ours grasped the mug in his hand, his grubby palm covering the equally foul cup so that the coffee wouldn't slosh out or the gunner get salt water to drink instead of coffee. With the other hand he covered a soup spoon full of sugar. The harpooner first took the sugar in his mouth and only then slurped up the black, boiled coffee. (That's how the Norwegians are used to drinking their coffee, and my shipmates always found it an affectation that I stirred my sugar in.)

Meanwhile, all the men's eyes were aimed straight at the spot where they suspected that the whale would surface. Although the salty spray slapped them in the face and turned their clothes into icy suits of armor, they stood excitedly peering at an uncertain point in the middle of the tumbling waves, where they expected to see the smooth, shiny back of the fish emerge. They stood swaying on their strong sea-legs, calmly adapting to the rolling and pitching of the deck beneath their feet. That happened automatically; they knew nothing but vessels that never lay still on the water but were always in motion.

One is never certain where a whale will surface; very often it's in exactly the opposite direction than expected. Furthermore, it turns out that the blue whales, especially the solitary males, are particularly shy and difficult to approach. Although the animals are fairly obtuse, they often succeed in evading their pursuers for hours. Only when they're mating or feeding is it easier to get close to them; then they lose sight of all caution and notice nothing that's happening around them. The whales are especially easy prey when entangled in the nets of Amor. Sometimes they're so inattentive that chase boats sail right into them.

To get a good shot at a whale, the hunters must approach it from behind and to the side. That isn't very easy, because its small eyes, which are situated near the corners of its mouth, actually see sideways. The creature has no neck and thus cannot look in front or behind itself.

The distance for a sure shot is pretty short — ten fathoms at most. Especially in turbulent seas the chance of making a hit at a great distance is slim. And don't forget that the gunner and the cannon are usually standing on a wildly rolling and pitching ship. Add to this the difficulty of targeting the best place for an absolutely deadly shot: the armpit, as is the case with most animals, and with the whale, just behind the pectoral fin.

In our case, our prey seemed not to have noticed the boat. As far as we could see, the great *blaahval* appeared to give no sign of uneasiness and kept slowly swimming forward in an irregular zigzag line. This meant that the whale kept coming up in the most unexpected places, and so it required several hours of patient maneuvering before we came within shooting distance. We were constantly surprised to see where the whale would pop up to breathe after a long submersion.

So it was still unexpected when the colossus suddenly came up, almost directly in front of the bow. Luckily, Hartviksen, who was equally unsure where the whale would next appear, had turned the engine off ten minutes after the animal had last disappeared into the deep. The *Star 3* thus had almost no power and only glided forward, slowly and silently.

Einar, up top in the *tönne*, saw the vague, dark shape rise toward the surface, very close by, in front of the bow. He let out a warning cry, and the helmsman turned the wheel with all his might, hands and feet together, so that the wheel flew around, rattling. At that same instant he roared *"Tilbake!"* through the speaking tube to the engine room, but the men on deck had already shouted to the engineer through the hatch to let the engine run in reverse. Immediately we felt the characteristic shaking and vibration of the vessel as the screw began to beat in reverse.

A moment later Einar looked down from his elevated station onto the enormous head, which came slowly above water. He could clearly see the two clefts of the blowholes open up, whereupon, with a booming whistle, vapor streams thick as an arm were spewed out. Then we clearly saw the closely spaced nostrils snap shut again and pull together, furrowing, as the enormous head disappeared under a splashing wave. Then the broad, smooth back with the small fin placed far behind glided slowly forward, while the sickly scent of whale unpleasantly prickled our noses. The tremendous tail fin hit just above the water, so that the foam flew up, and the prey disappeared again.

The gunner had already taken off his mittens. Peering along the scope, he securely grasped the handle of his cannon and tried, when the fish came up, to aim the lurching, rearing murder weapon at a point just behind the pectoral fin, ready to fire as soon as the vulnerable spot should be exposed.

It was no easy task to hold the cannon steady, because the chase boat, which was now running under almost no power, rolled like a piece of cork over the onrushing seas, and over and over again the whale disappeared behind an upcoming wave crest. Now the hunt was getting exciting; the climax had to come soon, with the gunner seeing his chance and taking it. Hanging on to the rigging and spars, the whole crew followed with taut attention all the movements of the gunner and his prey, especially the latter.

What the harpooner would do depended, of course, on the movements of the leviathan. And everyone knew exactly when Hartviksen would fire, even without looking at him.

Very carefully, so as not to frighten the animal, the engine was slowly maneuvered to bring the vessel to the desired distance from the colossus, while the man at the helm, without letting the whale out of his sight for an instant, turned the wheel so that the boat slowly approached it from behind.

The great *blaahval* had already blown three times. Now a favorable opportunity had to present itself quickly; otherwise the animal would dive again. Then the chance would be lost, and who knew how long it would be before another good opportunity presented itself?

In silent excitement the men stood watching. The only exception was the cook-steward, who was not an old hand at this: he had deserted his miniature galley and was so excited that he was standing on tiptoe in order to see everything.

He had to hold on to the railing with both hands in order not to fall down from pure excitement, and he uttered all sorts of strange noises; he didn't notice that the *Smöregröd*[3] was still burning. But the seamen stood watching silently at their posts, heedless of the water pouring over them, and poised for immediate action.

Finally, after the fourth *blååst* — it seemed to those watching to have lasted for hours — the dripping flank of the sea monster came above the waves for a moment. THE moment to fire! The gunner hesitated for a fraction of a second because he saw in that same moment that the prow of the chase boat was going to bore into a wave. But the chance was too good not to take.

3. This is Norwegian for "butter porridge."

While the bow splashed down and the leviathan was hidden from sight by a thick curtain of onrushing water, the gunner fired. An orange bolt flew like lightning straight through the cloud of spray. There was a dull bang and the sharp smell of gunpowder smoke. Wrenched along with the harpoon, the harpoon line shot off the platform, swinging wildly back and forth.

The rushing water had prevented the gunner from seeing where the harpoon hit when he fired. The cloud of gunpowder smoke first had to be wafted away by the wind before he could see that the harpoon had penetrated too high in the mighty body and had made only a flesh wound.

The struck animal remained lying motionless, as if he felt nothing or as if he were crippled. Then we heard a muffled bang, and a shock ran through the giant body: the grenade had exploded. Now the chase boat drew close to the whale. Suddenly the great beast began to flounder heavily, and a moment later dove underwater with an enormous splash. The tremendously wide tail swayed high up, right above the gunner's head. The observers all caught their breath; in their imagination they already saw the man as a bloody pile of shattered bones washed off the platform into the sea. Luckily, the wounded whale dove straight down without lashing his tail.

That probably would have cost the gunner his life. The power that resides in such a gigantic body is tremendous. You have to see such a sea monster up close in order to grasp the enormous amount of energy that can be summoned by the tremendous masses of muscle.

It turned out well, however. Only the portside anchor davit was struck by the tail flopping down, which snapped the cast-iron thing — as thick as a strong man's arm — like a match.

When, along with the whale, the danger had disappeared again, a sigh of relief went up. When the tension eased, the men laughed at the situation and, as is the nature of seamen, made loud, coarse jokes about it. As always, they were ashamed that it might have looked as if they were afraid.

The fish was secured, although he was evidently not mortally wounded. Now it was just a matter of time and patience to subdue him, to which end the harpooner might still add another stripe of gunpowder to the row already there on the side of his prey.

Naturally, the seamen's hands were not idle. The man at the winch had already turned loose the clamp, and while the whale plunged toward the depths, the harpoon line ran out quickly, rumbling over block and guide wheels. The desperate animal swam quickly right to the sea bottom, hoping to

Pulled along

get rid of the thing that was causing him such torturous pain. The harpoon line ran out steadily, hundreds of fathoms. After that the pressure on the giant body was evidently too great, and the animal swam farther in a horizontal direction. The line didn't stretch straight anymore but took an increasingly slantwise position. Gradually the slack was taken up, and the chase boat began to move, dragged by the *blaahval*. The clamp was set increasingly tight, and soon the huge animal was dragging the vessel behind itself at the speed of eight knots. The engines were stopped and later even set in reverse in order to force the prey to greater exertion and so exhaust him as soon as possible. Luckily, he swam toward open water and not toward the ice. In his confusion the wounded animal, desperate as he must have been from pain, could just as well have sought the protection of the ice. But he didn't think of his enemies; swimming blindly forward, he tried only to escape the burning pain and get away as quickly as possible from the place where he had been pounced upon by that horrible thing that bit deep into his back.

Diving under the ice is, as it turns out, a tactic often used by stricken whales. They try to free themselves of the tormentor by grazing along the underside of the ice, just as they skim along rocks to rid themselves of an orca that has clamped onto them. Had the whale fled under the ice, he would probably have saved his own life. So as not to be crushed against the ice, we would have had to cut the harpoon line.

But our prisoner swam toward the open water, and since he had received only a large flesh wound, it could well be hours before he was worn out and a second shot put an end to his suffering.

Meanwhile, the cannon was reloaded, and a second harpoon rope was threaded through the blocks and over the grooved head of the capstan on the other side. We expected that more harpoons would have to be shot into the giant body in order to kill the Goliath — certainly at least one.

Diving, the whale had reached a great depth, which required tremendous effort, as did dragging the heavy chase boat behind him. So the air in his lungs was quickly used up, forcing him to resurface quickly: he surfaced again after only five minutes. Still, he raced with undiminished speed toward the north, toward open water, in the fruitless hope of being able to flee his unbearable pain.

Even before he reached the surface, the whale blew out the compressed air with a heavy, powerful *blååst*, but it wasn't yet colored red with blood. If a whale spouts a red stream, then his vital organs are hit, and the fate of the giant is quickly decided. With unlessened speed the animal, fearing for his life, sped farther for a long time, pulling the vessel straight through the onrushing seas. Gradually, though, he began to shows signs of exhaustion: he blew less powerfully and many times in a row, and the speed with which he dragged his executioners forward gradually decreased. Yet even though the engine was going at half-power in reverse, the mighty animal was still so strong that he was able to keep pulling the boat for more than an hour at a speed of five knots through wild seas.

Then, unexpectedly, the whale, as if worn out, floated on the sea's surface, silent and motionless. He lay rolling powerlessly on the swell as if dead. He stopped moving forward so suddenly that the chase boat, which had still been following a long way behind, nearly collided with the floating colossus. We still took care to remain a considerable distance from the powerful tail. That was a good thing too. The temporary paralysis was quickly over, and the animal, crazed with pain, thrashed around wildly. Waves of blood streamed out of the gaping wound, which had been carved in deeply by the long pulling, although the great hooks prevented the harpoon from coming out.

The bloody foam carried by the wind flew like red rain over the boat.

The tremendous body rolled over and over convulsively in a pool of foam. The blood continued to flow out of the wound that the grenade had made in the enormous body. The animal was desperate with pain, yet he didn't think of attacking his tormentors. With all his might he struck out left and right around him and twisted into all sorts of curves to shake off that thing that burned like fire in his body. Once the colossus even sprang completely out of the water, a hundred thousand kilos [a hundred tons] of bone, flesh, and blubber, to fall back in with a tremendous smack. It looked as if a huge bomb had burst; the foam flew out over the mast.

The death struggle of this enormous animal was dreadful to behold — all the more because, his unbelievable dimensions notwithstanding, he was in fact completely defenseless. Involuntarily the men felt a deep sympathy for these gentle giants when they were finished off so mercilessly. Such scenes were always unusually repulsive, and I was never able to bring myself to choose such a bloody slaughterhouse drama as the subject for a painting. It was just too cruel for that.

For more than a quarter of an hour the convulsive wrestling with death continued. The creature was no longer trying to escape the chase boat or the harpoon; he wanted to shake off death, which he felt approaching, using the last of his powers. He dove again a few times, but he didn't remain under for long. But even though his life was flowing quickly away, he kept on thrashing the red-colored waves with his fins and tail, chasing the bloody foam high.

Meanwhile, the boat crept closer, very carefully: one slap of the giant tail could cause ugly damage and accidents. The closer the boat came, the more the slack of the harpoon line was taken in, but in such a way that it

In the throes of death

could easily run out again. It was necessary to hold the rope as taut as possible in case the fish suddenly lurched forward or dove deep. If the rope were hanging slack, then it would suddenly pull taut with a jerk that would snap it, and the catch would be lost. But the winch man was at his post, ready to play out line if it was necessary.

Gradually the leviathan's twisting movements weakened, and finally the mortally wounded giant lay completely still. With the utmost caution, watching out for the least movement, Hartviksen now brought the *Star 3* alongside. He knew all too well that the whale, however exhausted by loss of blood, wasn't dead yet, and everyone stood ready for immediate action in case the creature might revive. Then the whale would probably go at it again fearfully. But he didn't give a single further sign of life.

When the chase boat came within shooting distance again, nothing indicated that the whale, being tossed to and fro on the waves, was still alive. His little eyes weren't visible; if they had been, we probably would have been able to tell that not all life was extinguished quite yet. To be completely certain, the harpooner still preferred to deliver a mercy shot to put the whale out of his misery. Looking along the sights, he aimed carefully and was ready to pull the trigger when Einar, watching from the crow's nest, suddenly let out a warning cry: *"Paspaa!!"*

The shot did not go off.

Einar had noticed a weak movement of the tail, although the whale did not stir further.

Then suddenly the enormous tail waved high above the water, and the gunner was almost washed away by the wave that rose up as a result. But at the same moment, the shot rang out, whistling and hissing when the high-pressure gasses flashed straight through the water. The rumbling boom made the whole vessel shudder, while the sharp stream of fire shot flickering through the dense cloud of gunpowder, foam, and steam. The harpoon line shot in skittish coils after the deadly projectile. With a jerk the wind swept the foam and gunpowder smoke away, and the men, who were leaning over the railings craning their necks, saw how the shot had hit. A unanimous cry of joy went up; the harpoon "sat." Directly afterward a dull explosion rumbled.

Burbling, ripping sounds rose up out of the tremendous body of the giant of the seas as the grenade exploded deep in his innards. A shudder went through the gigantic body, which for a moment swelled up powerfully under the great pressure of the loosed explosive gasses. For an instant, the beast lay

Mortally wounded

motionless, as if paralyzed. Then he dove lightning quick toward the depths with such force that it wrenched the harpoon line, which rattled and clanged in the blocks until smoke curled up from the guide wheels. We loosened the brakes to give the fleeing whale as much line as he wanted to pull along, and we turned around with the engine in order to give the now mortally wounded whale as much space as possible when he came to the surface again.

In his death struggle he would no doubt go at it frightfully. Fifty — one hundred — one hundred and fifty — two hundred fathoms the manila rope ran out with dizzying speed; the smoking blocks shrieked and groaned. After that things went a bit slower. The whale couldn't possibly dive farther without drowning or bursting from the enormous pressure of the water at such depths. The pressure of his sundered innards must have caused the poor creature hellish pain, but of course the whalers didn't think about that at this point. They reckoned only with the practical side of the situation. When the animal dove no lower, and the rope ran out only with little fits and starts, the skipper beckoned to the winch man to pull on the brakes and not give out any more line than was strictly necessary.

Soon the rope didn't pull at all anymore and hung down right in front of the bow. The gunner looked in amazement at the loosely hanging line and commanded, *"Agterover, halv fart!"* ["Reverse, half speed!"]. He said a whole lot more that is definitely not proper to repeat here. He had absolutely no control over what the *blaahval* would do next. Scarcely a minute had passed since he dove with a quantity of air in his lungs sufficient to let him stay underwater for a quarter of an hour, but there was every sign that he already wanted to come up again, and it was advisable to keep a respectful distance from him during the final convulsions of his tremendous body.

Then suddenly a red stream of water spouted up out of the waves at some distance. It was the wounded whale, already blowing before he had reached the surface — a proof of fatal exhaustion — and the expelled air was mixed with a fountain of blood. Right after the first breath the massive head became visible, and again a thick red stream came spitting out of the nostrils of the mortally wounded creature. The blood, mixed with water, gushed over the high-held head. The exploding grenade had apparently ripped open the whale's lungs, and the fact that he spouted water also showed that he was nearly drowned.

It seems strange and unlikely that a whale could drown, and yet that is in fact truly possible. A whale drowns just like any other mammal if its lungs fill up with water. The whalers actually make use of this sometimes, if they don't want to shoot off more than one expensive harpoon. They will often simply drown a small whale that hasn't been fatally wounded by the first shot but still has the harpoon firmly hooked into its body. First they drive the chase boat full speed ahead in the opposite direction to that in which the wounded animal is fleeing. Then, as they put it, they steam over its head, and the whale, pulled forcefully by the boat, can't surface to take a breath. Consequently, the whale drowns in a relatively short period of time.

It appeared now that the torment of our victim would soon end. He rolled powerlessly from one side to the other, and the waves broke over him as over a helpless wreck. His breathing grew difficult and ragged, while fountains of blood thick as arms welled up out of his trembling nostrils. The leviathan could no longer produce a powerful stream; his sundered lungs were filling with blood and seawater. The end was near. Gasping for breath, the animal lifted his mighty head completely out of the water; his mouth, out of which streamed waves of blood, stretched wide open like a gaping abyss. Red streams flowed among the baleen and clouded the gray waves. In a desperate attempt to suck a breath of fresh air into his destroyed, blood-drenched lungs, the whale gathered his last strength and pushed his head even higher out of the water; but soon, exhausted and powerless, he let his head sink down again. Once more his tail swayed high and threatening, only to splash down limp again on the romping waves.

Life ebbed quickly out of the giant body of the king of the seas; the swell heaved it to and fro like a lifeless rag. Still, Hartviksen didn't dare get closer — we were holding off at a good hundred meters' distance [over 300 feet] — because the giant still lived. If he were dead, he would have sunk, but he still floated, even if the waves buffeted him and streams of blood kept welling up out of his widely flared nostrils. The fish was still breathing, and so there was still the threat of dangerously powerful convulsions as the animal neared the end of his death struggle.

It turned out to be a good idea to wait awhile.

Suddenly the seemingly dead whale revived. Absolutely motionlessness an instant before, the animal unexpectedly rose to mighty activity. He came rushing forward turbulently, a pool of foaming water behind him, headed right toward the chase boat, as if he wanted to ram it into the ground. It was a final flickering of his quickly fading vital powers.

Blindly, desperate with pain, the giant chased forward, trying to evade the death he felt approaching by fleeing the site of disaster with amazing speed, racing away from the searing, piercing pain that burrowed in his shredded innards.

The *Star 3* lay directly in his path.

When the sailors told the story later, they swore they had seen the little eyes that lay aslant the corners of the mouth flickering malevolently; but that was pure fantasy. It isn't in the nature of the *blaahval* to harbor such feelings. There isn't a single known case of a *blaahval* approaching a vessel with intent to attack.

But whether or not the whale's eyes flickered, it was a fact that he came storming at the chase boat with the speed of a torpedo; a collision could no longer be prevented.

"Full speed reverse!" bellowed the gunner, while he raced to the stern. The frantically racing colossus was headed straight for the ship. Stumbling and slipping on the ice in their haste, the sailors followed him, keeping one eye on the whale storming toward them. The helmsman decided that he wasn't safe up on the bridge, either. With a mighty jerk he turned the wheel full speed, rattling, while yelling one last order through the speaking tube to the engine room, and then sprang below, ignoring the ladderway in his haste. Wonder of wonders, he didn't break his legs, and he ran to the stern, where the others had already clamped on tight to props and other handholds to await the shock that inevitably was to come. It didn't matter that the engine immediately rammed away in reverse. The racing whale had built up such an incredible speed that the boat just couldn't get out of the way fast enough.

But when the violent creature was not a meter's distance [three feet] from the vessel, his powers appeared to suddenly and totally collapse. With convulsively extended fins he held his enormous head up out of the water in a last, pitiful attempt to fill his lacerated lungs with air just one more time. The dying titan was desperately stifled, feeling death by suffocation at hand. He gasped for one small, fresh, life-giving breath. His muzzle, splayed wide open, gaped like a dark cave, streams of blood still gushing out of it.

Because of the unbridled speed with which he had come storming on, the heavy mass of bone and flesh still shot some distance forward.

His thirty-ton head came roaring down over the bow, pushing it completely underwater. With a jerk the boat swerved a quarter-turn around, rolling heavily, so that the men on the rear deck lost their grip and tumbled head over heels over each other.

For a moment the boat was in a precarious position. The bow, where the cabins and cable housing were located, filled with water through the cabin door, which was destroyed, along with the cannon platform, the anchor davit, and the railing.

The whale was now dead. His tremendous assault had used up the last shred of his vitality. Powerless, the enormous head began gliding back into the sea, and the boat righted itself again, while waves of blood streamed over the deck. Twisted and broken pieces of iron plowed deeply into the meters-wide lower jaw, tearing off bloody slices of flesh and blubber, which remained hanging on the protruding pieces of iron while the colossal carcass slowly sank away into the depths. Although the chase boat wasn't seriously damaged overall by the attack, it was a real shambles on the foredeck. A piece of the cast-iron railing was bent and torn, the platform was destroyed, and the cannon had vanished from its pedestal. The cabins went under completely; sea chests, clothes, and benches bobbed about in the dirty, bloody water. One of the harpoon lines had also given way; luckily, the other one remained intact, and now the whole leviathan hung on it, but the winch man let it out carefully, a little at a time, until the animal didn't hang on it too heavily.

The end of the giant

Quickly the worst rubble was cleaned up, and then the men worked to secure their prize. Gently the giant was hauled up on the harpoon line. That demanded great caution in the turbulent seas in which the *Star 3* lay riding. If the bow rose up on an onrushing wave, the line sprang taut as a violin string with a jerk and had to be cautiously eased out a bit. But finally the fish came to the surface anyway, and then it was maneuvered so that the *hval* finally came to lie alongside with the tail facing forward.

A length of chain was slipped over the base of the tail and secured to bollards. As soon as the fish was secured, it was pumped up to give it a bit more flotation. For this purpose a sharply pointed pipe was driven right through flesh and blubber, deep into the body of the giant, after which air was pumped into the abdominal cavity with a hose from the deck pump. Meanwhile, the long ends of the tail fin were cut off. The flapping tips only hinder sailing. In the thick edge of the tail two notches were carved to indicate how many harpoons had been shot. These could later be found and cut out. Harpoons are expensive, and if possible they are retrieved and reshaped at the smith's so that they can be used again. But often they're so damaged that they can't be repaired — as, for example, when they're twisted into giant corkscrews.

It appeared to be a strong fellow that we had captured; more than ninety feet long, truly prehistoric dimensions.

The cannon was indeed lost, but that didn't matter; it was quickly replaced by a reserve cannon. Nevertheless, Hartviksen saw himself forced by circumstances — compelled against his will — to turn back to Discovery Inlet and the *Ross* with just this one fish. The coal and provisions were beginning to run low, and it was urgent that we return to the mother ship to replenish our supplies.

The crew of the chase boat wasn't exactly pleased with the result of their five-day trip: just one whale, and lots of damage on deck. For me the trip had been more successful. In the midst of everything I had been able to make many studies in my sketchbook, which luckily had lain in the chart room. Had I kept it in my bunk, as I usually did, there wouldn't have been much of it left over after the cabins were inundated. Several of these scribbles illustrate this chapter. My bony shipmates in their rough work proved picturesque enough to make desirable models.

After the catch was secured and the decks cleaned up, it was bottoms up, as was customary. The men had honestly earned their rum ration, and they naturally roared with approval at the idea.

Thereafter, with our hunting prize secured alongside, we headed back at full speed to Discovery Inlet to deliver the whale to the mother ship.

Rum ration

CHAPTER TWENTY

Whale-Hunting in Earlier Times

Sperm-whale hunt (after an old painting)

—⧈⧈⧈—

Although nothing is known with certainty about whether whale-hunting was done in prehistoric times, humans probably hunted whales already in the far-distant past.

Eskimo practices suggest that this is the case, since they use relatively primitive methods to hunt for and capture whales. They manage to catch the giant of the sea using their one-man kayaks and simple weapons. Of course, it costs them a tremendous amount of effort, but that effort is richly repaid. Once a whale is captured, they have a large quantity of meat and blubber that can feed a whole tribe for a long time. That's quite something for people who often have to contend with food shortages during the long, dreadful polar winter.

Almost as much whale meat is eaten along the South African coasts as along the coasts of the Arctic Ocean. But the Hottentots don't catch the colossal animals themselves, like the Eskimos and the Alaskan Indians do. They calmly wait until the sea throws the animals high and dry onto the beach; then it's feast-time.

It was the people of the Bay of Biscay, the Basques, who laid the groundwork for the great whale hunt as we know it, although it remained a small and flawed enterprise by our standards. They hunted primarily North Cape whales, which have this fact to thank for their scientific name of *Balaenae Biscayensis*. Already in the Middle Ages the Basque fishers had numerous land stations along the Spanish and Portuguese coasts and supplied all of Europe with baleen and oil. On their voyages they ventured far into the Atlantic Ocean and even got as far as the Arctic Ocean, past the North Cape. Later, around the year 1500, they changed their hunting area and carried out fairly extensive hunting near Newfoundland and Iceland; they even had permanent land stations in the north of Norway, the modern Finnmark. In the sixteenth century, sailing reached a breadth and a flowering as never before. Explorers had found a sea route to the East, and the New World had been discovered just a short time before, so the people of Europe slowly began to realize how large our earth really is. The great oceans offered avenues of unlimited possibilities. Trade broke new ground, and the riches of the newly discovered lands made mankind bold. Trade ventures and shipping companies were established, and expeditions were mounted to discover still more lands and to search out new routes to those lands that had already been found. The geographic knowledge of our earth broadened steadily, and along with it grew economic progress.

The earlier pathbreakers in the areas of trade and shipping, the Portuguese and the Spanish, weren't in a position to hang on to the headstart that their great seamen and explorers had given them; because of various political developments, new seafaring nations soon set foot on the world stage. These nations set to work with great energy and effort. It was the Dutch and the English who subsequently became the great seamen and pioneers of the seventeenth century. They also laid the groundwork for whaling on a grand scale, after the Basques had hunted North Cape whales on a small scale. It's interesting to review this period of whaling history.

Toward the end of the sixteenth century, both the English and the Dutch sought a new sea-route to Asia, a northern route. The Spanish and the

Portuguese were giving them too much trouble on their old, familiar route around the Cape of Good Hope. Along the new so-called Northeast Passage, explorers hoped to be able to reach China and India and all the fabled treasures of the Far East. (In those times people still had entirely mistaken notions of geographical relationships and distances.)

Between 1533 and 1584 several expeditions left from England to find the coveted northern passage, but not a single one of them reached their envisioned goal. Meanwhile, the Dutch had also begun broadening their reach. In 1565 a ship from Enkhuizen had already set up a station on the Kola Peninsula in the White Sea.

When in 1584 the king of Spain prevented all trade between Portugal and Holland, the Dutch became all the more interested in finding their own way to India so that they could procure the spices they could no longer buy from the Portuguese. In 1584, 1594, and 1595 three attempts were made — all fruitless. Then, in 1596, a small expedition of only two ships departed from Vlieland, under the direction of Baerentsz. Both Bear Island and the Spitsbergen islands were discovered, and the voyage ended with Barentsz and Heemskerck overwintering on Novaya Zemlya, which is still regarded as a splendid episode in our seafaring history. On all these voyages to the north, men had consistently come across many seals and walruses in the cold oceans, as well as along the coasts of the various island groups, but apparently no attention was given to this discovery at first. Eyes were opened to the wealth of Spitsbergen only in 1610, when Henry Hudson found many whales along the coasts and in the fjords of that area. Thereafter the English whalers took a rest, and at the same time the Hollanders and the Spaniards began to take whaling in that area seriously. When in 1612 ten English ships arrived in Spitsbergen, they encountered two Dutch ships and one Spanish ship that had already begun processing oil there.

Naturally, differences of opinion immediately arose about the right to hunt there. The English maintained that the right was exclusively theirs to exercise because they had first begun hunting there the year before; the Dutch thought that they had at least as much right because the islands had been discovered by a Dutch expedition. The dispute ended with the English driving out the Dutch. (They were bitter rivals at the time.) The Basque ship was allowed to stay and fish.

The following years witnessed many quarrels, which sometimes ended in bloody fights among the different nations. In the beginning the British had the upper hand; in 1613 they sent seven warships to Spitsbergen to protect their interests. Expeditions from various other nations came that year to take part in the hunt: the Dutch, the Spanish, and the French. But their ships were hunted down and plundered by the English without mercy (except for a pair of Dunkirk bottoms, which managed to conceal half of their catch from the English).

The Hollanders, who had first developed their seafaring capabilities during the Eighty Years' War, couldn't leave it at that, and the following year they showed up on the scene with a large fleet that was fully protected by armed ships. Their opponents became aware of these and kept their distance. The season unfolded without any disturbance and delivered rich results.

The stream of gold that flowed from whaling awakened the disapproval of Denmark. Greenland belonged to the realm of the Danish king, and in those times men were inclined to regard Spitsbergen as belonging to Greenland — in fact, Spitsbergen was still called "East Greenland." On these grounds, Denmark wanted to exercise a monopoly and let the riches of the newly dug Spitsbergen fountain stream into the Danish treasure chest. So in 1615 the Danish king sent three warships there to levy a toll on all foreign hunters. They succeeded in seizing a couple of Basques, but beyond that the Danish claims were supported by too few cannons, and the adventure turned into a fiasco, as could have been expected.

With the growth of the yearly yield, the hunt also intensified the rivalry

Whale hunt (after an old print)

between the Dutch and the English. In 1617 the English had an especially good catch, but with jealous eyes they saw that the Dutchmen had met with equal success. They didn't want the Dutch to sail home with an equally rich cargo, so they sought a provocation in order to overpower the Hollanders, who by chance weren't protected by warships that year. The English wanted nothing less than for the Dutch to quit hunting; when the latter didn't willingly consent, they were driven off violently, with weapons, and a Dutch vessel was seized.

In the Low Countries they now wanted to put an end to this abuse once and for all. The following year a strong fleet sailed out and divided its ships among the fjords where the English wanted to anchor. In several places the ensuing altercations came to blows, and near Voorland a fierce sea-battle developed in which many lost their lives. The English ships were seized, although they were later given back. It became clear that things couldn't continue this way, and so the hunting grounds were divided. The Hollanders, the English, and the Danes assigned themselves the best portions. Meanwhile, the Basques, who as the teachers of all other whalers surely deserved something better, saw themselves assigned to the bleak north coast, which was largely inaccessible because of ice.

Peace was thus secured. Now a time of great growth began for Spitsbergen. Whole fleets — sometimes hundreds of ships together — went on the hunt. The Dutch stations on Spitsbergen and on Jan Mayen Land (Mauritius Island), discovered in 1614, belonged to the "Northern Company," which in 1614 received its charter from the States General. Its plan was to pull the captured whales onto dry land and process the oil on location.

Not much is known about how the Northern Company worked during those first years. What is known is that in several carefully chosen places, tents were set up as shelter for the sailors who processed the oil onshore. These tents were later replaced with wooden lodges, which were still always called "tents." In this way permanent oil factories were gradually built, so that the industry spread out more and more. In the summer the tent camps were inhabited like regular settlements that had to be defended against the English, the Basques, and the Dunkirkers, who begrudged the Dutch their success. Because of this, small forts were set up on Jan Mayen Land and Spitsbergen.

Only during the hunting season in the summer was there great activity in these oiltowns. During the winter they lay deserted. Then the tools were

The oil factory on Jan Mayen Land
(after Cornelis Willemsz de Man, 1639)

stored in the tents, the chase boats were pulled high up on the beach, and the quantities of blubber and oil that the men couldn't bring with them were safely stored.

Smeerenburg, as the Dutch establishment on Amsterdam Island was very fittingly called,[1] was the most prominent of all the settlements, and sometimes counted a summer population of twelve to fifteen thousand souls. To this day the remains of it can still be found as witness. A certain whaler named Zorgdrager described Smeerenburg — not unkindly — this way:

> Alle the Try-pots and Wayrehouses formed together a Neighbourhoode or smalle Village, which was called *Smeerenburgh* moste suitably after its manner of Trade. After that the Shippes voyaged here and redoubled the Folke, then it came to passe that those in the Ships, the Sloops, and on the Lande were daily fulle of Industrie; there arrived also in these Shippes, along with the Army, some Merchaunts, who sold their Wayres sutch as Brandy-Wyne, Tobaccoe, and other sutch thinges in theyr owne dwellinges or in the Wayrehouses; also there came Bakers to bake Breade, so it came about that in the morninges when the warme Rolles

1. "Smeerenburg" means something like "Oiltown" or "Greaseburg" or "Blubber-ville."

and Loaves came out of the Oven, there was a blowninge upon the Horne, so that in this *Smeerenburgh,* established in the same tyme as *Batavia,* there was pleasauntly muche to do, albeit not in comparison with that Javanese Capitalle; neverthelesse theyre was a fayre bustle about and the chaunce to obtaine a fitting amount from the Lande, and the Wyne and Brandy-Wyne were reasonable cheape.[2]

I found this description in the introduction to *Walvischvaarten, Overwinteringen en Jachtbedrijven in het hooge Noorden, 1633-1635* by S. P. L'Honoré Naber.[3]

Occasionally several men overwintered in Smeerenburg to keep an eye on the possessions of the Northern Company. The diaries of some of their overwinterings have been preserved. Unfortunately, such experiments often ended in tragedy. Cold, scurvy, and hungry polar bears were the reasons why only frozen bodies were found the following summer.

Perhaps you'll be surprised to learn that our greatest naval hero, Michiel Adriaanszoon de Ruyter, was also a whaler. No wonder, for de Ruyter was at this time just an ordinary steersman; only later did he become the great admiral whose glorious deeds made our land famous and feared as a first-rate sea power.

Included in the work mentioned above by Naber are journal excerpts from two journeys that de Ruyter made as a steersman on the ship *De Groene Leeuw* [*The Green Lion*] that was fitted out for whaling in the waters off Jan Mayen Land.

From the journals it appears that the Hollanders still employed Basques, the most experienced whalers of that time, even though our compatriots had apparently already developed a certain seaworthiness of their own. This is clear from the following citation, in which the old Dutch sounds so pretty and congenial:

Item the 30th of the same in the evening alle our shippes ventured into the sea towards the southe and on the first of Juinne one of the Basques

2. In this and the following excerpts, I've attempted to convey something of the delightfully antique flavor of the spelling and phrasing of the original early-seventeenth-century Dutch that Van der Does quotes by translating the passages into equivalently antique English. My thanks to Nancy Van Baak for her help in this undertaking.

3. The English translation of this title is *Whaling Voyages: Overwintering and the Business of the Hunt in the Far North, 1633-1635.*

shotte a fishe. Item 2nd-3rd-4th Juyne without the baye was it fulle with ice and on the 5th, Sunday we muste needs go ashore the baye being so fulle with ice we came and there we moored untille the 6th and from the 6th unto the 7th, when our Biscaeyannes broughte their fishe by the baye which they hadde shott and the 8th Junne in the morninge broughte they them further into the baye and the same day in the morninge the ice wentt out of the baye and we went again out onto the roades but there yet laye alle aboutt us muche ice and on the 9th Juyne in the morninge early we returned once more to the lande by reason of all the ice and the 10th Junne broughte Mols' Biscayans yett another fishe into the baye and we laye theyre untille the 13th Juinne. Then broughte the Germayen harpooniers from *Amsterdamme* the thirde fishe in the baye and laye further in the harbour in as much as the baye was so filled with ice. Item the 15th Juyn in the eveninge we did give chace on a fishe but Hans Duyvel from *Hooren* did shoot him, but we received fifty gulden for that we didde help to kille it harde by the *Grande Cape* and we came furthermore that night on boarde.

From the extract from the second *Joordenael* [*Journal*] that dates from 1653, it appears that the Dutch didn't really trust the Basques. One day as they lay at anchor near Jan Mayen Land, they saw a sail in the sea. They thought it was one of the chase boats coming in with a whale. "Then theyre wentt," reads the *Joordenael*, "Delfs' sloope toward the saylle, thinkinge that it was our whale-boate and when he came on boarde it was a Biscaeyan and ranne away Northwards againe. Item the 3rd Juilly we made ready oure defence on the N. forte." It was an evil welcome that they had in mind for the Basques. The relationship certainly wasn't a very friendly one.

The old Spitsbergen sailing vessels were three to four hundred tons heavy and were built as sturdily as possible, with an eye toward sailing through the ice. There was a lookout in the foretop, and in the hunting grounds the boats were kept ready so that they could be manned and launched within a few minutes.

The ships were fitted out during the winter, and the fleet departed for the north in March or April. The crew of each ship numbered forty to fifty heads. All had a financial interest in the undertaking, as is still the case today with whaling.

In the olden days the ships neared the sea ice toward the middle of May.

The customary hunting grounds weren't usually reachable then, and so the men simply began the hunt along the edge of the ice, where in fact whales can always be found. The hunting grounds, which were originally limited to the fjords of Spitsbergen, were quickly expanded, and soon the hunt was being carried out between the 75th and 80th degrees of latitude along the entire edge of the ice, even all the way up to Greenland.

The whales were attacked from boats that were launched from the great hunting vessel. A whaleboat of this sort was light and strong and offered enough space for six to seven men and several hundred pounds of harpoon line. The usual hunting tools were harpoons and lances. The men understood that killing a whale this way was often far from easy work — not because the whale so heartily resisted the process but because it had such tremendous dimensions, which meant that doing it in with hand weapons made for numerous difficulties.

As soon as a whale was spotted, the boats were manned and launched. Because a whale doesn't hear well but can see fairly well, the hunters tried to approach it from behind. They had to exercise a great deal of care in doing so, especially in calm weather. When the fish was killed, it was fastened to a boat, after which it was towed to the hunting vessel by the hunters' combined strength. That was hard work: it took several boats to tow a large whale at the rate of one knot. For flensing the cadaver was fastened alongside the ship with the tail facing forward. Flensing was done along the length of the carcass, and when necessary the creature was turned with the help of tackle. The flensed blubber was shorn of hide and meat scraps and then cooked out on the beach or in open kettles onboard. Or it was stowed onboard in barrels to be cooked later, back in the home country in the oil factories of the harbors from which the ships had sailed.

It was especially the Hollanders who grew formidable in whaling; from the beginning their profits far exceeded their expectations. Great quantities of building materials were brought to Spitsbergen to build oil factories, warehouses, barracks, and shops, so that Smeerenburg and the nearby Harlinger Factory grew into formal cities.

The great slaughter among the whales resulted in their becoming steadily scarcer and very timid. They avoided the coastal waters and retreated to the open sea and into the pack ice.

Accordingly, the hunt moved increasingly into the open water, and the land stations on Spitsbergen and on Jan Mayen Land fell into decay because

The cabins in Smeerenburg (after an old engraving)

the ships kept the blubber in vats onboard. The unilateral hunting concessions that had once caused so much disagreement lost their reason for existence: in the open sea, everyone had equal rights. Thus there arose an era of new and unexpected flourishing for the Spitsbergen trade. In earlier times, perhaps 30 whaling ships took to the sea every season. But between 1640 and 1770, about 150 Dutch ships took part in the hunt. The hunters carried out the so-called ice catch toward the west as far as Iceland and Greenland, even in the Davis Strait and Baffin Bay and west of that. Eastward they hunted as far as the waters off Novaya Zemlya.

Until about 1740 it was the Hollanders who were in the forefront of whaling and earned the greatest fortunes, but thereafter, between 1740 and 1750, the English pushed themselves to prominence again, lured by the stream of gold. Just as the Dutch had, the English enjoyed a period of previously unheard-of wealth. Toward the end of the eighteenth century, however, whaling began once again to fade due to several factors.

Napoleon's continental system drove the Dutch and the French whaling industry entirely into the ground, helped in this matter by the English, who undauntedly captured ships from all the continental powers. The British had the riches to themselves from then on, and until about 1814 the yield of baleen and oil kept rising. This threatened to completely wipe out the whales in the far north. At this point Spitsbergen had long since been deserted, and the hunt transferred to the waters off west Greenland.

The number of whales in the Arctic Sea diminished steadily while at the same time the hunt went over almost totally into American hands. The waters of Greenland were also deserted by this time, so the Yankees began trying their luck in that part of the Arctic Ocean that is reached by way of the Bering Strait. (The whales leave the polar sea in September as the sea ice begins to freeze up; they then go through the strait toward the south.) But the hunt in the Bering Sea proved much more difficult than that in the European Arctic. It was impossible to go farther than the 74th degree of latitude, and so the whaling there remained a sort of coastal fishing, as in the olden days near Spitsbergen. Ships always faced the danger of being crushed by the ice, and the return voyage through the narrow Bering Strait was difficult, especially if new ice had already formed. Ships were lost more than once. Frequently the hunt degenerated into a scandalous scramble for plunder. Because the baleen had more value than the blubber at this point in time, hunters often simply cut out the baleen fringes of a captured whale and let the rest float away; men worked this way especially if the hunt went well. Now that the baleen no longer has any value, this no longer occurs.

The hunt in those regions is also steadily declining now, probably because the whales are retreating more and more into the ice, just as was the case near Spitsbergen.

In the first flourishing era of whaling, it was especially the North Cape whale that had to suffer for it; in the second rich period, it was the Greenland

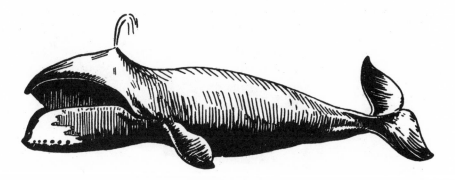

Greenland whale (after an old print)

whale that men attacked. Thereafter came the third era, the American whaling period, with the sperm-whale catch.

In the English colonies in North America, whales had been hunted for a long time already, along the coast and in the many bays. Already in 1650 a regular hunt was carried out on Long Island, bringing the inhabitants considerable profits. In Southampton the business took off so quickly that all the adult men took part in it. In 1668 a company was established that enlisted Indians as harpooners. Later Nantucket took the lead, and New Bedford and Cape Cod also became more prominent.

In the beginning the whaling was limited to coastal fishing, but as the animals grew scarcer along the coasts, men began to outfit special ships, just as in Europe, and also began to hunt sperm whales. This deep-sea whaling began near the end of the seventeenth century and soon was carried out along the entire coastline, from Newfoundland to the Bahamas. Ever larger and better-equipped ships were brought under sail, and the American whalers crossed the whole Atlantic Ocean, both south and north of the equator.

The Revolutionary War dealt the death blow to the American whaling industry. The English captured the American ships and even the sperm-whale catch. To the British also goes the honor of having added the Pacific Ocean to the hunting grounds. In 1788 an English whaler navigated around Cape Horn and sailed home with a rich cargo of oil out of the Pacific. Soon it was also the Indian Ocean's turn, and then sperm whales weren't safe in a single ocean in the world. When the United States began to flourish again after the war, the American whaling industry revived as well, growing even stronger than before — at the expense of the English, who gradually and

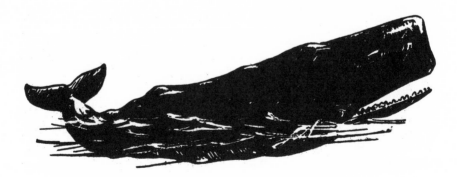

Sperm whale

steadily withered away. The Yankees let the Stars and Stripes wave in any and every ocean where sperm whales were to be found. In fact, the Americans carried out the hunt so intensively and with so many ships that sperm whales threatened to disappear completely from the world's oceans. And thus the American decline began. In New Bedford, hundreds of whalers had once been fitted out, but by 1920 the whole fleet consisted of only ten ships in the 100- to 300-ton range. Now most likely not a single one of those ships remains.

In earlier years the whaling business was dominated first by the Basques, then by the Hollanders, then by the English, and then by the Americans. But today this specialized branch of seafaring is predominantly a Norwegian business.

In general it is also other species of whales that are hunted these days. In earlier times, with the exception of sperm whales, men caught only the smaller types — in sailor's argot, "right whales." The hunters hadn't tried to catch the larger fin whales (with one exception), and once they attempted it, the results were mostly discouraging.

The modern whale hunt, in accordance with the spirit of the times, has totally become a big business, and much of the romance that was bound up with earlier whale-hunting has been lost. The romance isn't gone completely, of course, as can be seen from the previous chapter. Whaling is still one of the most adventurous and risky businesses. But in the past, circumstances made it far more challenging: men hunted the giants of the sea with hand harpoons and lances in open boats, and it demanded a great degree of tenacity and seamanship to catch the powerful animals with such simple weapons.

If whales weren't such defenseless simpletons, it probably would never have worked to hunt so many this way. One slap of the tremendous tail is enough to smash much more than an open boat to splinters. It actually almost never happened that a whale truly attacked a boat. A wounded whale almost always quickly took flight, diving deep underwater to try to escape the place where disaster had struck. It has happened that a stricken animal dragged the chase boats behind itself for more than two days in its flight, but it didn't turn on its pursuers. Only the sperm whale isn't always so goodnatured. It will sometimes go on the attack, and it has sunk many a ship. It has been reported that sometimes a sperm whale would take a run of several hundred meters and come shooting toward a ship like a torpedo, with a wide track of foam trailing behind it. It would storm the vessel, ramming the doomed ship with its massive, square head so that leaks sprang up in every joint and seam and the masts went overboard from the violent collision. Many a ship has gone down with all hands this way. After the ship was sunk, the furious whale would cool his wrath on the full whaleboats, which it cracked between its enormous jaws and smashed into wreckage with its powerful tail. The men were crushed in the tremendous maw.

The old whaling industry was thus truly rich in danger and raw romance. Today, now that the ships are so much larger, the hunters aren't in so much danger anymore, and with harpoon grenades the whales are also killed much more quickly and surely.

The dangers of sea and ice have of course not diminished. In fact, they have increased as men have been obliged to penetrate ever deeper into the world of the permanent ice in order to find the whales that have been retreating ever farther. The modern whale-hunt is almost exclusively restricted to the Antarctic Ocean and has reached greater heights than ever before.

Today the hunt is exclusively about oil and nothing else. It's true that the world production of whale oil makes up only 5 percent of the total of fats handled on the market, but since 1920 this production has risen ninefold. The number of whales that are killed annually for this purpose number about 25,000 to 30,000, while in 1930 the catch reached the startling number of 40,000. In the past few years the hunt has been carried out with the use of airplanes, with one or two taken along on each mother ship. The airplanes serve only as reconnaissance. They track down the whales, which from the air can be seen from a great distance and deep underwater. It appears that the family of whales has by no means been wiped out yet. Still, the experts predict that in less than twenty years the animals will practically cease to exist if men continue hunting them in the same way that they have in the past few years.

The malaise [The Great Depression] that caused so much unspeakable suffering was a blessing for the whales. As was the case with most raw materials, oil was overproduced. Then the market was flooded, and the price sank accordingly, so that oil had to be sold below its production cost. The result was startling: in 1931 the great Norwegian whaling companies didn't send a single ship out to the Antarctic — only a few English companies did. As a consequence, the huge slaughter of recent years didn't take place. But that's only a temporary stay of execution. As soon as the Depression is over and business and shipping revive, then things will be just as they were before. Every autumn the great whalers, equipped with the latest inventions, will depart from the Norwegian harbors to the various hunting grounds in the Antarctic Ocean. In the last few years measures have been taken to prevent the whales from being completely wiped out, but I fear that there isn't much that can be done about plundering. It's impossible to control how many fish are shot in the sprawling seas and in the far south, even if specific quotas are assigned to each ship and land station. The whales are creatures that are doomed to disappear. Their death provides mankind with too many advantages, and history teaches that all species for which that is the case inevitably disappear from the earth, despite all legal measures taken to prevent it.

CHAPTER TWENTY-ONE

The End of the Polar Summer

Midnight sun

N one less than Shackleton, an essential authority on the subject of Antarctic weather conditions, considered February a bad month in the Ross Sea. And the weather seemed bent on proving right this opinion of the polar explorer who died too young: February began with a heavy snowstorm.

Already the evening before the storm it began to blow hard, and along with that it froze twenty degrees below zero Celsius. That temperature by itself isn't so bad, but if alongside that the wind develops a speed of a hundred kilometers per hour [sixty miles per hour], then it begins to be unpleasant.

The cold caused a thick frost-smoke; dense mists came alongside and over the ship and hindered all visibility.

Naturally we kept a watch in all directions, not only on the bridge but also on the bow and the stern. A solid wall of ice threatened us both before and behind, and the danger of floating icebergs was ever-present. But the worst thing was that the frost smoke was so thick that if we did spot danger, it would already be too late to deal with it.

Both anchors appeared to be useless; with a foot on the steel anchor cables one could tell how hard they dragged. The shocks one could feel were clearly caused by the dragging over an uneven seafloor. When the wind whipped into a howling snowstorm, the decision was made to weigh the anchors, since their movements only hindered the ship. With a great deal of difficulty we hauled onboard the anchors and the chains, hundreds of fathoms long. The engine ran in reverse while we did this; otherwise it would have been impossible for us to undertake this task because of the force with which the storm drove the ship back.

Only after four hours of toil were the anchors safely lashed. Quite a while to raise anchor! But the conditions were unusual too. The anchors lay in about three hundred fathoms, and it was storming so hard that the men on the prow couldn't stay on their feet. Without a sturdy handhold they slid like fury backward over the frozen deck, and no sooner had the anchor cables come on deck than they froze.

It isn't an enviable business to handle frozen-stiff steel cables for hours at a time. Our hands went numb often and became useless, so we had to take frequent breaks to thaw them out. It was so cold that the men who were working on deck were soon completely unrecognizable because of the mask of ice that their frozen breath formed on their faces and headgear.

After the anchors were finally raised, the *Ross* lay heaved to, below the Southern Barrier, for a whole day and the following night. The high wall of ice offered a good lee; the sea was fairly calm there. In the open ocean a blizzard might well have swept up a formidable sea. Indeed, the four chase boats that were out must have had rather raw weather, unless they were able to temporarily shelter themselves behind the Barrier until the storm had spent itself somewhat.

The fierce wind drove along with it great quantities of hard, powdery snow, chasing it in horizontal flashes over the ship.

The man on the lookout at the bow was relieved every half-hour, and that was no excessive luxury, since whoever was at that post encountered the snowstorm firsthand. On lookout one needed to stand as forward as possible by the jackstaff, but it simply couldn't be done. I tried it when it was my turn, but as soon as I stuck my nose out over the railing, the storm cut off my breath, and it was impossible to keep my eyes open. The ice crystals that the wind slapped into them hurt like steel splinters blown forcefully into my face.

The drum of the anchor winch offered good cover against the blizzard, although that restricted my forward field of vision, and I still couldn't keep my eyes open against the storm for longer than a minute. By then I was forced to turn my head away from the wind to give my eyes a rest and to remove the snow and ice from my eyelashes.

The howling storm chased forward one thick cloud of snow after another with whistling speed. Everywhere around us there was nothing but the constantly onrushing snow, and we could see nothing but horizontal white stripes shooting by through the atmosphere.

To give the ship a bit more maneuverability, we steamed toward the broader entrance of the bay, which lessened the danger of colliding with the Ice Barrier. It wasn't advisable to remain lying outside the bay; as we could see now and then, numerous icebergs whirled by at great speed.

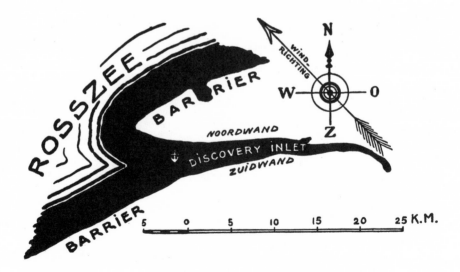

The anchorage in Discovery Inlet

Under the lee of the Barrier where the sea was relatively still, a thick layer of slushy ice quickly formed on the water. In calm weather that would have grown into a solid layer of ice in no time, but now there was too much movement in the water for that.

After raging unbroken for about twenty-four hours, the fury of the storm quieted somewhat. The rush of snow grew thinner, and we saw sky and clouds above us again. When we could see the Ice Barrier again, it didn't seem nearly as dangerous as it did during the storm, when it wasn't visible and thus was all the more threatening.

The force of the wind fell off remarkably quickly. The thick snowbanks drove off toward the open sea, and even though the snow kept whirling, we could again see where we were.

During the storm we really navigated only by feel. Now and then we did get a glimpse of grayish-white ice cliffs, but that didn't give us much help in determining our location, since the Ice Barrier looks exactly the same everywhere. As it turned out, the *Ross* hadn't wandered far. The ship lay just outside Discovery Inlet, under the protection of the Barrier, and soon we brought it back to anchor at its former location.

It is surely an unusually rough climate where such blizzards are part and parcel of summer. Isn't it almost impossible to imagine that there have been times when Northern Europe presented the same cheerless picture that the land of the South Pole does now? And yet it is a fact. During the last ice age, estimated to be about 50,000 years ago, Northern Europe was one great wasteland of snow and ice. Just like modern-day Antarctica, it lay buried under a heavy shroud of ice. The lands that are now covered with fruitful farms, blooming fields, and green forests — at that time they lay buried under the eternal ice, which thus turns out to be not absolutely eternal after all. Where now the noise of labor rises out of thousands of densely populated cities, then there was no other sound than the hissing and whistling of driving snow. But no ear heard the lonely voice of nature; neither man nor beast could yet live in the endless, deadly wastelands of snow, over which the god of winter blasted his all-benumbing breath, age in and age out.

One tremendous glacier covered the entire northern half of our hemisphere. From the Scandinavian highlands the stream of ice pushed ever further southward, and the outermost edge of the ice reached our land [the Netherlands]. The hillocks of sand and gravel in [the provinces of] Utrecht,

Gelderland, Overijssel, and Drenthe arose when the ice melted and the glacial till remained behind. All that material was ground off the mountains of Scandinavia by the flood of ice and carried along over all that distance. The Dogger Bank in the North Sea must also be seen as a terminal moraine from that same layer of ice.

During the last ice age, about the same conditions must have existed in Holland as do now in Antarctica. One has to admit that the weather has improved remarkably since then, even though people often find reasons to complain about it.

With the wobbling of the earth's axis, the poles shift, but that happens so slowly that you don't even notice it. So you don't have to worry about being overtaken unexpectedly by a new ice age. And it's not necessary to have yourself measured for polar clothing just yet.

Just as Europe has known ice ages, so the South Polar Region has known warmer eras. The layers of coal that have been found in Antarctica provide convincing proof of that.

THE SNOWSTORM seemed to have been necessary to restore the balance in the atmosphere. For days afterward we had steadily pleasant weather and an excellent opportunity to work day and night without interruption. Whales were brought alongside in sufficient quantity, and on such days many a barrel of oil streamed from the boiling kettles into the tanks. The rising number on the blackboard, indicating the quantity of processed oil, brought a smile of contentment to many a weatherbeaten face. The oil processing was going well. Good thing too, for it was as good as certain that the new ice at the end of February would force the whales to leave the Ross Sea to look for warmer waters. Then it would make no sense for us to stay any longer. In addition, the growing ice would present too great a danger for our unprotected ship.

Even though the weather was excellent for days on end, the sinking sun undoubtedly foreboded the approaching polar winter. And because the sun skimmed steadily lower along the horizon and gradually gave less warmth, the temperature also sank steadily. Every night the sea was covered with a heavy layer of smooth new ice; fortunately, every day, as the temperature rose and the wind increased, it was crushed by the waves again.

Still, it grew colder, slowly but surely. By day the thermometer indicated, on average, five degrees below zero Celsius, and by night twenty degrees below. Finally, even by day, new "black" ice lay around the ship, even though the moderate wind was easily strong enough to work up sufficient wave action to pulverize the ice layer.

Remarkably enough, as the temperature fell, the number of whales that the hunters managed to seize increased, even though precisely the opposite might have been expected.

Because of the mounting cold, the bay froze completely solid at night, while by day its surface remained covered with thick pancake ice.

In very still weather the frost smoke, which rose up from the congealing water, formed such a thick mist that the steam whistle had to keep blowing constantly so that the chase boats coming in could locate the mother ship. When by chance a pair of boats came to deliver their prizes at the same time, one could fancy himself in the North Sea or in the Channel because of the droning of steam whistles that answered to the heavy voice of the *Ross*.

In those days, when the sun seemed to rest on the horizon at midnight and painted the southern sky the whole night with a welter of warm, beautiful hues, I often climbed up to the *tönne* in the foretop to dream undisturbed and to enjoy the wondrous, delicate beauty of the colors of the midnight sun. The midnight meal offered plenty of opportunity for that. I could quickly work my way through the simple supper of whale meat, frozen potatoes with gravy, and tinned vegetables, generously washed down with black coffee, so that I'd have enough time left over to go high above the uproar of the penguin deck into the crow's nest to dream and to enjoy the rare beauty of the autumn night. From the deck, one looked up at the steep wall of the Ice Barrier. But from up above, one could see the surface of the Barrier, and also the sun, which seemed to roll forward along the horizon like a glowing ball, surrounded by a wide wreath of warm sunset hues. The cloud formations changed constantly, and as they changed, so did the light and the colors, which sometimes set the whole sky glowing.

Nature puts much more tempered colors on her palette in the polar area than she does between the boundaries of the tropics. The immense, completely empty snow surfaces lost much of their disconsolate aspect under the welter of warm tints, but still I always felt the impact of the hopeless desertion of the endless, deathly wilderness of snow and eternal ice, on which not the least sign of life made even the smallest variation.

The garment of snow with which the Antarctic has been covered through the ages and seasons was then no longer white. Through the play of light and color in the sky, it sometimes took on the most wonderful hues.

Still, that couldn't prevent a nameless oppression from emanating from the endless, deathly expanse of the empty snow plains.

Always, under all conditions, Antarctica remains the kingdom of eternal silence and cheerless desolation. This dead, chilly world exudes an almost tangible mysteriousness, and therein lies the irresistible fascination that the polar environment holds for some: the silent loneliness of the landscape that doesn't seem to belong to our earth but rather resembles the images one conjures up of a long-extinguished planet.

There, high up in the crow's nest, high above the noise onboard, I got the feeling that we — with our boisterous labor, stinking smoke, and clouds of coal dust — were profaning something sacred.

And that we were too! Is this ice-armored end of the world not the last bulwark of nature, where she tries to keep herself untainted? One feels the eternal stillness of the polar region as something consecrated. Here, where nothing moves other than the icy snowstorm, one fancies he is experiencing the death of the world. Each banal sound seems to profane the sacred stillness, just as a babbling drunk would desecrate the earnest silence of a funeral procession.

We are accustomed to identifying deep cold, the kind that defines the polar regions, with the chill of death. But Antarctica as a whole isn't nature's death-chamber. In fact, it's quite the opposite. The cold of the polar regions is one of the most important factors determining climatological relationships all over the world. It was with the goal of gathering more reliable data about this that in 1911 the Australian South Pole Expedition under Sir Douglas Mawson went to Antarctica.

On the *Ross* the scientists gathered masses of material on this subject as well. And they didn't just collect tables of numbers. Sometimes they went out for a day or so with a chase boat, and as a rule they climbed up the boarding ladder of the ship with beaming faces and baskets full of stones and sea creatures. All those things hauled up with a dragnet they carefully arranged and prepared so that they could be researched by experts later.

GRADUALLY THE INCREASING cold began to be troublesome in the processing of the blubber. As long as the blubber sat on the cadavers, it remained manageable because of the warmth given off by the process of decay. But as soon as a long strip of blubber was hewed off in the fierce cold, it froze as stiff as a board. Then not much could be done with the flensing knives, and axes

Flensed cadaver

had to be used to divide it into usable pieces. Frozen blubber was as stiff as hard soap and looked like it too; frozen whale meat looked like dark red, white-veined marble, and a strip of beefsteak could be secured only with powerful strokes of the axe.

All sorts of things pointed more and more to the approaching end of the polar summer. Even though a great deal of heat was generated onboard for the oil processing, the snow didn't disappear from the decks but steadily increased. Heavy rime added to it.

The cold caused a lot of trouble with the steam pipes and the deck-rinsing pipes. The steam pipes had to be thawed over and over again, and the deck-rinsing pipes slowly become permanently unusable.

Repeatedly a high swell ran into the inlet that made outboard work impossible, even if the "Ice Cellar" itself had the best weather one could imagine. That meant that on the Ross Sea it was storming somewhere. Often because of that, a number of whales couldn't be processed before they decayed. The decomposition destroyed huge quantities of blubber, and because of the warmth of the decay, the fat melted and streamed in jets out of the cadavers. A lot of precious oil was lost this way — and a lot of money. The oil that could be processed from a single whale was worth about ten thousand guilders. So with sorry eyes we had to watch more than one whale fall into such an advanced state of decomposition that it became worthless to us. We then simply let the rotting giants float away; the orcas must have had a real feast with them.

Even someone who wasn't used to doffing his cap at a full moneybag must have found it a pity to see something so valuable go to waste. But there was nothing left to do but to go at it harder than ever on the days when the sea didn't prevent us from working, in order to produce as much oil as possible during the short time that remained to us.

Day and night we worked without interruption, and the oil kettles in the forward and rear holds were used exclusively to boil oil from blubber. At first from the flensing deck on back only *kjödt og ben* — flesh and bone — were processed, but that resulted in a far smaller percentage of oil. So after that we processed only the blubber of the whales, and we worked on them both fore and aft. We worked feverishly around the clock, and soon ten thousand barrels of oil stood notated on the board.

Another less pleasant result of this unusual diligence was the unspeakable filthiness into which the whole ship unavoidably fell, and with the men it didn't go much better. From stem to stern, from crow's nest to the bottoms of the tanks, the *Ross* was covered with a layer of foul, slippery fat. Impregnable barricades of quivering blubber obstructed the hold decks. Fat and filth spattered about as the men cut and hacked the enormous sides of blubber into more manageable pieces. Tall rubber boots were indispensable, since the men were forced to wade up to their thighs in the heaped masses of blubber. Ropes and cables were dragged through it, and countless footsteps spread the filth to every corner and hole, because the dirty, fatty tangle stuck to men's legs in clumps.

The *Ross* became a beastly greaseball, the filth ten times worse than the most vile befouling that you can imagine. Not a man could be spared to clean the ship, and the continuous strong frost prevented the filth from running out through the scupper holes. The mess made everything on the ship slippery to boot. There was nothing we could lay our hands on that wasn't slippery. To be able to use axes, knives, and other tools, we first had to scour them with sawdust. Without the sawdust, you couldn't possibly make a decent cut with a bone-axe; it was sure to slide out of your hands by centrifugal force and fly overboard in a graceful arc.

Buckets and barrels of sawdust stood on hand every place we were working. Even the flensers who were cutting strips of blubber from the swollen cadavers outboards took care so that, in addition to their knives, spades, hooks, and whetstones, they also had a barrel of sawdust on the platform to help them keep a stiff grip on the shafts of their tools. When the day's work was done, the men brushed each other off with sawdust in order to remove at least the very worst filth from their clothes. And they were still so completely foul that they were unrecognizable.

After work was set aside, a bath wasn't a luxury but a pressing necessity. Only those who had developed refined skills in obtaining hot water could snatch a place in the bathhouse. Anyone who wasn't that fast looked someplace else for the chance to carry out the ritual washing: in the forepeak, the sailroom, or the smithy. But it was often a real feat to get to the cabins spotless again, where with united effort and resistance we maintained a comparative neatness.

We readily endured all that trouble without much griping. There were, after all, a lot of whales alongside — sometimes eight at a time — and the oil poured from the smoking kettles into the waiting tanks in thick streams like liquid gold. On good days we processed five to six hundred barrels of oil, sometimes even more. Such results powerfully fed the desire to work — understandably, since a portion of the stream of gold would ultimately land in the sailors' empty purses.

THE MONTH of February, which had such a bad reputation for nasty weather, didn't give us much cause for complaint at first. For days the weather stayed constant and clear. Above the open sea the sky was gray and cloudy, while above the Ice Barrier there wasn't a trace of cloud, except for a few very high cirrus feathers. The separation of these typical water-skies and ice-skies was unbelievably sharp. The boundary of cloud above the sea ran in a high arc from the east to the west, through the zenith, and closely followed the line of the Barrier.

For a time the weather remained favorable, even to the point where we hoped that the *Ross* might still get up to a half-load of oil.

That would have been all too nice. To drive such unwarranted optimism out of our heads, a powerful snowstorm howled up over Discovery Inlet on the sixteenth of February.

We quickly weighed anchor when it looked like it was going to be bad, but the wind rose so fast that we added an anchor, along with several hundred fathoms of anchor cable.

As long as the blizzard raged, we hid away, with the ship behind the south wall of the Ice Barrier, which took most of the force of the storm. When the storm had exhausted its powers, the wind changed, coming from a northerly direction. This breeze from the open sea drove the temperature so high that for the first time since we had lain in the bay, the mercury rose above the freezing point, even though it was by only half a degree. That "high temperature" felt downright unpleasant after the cold to which we had become accustomed.

Thereafter the sky remained constantly clogged and gray, and a fair amount of snow fell every day, sometimes unusually large crystals in six-pointed shapes. Ice crystals also whirled steadily out of the low-hanging, gray clouds, or sago snow fell, like soft hail. The Barrier kept on calving. On windless days we could clearly hear the dull booming of shifting ice around us. Many young icebergs sailed past the mouth of the inlet, and the ice walls, which formed the shores of our harbor, changed their shapes daily as there were smaller or larger calvings.

Not many icebergs were born in Discovery Inlet, probably because the unusual formation of the glacier at that spot was so compressed that the ice masses were pulverized. In most calvings the ice wall, over a larger or smaller distance, collapsed into the sea as rubble. Sometimes the calvings stretched out over several kilometers. The glacial debris formed extended ice-fields, which sometimes were a nuisance, since enormous blocks often floated among the smaller pieces of crushed ice. We had to avoid such monsters so that the whales alongside the ship wouldn't be torn loose.

One day I was shocked awake during my watch below because I was thrown out of bed, and I landed rather ungently on my sea chest. I could hear the noise of swaying and falling objects on deck, and the *Ross* was pitching violently. The entrance of the bay was invisible because of thick, swirling clouds of powdered snow, from which arose the sound of a cannonade of ice masses collapsing into the sea. This caused the vicious swell that had immediately set the ship to turning so violently. When calm was restored and the clouds of snowdust floated away, the promontory on the northern side of the bay entrance appeared to have vanished, and an extended field of glacial debris completely blocked the entrance.

Because of the multiple calvings, the surface of the inlet was almost completely covered with a continuous field of glacial ice. All that ice dampened the swell of the waves, so that at night the water could quietly freeze. That it did too, and it looked as if the great freeze had suddenly begun, which would necessitate our immediate departure. If winter made a sudden attack, we would have to leave the inlet immediately, because its fairly protected position meant that the new ice would readily freeze solid there. Once the ship was frozen in, it would be difficult — probably impossible — to get it out of the inlet.

In several hours the fields of glacial debris were frozen together; all the gaps were filled in with new sea ice. As we were making preparations to raise anchor at a moment's notice and head for the open sea, a blizzard rose up out of the southeast. All previous snowstorms had been received with loud curses, but this one was greeted with rejoicing, because it didn't take long for the storm to break up all the new ice and drive it forward to the open sea. In a few hours' time the inlet was free of ice again, and the *Ross* remained lying at her old anchorage, fighting against the fierce pressure of the wind. It was now

The fate we wished to avoid

very clear that our days in Discovery Inlet were numbered. But we would stay there and continue to work until the last possible moment in order to keep producing as much oil as possible.

Meanwhile, it was undeniable that the situation was getting serious for the ship. The effect of this on the crew was very easy to notice. The men began to get restless, and voices arose demanding that Captain Larsen give the order to head for the north and leave the dangerous "Ice Cellar." The increasing cold, which put ever greater difficulties in the path of the work, did nothing to improve the mood, either. Slowly a spirit of resistance arose among the crew, and the voices demanding that the *Ross* raise anchor grew ever louder, so that they were probably also heard amidships.

This same uncooperative feeling undoubtedly also played a role in the short-lived strike that broke out on one of those days — a peculiar incident that also had its sympathetic side. The first mate, Olaf, who was the leader of the proceedings, devoted himself willingly and deeply to Bacchus whenever he managed to get a chance. Then sometimes he wouldn't be seen on deck for several days. The work continued anyway, but naturally it wasn't up to par. The *bestyrer* [captain] had already taken Olaf to task several times, but without result. When it happened again that Olaf was indisposed for several days in a row, Captain Larsen decided to demote him and put him on a chase boat as a steersman. This decision was made at night, and the next morning Olaf got ready to transfer onto the small boat. He was standing with his sea chest by the boarding ladder in his famous moss-green pants when the day crew that was just about to start work noticed what was going on. The men liked Olaf a great deal, and to protest his demotion they went on strike on the spot. No matter what Captain Larsen proposed, nothing helped. The men simply refused to work if Olaf disembarked. The men certainly wanted to work, but only on the condition that first mate Olaf stayed on the *Ross*. There was nothing to be done for it, and Olaf stayed. Did this involve a loss of prestige for the captain? That depends on your point of view. But in any case, by giving ear to the men's demand, the captain avoided the sudden termination of the whale hunt. He still hoped to get several thousand more barrels of oil in the tanks before the whales, which were already beginning to grow scarcer, disappeared completely, and before the incoming winter forced him to end the hunt.

CHAPTER TWENTY-TWO

Antarctic Poetry

The poet

P oetry with a question mark and the pronounced aroma of oil! It's Bullet's
fault that this chapter was written. Bullet, the Benjamin of the Tasmanian
crew, was on a more or less strained footing with his mother tongue, and
without doubt he had never read a single line of poetry; his educational process hadn't yet gotten that far. And yet circumstances led to his being temporarily under the illusion that he was poet laureate. That said, be prepared for
the worst.

It was on Paddy's birthday that we detected the first portents of the poetic river that soon streamed through the penguin deck and later even took on such grand dimensions that without exaggeration one could speak of a true *bandjir.*[1] We liked Paddy — the quiet, good-natured Irishman — a great deal; he was a hard worker and a good companion. But there was one thing that we sometimes took him to task for: his ceaseless and irritating training on the punching ball, which he had, *nota bene,* brought into his bunk, and which he faithfully tried to beat to a pulp every single day with unflagging zeal. Since he was a boxer by profession, we gladly granted that he had to remain in good condition, and there were always fellows who were happy to go a few rounds with him. But his monotonous slapping against the ball often grew unbearably annoying — and then we'd make a prompt end of it. We knew it was safer to avoid his steam-hammer hands, so we rendered him harmless with a couple of cleverly thrown blankets and then lashed him into his bunk to cool off.

Despite that, he was everyone's friend. When by chance we discovered that it was his birthday, he found all sorts of little presents next to his tins of food: a shaving razor, a cigar, pieces of soap, and a milk bottle of brandy. Paddy was visibly moved by these tokens of affection, and the journalist onboard, inspired by the feeling of camaraderie, made up this occasional rhyme on the spot:

> 'Tis Paddy's anniversary,
> The first day of this kind he ever had at sea.
> Oh Paddy, old thing,
> You pride of the ring,
> This memorable day we want to report.
> We reckon you are a real good sort.
> You are, we think, the smartest Irish blood
> That hails from the island of shamrock and spud,[2]
> And Paddy, old bean, in our own hearty way
> We wish you many a happy return of the day!

It's likely that nobody had ever taken any notice of Paddy's birthday, uncivilized wanderer that he was, and when the flattering cripple of a poem

---

1. This is an Indonesian word meaning "flash flood."
2. For his Dutch readers, the author adds that "spud" means "potato."

was declaimed over him with the necessary pathos, he blushed from shyness and emotion right up to roots of his red hair. Especially the phrase "pride of the ring" must have rung like music in his ears. Wrapping the ditty carefully in a piece of newspaper, he hid it like a precious treasure in a grubby wallet in which he kept all sorts of well-thumbed papers.

This was all normal and reasonable, but Bullet, who had recited the poem, must have had some very peculiar twists in his brain. Although he had succeeded in reading this artistic masterpiece only with all sorts of help, he considered his performance so successful that he quickly puffed up with pride. Soon he was not only convinced that he had put the ditty together all by himself, but also certain that he could shake poems out of his sleeve just like that. The most remarkable thing was that he actually believed it. The fact that all refinement was alien to him, so that he wasn't even in a position to read or write his own language decently, eluded him completely. He was soon so sure of his poetic genius that he spent all his free time making verses — "verses" in quotation marks, that is.

If with heavily furrowed brow he discovered two words that more or less rhymed with each other — he didn't require it to be all that close — then there was another poem, according to him, and his enthusiasm knew no bounds. This was amusing to watch, so everyone helped him string together a few lines of rhyme, as good and as bad as it got. The intentions were good, but you can imagine how pathetic the results were. Often it was downright frightening, but nobody minded. As long as the poem rhymed just a little bit, everything was all right. The poet himself was bothered by this least of all; he was too busy exercising his divine gift. Evidently he even forgot that he hadn't hatched these creations by himself in the first place.

If and when a poem was ready, he set to writing it down. He sat down on his knees in front of the hatch, which served as a writing desk, his tongue clamped between his teeth, working for hours at a time to put his brainchildren down on paper in a laborious and nearly illegible scrabble. He was a great and very naive child, Bullet was.

He attempted to perform the poems with great pathos, even though he often didn't comprehend their meaning, and his word accents sprang all over the place like a frisky colt, and he stumbled over unfamiliar words — which in addition he corrupted pitifully.

His only regret was that he had no decent mustache to play with, something to boost his self-confidence as he declaimed his verses. All real artists dramatically finger their mustaches as they offer up their works to the people, someone had assured him. No problem — an enviably masculine and artsy decoration was made for him out of a piece of bearded sealskin. With a little piece of iron wire, it could be made to stay wandering pretty much in the general vicinity indicated for it by nature. But if, in the rapture of artistic performance, Bullet fiddled with the device a little too energetically, it showed dissolute tendencies and then fell onto a mess bench or into the mush of oil on deck. But the poet didn't let this distract him from his great rendition. Undaunted, he simply stuck the recalcitrant artistic emblem back on his upper lip.

The fellow really was grotesque in his unbelievable naiveté. Despite all the absurdities, he was absolutely serious; not for a moment did he doubt his genius. Because of this, he didn't actually lose sight of all sobriety. He signed all his would-be brainchildren with this full flourish:

Herbert Williams.
Temporary residence
Discovery Inlet Southpole.

No minor mark of vanity! And after someone let him know that this was necessary to prevent theft, he also added "All rights reserved"!

It goes without saying that the rhymes were mostly inspired by the work being done and the circumstances in which the men lived. Unfortunately, the language employed was as a rule so coarse and uninhibited that I don't dare to present most of the stanzas of this Antarctic poetry to you.

Of innocent verses like this one, there weren't many:

Frostbitten feet, hands frozen stiff,
Long icicles drooping from his ziff,[3]
The flenser is forever cutting from the whale
Long strips of blubber, from jaw to tail.

The man who wrote the following lines had clearly had more than enough of coal-trimming and was longing for home when he made this farewell address ready in advance:

3. "Ziff" means "beard."

Farewell to the Ross

I shall remember you when I go down
Back home to good old Hobarttown;
You and all the dirty jobs I've done
Aboard of you, by the flaring, icy midnight sun,
When chilling blizzards, rough and cold,
Were challenged by the Tassies bold,
And the night gang in the dusky hold[4]
Was shoveling damned dusty coal.

Some of the poems were more personal, such as this one, which contained a warning to me — a wink not to go after the boys quite so hard:

To Bill the Boss

Don't swear when I can't get a hold
On a damned wire that's slippery and cold,
Not even when a big whale drifts away[5]
After escaping the careless watchman's eye!
Don't blame us as we have a spell,
As working in the blooming coal is hell;
Or when the frozen winchman lets
A ton of it drop on the decks.
I wonder if you will believe when told
That all the speck[6] is frozen stiff with cold
And only a bone-axe be strong enough
To split the beastly rotten stuff.

Bullet's thirst for poesy seemed to be unquenchable. He asked for more and more, but his own springs of poetry were quickly exhausted. In some old magazines, however, he found an ample assortment of poems that, with small changes, he could easily adapt. Sometimes they sounded rather odd, but the rhyming words and the flowing rhythms of the melodious sentences enchanted the simple ears of our polar bard. Naturally he failed to notice the

4. The author adds this note: "to be pronounced as 'hole.'"
5. The author notes that in Tasmanian pronunciation "away" rhymes with "eye."
6. "Speck" means "whale blubber."

many questionable combinations, not to mention the laughably tortured language. So arose, out of a poem entitled "Pumas," this curiosity, which we listened to with open mouths:

Ode on the Blue-Whale

Hushed, cruel, amber-eyed,
Before the time of danger of the day,
Or at dusk, along the ice-clad barrier-side,
Big-jawed, lithe-bodied,
With mighty tail, as chiseled for love or hate
In chilly oceans, berg-strewn and ice-pack-rimmed,
The great whale seeks his mate.

Rippling, as water swerved,
To heavy pressure-ridge in greenish deep,
Or secret caves where the barrier front is curved,
The great fish goes for sleep.

Seeking the mate or prey,
Spouting blast 'pon blast into the frosty skies.
Man, who is made more terrible than they,
Dreams he is otherwise.

Following is another specimen that we received with slack-jawed amazement:

Call of the South

I'm hungering in the city for the smell of fresh-shot whales,
For "kokeries" where the blubber-smoke goes curling
    through the shrouds,
For the countless miles of barrier wall, where the green waves
    kiss the ice,
In the land of ghost-white snows, beneath the cold grey clouds.

Where the skua pipeth shrilly, and old memories come to stir you,
Where ne'er twilight lowers the purple veil that city folks call night,
But oh, the miles of thund'ring waves that shut me from the pack,

From the endless leagues of wild-pressed ice, from the sun
  of midnight.

It's there my heart goes straying, to the splendour of virgin snows,
Where the whales leap in the Inlet, and see their cloudlike blast,
Where I'll vision all the folly, all the noise and pain and tumult
As a fevered dream that's vanished, ne'er to return at last.

The final stanza was the icing on the cake:

For the cold winds murmur comfort to the hearts that know
  their music,
In the great, white, silent spaces, where the quiet sets one free
From the gold-greed of the city, from its sins, its strife and clamour;
And the pure breeze of Antarctis washes clean the soul of me.

It was priceless to see the faces of the audience when our poet mounted
his Pegasus and gave such grandiloquence his best. Nobody, including the
poet, had any idea what it was about, but they still thought it was really very
nice anyway — and the need for washing was something they understood
very clearly. With serious faces they nodded yes — not to washing their
souls, of course, but to washing their oil-soaked clothes, which loudly called
for soap and boiling water.

Rhymes whose tendencies lay closer to the ground were of course a
much bigger success and were greeted with unbridled joy.

Making poetry — or letting poetry be made, I should say — became a
matter of life and death for the enthusiastic Bullet. He rewarded a suggestion
for a verse or a pair of rhyming words with a pack of cigarettes. And the hon-
orarium for a complete verse was a pipe or a pack of tobacco, your choice; a
fearful lot of smoking went on during those days. The poet wasn't really particularly critical — no more so than his public. As long as there was rhyme,
everything was fine, and the more muscular the language, the better. On that
last point there certainly wasn't much to complain about: the Tassies' choice
of words left nothing to be desired as far as unrestrained expressions and
forcefulness went, to put it mildly. For this reason — alas! — most of the
verses they created with their combined strength are absolutely not salon-
worthy and not fit to print.

Epigrams of a certain sort were very popular. This one especially enjoyed great success:

> God strike me dead!
> Old Larsen said,
> As Thorsten shot a whale.
> The bastard aimed at the head,
> But he hit the blooming tail!

Countless variations were made of this one, none of which left much to be desired in terms of clarity, but which sometimes seriously overstepped the bounds of decency.

After wallowing in poetry of this alloy for a while, the men finally had their fill of it. The supply of tobacco and cigarettes was also exhausted in the end, so that the stream of poems died down and finally dried up. But Bullet had written up all the ditties and carefully preserved them, with the idea of publishing a volume of poems — Antarctic poems — once he got home.

I don't know if he ever actually tried to do it. It would have been priceless to see the face of the publisher when he received the volume for examination, a taste of which I've given here in a modest anthology of tame and chaste selections.

This poetic episode was naturally more than laughable, and I only men-

As Thorsten shot a whale

tion it here because it gives an interesting glimpse into the mentality of the fellows who populated the penguin deck and the mutual relationships in the very primitive society of the fo'c'sle.

It was impossible for me to reproduce Bullet's original spelling. Without correction it wouldn't even be legible, for the poet entertained very singular ideas about the grammar of his mother tongue, and on top of that he was a devoted follower of phonetic spelling. So, for instance, he wrote "blooale" instead of "blue whale." "Ale" was doubtless a sound that awakened pleasant memories for him. "Ocean" he spelled "ohshun"; of "terrible" he made "turble." And after a long investigation we discovered that this incomprehensible series of letters — "wornerrtwaylay lorseer pewpelfeel" — had to be translated as "where ne'er twilight lowers her purple veil." But general education isn't an essential commodity for a coal-heaver on a *flytende kokeri*, even if he sometimes ogles the Muses freely and frankly.[7]

7. Alan J. Villiers, the Australian press correspondent who joined the expedition in Hobart, Tasmania, recounts this incident in the book he wrote — and he gets the last laugh in this story by uncovering the secret that Van der Does is hiding: "We had known for some time that Bullet had not written a word of his 'poems,' weird and wonderful as they were. 'Billy,' the Hollander, cabin-mate of our friend, had written them all, and Bullet had copied them, more or less inaccurately. With this information we suddenly confronted the important 'poet,' to his complete undoing, and thereafter, although he tried to explain that Billy was only his assistant and had but helped him in the spelling of the words, he wrote no more poems, nor did he press for payment for those that had been delivered." See Villiers, *Whaling in the Frozen South: Being the Story of the 1923-24 Norwegian Whaling Expedition to the Antarctic* (Indianapolis: Bobbs-Merrill, 1925), p. 147.

CHAPTER TWENTY-THREE

Driven Out by the Ice

Ice grotto

On February 22 the sun showed itself at midnight above the horizon for the last time. A little segment of sun just managed to show like a pale red arc through the mists that hung over the Ice Barrier, peeping through and tinting the wandering mists and frost smoke a soft pink. Sad, pale-red light filtered through the veil of frost vapor that rolled over the freezing bay and reflected brokenly in the smooth new ice that covered the surface of the sea.

Nothing more could be seen of the mighty ice wall than a vague straight line where the upper edge of the wall stood out against the light-streaming mists above it.

It was a wonderful, quiet, strange night, full of pale, pastel hues. Everything was peaceful and quiet: no breeze moved, and the sea was so still that without any resistance it let the prince of winter put it into a suit of brand-new ice armor. This great quiet, made greater still by the wild silence of the stark, unspeaking polar landscape, was truly so overwhelmingly deep that it grew highly oppressive.

And the wealth of fine, tender colors with which the departing sun filled the atmosphere in no way drove away the comfortlessness that the completely empty desolation of the polar region awoke in the soul.

The polar winter was approaching, but for several days in a row the good weather continued. By day the sun shone, and there was a scarcely perceptible coolness out of the south. By night it was usually dead calm; then it froze hard, and the new ice grew quickly, but it was still carried by the current out to sea.

It wasn't really cold, even though the mercury column pointed to 20 degrees below zero Celsius. We were already so acclimatized that we felt rather warm in the middle of the day if it was about 5 degrees below zero! Now and then we washed our hands with snow to freshen up a little and slept with the portholes open, lying under a single blanket.

That probably seems unbelievable to you — which is understandable. Before I was in the polar region myself, I didn't believe it when a well-known Greenland explorer assured me that he had often seen Eskimo babies crawling out of their igloos stark naked and romping about in the snow, crowing with joy.

On such calm, lovely days, if work didn't claim me, I often went out on a flensing flatboat to row along the Barrier and take a look at the many grottoes that the sea had carved out of it. It wasn't risk-free to come that close to the foot of the tremendous wall, and it was essential to avoid those portions of the glacier that showed any sign of action. It would have been decidedly unhealthy to have a couple of tons of ice fall on my head unexpectedly from sixty feet up.

Up close the ice wall made a much mightier impression than it did from a mile distant. From that vantage point it really didn't seem so enormous, especially if you kept looking at it every day. That's because the Barrier stretches from one end of the horizon to the other, so that its horizontal dimensions make a much stronger impression than its vertical ones. But if you see the Barrier close up, it makes an overwhelming impression. When you tilt your head back, you're looking at ice cliffs that are sixty feet high, rising straight up out of the sea.

But the shimmering depths of the grottoes held an irresistible attraction for me. In them the faintly swelling sea, which rolled endlessly to and fro between the smooth, glistening walls, sighed and murmured with strange, muffled sounds. Rowing into an ice cave, I found myself shuddering involuntarily. It wasn't pitch dark, as it is in an ordinary cave, but the atmosphere inside was very mysterious. The depths were obscured in vague, deep blue shadows.

The subdued light, which penetrated through the ice and was reflected back through the water, was an intense cobalt color in the ice grottoes. The farther I went in the cave, the more everything lost itself in those cold blue shadows, and altogether it looked like a picture painted in Delft blue.

As soon as my eyes were accustomed to the strange, diffuse light, I could easily imagine myself in a fairy-tale world. On the walls, myriad ice crystals shimmered like countless gems that gleamed and then were extinguished, according to the pleasure of the softly swelling sea. The sunlight skipped from the entrance inward over the tops of the lapping waves and threw whimsical pendulums of light along the sparkling walls, so that long, living strings of scintillating diamonds seemed to whirl over the walls of the fairy palace. The sunlight stood like a haze of transparent gold over the entrance of the grotto, and living fire seemed to spring out of its uncountable facets. The ice itself was such a beautiful translucent blue that the entire cave seemed to be carved out of one tremendous block of turquoise.

The exquisite play of cobalt-blue shadows and sparkling gold light was so fairylike, of such an unreal beauty, that I lost myself in that wonderful dream-world in which fairy tales and sagas become living reality. Sometimes I awoke from that half-conscious state only because the oars had slipped out of my benumbed hands.

A grotto like that was a true ice cellar, because the encircling ice radiated a large part of the cold that it accumulated during the long polar night.

THE DISAPPEARANCE of the midnight sun was evidently a sign for summer to take its leave and at the same time an invitation to the polar winter to claim its rights with more force. During the day too the sun was only seldom visi-

Ice in Discovery Inlet

ble; the temperature dropped steadily, and fog and frost smoke shrouded the already very somber landscape in a drab gray garment that took away the last trace of nature's cheerfulness. Storm- and snow-showers alternated with each other endlessly, and the sea was made so turbulent by the rapid succession of blizzards that the massive ice cliffs of the Barrier could no longer hold out against the power of the relentlessly battering waves. The enormous ice walls calved almost constantly. Thundering, they collapsed over great distances, chasing the restless waves even higher and filling Discovery Inlet with vast fields of glacial debris and both large and small icebergs, which formed a constant threat to the *Ross*.

Under normal circumstances the ship seemed so large and so safe to us, but when winter made its entrance with blowing blizzards and mighty masses of ice, we felt all too keenly that the safety which a steel ship such as ours had to offer was extremely relative and, yes, almost even imaginary. The bad weather not only produced ice that made us anxious but also made the circumstances under which we had to work unusually difficult even for the most hardened men. Frozen noses, ears, and hands were the order of the day, and the whales alongside the ship rolled so frightfully that the flensers were always in great danger for their lives.

As chance would have it, it was precisely during this period of raw weather at the end of February that quite a few whales were captured; naturally, it was unthinkable not to process them. The hunting season was coming to a close, and the days in which the prince of winter would tolerate us in his domain were numbered. Every barrel of oil that ran from the fat kettles into the tanks might be the last. So we kept on working with grim stubbornness, completely ignoring the almost insurmountable difficulties. Like bulldogs, the flensers clamped themselves down on the pitching, ice-covered cadavers, with spray freezing solid over them, while wind and sea were sometimes so turbulent that the wrenching giants broke loose from their chains and floated away, men and all.

One time, to our consternation, a chain got tangled in the propeller. The weather was so rough that the engine had to be kept running forward at half power to keep the *Ross* in the desired position. We shut off steam immediately, but the chain had already worked itself around the screw — how far, we couldn't tell. The situation was tense and more than dangerous, considering that we might be forced to depart any minute, compelled by the inevitable freeze-up. Then every moment would be more precious than gold, and we would have to entrust our lives to the power of the engine, which had been put out of commission so suddenly. Getting anxious and upset about it wouldn't help, either. So, with feverish haste, we immediately began to try to free the propeller.

We thanked heaven that the anchor chains didn't break. If they had, the ship would have been irretrievably lost and helplessly smashed to bits against the ice wall. While the men worked hard to free the screw from the chain, we expected at any moment that the anchors would give way. But they held, against all expectations, and to our great joy and amazement it appeared that the chain had only wound itself around the propeller for a few turns. In less than an hour it was free again.

Not much was said when the engine's trusty stamping was heard again, but with that sound a load as heavy as lead was lifted from our hearts. During that fearful hour when the propeller was stuck, many an anxious glance was cast at the threatening, enormous Ice Barrier and then back at the work being done. The men worked so fast and furiously that they dripped with the sweat of exertion despite the cold. But when the danger was finally averted, they laughed at their own fear, as sailors do, even though it had most certainly been warranted. That's what the rough life of whalers is like. So many dangers confront these men every day that they learn to take them lightly and forget them again as quickly as they're over.

IN THE FIRST days of March, the whales suddenly seemed to withdraw from the vicinity of the Ice Barrier. The chase boats frequently came back without any catch. That was an unmistakable sign that the polar winter was near. The ice in the sea had doubtless already grown so heavy that the creatures felt winter approaching and had begun the trek to the north, to warmer seas.

One blizzard was followed by another even more severe. It snowed almost continuously, and it grew colder and colder. None of this improved the morale among the men. Those of weaker character became melancholy, and it was remarkable how often they reported in sick without actually having any real complaint. They became irritable and showed all the typical symptoms of depressed morale.

When the howling snowstorms and the growing masses of ice put a stop to oil processing, there was nothing standing in the way of giving the fellows a few days off; they could then recover from the bitterly hard work and retreat for a little while from the depressing effect of the rough weather.

During particularly bad weather, the flight from the polar climate was so universal that sometimes I was alone on deck with the steersman of the watch for whole days at a time. As good and as bad as it got, the two of us did whatever most had to be done. That was fine as long as the storms prevented work.

Rough dramas

But when the weather abated enough for work to be possible again, then the men had to get going. Sometimes it wasn't at all easy to get them moving again. To the command *"Paa'n igen!"* many men simply didn't react. Among the best men an appeal to their honor still had some effect, but there were fellows among the men who couldn't be brought to reason any other way than by force. That often made for some rather rough drama in the cabins. Without benefit of trial, a laggard who was healthy was hauled out of his bunk, and not carefully, either: this was done with one determined tug. Because such a gent was in no mood to put up with this kind of treatment willingly, it was smart not to give him any opportunity to use his fists or his feet. If he showed even the slightest sign of attacking, he was simply slammed onto the deck. That was simple self-defense; it was the only way to smother any resistance in advance. If such a rough, embittered client was allowed the opportunity to use his fists, there was a chance that a violent fistfight would break out — maybe even a mutiny — and that couldn't be risked under the circumstances. And so the blows that he had to be given hit home, and hard. It was typical of the mentality of these rough chaps that they usually held no grudges after having been fearfully manhandled, but simply recognized defeat and went to work without further protest, their eyes bruised or even swollen shut.

Such dramas made me think of the "hell ships" of earlier times: sailing ships on which the press-ganged members of the crew were driven by cruel officers with the force of fists and seaboots in what was surely an already heavy struggle against the pitiless elements. During these days the *Ross* sometimes seemed quite a bit like a "hell ship," and was often called that too. We certainly went through plenty of tense moments when we feared that the men would take sides on behalf of a shipmate who had been called to order so roughly. But luckily everything kept going well.

The weather made it clear that our departure couldn't be postponed any longer. So the decision was made to leave the Antarctic Ocean. This cheered the men up. High spirits reigned all over the ship, as they always do when a departure is at hand, and I don't think that anyone could have been happier or could have thought of money even if at that moment hundreds of big fat whales had come alongside the ship.

WAS IT by chance that the great freeze-up suddenly began once the decision to leave had been made? In any case, immediately thereafter, on March 7, winter began in deadly earnest.

A medium storm raged. The air was thick with snow and frost smoke, and the ship was stuck solidly in the new ice that had formed since the previous day, even though the engines had been running nonstop all that time to support the anchor. The solid ice stretched out for a ship-length forward of the bow and visibly grew as the wind piled up great masses of slush and snowy ice against it. This tangle of ice solidified immediately into one compact mass as soon as it came up against the solid ice and was compressed by wind and waves.

After several hours the solid ice had already grown several cable-lengths, and the wind and the sea put steady pressure on the ice, pushing the floes over each other, making the ice layer that completely surrounded the ship grow steadily thicker. The ice backed up against the northern wall of the Ice Barrier, behind the ship, and soon Discovery Inlet was covered for half its width with a layer of ice that was on average a meter thick. Luckily, tidal currents and the pounding of the waves prevented the ice from freezing together into one compact whole. In other words, we had the storm to thank for saving us from being immediately frozen in. Then we would have been helpless: the temperature was so low and the seawater solidified so quickly that any attempt to saw the ship out would have been completely pointless.

The freeze-up we had feared was here. Not a moment could be lost now. If the storm died down, the *Ross* would be immediately and irrevocably frozen in and thus be irretrievably lost. In great haste those chase boats that had come in were stuffed with provisions and coal for the return trip to the Ross Sea. On the way there would be no opportunity to provide them with the necessities; we were figuring on unusually raw weather.

Bunkering the boats wasn't pleasant work in the icy storm, since it was more than 20 degrees below zero Celsius, even though the work flew by more easily than usual. On other occasions the little chase boats usually pitched so heavily that a great deal of the coal was lost. But now both the *Ross* and the chase boats were jammed rock-solid in the ice, which made provisioning much easier. We waited impatiently for the two chase boats that were still out, and we noted with concern that the barometer was no longer falling. We needed continued bad weather so that the ice couldn't set completely. When the mercury slowly began to rise and the wind died down, until it only blew hard during squalls, the position of the ship grew precarious. And so the first absent chase boat to appear was greeted with cheers when it tried to come alongside to be bunkered, wrestling with the ice. The plucky

Chase boat in the ice

thing wasn't actually strong enough to break through the ice, so the *Ross* came as close to it as possible, running full speed in reverse and dragging after its anchor. The *Star 1* was actually the most powerful of the chase boats. It had writhed laboriously through twenty miles of heavy new ice in order to reach Discovery Inlet. It had lain in the Bay of Whales during the most recent blizzard along with the *Star 5*. That boat had a weaker engine than the *Star 1* and so had had more trouble working its way through the pack ice. We decided to wait one more day for the latecomer. If it didn't show up, we would have to go looking for it.

The ice piled up in the inlet by the powerful, stormy gusts began to freeze more and more solid and began to grow so heavy that it looked serious for the *Ross*. It was getting to be high time to escape the fast-growing ice and save the ship. Delaying any longer would make the chance of freezing in too great. We knew at this point that the whole bay could freeze shut in less than twenty-four hours so that it would be impossible to get the *Ross* free. It would be safer to wait outside the bay for the return of the *Star 5*. In open water the ice couldn't be as heavy as it was in the bay; for the time being the sea swell would prevent the ice from developing into thick pack-ice.

So we came outside, steaming eastward under and along the Ice Barrier, heading for the remaining chase boat. Under the lee of the glacier the sea was calm enough, and in the afternoon the *Star 5* finally came into view. It hadn't been at all easy for the chase boat to make its way through the hard new ice, and when it was finally fastened alongside the ship, it was clear that its trip from the Bay of Whales to the inlet hadn't been a pleasure cruise. Its entire foreship had become a single formless mass of ice.

The return of the *Star 5* was greeted with cheers. After all, that was the sign to begin the long-awaited return to milder climes! Now all thoughts shifted from the ice and were drawn with irresistible force to the north — to Norway, to Tasmania, to all those held dear, to everything that was lovingly bound up with those thoughts to each man personally.

Never was a chase boat supplied so quickly and with so much gusto with provisions and coal. All five chase boats now came alongside to receive their orders and to have their supplies replenished for the last time. Everything that they could need was amply provided, since it was impossible to guess how the return trip would turn out, and whether the ice would offer much obstruction in our path. In any case, we knew that there was much raw weather to expect at this time of year.

WITH AN EYE on Neptune's evil humors, the *Ross* was made completely seaworthy. Everything on deck was securely fastened, and the ship was ballasted for better steering by filling up several of the aft tanks. A voyage through the seas of the high south in March can't be regarded as child's play. We couldn't neglect anything that could increase the seaworthiness of a ship that had to brave such a journey; of the few ships that had ever been in the Ross Sea, none had ever left so late in the year as the *Ross* did. Bad weather and the steadily thickening pack ice weren't the only reasons why men had always returned to warmer regions much earlier. They also wanted to leave before the midnight sun disappeared. After that happened, the nights grew steadily darker, and navigation through the ice was unusually dangerous, as can well be imagined.

The men on the chase boats were also busy making their crafts as seaworthy as possible for the long, difficult return trip. As soon as the boats were freed from their icy suits of armor with the help of steam and pickaxes, all five of them were secured behind the ship with strong towropes. That was necessary to keep them together; otherwise, the least powerful vessels might hold up the convoy in the ice.

Every day, every hour the ice grew thicker and heavier. Saving time meant preserving safety. Finally, toward noon on March 8, the fleet was ready to sail. It steamed northward, its next destination being Campbell Island, which lies all by itself in the wide, deserted ocean, several hundred miles south of New Zealand. Our intent was to go fishing in the surrounding waters if it looked like the whales were pausing near that island on their northward trek.

Standing guard

Underway along the edge of the pack ice that we expected to find outside the Ross Sea, we would also keep an eye out for whales in order to get some more oil into the tanks. Up until now we had processed about 17,000 barrels of the precious oil, but a full cargo was around 65,000 barrels. So we could really use some more oil.

The wrath of the winter god, which was designed to chase us out of Discovery Inlet, seemed to cool as soon as we raised anchor. In the "Ice Cellar" the storm roared, and it was cold enough to freeze bricks. But as soon as we passed the old weathered iceberg that stood guard in front of the bay, the weather changed completely. A high blue arch of sky vaulted itself over the sun-bedecked world of ice and water, and the ice-covered sea rolled in a long swell. It wasn't cold in the open sea, either: it was only a few degrees below zero, and to us it felt so warm that we couldn't keep our thick winter clothing on. So all of us got out our summer clothes.

It felt strange to see the Ice Barrier slowly disappear out of sight. We had gotten so accustomed to that tremendous glacier that we really weren't focused on the fact that we found ourselves across from the mightiest mass of ice that our earth knows; we had gotten used to thinking of the Barrier only as a constant threat to our safety. Our glances at it had only seldom expressed amazement and awe. Well, awe — yes, but followed by a sense of the danger we faced. When the Barrier slowly sank below the horizon and no longer represented a threat, when it was no more than a long, shining white band that floated from east to west on the retreating horizon, then we could see the enormous glacier with different eyes and other thoughts. We realized that one of the mightiest wonders that nature has to display was disappearing forever behind us.

So it wasn't without sadness that we saw the long expanse of white sink below the horizon. We felt an emptiness, a vague sense of loss. Along with all the dangers and worries that it had brought us, the mighty Ice Barrier had clearly left an indelible impression of its greatness on our souls. Our lives had been made richer by this incalculable discovery. But now that adventure was at an end.

NORTHWARD! To the sun!

The weather was improbably mild when the fleet turned its back on the Ice Barrier. Bright sunshine, a calmly swelling sea, and a good water-sky ensured that the return trip began with morale very high. The ice was light beyond all expectations, so light that it caused no serious hindrance. In fact, on the second day there was no ice to be seen at all, and the weather remained mild. We saw no trace of any whales; not a single *blååst* was spotted. That got us thinking that the whales had already gone north. The penguins that we saw were also leaving in great schools, heading for the ocean. They romped and frolicked like porpoises, speeding northward, shrieking and screaming with glee as they dove up out of the water in graceful arcs. Only spread-out strings of new ice and a few lonely icebergs gave proof that we were in the Antarctic Ocean.

As the latitude decreased, the nights soon lengthened. The darkness also quickly grew deeper now that we were no longer surrounded by a world of snow and ice, which reflect so much light. For the first time in months, we saw the stars flicker in the heavens. It gave us a pleasant feeling of security to see these good old friends winking at us in confidence again.

The darkness did make navigation more dangerous. Even though we could see no pack ice, we did pass by many icebergs of all sizes and shapes. On nights when the sky clouded over, the friendly stars spread no light, and dark squalls rushed low over the water, it would have been irresponsible to just keep on sailing through the night. The ice was difficult to see then, especially the layer of ice that could so easily be mistaken for white-breaking waves in the vague, dusky darkness of the night. So on dark, starless evenings, Captain Larsen kept the engine running, but dead slow, just enough to keep the ship on course and to allow us to maneuver immediately if necessary. When it snowed and nothing was visible, the steam whistle was blown regularly, and after the heavy drone died away, many a sharp ear listened to see whether an iceberg would throw back a weak echo.

Extremely careful navigation was certainly called for, since we were in nearly unknown sailing waters, and the charts for it were still very incomplete. Especially by night one could suddenly catch a surprise in front of the bow in the form of islands or reefs that one wouldn't so easily run into by day. Needless to say, at night this would make for a less-than-pleasant encounter. There was a stiff breeze blowing, with so much swell that any disturbances in the sailing waters would be betrayed by breakers. Still, it was better not to run any risk, since there was no help to be had if the ship met with an accident. The vague shadows of icebergs, which kept looming up out of the darkness only to be swallowed up again just as quickly, constantly reminded us to remain unflaggingly vigilant. Silently we stared at the threatening ghost shapes until they were sucked up again into the night, out of which they had glided into view so unreally and noiselessly.

Our northerly course wasn't the only thing that showed we were headed toward the civilized world again; all sorts of other things indicated that as well. On Sundays, if we weren't working, the *Ross* looked like one big laundry. Everyone was busy with their kits, which needed cleaning very badly. Over the past few months there hadn't been time for this, and given the unprecedented state of filth into which the ship had fallen, there had been practically no point in it.

Many a long beard and much long hair, which in the cold the men had gladly let go wild, fell victim to the ship's Figaro. Attempts at civilization of this sort were part and parcel of nights off. We were so used to the luxuriant locks and patriarchal beards that we sometimes didn't recognize one of our own who had been stripped of such adornments. It led to much hilarity when suddenly a strange man appeared on deck.

At this point we saw a few whales, but we left the animals in peace. It would have been impossible to process the animals on the high seas, and even less could we think of towing them to Campbell Island. It would take too long, and the bad weather that doubtless awaited us also ruled it out in advance.

There was no doubt that raw weather lay in the offing. A long swell out of the northwest, which was at first scarcely noticeable, was already running higher. It gave us trouble with our towing. The lines kept breaking and forced us to travel more slowly. Finally we let loose the *Star 1*, which was strong enough to be able to follow us. That would allow us to maintain a faster rate of travel.

The cloud formations also pointed to a change in weather. The sunsets were glorious, the kind of great and majestic occurrences that one can admire only at sea or in the desert. The sky was covered with dark, threatening nimbus clouds that colored the rolling waves almost black. Fiery beams of light twisted between the low, driving masses of cloud and the dark, swelling horizon. Blood-red tongues of light shot up out of the turbulent waves, and the edges of the thickly massed clouds gleamed like red copper. The scene was so impressively beautiful that even the most sober of us kept looking at it, enthralled. But the fierce strip of light above the horizon pleased us less. It looked suspiciously like iceblink. That meant there would be pack ice ahead; we could scarcely expect anything different.

At night, however, the wind blew the clouds away, and then the stars looked down on us again like trusted old friends. The jewels of the Southern Cross, which in the tropics we could see for only a part of the night, sparkled with all their beauty in the zenith. The Scorpion with its long, curled tail and the Ship Argo with Canopus flickered on the velvety black night sky. Boötes stood low in the east, while in the north the Great Lion appeared with Regulus, and in the west Procyon shone in the constellation of the Little Dog. More to the south shone Sirius, the leader of the starry lords. Jupiter stood as calm and still as a distant light that had been hung high up on the southeastern vault of the sky. The atmosphere was clear enough that we could see a large part of the Milky Way and most of the constellations, such various signs of the Zodiac as Cancer, Leo, Virgo with Spica, Libra, and Sagittarius.[1] It did us good to see all those old friends again, which so often had been our only companions on lonely nocturnal trips in the mountains or at sea.

It was too bad that the moon didn't also appear in the roll call; we would have loved to enjoy a moonlit night on the pack ice.

Naturally all sorts of conjectures were made about the pack ice that we were sure we would encounter. But four days after our flight from Discovery

1. The Dutch words for these constellations are *De Kreeft* ("The Lobster"), *De Leeuw* ("The Lion"), *De Maagd* ("The Maiden"), *De Weegschaal* ("The Balance"), and *De Schutter* ("The Archer"). The Dutch word for the Zodiac itself is *De Dierenriem,* meaning "The Belt [or Band] of Creatures."

Inlet, no more ice floated on the gray waves, and not a single iceberg interrupted the straight line of the horizon. A faint iceblink did appear on the port side, but it could well have been attributed to the solid ice that covered South Victoria Land. Even if it was caused by sea ice, our course ran well free of it. Five days after our departure, at least thirty soot-gray albatrosses hovered over the ship, a sure sign that there wasn't much pack ice. The albatrosses are birds of the open sea and would never fly over large expanses of thick ice. Other heralds of the open water were Cape doves — whole flocks of them — and silver-gray petrels. The birds seemed to seek out the ship; they often skimmed overhead.

That portended stormy weather. And indeed, shortly thereafter, just after a wonderfully beautiful but wild sunset, a true snowstorm began to rage. It quickly swept the sea up high so that the *Ross* began to labor hard, and we worried about the towed chase boats. The towropes kept breaking, and it was far from easy work to keep getting out new ropes in the dark in such heavy seas. Every sailor understands that in cases like this you have to cuss to keep up your morale.

Although the towed chase boats helped to the best of their ability, with their engines on full power, eventually we couldn't hang on to them. One by one they broke loose, and the weather grew so bad that it became too dangerous to continually bring out new ropes. Fortunately, four of the five chase boats were seaworthy enough to be able to save themselves. So we let them slip away and follow the mother ship under their own steam. The least powerful one, which would have been left helplessly behind and would have held up the whole flotilla, was fastened with more and sturdier ropes so that it had no chance of bolting.

The crew and the boat really had to undergo rough treatment. Against the rhythm of their own violent movements they were being dragged through heavy seas by force. It was a good thing that they were so seaworthy. We could see how they were more under water than above it; on that boat it was more than life-threatening to be on deck. What made things worse was that the *Ross* was heaving so violently that it was difficult to steer. The helmsman was forced to steer by the compass because of the foul weather. Things were already wild because of the ship's heavy rolling, and they were made even worse by the immediate vicinity of the magnetic pole, so that the horizontal directional power of the compass was very weak. On the dogwatch the storm reached its peak, and we had to cut the towropes to the chase boat in order to save the vessel and its crew. It must have been a relief for the men, since the boat had been more like a submarine than a sailing ship. Once free in its movements, it didn't take on nearly as much water, and it stopped being in continual danger of seeing its whole topside get slammed away. The *Ross* itself was taking on a lot of water; huge green sea surges swept overhead, and everything was covered with a thick crust of mushy, salty ice. In fact, wind and sea were so turbulent that both the *Ross* and the chase boats were forced to heave to for two watches until the weather had calmed down.

WE FOUND ourselves off Cape Adare. We had reached a latitude where we had expected pack ice, but there was none to be seen. There were a number of wildly dancing icebergs — or rather, the remains thereof: large, foam-spattered clumps of ice, swiped smooth by the sea, that capsized with thunderous force.

No wonder there was no sign of pack ice. The sea ice that may have formed in much calmer weather was naturally destroyed by the turbulent seas. When we saw how the icebergs were battered by the bellowing seas, we understood that these massive giants couldn't offer resistance for long. It wasn't primarily the warmth of the sun that affected the bergs, but rather the ceaseless and constantly fierce pummeling of the waves.

What remains of an iceberg

After a day the chaotic violence of the storm had exhausted the powers of the blizzard. The storm turned into a moderate southern cold front, the sea improved quickly, and it began to freeze hard.

We had now arrived at a latitude at which we could expect to find the sea sown with icebergs, and extra posts were put on lookout. This was no superfluous luxury, as soon became apparent. In every wind direction the icebergs seemed to shoot up out of the waves like weeds, and at night great vigilance was imperative. If the drift of an iceberg crossed our course, then we gave a couple of blasts on the steam whistle to alert the chase boats to the approaching danger. On the tall mother ship we saw the bergs earlier than they did on the much lower-lying chase boats.

The snowstorm had purified the air. Wind and sea came to repose again, but it froze hard with the wind coming straight out of the south. We saw whole schools of penguins traveling north at great speed and countless whales that were headed in the same direction. All living beings fled, just as we did, from the fearful polar winter, seeking less fierce climates so as not to perish, lashed into King Frost's icy suit of armor. At the latitudes where we had struggled through the ice with such difficulty on the trip out, there was now not a single floe to be seen, nor was there any sign of iceblink. All around us a dark, unmistakable water-sky stood above the horizon. There was no pack ice, as the many albatrosses that hovered over the ship also assured us.

The true polar region lay behind us!

CHAPTER TWENTY-FOUR

The Lives and Loves of Penguins

Molting King penguins

It would be ungracious to leave the polar regions without taking leave of our friends the penguins, those comical birds who in fact are the only true inhabitants of those wild, icy domains. It is only fair to dedicate a chapter to them in order to sketch some of the curious peculiarities of the lives of these true polar dwellers.

So far as we know, penguins are found only in the Southern Hemisphere. There are more than ten different species, two of which are found only in the Antarctic Ocean. The birds absolutely cannot thrive in warm areas. The Adélie and emperor penguins only feel good in the middle of snow and ice. (The penguins one sees in the European zoos belong to other species that are born in more temperate climates.)

I've already described our first meeting with emperor penguins in the Bay of Whales. These birds are rare, unlike the other species, which live cozily together in colonies of tens of thousands. It's no wonder that the fine, princely emperors, which grow to be 1¼ meters [nearly four feet] tall, are so scarce. Driven by a still-inexplicable instinct, these remarkable creatures breed in the middle of the long, icy polar night, when it is wretchedly frozen. And for this purpose they do not, like the other penguin species, search for an area where the climate is milder; they stay in the place where they themselves were born, where their whole lives play themselves out: the heart of the polar region. It is incomprehensible that the species still exists when one thinks about the circumstances under which the birds breed: during the long, somber polar night, when it is pitch dark for months on end, and the most terrible snowstorms rage, which no other living creatures are able to survive. The temperature can sometimes sink to eighty degrees below zero — as far below zero as in Java, on average, it is above zero![1]

Maybe you think that the penguins build ingenious nests that effectively protect them against the more than harsh climate, but nothing could be farther from the truth. In all of the endless polar region, there is no material to be found out of which a proper nest could be made. So the birds live and breed on the bare snow without the least bit of covering. Their only protection consists of the layer of snow that the snowstorms spread out over them. This shelters them from the deadly, biting cold of the blizzards, in which no life is possible.

The single egg that the female emperor penguin lays can't be hatched in the normal way — with her lying on top of it. Since the egg would be lying on the ice, it would quickly freeze. So the mother broods while remaining in a standing position. The precious egg is concealed in a downy fold of hide and rests on the mother's feet.

The struggle to survive is indeed unusually difficult for these extraordinary birds. In the incomparably harsh climate, in which only the most hardened men can overwinter, and then only with the help of numerous resources, the females sit resignedly brooding as if it were the most ordinary thing in the world. It may seem strange, but the best thing that one could wish for emperor penguins is an abundant snowfall and many snowstorms. The temperature always rises considerably during a blizzard, and when a

---

1. Presumably Van der Does is speaking in terms of Fahrenheit temperatures: 80 degrees below zero is -80° F, a standard Antarctic temperature, while 80° F is a standard temperature for Java.

thick layer of snow covers the animals, they are warmly blanketed, protected against the fierce wind. These aids notwithstanding, the enormous endurance of the emperors is truly amazing.

The almost unheard-of circumstances under which these penguins breed are the reason that they're so scarce. A large percentage of the young birds must inevitably succumb to the merciless cold, and doubtless many eggs freeze. Even if it doesn't freeze more than forty degrees below zero, if the mother leaves her egg for even an instant, it freezes on the spot.

Despite these all-but-insurmountable difficulties, the female penguins display an unusually strongly developed maternal instinct. Dr. Wilson from Scott's expedition saw some hens nurturing egg-shaped pieces of ice in their belly folds. These were hens who had lost their eggs, and the poor creatures were trying to hatch these pieces of ice. In the deep darkness of the polar night, Wilson first mistook these grubby ice balls for real eggs. Only when he picked up one that a bird had let fall did he realize his mistake.

It is understandable that not all the birds who begin to brood also come to know the joy of motherhood; many hens remain childless. In their vehement longing for a child, they let nothing stand in their way. They'll even try to steal a youngster from its mother. They often fight life-and-death battles in an attempt to seize one. If an imprudent mother leaves her downy offspring unattended for just a moment, the childless hens, who wait for just such an opportunity, descend on it. Then they all try to take possession of the de-

The fight over the chick

fenseless youngster, and not infrequently it happens that the poor chick is torn to pieces by the vicious hens, who in their covetousness pull and jerk as hard as they can from all sides.

Our scientists thought that the desire for preservation of the species led the emperor penguins to brood in the coldest season of the year. That seems absurd at first, but on second thought it makes sense: it's the only way the birds have to ensure that the chicks will be old enough and large enough toward the end of the short polar summer to look after themselves. The young molt then, and after they've exchanged their woolly down coverings for complete polar outfits, they can brave the coming winter successfully.

It is really incomprehensible why these birds don't seek a more bearable climate, one that would present fewer dangers to their species. One has to assume that the creatures are obeying an ancient instinct when they so steadfastly remain true to the same breeding-grounds where their distant ancestors came into the world, in long-vanished centuries, when Antarctica was not yet completely covered by glaciers, and the land could still support animal life. The ever-advancing glaciers, which finally covered the land completely, drove the birds out ahead of them, until they were finally forced to put up with the sea ice as a breeding ground. During very harsh winters, when the solid ice extends for miles out into the sea, the creatures must often have a rough go of it. Then the males must have to make frequent long trips over the sea ice to reach the open water to get food for their families. Anyone who knows the terrors of a polar blizzard understands what that means and has to be amazed at the nearly unparalleled stamina that the animals display.

THE EMPEROR penguins are admirable aristocrats, always dignified and calm, their bearing like that of self-assured patricians.

The Adélie penguins represent a wholly different type: they're more middle-class and jovial. They are happy, lovable creatures; we regarded them as friends from the moment we first encountered them in the pack ice. These humorous birds drew many a hearty laugh from us, especially in circumstances in which we really needed a bit of cheer.

As soon as we saw the first penguins, their comical manners and boundless curiosity attracted our attention. The interest was mutual, and we always welcomed the funny birds when they came to visit and curiously inspect the ship.

It didn't surprise me when the professor, after having studied the life of the busy creatures for hours, assured me that he would gladly make another trip to the polar regions just for the penguins. One really doesn't tire of observing their almost human behavior. One is inclined to suppose that creatures enduring such a merciless climate would be bowed down under the pressure of their difficult living conditions, but that simply isn't the case. They're a happy tribe, not in the least bothered by the cold, which for them is as natural and necessary as warmth is for animals that are at home in the tropics. You just have to see how the chicks enjoy their young life!

When we set up the depot on the sea ice in the Bay of Whales, the penguins quickly came waggling up from all sides, taking stock of the strange beings in amazement, but remaining calm for the time being. Later on, the half-grown chicks joined the group and didn't even try to disguise their curiosity.

Screeching from nervousness, tripping over their little feet in their haste, they came out holding their breath, just like street urchins when there's "something to do" in the neighborhood. They gestured excitedly, calling out observations and remarks to each other, and ran alongside the sledge, beside themselves with excitement. No wonder; they had never seen something so unusual. Strange things had been happening in the Bay of Whales recently. Life was full of surprises, but this topped them all. These strange new beings were evidently afraid of water. Unbelievable! Where did they get their food from, then? All the animals they knew lived in the sea, but these queer creatures wouldn't even think of leaping into the water the way all the birds and seals did.

On the previous day, they had stood looking amazed at some Weddell seals that were getting up out of the water and on to the ice with great difficulty. They had secretly laughed at the clumsy creatures. Why didn't those fat lumps of blubber spring up like jacks-in-the-box, the way they themselves did, just like that — hop! — with a plop on top of the ice? They had even demonstrated the maneuver for the dumb seals a couple of times, but the simpletons just grunted and sighed and kept plodding and spluttering in their own silly way. The Weddell seals meant the penguins no harm, so there was no need to call out to mother if one of the seals blew against a young penguin or roared loudly if a penguin chick that was too lazy to step aside wandered calmly with its pattering feet over the seal's fat, round body.

The chicks had also seen a sea leopard once. They remembered very well how violently upset their mothers became when they saw the predator in the distance. All the chicks were just happily playing tag, a whole gang of them, and the game was going just swell. Madly they chased each other underwater, and when one chick was almost caught, he dove right up — bang! — and shot a bit above the water. That was always terribly funny to us, because sometimes the chick landed right on the ice, and if he plunked back into the water, he had to hustle to get away before he got nabbed. The chicks also swam in a row behind each other, now and then diving up and down in unison. The best thing was the frightful shriek that they sometimes let out all at once when they were flying in an arc through the air.

It was at a time like that, when their game was in full swing and they were having the most fun, that one of the gruesome leopards came to disturb their play. The mothers had screamed with fright and had fled onto the ice as quick as could be, meanwhile calling to their children to get out of the water — quick, quick. Greatly upset, the chicks hurried after their mothers. Once up on the solid ice, they still had to take a quick look around. But then they were even more frightened, so scared that they couldn't budge because their feet were quivering so violently. They saw a large, spotted seal with a long, lean body swimming frightfully fast after them. The youngest penguin chick could only barely escape the monster. At the same instant that the little one sprang up on the ice, the bandit snapped at it. The gleaming tusks snapped together right behind the penguin's stiff tail. As the chicks thought about it again later, they started to quiver with fear, so fiercely had the eyes of the leopard seal glittered.

The orcas, the great killer whales, knew about the young penguins too, but the penguins weren't so terribly afraid of them. Orcas do have tremendous mouths full of teeth, but they're so big that they can't twist and turn nearly as fast as penguins can, and so are easy to evade. Things only get dangerous if a penguin tries to escape the deathly jaws by swimming hard, because an orca swims much faster.

"If there are orcas in the area," the penguin-hens always impress upon their children, "it's wise to climb as fast as possible onto a thick ice floe, and get as far away as possible from the water." If a penguin stays on the edge of a floe, then he's sure to be snapped off by a hungry killer. One time a flock of young penguins saw how the baby of a Ross Sea seal, playing unsuspectingly at the edge of a floe, was devoured by an orca.

The chicks were romping in an open channel when they suddenly saw a big, black fin come up right by the floe where the young seal lay playing. Quickly they fled up onto the ice, and they called to the baby seal to get a move on, but the playful thing paid no attention. Sneezing and snuffling with pleasure, the little one slid over and over again into the water, while his mother lay peacefully sleeping a little ways off. When he dove underwater with a splash, he quickly scrabbled back up onto the floe, repeating the same game over and over until he thought of a new one. For a change he decided to slide into the water in reverse, so he crept clumsily backwards. When his little tail stuck out over the ice, and its little owner peeked around a moment to see if the coast was clear, he gave a dreadful shriek and immediately disappeared. The orca had noticed the little one playing and had swallowed him up. The penguins, who stood a little farther off shivering with fear, had clearly seen the wide mouth with its two rows of glistening teeth. Brrr . . . !!

Earlier on, the penguin mothers had gravely warned their children about the skua gulls that almost always hovered above the penguin colonies, but now the chicks were already so big and strong that they didn't have to be afraid of the feathered freebooters anymore. The skuas looked mostly for young chicks and for eggs.

The penguins knew precisely which creatures lived in the water, ice, and air of their birthplace, but humans, those creatures walking in front of the sledges over the ice, were completely foreign to them. They could never run out of things to say about them. They found humans to be very remarkable creatures, and with their natural curiosity they noticed all sorts of interesting characteristics of these beings that were new to them. Their clever eyes just about popped out of their heads!

The unusual visitors did incomprehensible things, but the penguins agreed that the strangers must also be penguins: after all, they walked upright on two feet! But oh, were they ever dirty and grimy! Their front side was just as dark as their back side. Surely they had crawled around the breeding grounds on their bellies, because who had ever seen a penguin without a white breast?

A fight threatened to break out over the question of whether these rare penguins could catch fish, since they had no beaks at all, and their faces were as flat as mussels. "Oh, look!" they called to each other, surprised. "That first one is just like a whale blowing — smoke is coming out of his head!" "Do you hear what crazy sounds they're making?" one asked, amazed. These are the sorts of comments that the penguins must have made to each other when they saw the sailors smoking and talking while they walked in front of the sledges. What the inhabitants of the Bay of Whales must have wholeheart-

edly agreed on, though, was that these were queer ducks, these huge penguins that had suddenly fallen out of the sky.

The peculiar ceremony with which humans are received in a penguin
colony is something I've already described in a previous chapter. In every
penguin city that we visited, we were greeted in nearly the same way and with
the same courtesies, from which we got the strong impression that the com-
munal life of penguins has reached a fairly high level of development. Over
and over again we were struck anew by how human the behaviors of these
birds were, and that's why it was a pleasure to observe their private lives from
nearby. The similarity always came strongly to the fore.

Once the official welcome was over, the animals took little more notice
of the strange visitors, as long as we behaved ourselves and didn't disturb the
public peace. Then we could study the life and work of the penguin city unhindered. The brooding hens and the mothers with children were usually
busy enough caring for their progeny while also keeping a watchful eye on
the thieving skua gulls, who, hoping to espy a tender morsel, circled above
the colonies. From bitter experience the birds had learned that a single instant of inattention provided opportunity enough for one of those drab-
colored thieves to drop like a stone onto a nest and then disappear quick as
lightning with a stolen egg or chick in its beak.

The lords of creation usually stood in little groups discussing things,
underlining their arguments with sparing gestures. When the hungry youngsters began to call loudly for food, the fathers of the house were sent by the
wives to get lunch. Dutiful heads of the household naturally didn't need to be
urged on, but there were also those who were less energetic and had no desire
to run errands; they wanted to nap a little longer. The wife of such a laggard
would get up in front of her brood and, in blunt language, point the slothful
spouse in the direction of his neglected fatherly duties. She shook the lazy-
bones awake with sharp pecks of her beak and shoved him quickly onto the
street, where he, mumbling under his breath, trudged onto the path that led
to the sea and trotted away.

Among penguins, just as among people, there are great differences in
temperament. Some are lively by nature and stand up for themselves,[2] while

---

2. Here Van der Does expresses the meaning of "standing up for yourself" with the
charming Dutch phrase *laten zich de kaas niet van het brood eten*: "not letting anyone eat the
cheese off your bread."

others who are more good-natured and trusting are taken advantage of by the sharper ones. So, for example, in a colony of Adélie penguins there was a father of the house who cared for his family very well. He and his wife, a real drudge, were more than busy with their two fast-growing sprouts. Their task was truly not a simple one. The youngsters had already grown so large that the careful mother couldn't hold them under her wings anymore, and the chicks, who wanted to go out into the wide world, began to chafe under the tender care of their parents. They were tremendous fidgets, even though they couldn't even walk very well yet, and the parents had their feathers full making sure that the rascals didn't run out into the street. It was an almost hopeless situation. Sometimes the harried mother in her despair simply sat on her offspring, with her feet on their backs. But even that didn't help; the vivacious chicks kept wriggling out from under her and waggling out of the nest, stumbling over the ring of loose stones that formed their dwelling. The father stood assessing the situation for a while; with stooping shoulders and a thoughtful look he stood pondering what changes might be made. Finally he shifted in his indecisive stance; he appeared to have come up with something. Yes, indeed, that was it. The nest was too small! Why hadn't he noticed that before? Thoughtfully, like a man who goes about bent under the weight of heavy cares, he walked away to implement his plans.

Another penguin, unnoticed by the care-worn parents all this time, had stood nearby very unobtrusively, as if deep in meditation. But when the father left, he seemed to come suddenly awake. And while the mother was busy washing the feet of one of her muddy youngsters, the rascal quickly stole a stone away from the nest. The hen was so busy that she didn't notice this, and the thief walked away with his booty with an air of having done nothing wrong. He lay the stolen stone quite calmly by his own nest, and then came with an innocent face to stand again, in apparent thoughtfulness, near the mother with the unruly children.

A bit later the father came back with a nice new stone that he had found. With a certain pride he showed his find to his wife, who nodded approvingly, whereupon he added the stone to the nest with a great deal of fuss. He rearranged all the stones repeatedly, each time waggling a distance away, then cocking his head and appraising his work critically. Finally he was satisfied. Then he muttered a short greeting to his wife and went away to get more stones.

Scarcely had he turned around when the thief, who had appeared motionless, stepped closer. He was just about to take possession of another stone when the father turned around. Apparently he had had second thoughts and wanted to rearrange the stones again. He was lost in thought and so paid no attention to the thief, who kept standing in the same position without moving a fin, his beak almost on top of the stones, as if he were short-sighted and attentively admiring the quality of the construction. He took his impudence so far as to address the man of the house. His chatter probably meant something like, "Well, well, neighbor, aren't you quite the clever handyman!"

The father, however, was much too busy to waste his time with chitchat and muttered, "Yeah, yeah, but I'm not happy with it." Then he turned around and trotted off, looking for more building materials for his house. Scarcely had he lifted his heels when the thief quickly plucked up another stone and stepped away, his face as innocent as a lamb's.

It's doubtful that the honest house-husband ever succeeded in fully expanding his home, but meanwhile the crafty stone-thief easily made a nice nest in a short period of time.

As SPRING comes to penguin land, there's life in the colonies. The temperature isn't very springlike to our way of thinking, and there are no budding trees, singing birds, or opening blossoms to evoke a springtime mood, but the penguins think otherwise. To these creatures it is enough that the sun is again visible and their land of snow is lighted; this puts them in a happy mood again.

The coming of spring has the same effect on penguins that it has on all living creatures elsewhere and anywhere. Their blood races faster, and they live out their simple romances. The young cocks then court the hens, and *Amor* abounds. But this is a peace-loving, mild-mannered folk; all this courtship seldom gives rise to fights of amorous envy, which are normal occurrences among so many animal species. It's an exception if two cocks get into trouble with each other over a female. It happens only occasionally, when the whole penguin city is in an uproar. That's when Cupid seems to be powerfully at work, busy shooting arrows in the breeding grounds. Then the penguins' blood rises to their heads, and a general fracas arises that inevitably spills over into tussles.

When the spring air has brought the young, marriage-hungry birds into a state of confusion, they sometimes engage in a peculiar custom. Stand-

ing up straight, they stretch their beaks up, wave their fins, and make soft, humming sounds. One gets the strong impression that the birds are warbling romantic songs of spring and love in an ardent tone. The ecstatic state produced by this singing is evidently very contagious. As soon as one of them starts crooning this spring song, the others fall in immediately, and soon the whole of penguin youth stands singing in chorus, their bodies swaying softly to and fro, their fins waving.

We also saw young pairs enveloped in rapture in the same way. They looked just like betrothed couples in joyous ecstasy over their newfound bliss. But mated and brooding hens sometimes behaved this way too, and many males and females also crooned together, so it was difficult to determine what this curious custom really meant. But apparently it was a behavior that had some relationship to mating, since it happened only during the breeding season.

Duet

Toward the end of the mating season, when most of the young hens had set up their nests or even sat brooding already, there were always a number of young ladies on whom no young penguin lad's eye had yet fallen with favor. These passed-over maidens stood somewhat forlorn and alone next to abandoned nests or hollows that they had made in the hope that a house of their own might still come of it. Quiet and resigned, they stood waiting for their knights to turn up, ready to take them from thenceforth for better or for worse.

Penguins are more or less shy in their love-play; as a rule the cocks don't play the impetuous Don Juan. When a penguin youth meets a hen who manages to charm him, he makes a formal request for her heart and hand. The ceremonies that go along with this request are of an unmistakably symbolic nature, and the whole formality is touchingly naive and thus very human. So it's hard to fathom that this is an animal, since it seems to perform in such an apparently conscious manner. If a future penguin-bridegroom has found the bride of his choice, then he doesn't begin by declaring his love to her in glowing language — he wouldn't think of such a thing. Instead, he expresses his feelings in the form of a symbolic gesture, a deed that is far more convincing than a stream of pretty words. Immediately he takes his hands out of his pockets and sets to work to convince his intended that he is serious.

He goes looking somewhere for a stone to offer his chosen one as proof that his intentions are honorable. If after much deliberation he finally finds a stone that seems to him to express his feelings as fully as possible, then he plucks up his courage to take the stone in his beak to go offer it to "her." First, however, he subjects his outfit to a thorough inspection and takes care that his appearance can do no harm to the results of his efforts. Usually the penguins look shabby, their white-and-black costumes hanging on their bodies like cheap, off-the-rack suits. But for important occasions this changes quickly. Then their bearing becomes lively, and the sloppily worn uniforms seem to be transformed by a stroke of magic into something out of a first-rate men's fashion magazine. Then all the penguin gentlemen are immaculately clothed, with wide, smooth, starched shirts.

When a young penguin is suitably attired and is bearing the stone he's picked out, he goes to ask for the hand of his chosen one. Arriving at the fair one, he lays the stone down at her feet and waits to see how she reacts to it; the decision appears to lie completely with her. If she accepts the stone, then the worshiper is received graciously. The wedding ceremony is thereby completed, and without further ado the pair begins to build their nest, whose first stone has been laid down as the marriage proposal. Of course, it can just as well happen that the penguin lass doesn't harbor the same feelings for him as he does for her. The unappreciated knight then droops away reluctantly.

It is wonderful to experience such events in the lives of the penguins from close at hand, and to see how differently individual penguins react to the same event, depending on their nature and temperament. The response to a marriage proposal can be quite varied. We saw both bold and shy lads among the penguins, as well as both free and timid lasses.

For instance, we saw an audacious young fellow who took the whole matter rather lightly. He came diving up out of the sea suddenly, sprang onto

The proposal

the ice, quickly shook the water off himself, and then stepped right into a group of waiting maidens. He walked calmly around the first one, giving her a critical glance from top to bottom. Apparently she didn't please him, and the young charmer, who hadn't even taken the trouble to bring a stone along for his future bride, gave the same once-over to at least ten more young ladies, one after the other. Some took no notice whatsoever of the self-assured fellow; others looked at him with suspicious glances; one was disappointed and visibly upset that she had been treated so rudely.

The spoiled Don Juan, who was carefully weighing the charms of various females with his eyes, was apparently unable to choose, and kept walking carelessly until he suddenly stood in front of a penguin beauty whose charms seemed to destroy his cynicism with one blow. He was so struck by her that he kept standing there dumbfounded and staring at her in undisguised amazement. His surprise was equally measureless when the young lady considered his glowing glances worthy of no attention. That had never happened to him before. She must have become a little bashful, he thought. Then let's try it in the traditional way! He picked up the first stone he saw lying there and laid it right in front of her. Still, the maiden clearly felt nothing for the attentions of the charmer, who on the whole she seemed not even to notice. She considered him unworthy of a glance and turned her head away with a contemptuous gesture. At this point Don Juan realized that he had been jilted. He was furious, apparently taking her rejection as an insult. With an angry glance he called out "Kraak!" at the recalcitrant beauty. It was surely no endearment that he snarled at her. With hasty steps he went on to the next potential bride, now having evidently decided that all this nonsense had to stop.

The lady to whom he now offered his favors was perhaps frightened by his ungallant behavior toward her neighbor-lady; she probably also didn't set much store by this young gasbag. At any rate, she didn't wish to take any notice of the stone that he lay at her feet with a flattering "Kraak!" That might have been because he had simply taken the stone from the nest that she herself stood guarding. It was understandable that she expected the man who desired her as his bride to show good faith by at least taking the trouble to look for a stone himself. But the ladykiller wasn't about to let himself be sent away just like that. He took another stone — again from the chosen one's nest — looked her in the eyes, and called "Kraak!" again, louder and more urgently than the first time. This little game played itself out another five or six times as the incensed lover tried to attract her attention with increasingly emphatic screeches, all without success. The young lady refused to notice him and remained calmly looking in another direction.

That made the spoiled young fellow completely enraged. With a hasty gesture he picked up yet another stone, threw this one down with the others at her feet, seized her by the neck, and pushed her beak into the stones that he had offered her. Your love or your life, he seemed to be saying. The frightened

Jilted

A happy marriage

maiden was apparently given no choice. She seemed to resign herself to the inevitable, and together they began to arrange the stones for the nest.

There are also penguin ladies who don't let themselves get caught off guard like that. We saw one such young lady who must have been Xanthippe's older sister.[3] She snapped at a suitor who didn't appeal to her, and when the ardent young chap didn't cease and desist but kept on with his attentions undaunted, she actually attacked him like a real hell-cat. It was touching to see how the battered lover tried to appease her with loving words and tender gestures. He actually managed to calm her down, flattering her and voicing his affections until the little vixen sat meekly and let the persistent suitor go on. Did he manage to lead her to the altar? We shook our heads over that one.

It was interesting to observe such love stories and to watch how varied the penguins were by nature and temperament. It wasn't only courtships that played out before our eyes; we also witnessed charming, homey scenes.

Close to the penguin nest where the thief had come stealing stones there lived a newlywed couple that was definitely happy, to judge by the behavior that we saw. The young female sat still, already brooding. Ha — there

3. Here Van der Does uses another charming Dutch phrase: *die beslist voor Xantippe uit het ei was gekropen:* "who certainly crawled out of the egg ahead of Xanthippe." (Xanthippe was the wife of Socrates; her reputation for ill temper is such that her name has come to stand for any shrewish woman.)

came the young spouse. He toddled closer with rapid steps, and before he reached the nest he muttered a long story with tender, murmuring throat noises, and she greeted him in the same loving manner. Softly cooing, he took her beak in his very carefully: the welcome-home kiss. Then the new husband stood right next to his wife, and with purring sounds they said all sorts of lovely things to each other. It was unmistakable that the birds loved each other, and to make the correspondence to a loving human couple complete, they even embraced each other with their fins. Finally they both went into rapture over all the sweet things that they were whispering to each other. Visibly moved, the cock made some deep bows before his companion. He gargled in his throat and shuddered from emotion. Then he stretched his neck and, still gargling, turned his head back and forth. Immediately his mate joined him; ecstatically they sang together of their unwavering love.

After a while they both returned to sober reality, and the proud husband began to discourse loudly. He seemed to be attempting to convince his wife that she needed to take a rest. The careful wife wouldn't hear of it; she was oh-so-fearful of trusting the two precious eggs to the care of her partner. Men are always so hopelessly clumsy in such matters!

Then the crafty husband resorted to a trick. He so wanted to see the sweet little eggies once again. Could he? Just for a moment. Yes, that would be all right, said his wife, but not for too long — otherwise the dear love-pledges would get cold. Carefully the hen stood up, and together they stood looking thoughtfully at their treasure. Their dedication was moving to behold. Now that lovely wife was standing anyway, father really would like to take care of the eggs for a while to give his consort the chance to go out for a breath of fresh air. But lovely wife wasn't at all sure about this, and it cost many more flattering words to convince her. Finally she gave in, even though it was with undisguised displeasure, and she kept standing there, watching how her husband lovingly arranged the light-green eggs and carefully sank down on them. Only when she had convinced herself that everything was in order did the young wife take her leave — after first ensuring once again that her spouse took it to heart above all to watch out for the thieving skuas. That very same morning an egg had been stolen from the matron who lived yonder in the oil barrel that had washed ashore! So the young wife stepped out to the sea just to grab a bite of shrimp, but she kept looking back anxiously to the nest, where her husband devoted himself to his task very seriously.

The young wife had good reason to be concerned, as we soon saw when our attention was drawn by a commotion in another part of the penguin city.

On our way there, we witnessed a bold street thief. Behind us we heard sudden, excited penguin squawking, and as we turned around we saw a skua gull with an egg in its beak flying away, with the furious penguins screeching after it. The desperate mother screeched at it as she stretched up on her toes and made fruitless attempts at flying. She wanted to go after the brazen thief and snatch back her most precious possession from the miscreant.

The skua soon disappeared from sight, and the robbed penguin sat still, as if stunned, protecting her one remaining egg, while her neighbors, gesticulating wildly, stood around discussing the event. To soften the sorrow of the grieving mother, we gave her one of the eggs that we had collected in the interests of science — that we had snatched exactly as the skua had done. We invoked the need to do scientific research, but the skua would have considered its empty belly a much more effective excuse.

The quarreling farther on turned out to be a normal neighborhood brawl: two penguin matrons had come to blows. Their nests lay quite close to each other, and therein probably lay the source of their differences. An overly close contact easily leads to discord. Without standing up from the eggs they were protecting, they slashed at each other with their beaks so that feathers flew about and blood dripped from their battered heads. Finally the one grabbed hold of the other's tongue and held on tight, surely to punish her for all the ugly things that she had said with it. The spouses of the ladies had meanwhile also joined the battle and fought merrily all on their own. They had grabbed each other firmly by the neck feathers and were raining blows

The grieving mother

on each other's ears with their hard fins; they boxed each other around so fast that we couldn't even follow their movements. We separated the champions, but they were so eager to do battle that, forgetting their own disagreement, they fell blindly on us, the blows clattering on our seaboots. Finally they noticed that they had mistaken their man. Dazed, they looked up at us, called out a disdainful "Kraak!" and waggled off reluctantly, confused.

So you can see that the lives and loves of penguins are as full of variety as ours are, and that the relationships among these birds bear a remarkable likeness to those of humans. Their behavior displays a striking human element, so that one is inclined to ascribe to them almost human reason. That is, of course, incorrect. And yet the similarity to humans is in many respects unmistakable. That's what so powerfully attracts our interest in these creatures and makes it difficult for me to resist the temptation to tell many more interesting tales from the lives of penguins. But the scope of this book compels me to restrict myself!

CHAPTER TWENTY-FIVE

The Island of the Sea Lions

Sea lion

—◦◦◦—

The whole trip home was stormy. One really couldn't expect anything
else in the region of the "Shrieking Sixties," the seas that lie between 60°
and 70° S latitude. As the name implies, they don't exactly enjoy a favorable
reputation among seamen.

The "Shrieking Sixties" are worthy sisters of the "Roaring Forties," and they did their best to deserve that name.[1] Day and night, ceaseless snow, hail, and rainstorms screamed and moaned over the ship and whipped up huge, roaring mountains over the wide, dark surface of the water. For about fourteen days in a row the *Ross* and the chase boats wrestled with the wrathful ocean, over which tremendous surging waves constantly rolled forward, bellowing. The giant, white-capped breakers broke against the ship with turbulent speed, crashing down with thunderous force and smashing tons of ice-cold water overhead.

The chase boats had especially rough going during this siege. The wild waves often rolled over them from stem to stern if the vessels weren't able to climb one of these steep, seething mountains of water fast enough. The gallant little ships were tossed to and fro like flotsam and rammed about by the turbulent seas. The poor little things, which were more underwater than above it, took on the look of submarines. Needless to say, it was extremely dangerous to come on deck with the violent waves dashing overhead.

The *Ross* steered badly too. The ship was too lightly laden to sit tight, and it pitched and rolled so fearfully that experienced sea-legs were indispensable for staying upright; even so, a fair amount of acrobatics came into play. This led to some funny scenes that we laughed at heartily, all the more because our inclination was to look at these things from an optimistic point of view now that the prow of the *Ross* pointed in the right direction — north. Given this state of affairs, it was out of the question that the hurricane, which tossed the ship like a toy ball for days on end, could dampen the cheerful mood that reigned onboard. All thoughts hurried far ahead of the toiling vessel and occupied themselves with things that awaited us in the inhabited world, in New Zealand. For some this was above all letters from home. For others it was meeting new people, seeing trees and flowers again, and maybe taking in a movie. And then there were those simple souls whose desires aimed no higher than a bottle of spirits.

Because the *Ross* was so lightly loaded, it stayed nice and dry in the tremendously high seas. Heavy bursts of spray clattered over the ship, but it didn't take on much water. Although the ship heaved and pitched heavily, it rose up lightly and easily on the mighty mountains of water. Had it been heavily loaded, we wouldn't have gotten off so easily.

For three days in a row the hurricane raged with increasing wrath, so that

---

1. In between are the "Furious Fifties."

safety demanded heaving to. Later, when the winds whipped about and swept up a wild sea running at itself from all directions, our position grew even more difficult. Wind and sea then came out of various directions so that mighty waves unavoidably struck the ship; this not only sorely tested its seaworthiness but also repeatedly caused damage and made passage on deck life-threatening, even nearly impossible. Without a lifeline around his body, no man dared to make the trip over the tweendecks. The line prevented a man from washing overboard, but the chance of breaking arms and legs remained great.

The ocean in its fury delivered a splendid show that I never tired of admiring. An exalted beauty lay in the rolling advance of the majestic mountains of wildly agitated water. I could see a tremendous wave arriving already from far off, leaving a long white path of bubbling and churning water behind it. This sort of living hill moves forward with surprising speed, while the steep top curls over and a seething mass of foam covers the wave's crown, so that the onrushing mountain of water pulls a long, wide trail of boiling foam over the broad, swelling surface of the sea.

When the storm has developed its full strength, the entire ocean is covered with swelling white paths left behind by the breaking waves. From a distance a "graybeard" like this doesn't seem particularly dangerous; then you see only the wide, curly white head sticking up above the tumbling waves. But once it comes near enough that you can see over the whole mass of water, then the sight is so powerfully impressive that it's impossible to turn your gaze away from it, and you remain captivated watching the titanic play of the unchained elements.

A graybeard

Higher and higher the "graybeard" lifts up its ragged head, far above the ship, and it looks as if the whole enormous mass will soon drown the vessel under thousands of tons of boiling, seething water. Where the translucent wave-crest curls high in the air, the water is a beautiful emerald in color — just before the piled-up crown hits and shoots down like a thick layer of seething foam along the lee rail, while the fierce wind tears off whole pieces of the crown and chases them forward like salty rain. As soon as the foot of the wave reaches the ship, the vessel immediately rises up against the slope; the fearfully threatening mountain of water quickly loses height until the wildly moving wave-top rolls under the ship, usually without doing any damage. Then the ship glides down again along the opposite slope.

While the storm lowed and whistled, biting through the rigging, and the tops of the masts described wide, whimsical arcs against the chasing black clouds, the albatrosses sailed with the greatest calm alongside and around the ship. Judging from the unruffled nature of these birds, one wouldn't guess there was a hurricane raging, sweeping up air and water into a state of full-blown anarchy. In the howling storm, the albatrosses skimmed over the seething, roaring waves in absolute peace and with perfect self-assurance. The storm and the albatross are faithful, inseparable companions in the wide seas of the far south.

Without any apparent effort the majestic birds sailed over the wild, climbing waves, following the profile of hill and dale closely but always staying just high enough above the seething surface so that the spattering foam never reached them. Stately and stoic, they hovered over the wild waters. In winds that would force a man to hold tight to the ship's rail with both hands so as not to be blown away, they appeared to hang motionless in the air with unmoving, outspread wings. It was marvelous to see how these allies of the Great West Wind have mastered the art of gliding. Without any noticeable effort they sailed for a while against the storm. Sometimes they slanted over a little bit so that the wind hit the underside of their wings; then they sailed away on the crosswinds, or let themselves be driven before the wind like ships running with the waves, afterward turning into the wind with gracious, sweeping gestures. All this they did with the greatest assurance, without their outstretched wings moving even a slightly perceptible bit.

ON THE THIRD day the wind turned around to the west and thereafter kept blowing from that corner with unlessened force. The waves couldn't get any higher, but with the changed wind direction they went wildly and irregularly through each other and ran across each other so that enormous quantities of water constantly and forcefully washed over the ship with an ominous wailing, causing a great deal of damage.

Part of the railing was smashed flat against the deck, and heavy iron supports were bent. On the bridge deck, cast-iron bulkheads were pushed in like cardboard. We feared that the hatches would give way. Wonder of wonders, they held up well, but we looked with fear and trembling down below as yet another whole top of a wave thundered over the foredeck. It was a real relief when we saw that the hatches were still intact after most of the water had flowed away and the hatch covers were visible again.

Still, the *Ross* couldn't have held out very long in such a sea; the ship would have completely collapsed in on itself. The strenuous shifting it did do had already led to numerous leaks, though luckily not in the hull. But several tank supports had buckled, leading to the loss of a great deal of oil, which ended up in tanks filled with coal.

So nobody was sorry when, on the fourth day, the storm died down. A strong swell still rolled, but without the powerful force of the wind behind it, the ocean was like Samson shorn of his locks.

Whole flocks of albatrosses and other petrels appeared as harbingers of land, and the following morning, when the first light, pale and drab, broke through thick showers of rain and hail, Campbell Island came into view. Between the driving curtains of rain, we occasionally caught a glimpse of

Inhospitable coast

roughly hewn hills. As we came closer, the coast seemed to be a chaotic heap of stones and cliffs over which the tall waves crashed wildly, while gigantic fountains spouted up against the immovable rock walls, booming dully. It was a dangerous, inhospitable coast.

As the *Ross* came up behind the island, the turbulent motions of the ship suddenly ceased. It felt very strange to have stability underfoot after we had gotten used to the untrustworthiness of wildly pitching decks inundated by seawater. When we sailed into a narrow fjord, it was a boon to see real dry land again, not shimmering in the distance but close by. We saw no movable, unpredictable ice, but a solidly founded island with mountains and valleys and freestone rocks, with grass and even a little undergrowth here and there. For most people the effect of seeing land isn't that great, but to the seamen who for months and months had had to deal with uncertain, treacherous ice and equally uncertain and treacherous seas, it gave a deep, quiet joy. With eager eyes they feasted upon the faded autumn hues; happy as children, they pointed out to each other the silvery ribbons that shone in the tussock grass. Fresh water, a little stream! It would be nothing to the average person, but for them, under these circumstances, it was a significant thing.

THE *Ross* anchored in the middle of the fjord. We knew that the island was inhabited, that for a year now four men had been living there as shepherds. Our first visit had to do with them. Several of us rode in the motorboat to the end of the fjord, where two rude, primitive huts stood. The inhabitants were watching us come, clearly uncertain. No wonder they didn't know what was happening. They had already been on the island for twelve months without any connection to the outside world, and now suddenly they saw six ships — a whole fleet — in front of their simple homestead. They might well have thought that it was an optical illusion. They must have rubbed their eyes to convince themselves that they weren't dreaming. Were there really seven men coming toward them all at once?

The hermits clearly didn't know what to think of this. Later they told us that they had been truly frightened to see such a large crowd. After a year of not having seen a single human being, seven men looked like an entire army to them. They had become a bit man-shy; the unexpected and inexplicable visit made them stand hesitantly at a distance. Only when we moored at the rickety pier did they slowly come nearer, like wild things that didn't know whether they should be happy or afraid.

They willingly helped secure the boat. But their reticence vanished only after we had told them in a few words that we had come to their island looking for whales and weren't pirates but were honest men to the core.

They were thankful even for a few old newspapers, but their eyes really shone with quiet happiness when we told them that we had received their request via wireless to bring them back with us to New Zealand. The youngest, a fellow scarcely twenty years old, for whom this voluntary exile must have been especially hard, had tears of emotion rolling down his cheeks. He took us to his miserable wooden hut and showed us the walls, which were covered from top to bottom with pictures of women cut out of magazines. With a shrug of his shoulders he admitted that these had been a poor substitute, only enough to make the somber winter nights a tiny bit less desolate, an artificial oasis in the hopeless monotony of their colorless existence.

It was agreed that the shepherds would deliver us 150 slaughtered sheep. We had no fresh food other than whale meat at this point, and as a consequence, many of the men showed symptoms of beri-beri and scurvy. The lamb would be the cure. So many sheep wandered around the island in a half-wild state that the shepherds themselves couldn't estimate their numbers to within a thousand, so it was no problem for them to fill our meat lockers with legs of lamb.

The westerly storm, which after a day of rest had begun to blow with renewed strength, forced us to get back onboard quickly. Apparently it had

The stormy West Wind

stuck in the West Wind's throat to let us have an undisturbed day, so he angrily hurled one hail shower after another over the *Ross* and shook and tore at
the rigging and stays with such fury that they screamed sharply. Such fierce,
ripping winds howled through the valley of the fjord that it was at times impossible to stay on one's feet, even if the ship lay still. In fierce gusts of wind
we measured a pressure of more than 150 kilos per square meter [over 30
pounds per square foot], and we considered ourselves lucky to be safely in
the roads.

In the open sea, every vessel would have had a hard time of it in such
weather. Not many ships would have been able to withstand for long the
force of the murderous sea that goes along with such wind power.

THE FOLLOWING DAY, when the storm had died down again, we went ashore
in the early morning, this time to a bay on the west coast where an abandoned seal-hunters' hut was supposed to be standing. Because of the tremendous surf that broke thundering over the rocks on the western coast, we
couldn't reach the bay by water, so we sailed up the fjord in order to start
from the shepherds' huts and go over land to the west coast.

Just as we had been the previous day, we were amazed at the pristine
state of the island. The four lonely herders were clearly friends of the animals.
At our first landing a cormorant came up to us completely good-naturedly
and let us pet him, unafraid. Skuas and other gulls also approached us, curiously and without hesitation.

It was ebb tide, and on the dried beach the sea had left much behind
that thrilled our zoologist. We helped him pluck red and pink sea anemones
and collect mussels, snails, oysters, crayfish, and all sorts of other saltwater
creatures. Luckily, the rising tide put an end to this business; otherwise, we
would have had to haul even more ballast over the difficult terrain. Already
we each had forty kilos of supplies, since in addition to taking provisions for
three days we had also taken along extra clothing, cameras, painting materials, binoculars, geology hammers, and all sorts of other things.

An almost obscured path led over the rocks and grassy hills toward the
southwest. After crossing a high ridge, we left the path to look at the white
patches on the tussocky hills — patches that we first took to be remnants of
snow but that turned out to be albatross nests. We had ended up in a breeding ground of king albatrosses, which, as far we know, breed only on Campbell Island. As we walked around the island, we saw many of these birds, with

wingspans of more than three meters [about ten feet], skimming calmly as can be over the turbulent waves, and during our wanderings we were able to observe all the birds' doings on dry land.

If we approached a nest, the mother sat completely still; only her black eyes betrayed her fear of these strange beings. If we made rapid movements, the mother raised her folded-up wings to protect her solitary offspring or sometimes clacked with her beak. Those were the only defensive measures that she made; she didn't think of fleeing.

The very simple nest of the albatross is nothing more than a rise on the land surface hollowed out a little and sparsely furnished with dry grass and twigs. The separate nests lie a good 100 meters [well over 300 feet] away from each other. There's nothing remarkable about the nests themselves, but their placement is special. Like the bird's free, spacious flight over the stormy ocean, the nest of the albatross lies open and exposed on the grass-covered slope of the hill, so that it has a view over the valley and over the wide ex- panses of the restless sea. It needs the broad, spacious hillside as a soft, slop- ing runway that will — along with the wind wafting under its wings — allow it to lift up into the air. Many times we saw an albatross with outstretched wings trip quickly along down the hill and then rise up like a flying machine as soon as it had built up enough speed.

Only in the mornings did we find the mother birds on their nests; that's when they feed their young, who have to get by on one meal a day. We wit- nessed such feedings many times; they went very simply. The mother doesn't hold the food firmly in her beak; she's swallowed it during her foraging. When she comes back to the nest, she takes the chick's beak in hers, so as not to make a mess, and disgorges the child's breakfast — a squid or something like that — which the hungry little one then greedily gulps down. Later in the day it was always the downy chicks that sat alone on the nests. They stood up helplessly as we approached and anxiously waved their bills back and forth. If we came too close to one, then it grew truly frightened and vomited a yel- low, oily mass. The adult birds did the same thing in similar circumstances. Apparently it was a kind of defense mechanism.

An albatross child has a largely solitary youth. It has neither neighbors nor playfellows, and if it isn't sleeping, it can only stare anxiously into the wide, empty distance. Its childhood is not only lonely but also long. Indeed, there are few other birds that have to spend so much time brooding on their eggs and raising their offspring. The female always lays just one white egg, on which she must brood for three months before it hatches. For nine months thereafter, between February and November, the chick stays on the nest. All that time the mother has to feed it, and only in the early days of November, when she lays a new egg, does she make a definite end to the lazy life of the youngster. Without much fuss she grabs the chick by the neck as it struggles in protest and flings it out of the nest. After that, the fledgling just has to look out for itself. So, without further ado, it spreads its wings and lets itself be carried along by the wind into the air, which from now on will be its home.

Inspecting the many nests took us much longer than we had originally intended, so it was already afternoon before we saw, from a high, rocky crest, the wild and crumbled west coast. By this time we had already wandered far from the path, and there was nothing to be seen of a hut. As we looked for shelter, we noticed for the first time how heavy our packs really were. It was a difficult hike, over rough masses of stone and through high moorland, full of deep pits, which were the cause of many an impious outburst as one or the other of us suddenly sank into a pool filled with filthy water.

A high, whistling sound, ending with a mourning trill, so biting that it was painful to the ears, put an end to our grumbling and focused our attention on a quartet of male albatrosses that had drawn up around a female, attracted by the mating call she had made. In her snow-white bridal attire, she sat among her admirers, who paraded around her awkwardly. An albatross's body is perfectly designed for free and easy movement in the air, but on dry ground the bird is as clumsy as a log. Without noticeable jealousy, the candidates stepped up to the bride one after the other and vigorously recommended themselves. One stretched his wings out wide to show her their huge size; another walked up and down a few times with measured steps. Still another, evidently of a more practical bent, tried to get right down to billing and cooing with his intended. The female put up with all these expressions of homage but remained unmoved. She only shook her feathers now and then. That seemed to increase her suitors' admiration to an even greater degree, and they were delighted when she again raised her shrill whistle with its melancholy closing chord.

We longed for warm food and a roof over our heads too much to wait for the end of the show, so we shouldered our packs again. From a bald, windy hilltop we noticed an easy escarpment that inclined to the west and ended in a bay, and soon we had the winding path under our feet again. It didn't look very far away, but the trail swerved around every stone and every tuft of tussock grass, and a marsh, through which a sluggish stream seeped, appeared to hide an endless number of mantraps and pitfalls in the form of pools, holes, and the submerged roots of scrub. The drab evening, lit by a single star, began to fall, and it spread a heavy gray veil of mist over sea, valley, and hills. But there was no sign of beach or hut. Experience had taught us more than enough about how long and cold a sleepless night by an open campfire could be, while threatening rain clouds also spurred us on.

Ha! Finally we came upon a bizarre rock, the 200-meter-high [650-foot-high] pyramid of stone that the shepherds had pointed out to us as "The Monument." The seal-hunters' hut was supposed to be somewhere near that.

And indeed, shortly thereafter we saw in the distance the corrugated iron roof of the hut, which picked up the last wavering light of the day. But we were misled by the falling darkness. First we ended up on a fresh, still-slippery landslide, and after that we plunged into thick undergrowth, where we had only the dull rumble of the surf to serve as our guide.

It was already eight o'clock and completely dark when, tired but curious, we opened the half-closed door of the hut. There was an open fireplace and some dry wood, precious things to us, and soon the flames were crackling merrily. As that night proved, all sorts of special thoughts and stories come up around an open fire; it seems that the flickering glow opens the heart and loosens the tongue. Such evenings by the fire, far from the bustle of civilization, are full of romantic enchantment. Youthful dreams become living reality, and it requires no effort to imagine oneself a Robinson Crusoe, a pirate, or a castaway.

Nobody said good-night that evening, nor was the door-opening closed with the large flap of sailcloth that lay outside and served to hold the warmth in at night. One after another we fell asleep from weariness, and we scarcely heard how the storm howled and dirges wailed through the many holes in the galvanized walls.

LOUD ROARING coming from the nearby beach woke me before day and dew. On the slope between the grass and the sandy bank there were groups of sea lions skirmishing. The news of this got the others up quickly and running outside. We had planned to spend the day usefully: the doctor was hoping to find fossils, the professor wanted to expand his zoological collection, and the two others wanted nothing more than to enjoy untouched nature to the fullest. But now we followed the sounds of the skirmish. The fighters paid little

Fighting over a female

attention to the first shot that a cormorant let fall, but after the second one the sea lions slowly backed off and left the beach free for the skuas and other gulls.

We had looked with astonishment at a hemp plant gone wild near the hut, asking ourselves what the seal hunters had used it for. On our hikes along the beach we figured out that they had used the hemp to make soles for their seaboots so that they wouldn't slip on the rocks as they went along the coast hunting seals.

Stumbling and falling ourselves, we followed the stony beach to the north, picking our way over the weathered, eroded boulders that lay dry in low tide. In saltwater pools the professor found all sorts of little creatures to his liking. Meanwhile, the others went farther along, and after an hour of acrobatic exercises, their efforts paid off: they found a stretch of open, sandy beach where fifteen sea lions, spread out in small groups, were fighting out their differences.

Under the cover of several large cliffs, we could spy on them from a distance of several meters. The sea lions were very excited. They were challenging each other over the sole female, a lovely, slender animal with a fine, light-gray pelt. She was totally indifferent to the action around her, not concerning herself in the least with the males' fight, even though it was about her. The bantams fought so furiously that a thrown stone wasn't enough to calm them down. They looked around for a moment and then immediately resumed the struggle.

Right near the bride lay two old veteran fighters. They were nearly toothless, with wrinkled, scar-grooved hides and short, rust-brown manes growing around their necks. These old codgers were unchallenged masters of the domain; all the younger animals had had to leave the field. Of course there could be no talk of a compromise here, and we didn't have to wait long before we saw the fight blaze up anew. The heavy bodies smacked against each other, while the heads cut to and fro, lightning quick, in far faster movements than one would expect from such large, fairly clumsy animals.

Each round lasted about ten minutes. Afterward they collapsed, panting, onto the sand to recover. Then they looked around morosely; love certainly came at a high price. The fights of the younger animals were probably intended as training for the championship matches, for which the purse consisted of the coquettish creature who now lay sleeping in the middle of the arena, while the sun shone like silver on her precious pelt.

Gradually the younger ones realized that they wouldn't be able to compete for the championship title anyway, and they went off to recoup in the sea with a generous breakfast. Some of them pulled back into the tussock grass to rest; others stretched themselves out on the beach and threw moist sand over their bodies with their fins to cool off. One had clearly exerted himself too much. Resting on his forefins, he made convulsive movements, then broke off, exhausted, to fall down again.

Only the two old wrestlers still challenged each other for the prize. The one pulled himself back more and more, while the other old gent harried his fatigued opponent in every possible way. It was an endless skirmish, and it made us laugh. It looked like a hand-to-hand fight between two mumbling men from an old people's home — a farce. Meanwhile, the female resignedly waited for events to run their course. She had no choice. Only the right of the strongest was valid here — as it is everywhere else, for that matter.

On the overgrown slope we found an old, dying sea lion between the high tufts of grass. He wasn't moving anymore, and his eyes were already split open; the end was near. The skua gulls knew that too; they had gathered around him and could scarcely wait for him to breathe his last so that they could begin their lugubrious feast. A *coup de grace* delivered the dying lion from his suffering. It was the sign for the gulls to attack.

In the few hours that we had spent watching the sea lions, we had seen the whole cycle of their existence unfold like a film before our eyes. Arriving, existing, departing: the three phases of all mortal life. This left a deeper impression on us than it normally would have because the events played themselves out in a place so desolate that our full attention was wholly concentrated on them.

The tide forced us to scramble high over the rocks on our way back, which required great caution, and only late in the afternoon did we reach the hut again, thankful that we had brought dry clothes along; the day's rain had drenched us to the skin. The kitchen elf in the group provided us with an excellent meal of cormorant, bread, and hot black coffee, and the sandman didn't wait long to visit us this evening, either.

THE FOLLOWING morning it was already late when we broke camp. First we replenished the supply of firewood for future users of the hut. After that we were held up for awhile by our sighting of the nest of a sooty black albatross, in which a pitch-black chick lay sleeping. The nest lay not in a tussock slope, like those of the king albatrosses, but on the rocks, high above the surf, and it was difficult to reach. Without the anxious peeping of the chick as a directional signal, we couldn't even have found the nest among the chaotic pile of rocks. The mother was hurrying to respond to her youngster's call for help, and she gave a mournful whistle that the little one, like a wailing echo, repeated to the father, who fluttered restlessly around the rock. Only when we backed off did he come sit on the nest, and with that the anxious peeping was instantly silenced.

After we finally left the hut, it grew misty, and without a compass we probably would have gone wandering again, as we did on the trip there. But then we hadn't actually known where the hut was, whereas now we couldn't possibly miss a deeply cut fjord arm. A well-trodden sheep path that we came across reassured us even more, and we sauntered on cheerfully, stopping by every albatross nest that we saw. Usually there was just a young bird sleeping in it. If the mother was home, she stood over the nest napping, but as soon as we came closer, she quickly dropped onto her child to protect it.

It was already rather dark when we reached the shepherds' hut, after which the ship's motorboat brought us back to the *Ross* in a rising storm. During the evening the wind grew to hurricane strength, but the ship lay so safely at anchor in the sheltered fjord that we gave ourselves up to rest unworried and let the tyrant howl through the rigging without troubling ourselves with his matchless fury.

WE STAYED on Campbell Island for ten days, not so much to take on fresh provisions or to give the crew a bit of a change as to find out whether the whales had stopped in the waters around the island. That wasn't the case; not a single one of the chase boats sent out on reconnaissance could report sighting even a single *blååst*.

Onboard during those days a number of fruitless attempts were made to enrich the menu with fresh fish. That didn't work; fish seemed to be unusually scarce. The only ones we could catch were inedible; the flesh was full of worms.

Still, the cooks were busy with all sorts of unusual dishes. They were gastronomes who made up dozens of recipes to make cormorant taste good. We also discovered that the bottom of the fjord was crawling with crabs, which we hauled up by the basketload. Coal-baskets weighted with grille bars, to which a piece of salted meat was fastened, were played out in the water until they hit bottom. When they were hauled up again after half an hour, dozens of crabs were crawling around in them — big, fat creatures. And the culinary pleasures they provided far exceeded any we might have expected from dining on fish.

Because of the crabbing, we witnessed a deadly fight between a sea lion and two sharks. It played out right in front of our eyes.

Seals don't seem to mind having a hearty morsel. Already on the first day of the crab catch, a big sea lion came around, attracted by the smell of the salt pork, curious to find out how things stood. The first basket that hit the water he left alone, the second one he sniffed at from all directions and with great interest, and the third one he relieved of its bait without even thinking about it. After that, he never missed the call at mealtime, and when the crab harvest began, he didn't hesitate to grab a tasty bite if he saw his chance. On such occasions we admired the velvety grace and the unbelievable suppleness with which he moved in the water. It has been claimed that a swimming sea lion can build up a speed of forty knots, and one is almost inclined to believe that when one sees what power and pliancy the beautiful creature possesses.

One fine day, also attracted by the tempting smell of the salted meat, two sharks showed up on the scene. They were formidable fellows, as we could tell from the giant dorsal fins that cleaved the water of the fjord, side by side. Excitedly we waited to see what would happen. We knew that sharks and sea lions are implacable enemies, so a life-and-death struggle was inevitable. In a fight between a sea lion and a single shark, the result is certain: the shark is torn to pieces by the seal, which has the great advantage of its fabulous speed. But here the seal would find itself up against two huge jaws instead of one, both with several rows of razor-sharp teeth. This heightened our excitement to no small degree.

We held the basket with the bait on the water's surface to make the sharks come closer. It was when they had come right up underneath us and carefully wound around the basket that the sea lion first noticed his enemies. Like a living torpedo, he shot off after them, and the sinister creatures took flight. One of them quickly reached safety on the other side of the ship; meanwhile, the sea lion attacked the other shark with incredible speed. There was no chance for the victim to get away. The sea lion struck again and again, lightning-quick, and each time tore a chunk of flesh out of his enemy. The seal, fluid as water, had no trouble avoiding the sharp teeth and the fearful tail of his victim. The water boiled wildly with the violence of the fight unfolding below, and it soon flowed red with the shark's blood.

Sea lion and shark

The unusually exciting fight was short. The shark was completely defenseless against the rapid, furious attacks of the sea lion, and there was no possibility of resistance — the sea lion didn't leave any time for that. The shark was simply murdered. Soon the water was still again, and the bloody, mangled body of that hated thief of the seas floated on the surface. The sea lion had finished off his enemy with unbelievable speed. And these are by no means toy sharks that threaten the coasts of New Zealand.

While we were still uncertain about the result

of the duel, it was already over, and before we knew it, the sea lion shot like a meteor under the ship and set out after the second shark — so indescribably fast that the victim didn't even get a hundred meters [300 feet] away. The sea lion dispatched this shark as quickly and as thoroughly as he had its companion. Scarcely two minutes later, two mutilated corpses floated on the water's surface. The sea lion swam away as cool as a cucumber, clearly not the least bit tired. On his way he even grabbed the piece of salt pork out of the basket that was hanging outboard. The creature was completely unruffled. Later we again saw triangular black shark fins in the distance — and apparently the sea lion saw them too. Just after our sighting, the water in the place where the fins disappeared was set violently in motion, and soon the stream ferried along toward the ocean the bodies of three mutilated sharks, accompanied by swarms of skuas.

THE CHASE BOATS, all five of which had looked in vain for whales day after day, were furnished with coal for the rest of the trip to New Zealand. The shepherds, in an excited mood, brought their baggage and dogs onboard, and after the bales of wool that they had gathered were loaded, the *Ross* took to the sea again.

Only a good 400 miles separated Campbell Island from Stewart Island, which lay to the south of New Zealand. The chase boats were going to overwinter there until the following spring, when they would travel to the Antarctic Ocean again with another *flytende kokeri*.

After a year of loneliness, the shepherds were happy to have other people around them again, and they talked a mile a minute. No wonder; after twelve months together, those four men had nothing new to tell each other, and their conversation must have grown lean indeed. But we didn't know their stories yet, and when they noticed that we actually wanted to hear them, then there was no getting them to shut up again, day or night. In the solitude of the dreary island, surrounded by nature's desolation, their fantasies had had free rein, and we quickly discovered that it was a good idea to savor their stories with the necessary salt.

They positively insisted, for example, that the famous "sea snake" had repeatedly been in their fjord. They had also seen a human-like form of supernatural dimensions running over the tussocky hills when it stormed: the god of the storm. And they were serious about that. The storm god usually appeared when there was bad weather, and that happened quite often on

Campbell Island. They saw the ominous form on the slope of Mount Paris, which rose up across from their huts. "Dinkum, Sir," they said, wholly convinced, "we saw the albatrosses fly up frightened from their nests when the god raced on down the slope."

They also dished up wonderful stories full of colorful, romantic peculiarities in connection with several deserted graves, recognizable from the tall mounds of stones on them, that lay at the end of the fjord. We had seen these graves and knew who lay buried there based on information in the sailors' guide. But the shepherds recited to us, with the fervor of conviction, a whole tale about a banished French princess who had lived in exile on Campbell Island and had there been the adored but cruel mistress of a band of blood-thirsty pirates who murdered and plundered over the rich islands that lay strewn over the Pacific Ocean. Immeasurable treasures gathered by the pirates must be hidden somewhere on the island, the shepherds insisted. They had often searched diligently for them, but of course without any results.

The facts in connection with the abandoned graves on the island are simple enough. The discoverer of the island, Hasselborough, was captain of a pearl schooner, the *Perseverance*. In 1820, the vessel was swept away far to the south in bad weather, until men on the disabled ship scouted out an unknown island, which was christened Campbell Island after the shipowner. In the fjord, which got the name of the schooner, they found a suitable anchorage, but in their attempt to land, four people lost their lives. The boat was capsized by a violent tailwind, the kind that can descend from the hills with hurricane force without the least warning, and Hasselborough, his wife, and two sailors drowned. The body of the captain was never found, but the bodies of the other three were discovered and buried on the island. Hasselborough's wife was probably the daughter of a Kanaka chief, and therein the legend of the princess undoubtedly found its origin. That she was supposedly a French princess was explainable by the fact that a French sailor was also buried there, a member of the French expedition that reached Campbell Island in the middle of the previous century. The man from the press in our Tasmanian crew industriously gathered all the fantastic tales of the shepherds in order to concoct an adventure novel — with a sequel.

CHAPTER TWENTY-SIX

Back in the Inhabited World

Scott's Memorial in Port Chalmers

<small>⤐øℓℴﬥ</small>

When we left Campbell Island, we had clearly left the region of the Great West Wind behind us also. Thick fog hung over the sea, and the island was quickly enveloped in mists, then vanished. Already the following evening we were in the vicinity of Stewart Island. We couldn't see the land, and since with the foggy weather we couldn't take a position, we judged it safer to wait for daylight. We took soundings from time to time all afternoon, until they indicated that we found ourselves near the southern point of the island, after which we anchored in ample water.

The next morning it was clearer. The sun drove off the last mists, and the island lay before us, suffused with golden light. We knew that it was inhabited, but it didn't show many signs of life: no houses, no smoke, not a single ship. All we could see was the sail of a fishing boat, far in the distance, outlined against the green of the wood that adorned the whole island with a rich, variegated garment.

Was this now the inhabited world, which had become almost a myth in the imagination of our raw Vikings? Where were the pubs and all the other things that together make up a sailors' paradise? "A good-for-nothing hole" was the judgment of the tars. With disdainful glances, they sprayed streams of tobacco juice in the direction of the wooded hills. For the moment, New Zealand was a disappointment.

After we weighed anchor, the *Ross* sailed past heavily wooded hills and picturesque, rocky islands into a beautiful bay, Patterson Inlet. The bay, which wove itself among green slopes and islands, pushed deep into the island with many branchings.

On this unusually fine autumn day, it looked as if nature had striven to make our return to the inhabited world a holiday. After having been deprived of gracious warmth for so long, it did us good to see the sun shining so happily on the almost tropically rich garb of the plants that wrapped the hills and mountains from head to toe in a welter of autumn-rich green, brown, and yellow colors.

Without doubt we found ourselves again in the temperate climates and in the inhabited or at least the inhabitable world. But, as lovely as the natural world of Stewart Island seemed to us, it still didn't impress the men as being a desirable place to live overall. Upon our arrival, there wasn't a single sign of life or industry. A few miles farther on lay Half Moon Bay, which as we knew was the only village on the entire island, a little fishing town of three hundred inhabitants. Why were we visiting this deserted corner instead?

The big event upon our arrival was the handing out of the mail. One of the chase boats had been sent immediately to Half Moon Bay to fetch it. It goes without saying that nobody showed much interest in work that morning. Everyone looked for a quiet spot to sit with their letters and find out how things had gone with those they had left behind. In the far south, which is completely shut off from the outside world, we had formed a completely independent community, but now the broken ties with relatives and friends — with the whole rest of the world — were restored. Captain Larsen still dearly wanted to go hunt whales on the west coast of Australia, a good hunting-grounds where the *rethval* (right whale) and the humpback whale are found in abundance. The crew was asked man by man whether they were willing to go there, thus extending the voyage by a few more months, but even with the prospect of higher wages and bonuses, the men nearly unanimously refused. After all, they had mustered on only for a trip to the Antarctic Ocean and back, and so they weren't required to pursue whale-hunting outside the polar region. And once back in the world and with the latest reports from home in hand, the men wanted nothing more than to return to their own hearths as quickly as possible.

Now that there was no more talk of whale-hunting, the decks of the *Ross* were cleared of everything that had served especially for oil processing: the wooden flensing decks were broken up, the flensing platforms and the ship's onboard boats were secured and stowed away, and all the machinery needed for oil production was carefully stripped of the prodigious layer of fat under which it lay. This made the decks look more normal. For days we worked tremendously hard to free the ship of all the filth that it had collected in the Antarctic Ocean. The seas washing over the deck had cleaned up the worst of it, but even all that water hadn't been able to remove completely the thick crust of fat that lay caked tightly over everything.

The five chase boats were left to overwinter in Patterson Inlet, which was completely safe. And because it was out of the way, it also possessed another great advantage: the boats didn't need to pay any harbor dues. For four days we were busy with the disarming and provisioning of the chase boats; they also took on all the munitions that were still onboard the mother ship. The *Ross* would run into trouble everywhere with such explosives onboard and get held up in every harbor because of annoying regulations. But the boats in this remote corner wouldn't be troubled by anyone.

Naturally we went out to scout the cheerful land with great curiosity. Half Moon Bay appeared to be a small but extremely charming watering-hole with a beautiful beach, sheltered by forested hills and fringed by groups of tall trees. It lay in paradisaical surroundings; it's no wonder that newlywed couples liked to spend their honeymoon there. One couldn't easily find another spot anywhere else in the world better suited for withdrawing completely from the sober world of the everyday than this heavenly village. It didn't surprise us to learn that in New Zealand, if young people say they're going to Half Moon Bay, it means that they're making wedding plans. There is no more ideal place imaginable for a honeymoon.

The news soon got out that the *Ross* lay in Patterson Inlet, and many people came to visit the strange kind of ship about which so many romantic rumors were circulating. The newspapermen came around too, looking for copy, and we told them the most fantastic tales, which to our amusement we later read in the New Zealand papers in even more colorful form. It's really remarkable that in general seamen can't stand journalists, whom they disparage as "penny-a-liners"; they show not the least respect for the "Kings of the Earth" who are so slavishly followed on dry land.

THE WEATHER was flawless during our days on Stewart Island. The sun shone the whole day and set with ravishing beauty at night, only to come up the next morning in glory again. During the day it was so warm that it actually bothered us, since we had gotten used to low temperatures. We would have loved to take a refreshing bath in the calm water of the bay, where many white stretches of beach, enclosed by clumps of rocks, offered tempting opportunities for swimming. But alas, we had to wean ourselves from the pleasures of swimming, since the bay was swarming with sharks. All too often we saw their dark, pointed dorsal fins slicing through the mirror-smooth water.

Sharks were always loitering about the *Ross*. These garbagemen of the sea love to hang around near ships, greedy for the kitchen waste. The smells of oil and whale refuse that permeated the *Ross* seemed to give their olfactory organs a pleasant prickling. We saw many of these hungry sea-wolves nosing around the vicinity of the ship, ready to swallow up anything that might be thrown overboard.

Once, by accident, our deck-washing hose fell into the water. It would have been a sin to let such a thing get lost, so I quickly sprang into the flatboat to pick it up again before the current carried it too far away. In no time there were a good ten sharks around the hose, contesting with each other for the tasty morsel, and long before I got there, the gluttons were already tangled in a furious fight over the delicacy. Two of them had grabbed it on either end, like chickens on an earthworm, while the rest of the pack tore chunks of flesh off the ribs of those lucky two in an attempt to force them to let go of the prize. The fighting ball of fish had almost made off with the hose when I reached it,

Troublesome sharks

and it took a good deal of trouble to force the sinister beasts to give back the ship's property. They snapped at the oar that I wielded as a weapon. Their razor-sharp teeth snapped a piece off from it as if it were a butter cookie, and I almost went into the water with the oar because I wouldn't let it go. I had to recover the hose foot by foot, ramming the thick end of the oar with all my might against the sensitive noses of those thieving fish. It was definitely not expressions of friendship that I was calling out to them as I worked on their snouts with a shaving razor. I had my hands full with them; meanwhile, the strong current carried the flatboat steadily farther out to sea.

Finally I completely recaptured the filthy, battered hose, but the sharks kept following the flatboat from a distance. Good thing that the dumb animals didn't think of attacking my little nutshell of a boat all at once, or things wouldn't have looked so good for me. Just one of those ravenous wolves could easily have capsized the boat. I didn't exactly feel at ease with a dozen sharks lying in wait around me, and I was done in by my long struggle with them, so I wasn't in any condition to scull against the current. So it seemed safer to land on a stretch of beach alongside which the current carried me, to wait it out a little bit before going back to the ship.

Seeing their chance for a feast evaporate, the sharks dropped off one by one. But I still didn't dare take a bath, even though I was in no small need of a refresher.

Not much came of resting up on land, even though I had gotten away from the sharks in the water; it looked as if I had jumped from the frying pan into the fire. Mosquitoes and sand flies ruled the beach so thoroughly and defended their domain so zealously that it was unbearable. In dire straits I got back into the flatboat as soon as the black fins had disappeared from the water and rowed back to the *Ross* with arms that seemed to be made of wood. Now I finally understood why the beach of the idyllically situated Half Moon Bay was so little in vogue and why it was the favored choice of honeymooning couples who wanted to spend their vacation time undisturbed. The mosquitoes and other tormentors on the beach spoiled the mood of the unsuspecting bathers so thoroughly that they couldn't possibly appreciate the beauty and luxuriant wealth of nature surrounding them.

The exodus of normal, sober people worked all to the good of the lovers, who thus got the kingdom all to themselves and found in the majestic, fairy-tale-like surroundings a most suitable backdrop for the romance of their young lives. They wouldn't be lovers if they didn't gladly brave the mosquito-laden plague of flies for the sake of some golden freedom. The dreadful power of these flies was indicated by the dead dwarf penguins that lay on the beach. No obvious cause of death could be seen; the birds must have been the victims of attacks by the myriads of sand flies.

From time to time we had the opportunity to go ashore, and we didn't pass up the chance. We left the beach unchallenged to the winged menaces and went farther inland, where they didn't bother us. The island was covered with thick woods in which eucalyptus species dominated; in the undergrowth stood many tree ferns. There were birds in unusual abundance, and the forest echoed with their warbling, in which rejoicing, pining, and exuberant chirping blended together into one lovely, melodious whole. One of the feathered singers that we won't easily forget is the bell-bell, or bellbird, whose bright song is reminiscent of a carillon. Its song, pure and prominent as fine bell-tones, penetrated widely and mysteriously among the tall trunks and filled the whole forest with cheerful sounds.

How rich and bursting with life the forests were after the barren environment of the polar regions! These were glorious days that we spent on

Stewart Island: clear blue autumn days, full of bright, sparkling light that re-fashioned the island into one great, dreamy garden, so beautiful that it could have been a pleasure spot for gods, fairies, and elves.

WHEN EVERYTHING had been put in order for the overwintering of the chase boats and we had taken leave of the men who were staying onboard to maintain them, the anchor was raised. Early the following morning, the *Ross* steamed up the fjord on which Port Chalmers lies, the harbor of Dunedin, which is the capital of Otago, the southernmost of the twin islands that together form New Zealand.

The hills that enclose the estuary presented a totally different landscape picture than the one we had seen on as-yet-untouched Stewart Island: fields and orchards covered the hills. And soon the ship was moored at a real pier with warehouses and train tracks alongside. Harbor officials came onboard, and curious townsfolk watched how this strange type of ship was made fast. A single police officer looked with undisguised displeasure at the rough Norwegians who went at it loudly now that they were finally back in the inhabited world again. The bobby surely had a feeling that these fellows were going to cause plenty of trouble — and he was right about that. With the harbor district so close by that they could actually investigate two or three bars, there was no holding the sailors back.

Some of them got the captain to give them an advance, and a few even had a few shillings of their own. Those who weren't so lucky went ashore with a suit of clothes to convert into cash.

Before the ship was even well and truly secured, a whole row of land-lusty Vikings descended the boarding ladder and ran to the nearest bar. They didn't care that they hadn't gotten permission to disembark, and they didn't care that the captain was furious and threatened severe punishments. The boat was moored, and they just simply went ashore. It would have been a clever fellow who could have stopped them.

Discipline was sorely neglected, and there were days when not more than three or four men from the entire crew were on deck. The rest roamed around the city, in and out of bars, and forced the sacred servants of the law to an unprecedented level of activity. Some of the men ended up in police cells or in their bunks onboard, snoring to the honor of Bacchus. The priest from the seamen's home made exemplary efforts to hold the sailors in check and organized party evenings and mild entertainments, but he wasn't very successful. Sankey songs,[1] jam sandwiches, and lemonade usually put Jack Tar to sleep rather than reviving him, as was the intention. The insipid fare clearly lay heavy in the Vikings' stomachs, and they began to yawn during the singing of the pious songs that they weren't so terribly fond of to begin with. In the bar, things were much better. Hadn't the Vikings from ancient times undertaken their daring exploits with the one goal of finding wine and women in foreign lands? In this respect the sailing Norwegians weren't very far removed from the past: they were unsurpassed drinking buddies, and, as far as the other matter goes, well — this rhyme expresses it clearly:

> All the nice girls love a sailor,
> All the nice girls love a tar;
> For there is something about a sailor,
> Why you know what sailors are!
> Free and easy, bright and breezy,
> He's the ladies' pride and joy, etc.

Since the quality of the ladies wasn't a smidgen better than the quality of the inferior alcohol that the drowsy sailors swallowed at usurious prices, the whole place was in an uproar at night from this invasion of the Norsemen. Captain Larsen would have preferred to head for the sea immediately to put an end to the scandal. But we were waiting for a couple dozen tons of coal to be delivered by a tramp steamer that was underway from Australia, and the steamer had been held up by bad weather, so we were forced to exercise a few days' patience. We needed the coal order to be able to reach European waters. En route there wouldn't be much opportunity to bunker, since, for economic reasons, we wouldn't be taking the shortest way — through the Panama Canal — but rather the long route around Cape Horn.

New Zealand, which is a very young country and still welcomes new citizens gladly, seemed to hold a great attraction for the Norwegians, and several dozen of them hankered to set themselves up there. Our harmonica virtuoso from the penguin deck was the first to depart; he'd been promised mountains of gold for his playing. Not only deserters shrank the original

---

1. Ira D. Sankey (1840-1908) was an amateur musician who for thirty years was Dwight L. Moody's partner in evangelism. He wrote a flood of egregiously sanctimonious and sentimental hymns, the most famous of which is "There were Ninety and Nine."

crew, but also the Tasmanians, who were mustered off here, since they were no longer needed. (They received free passage to their own country.) The four shepherds from Campbell Island also didn't stay onboard any longer than they had to. They had been away from home for a good year, so they went back to their own hearths and homes as quickly as possible.

It was a nice surprise for me one day to see a steamer from the Royal Dutch Merchant Marine sailing up the fjord on its way to Dunedin. This was the last thing I had expected to see there, but the flag and the type of ship were unmistakable. Since in earlier days I myself had sailed as a helmsman on ships of that line, this East Indies ship understandably interested me greatly. I asked for and received leave to go to Dunedin for a day in order to visit the ship that awakened so many memories of my East Indies sailing days. It turned out to be the *Ombilin*, and the captain, Pankouk, was an old acquaintance of mine. It did me good to hear the sounds of my mother tongue again and to chat with fellow countrymen. It's in situations like this that one truly realizes how strong a feeling of solidarity usually accompanies shared nationality.

Unfortunately, there wasn't enough time available for a trip inland, where I so much wanted to meet the Maoris, a strong, intelligent, and sympathetic race. The last remnants of this people, having grown out of their own culture, still exist in the volcanic mountain country.

After a long search in Dunedin, we were able to find some Maoris, but they wielded fountain pens in place of javelins, and their traditional stone axes had already been replaced by pocketknives from Sheffield. We would rather have seen these descendants of a proud and warlike race richly tattooed, performing a war dance around a blazing campfire, instead of seeing them owlishly bespectacled and wearing bright yellow shoes, tallying up figures in stuffy offices where they forgot that thick forests, smoking volcanoes, and silvery moonlit nights still existed.

The few Maoris that we met in Dunedin as bouncers in harbor bars were otherwise degenerated from their brothers, who had already sunk to the level of fountain pens and Harold Lloyd glasses. The once so proud and strong Maori folk seemed to be doomed to ruination. Since the first white traders had set foot on New Zealand soil at the beginning of the previous century, a dark combination of alcohol, infectious diseases, war, and modern weapons had all done their worst to wither away the once brave and well-established Maoris and reduce their number to several tens of thousands.

There was even a time when preserved, tattooed Maori heads formed a principal export article, of more interest than the fruits of the land.

Paddy, our athletic Tasmanian, discovered a boxing tent in Dunedin that was in league with a few Maoris who were willing to go a few rounds with amateurs. Would we like to see how he would chase those natives around the ring? Sure, we said, but when we saw the copper-colored giants with their supple, muscled bodies looking like Greek gods, even Paddy's own countrymen didn't bet on him; the odds weren't good. Ireland resisted like a wildcat, but he couldn't hold out against the good-natured giant who was his opponent. Finally, smiling sympathetically, he planted his mighty fist in Paddy's gut with such force that for a moment Paddy glided through the air and over the ropes, landing in the crowd, where he was out for the count.

Pisani, our Herculean motor-car driver, who had been the Norwegian wrestling champion, wanted to save the honor of the *Ross*. He dared the Maori giant to wrestle him. Meanwhile, the rumor that the Norsemen were in the boxing tent had already spread through the town, and the sporty Brits, keen for an exciting match, filled the hall to the rafters. It was quite the event: betting was heavy, and a deafening noise reigned. And it was a splendid show for this kind of thing too. The white arms of the Norwegian had the bronze body of the Maori in an iron grip. The wild man was not so well-versed in the techniques of the trade as Pisani was, but he was certainly as strong as Pisani and much leaner. It was a clash of titans, so it was a long time before both copper-colored shoulders touched the ground. So mighty was the struggle that at the end of it the two gladiators lay on the mat next to each other, exhausted. The spectators couldn't be held back. They stormed the ring and enthusiastically carried the champions to the locker rooms, shouting their praises. It was a good day for Pisani. Beaming, he said that he was going to buy a cozy little farmhouse near Trondheim later on. He was going to call it "Maori" in memory of the match with the brown Hercules.

We heard that races were being held on the racetrack outside of town. Since we were already in a sports-hungry mood, we naturally went to see what the New Zealanders were worth in the area of horse-racing. Thanks to Pisani's performance, all Norwegians were received as guests of honor at the racetrack. That was much too kind — not because the rough patrons didn't appreciate the hospitality, but because they made all-too-grateful use of it, in particular the free whiskey. As could have been predicted, the consequences

A good start

were disastrous. Grown wanton on a flood of whiskey, the rollicking sailors wanted to mount the horses and ride a lap. Now, horses and sailors are beings that are problematic in combination, and the jockeys were totally against having their horses so misused. The result was general confusion, and after a noisy fistfight, during which saddles and chairs flew through the air, the honored guests were ignominiously removed from the fairgrounds by an extra detachment of police and locked up to get sober: "the end of a perfect day." But for those officers from the *Ross* who also attended the races, it was less perfect. They were naturally held at least partly responsible for the behavior of their men. They had tried as hard as they could to calm the boys down, but it hadn't helped much; black eyes and bloody noses were their reward. These excuses were heard with sour faces.

IN NEW ZEALAND there is great interest in everything having to do with Antarctica; the country lies fairly close to the least unknown portion of the South Polar Region. Several of the most important expeditions had left from Dunedin or Port Chalmers, including Scott's undertaking, which had left from the latter port and met with a fatal outcome. On a hill from which there was a clear view over the fjord and over the ocean, which stretched out unbroken to the south until it came up against the eternal ice, a memorial had been set up, noble in its simplicity. It was dedicated to the memory of Scott and his fellow explorers who lost their lives on the Great Ice Barrier.

Long reports about our expedition brought droves of the curious to the *Ross*. The crowd was so large that it grew bothersome, and a guard had to be placed by the gangway to control the flood of sightseers that got in the way everywhere and ruined their clothes. In general the English aren't very strong in the area of geography, and they sometimes asked astonishingly stupid questions. The pack ice and the Great Ice Barrier were completely unknown to most of them; they knew only the ice that their grocery store delivered. They often held odd opinions about whales too. Once when I was on watch at the gangway, a lady asked me if I could deliver her ten pounds of whales; she had guests coming the following day, and she wanted to serve them fine seafood. With a steely gaze I told her that I was very sorry, but Captain Larsen had just had the last ten whales fried for his breakfast. A finely dressed gentleman looked offended when I doubled over laughing after he asked me in all seriousness whether he might take a peek in the tanks where we stored the whales. He apparently assumed that we brought the whales live to Norway to show them off like goldfish in aquariums in our living rooms. That man clearly thought that the whale was a sister of the smelt or the sardine.

I should report that the men who still suffered from scurvy or beri-beri quickly recovered as soon as we arrived in inhabited places and could get exclusively fresh food again. But even those of us whose health hadn't suffered from the one-sided feeding appreciated the abundance of precious fruit that autumn brought in New Zealand. The sailors before the mast actually didn't value this wealth of fruit as much as they might have. They would have been ashamed to throw away the few shillings they managed to get hold of on such nonsense when there were still alcoholic drinks for sale.

As much as we had enjoyed our stay, we were also happy when our coal finally arrived. The two thousand tons of condensed warmth of the sun were loaded as quickly as possible; as soon as everything was set and all formalities were completed, the trip home could begin. A large part of the crew wasn't actually present: the police had locked up the fellows who had thrown Port Chalmers into a state of confusion. But at the request of Captain Larsen they were released upon payment of the costs they had incurred. It wasn't a pretty sight when the bobbies led them back onboard. A lot of heads were bandaged. Some of the men had fallen into such a state of drunkenness that they literally had to be dragged onboard, and they all showed unmistakable signs of extended stays in the gutter; some of them were adorned only with underpants. No, it wasn't a crew to be proud of onshore, and it was certain that many sighs of relief arose from Port Chalmers when the *Ross* finally steamed out of the harbor. In fact, I wouldn't be surprised if the police were paid an extra bonus for the unusually heavy duties they were charged with on account of the Norsemen.

CHAPTER TWENTY-SEVEN

"Rolling Home"

On the high seas

The autumn sky shone pale blue above the oil-smooth fjord when Port Chalmers slowly sank behind us in the sweltering humidity that the afternoon sun spread over the city and its encircling hills. At sea the *Ross* was caught by a long swell, and it was beautiful to feel the ship rising and falling on the ocean's peaceful breathing again while the bow, calm and sure, cleaved the billows into which it steadily dove up and down.

Once in the open ocean, a sea boat really comes into its own; the wide

350

water is its only true element, the only surroundings in which it completely belongs. A background of buildings can often make for a picturesque scene, but one has to see a ship on the wide, surging water to be able to appreciate the full effect, just as one needs to see a bird or a fish moving freely in its own element in order to appreciate its true beauty. Every ship is lovely and great when, far from all land, small under the broad dome of the heavens, it plies its lonely way over the ever-swelling waves, a shining arc of foam before its bow. It's a symbol of human progress as the midpoint of the seemingly unchanging horizon steadily yields as the vessel moves forward.

If the *Ross* had found its true element again, this was no less true for the crew. The seaman is in splendid form only when the deck heaves under his feet, as nothing but the unmeasured breadth of air and water surround him and no land can tempt his simple spirit from his rugged, manly task. Onshore our men hadn't shown their better sides. But the salty sea-breeze soon washed unsavory thoughts out of their heads, and they went back to work with the same assurance with which the ship had re-entered the sea. In Port Chalmers they had behaved like a gang of pirates; the only excuse for it was that the sailors onshore were bereft of their trusted environment. On land, in the noisy bustle of a big city, they felt more or less like wild mustangs. Swaying over the rolling decks, our seamen had in a figurative sense firmer ground beneath their feet than when they were on solid ground ashore, where a sailor always remains for the most part a stranger and where he seldom knows how to steer a straight course.

The atmosphere of the land was now blown away as if by a wind, and our men became their true, sympathetic selves again. They were now the same stalwart, stouthearted old salts whose competence and good-naturedness we knew so well and valued so much.

WE WOULD see no land before the wild coasts of Tierra del Fuego appeared, and after that, nothing more until we reached our final destination, probably a West European harbor. Which one that would be nobody knew, since the oil that we were carrying first had to be sold. This didn't bother us at all; we would get more detailed orders later on, in Las Palmas or in the Channel.

Meanwhile, every turn of the restlessly grinding screw brought us closer to home, and the men were happy that for the rest of the trip there were no more harbors, which would only mean a delay and a postponed homecoming.

It is a special mood that holds sway on a ship that's finally turned homeward after a long journey. The happy prospect of soon seeing all that they love — friends, their homeland, all the good and old and familiar — naturally leaves its mark on the men. The *Ross* was no exception to this rule — all the more since we had both wind and sea working together to speed our voyage. Now that the goal of the trip had been reached and there were only several thousand miles separating us from our destination, ice and whales no longer demanded the primary place in our thoughts; our attention was concentrated more and more on the endpoint of our wanderings over the oceans. The longing for home grew stronger as the number of miles that still separated us from it grew smaller. So it wasn't strange that some could no longer hear anything in the stamp of the engine other than an endless and emphatically repeated *"Hjem! Hjem! Hjem!"* ("Home! Home! Home!").

The reigning high spirits came out in happy songs at work and in athletic exercises at the end of the day's tasks. The man at the wheel wasn't allowed to sing at his post, but one couldn't begrudge him quietly humming to himself as he steered the ship with sparing hand movements, doing his more-than-usual best to make the wake as straight as an arrow in order to shorten the way to Norway as much as possible. Strange droning sounds came from the cable locker, where the sailmaker, while he patched up the battered awnings and sails, also tried to sing paeans, his voice like a cracked pot on which a hefty wad of tobacco worked like a mute. On deck we sudsed and painted so that we could sail home with a clean and gleaming ship, the pride of every captain, and the sudsy sponges and paintbrushes danced happily up and down to the beat of the songs. The ship's boy, who on a swaying bosun's chair smeared the mast and the deck underneath it with paint, sang the highest song, high in the air, and the noisy lowing of the corps that toiled in front of the fires and in the bunkers to speed up the journey just another half-mile rose up through the ventilator shafts.

Never had there been so much and such animated singing on the *Ross* as during these days on the long, lonely stretch from New Zealand to Cape Horn. All sorts of real sailor songs from the old sailing days echoed over the wide waters of the ocean, which this time did not belie its peaceful name of Pacific.

The hurried tempo of modern steam sailing leaves little time for vocal relaxation. But on the sailing ships, which stayed at sea for weeks and months at a time and where the clock wasn't such a dominating factor, they sang a great deal. Among Norwegian seafolk there are still always many who have traveled on sailing ships, and these old salts often know a wealth of deep-sea songs that the young gladly take up. This probably happens because the romantic attraction that sailing undeniably possesses is usually expressed so artlessly in these old sea tunes.

Here is a typical capstan tune, an anchor-shanty from the earlier Cape Horn sailors:

> Pipe all hands to man the capstan,
>   see your cable is all clear,
> For today we'll heave the anchor,
>   and for England [home] we'll steer.
>
> Refrain:
> Rolling home, rolling home,
>   rolling home across the sea.
> Rolling home to dear old England,
>   rolling home, my land, to thee!
>
> When we heave it with a will, boys,
>   soon our cable we shall ship;
> Then across the briny ocean
>   we [wi]ll steer our gallant ship. [Refrain]
>
> Up aloft, among the rigging,
>   blow the fierce, exulting gales,
> Like a bird with snowy pinions
>   shaking out its snow-white sails. [Refrain]
>
> To California's fairest daughters
>   we must bid a fond adieu;
> We can ne'er forget the hours
>   [that] we've spent along with you. [Refrain]
>
> We must leave you our best wishes
>   ere we leave your rockbound shore;
> We are bound for dear old England,
>   to return perhaps once more. [Refrain]

Southward, southward, ever southward,
   eastward and around the Horn;
Northward, northward, ever northward,
   to the land where I was born. [Refrain]

Where the lass that I love [so] dearly,
   e'er is watching out for me,
And is praying for her lover,
   out upon the deep blue sea.

Refrain:
Rolling home, rolling home,
   rolling home across the sea.
Rolling home to dear old England,
   rolling home, my land, to thee![1]

Our fellows had the same feelings as those that gave birth to this song. There was something genial in the steady, resilient rolling of the *Ross*, we thought, as if the ship on this homeward course had caught the happy, contagious mood that reigned above and below its decks. The ship rolled calmly on the accompanying swell, and even if the masts didn't sway as regularly as those of a sailing ship that's supported by a cloud of wind-filled sails, we were still just as much on our way to old Norway.

The fourth stanza conveys more proof of boldness than of high-mindedness, especially in connection with the young lady in the last verse. It is to be hoped that our sailors forgot the New Zealand beauties and that the waiting maidens in Scandinavia never guessed their existence; otherwise, their homecoming would be a sight less joyful.

WHEN WE crossed the 180th meridian, we set the calendar back a day; two days therefore bore the same date. If we hadn't done that, then our

---

1. Van der Does transcribed this text a bit oddly: his stanzas were sometimes four and sometimes eight lines long, the refrains returned irregularly, and the poem didn't scan properly. This is a well-known sea shanty consisting of four-line stanzas, each of which is followed by a refrain. Here it's divided into the song's original four-line format, with regular refrains, and the missing words are supplied in brackets to complete the proper syllable count.

timekeeping would have ended up a day short when we arrived in Europe. When we sailed eastward, the ship's clock, measured every noon by the midday height of the sun, was set sufficiently far forward to give the true local time. Since a degree's difference in longitude corresponds to four minutes of time, we would have set the clock forward on the whole trip from the English Channel onward until we returned: 360 × 4 minutes = 24 hours, since we would have thus completed a trip around the world and passed all 360° of the circumference of the earth, steadily sailing eastward.

The whales, which we saw blowing a few times on the trip home, didn't arouse unusual interest in us anymore; we were no longer whale hunters. Now that the harpoon cannons were in hibernation and the oil kettles weren't smoking, we were just ordinary seamen on the way home.

And yet in the middle of the Pacific Ocean it did happen once more that we followed the movements of a whale with excited attention. But that was also an interesting case, a drama in the grand style that played out unexpectedly before our eyes.

One day, not far from the ship, we saw the *blååst* from a sperm whale. The animal itself remained underwater, but the slanting direction of the expelled vapor made us certain that it was a sperm whale, which subsequently came to the surface to breathe. That was nothing out of the ordinary, and we probably wouldn't have paid much more attention had we not noticed that something odd was happening with this whale. The creature was swimming with raging speed and churning the water to foam with its broad tail. The leviathan was being followed by a school of killer whales, and it was clearly fleeing them.

Even though the strong, combative sperm whale, armed with fearful teeth, is not unjustly called *havets kongen* — the king of the ocean — and even though in the whole wide world of the ocean there lives not a single animal that it fears, there are still some fish that will not make way for it. These are the bold orcas, who terrorize the southern seas, fierce thieves with a sturdy bite from whom no single dweller of the sea is safe, not even the fearsome sperm whale.

This mighty tyrant, who doesn't even hesitate to choose the monstrous giant octopus for its breakfast, has to yield to the orcas. These crafty wolves of the sea wait to find a solitary sperm whale to attack. Just like the real four-footed wolves, they prefer to hunt in a pack when it comes to large wild creatures. They first encircle the prey, then destroy it. This was the tactic they used here.

Clash of the titans

The sperm whale fled before the bloodthirsty orcas trying to close him in. Because the running battle moved in the same direction that the ship was going, we were able to follow the struggle for a long time with our binoculars. The sperm whale was often put in dire straits by its persecutors; sometimes the powerful animal sprang completely out of the water to avoid the jaws of its attackers. The *havets kongen* really did have to flee, constrained by the superior forces of the killer whales, but it was no panicked flight. The black giant was clearly no easy prey. Time and again we saw the orcas, muzzles gaping wide open, spring out above the waves, their backs like drawn arrows that are suddenly let loose. Such were the abrupt movements that the sea wolves had to make to avoid the mighty tail with which the sperm whale tried to demolish his tormentors when they got too close to his heels. Sometimes there was nothing to see but a wheeling of foam-covered waves, sliced through by the triangular fins of the orcas. This meant that the deathly tired whale was suddenly turning around again for a counterattack. Then the pursuers headed out in all directions, racing away from the flashing teeth that threatened them.

A titanic fight developed. The flailing bodies churned the water's surface into violent turmoil, and the whale's heaving tail spattered the salty foam up high, turning it red here and there. The whale defended itself bravely: sometimes it yanked its powerful tail up high with a mighty wrench to fling off the orcas that had clamped on to it. Then the powerful, trunk-shaped head would rise up again like a black rock above the waves, with a twitching orca crushed between the gigantic jaws, while the rest of the gang tore chunks of quivering flesh off the body of the desperate whale.

We didn't see the end of the unequal fight; the battlefield eventually disappeared completely from sight. But the result was beyond doubt: *havets kongen* would be devoured alive. It didn't have the least chance of escaping its bloodthirsty enemies. It must inevitably succumb to the superior forces, since the surging water offered it no hiding place.

Untroubled, the *Ross* meanwhile followed its course straight across the Pacific Ocean.

The shortest way home would naturally be a great circle. But that would have led us too far to the south, where we would have ended up sailing among the icebergs. Thus we set a course that didn't go south of fifty degrees [south latitude]. And so between New Zealand and Cape Horn we didn't see even a trace of ice.

CHAPTER TWENTY-EIGHT

A Sailor's Funeral

Reverent silence

———∽∾∽———

The fine weather that accompanied us for the first few days after we left New Zealand couldn't hold up for long at that latitude. So we found ourselves in a wide band where the Great West Wind rules, and soon one storm after another blew over the *Ross*. In general this didn't give us much trouble because the direction that the wind and the waves followed was about the same as that of our course, so the force of the breaking waves largely spent itself.

Within a few days, storms thundered incessantly over our heads. Although the decks were mostly impassable because of the surging rollers, that didn't bother us, because wind, sea, and storm all worked together to make our ship go faster, shortening the time to the home port.

We were less pleased with that favorable wind when it stirred up into a tearing storm. Then the sea could really get frightening. By day this offered an impressive show, as the mighty breath of the Great West Wind smashed the petulant waves wildly over each other so that they spouted high up in fierce, freakish fountains and licked with foamy tongues at the dark, chasing clouds. We could still avoid the most dangerous storm waves as long as it was light. But at night, when we couldn't see them coming, they had their way with the ship; then many a huge breaker came thundering over the stern. Even though we had reckoned on the *Ross* having to face heavy weather for several weeks, everything on deck that wasn't riveted down tight as a drum was demolished and swept away during those days. We went through many an anxious moment when, during a pitch-black night, a violent wave unexpectedly threw itself roaring onto the ship and buried it in such an enormous mass of water that it sometimes looked as if half the ocean had heaved over the decks. Then it took a while before anyone dared to go on the afterdeck to see if much damage had been done. An inspection trip like that was always dangerous, because in the darkness you couldn't see a surge coming in time to get out of the way. Only at the last moment did you "hear" one coming over, but you still would be uncertain where and how it would hit. Then you'd jump up on top of something somewhere and hold on tight, waiting to see what the sea felt like doing. These were tense moments, when in the darkness the dully booming roar swelled ominously and the whole ship shuddered. Sometimes the wave thundered on by, but other times it poured over the ship like a flood, nearly drowning anyone who didn't use all his strength to keep from being swept away.

Were anyone to be caught by surprise by such a gigantic wave, he would as good as certain be washed overboard, without any chance of being rescued. In the best-case scenario, he would come away with several wounds or broken bones. But everyone knew the danger all too well and took the greatest precautions, so we ended up not having a single accident to regret — even if that was more attributable to luck than to wisdom. Or did things always go so well because the doctor had laid out his splints close at hand, the way someone brings an umbrella along to be sure that it doesn't rain?

In fact, we were more worried for the ship than for ourselves. If it turned out that the *Ross* couldn't withstand the power of the sea, then not a single one of us would survive its sinking. Experience had taught us well that the ship could stand up to a heavy blow, but the danger lay in the long-term exposure to the force of the waves, which twisted the ship violently for weeks on end. A ship that isn't solidly built can't hold up against such an incessant test of power and sooner or later hopelessly breaks up. Many a vessel has been lost down to the last man this way.

Dark days and darker nights of storm followed one after another. The groaning, creaking ship was overrun and wiped clean by one surge after another. Ceaselessly the waves bellowed and shrieked over the vessel, while the high waves were as black and threatening as the thick, chasing clouds that hid the light of the sun and stars.

On one of those wild, ominous nights, Death came and claimed one of our men: Gamle Hans. He wasn't a victim of the turbulent elements, though. He died after a long time in sick bay.

He had been one of our best men on deck, a seaman of the old stamp who did all the ropework that came up as deftly as he packed the pipe that seemed to have taken root between his teeth. We liked the old salt for his outstanding seaman's qualities and his imperturbable good nature. But he was weak in character and couldn't withstand the temptations of Bacchus — such a shame for someone who was an excellent sailor in every respect. Because he so willingly offered himself up to the god of wine, he grew old before his time, and with his white hair he got the name of Old Hans, even though he wasn't old in years by any means.

Gamle Hans had come onboard without decent equipment. That didn't do any harm before we reached the polar region, but when we stopped in Tasmania, he sold everything that he could to get drinks, so he had almost nothing more than the rags he was wearing when we went from there toward the barren south. He did sometimes get warm, usable pieces of clothing from this or that person, but the incorrigible drunkard always bartered them away again for a swallow of aquavit. Not only did Old Hans have to suffer bitter cold because of this; he also froze his feet so badly during a blizzard that he couldn't work anymore after that. Once we were back out of the Antarctic, he didn't recover like the others who had been sick in the polar region. A blood clot from the frozen foot had lodged in a blood vessel in his leg, and the doctor had prescribed complete bed-rest for him to prevent the clot from being carried along to his heart, where it could have fatal consequences.

To sick bay

But Gamle Hans got tired of being bedridden so long, and one day he was so incautious as to leave his bunk and walk around a bit. That turned out to be a fatal mistake. We saw that he was getting deadly tight in the chest and dragged him to sick bay. But there was nothing more to be done; the blood clot had ended up in his heart, and Gamle Hans died shortly thereafter. A death on the high seas is always much sadder than it is onshore. The deceased has to be buried at sea, so there isn't even a peaceful grave to serve as a last material link between him and those who loved him. It's such a complete and final disappearance from life.

The dead man was transferred to the empty powder-house on the poop deck and, in sailors' fashion, sewn into a piece of canvas, with a grating bar put in to weigh down his feet. Two days later the burial took place during the afternoon, and all hands who weren't on watch got time off to attend the solemnities.

At the appointed time, we went, wearing our best clothes, to the after-deck. There in the railing a cargo gateway had already been opened, and two flag-covered chests stood there to support the bier during the funeral that Captain Larsen would hold. Next to them stood a little black chest full of sand.

Silently, with a vague respect for death — the invisible stowaway who would eventually call all of us to him — we spread out in a wide arc around the gaping opening, the doorway through which Gamle Hans would disappear on his way into the unknown hereafter. No one thought it strange that the path the funeral procession would take was decorated with multicolored signal flags, as if for a celebration. Superficially seen, such a festive fluttering of colors wasn't at all fitting for the mournful ceremony that would soon take place, but this was only an apparent contradiction. It is understandable, after all, that we felt a need to express visibly our inner feelings (difficult to describe) about the passing of a comrade. Onboard a whaler one searches in vain for black crêpe, flowers, and palm branches, so we — rowing with the oars we had — made do with the contents of the flag chest. Meanwhile, someone distributed hymnbooks to us as we waited.

When the bier left the powder house, the flag, which had flown at half-mast, was lowered completely as a sign of respect for death, to whom all are subject. The engines were stopped, and a great stillness fell over the ship, broken only by the sighing of the wind and the murmur of the waves.

Bedecked with the Norwegian flag, the bier was carried by four sailors at a solemn pace, coming slowly closer under the fluttering flag decorations, which were oddly etched against the dark, threatening sky. They put down the bier in reverent silence. Meanwhile, the wide circle of men swayed wholly as one with the swell under the ship, which began to roll harder after the engines were stopped, and with silent seriousness we watched how the bosun carefully laid a wreath on the flag that covered the mortal remains. It was but a humble floral tribute, consisting of a bunch of wilted asters that had stood somewhere in the salon since the previous harbor. They were held together with a paper ribbon bearing these words:

"HVILE I FRED. FRA DINE KAMERATER."
("Rest in peace. From your comrades.")

In the middle of the respectful silence, Captain Larsen, dressed in sober black, took his place next to the bier and requested the singing of an appropriate psalm. He started off himself, but the seamen, who weren't particularly well-versed in the Scriptures, didn't know the melody and didn't have the faintest idea how to read the notes in the book, so the hymn sounded rather hesitant and timid — until while singing somebody by accident landed on the better-known melody of the psalm "The Hunted Deer Fleeing the Hunt."[1] That went better, and we all sang along gallantly with that song, even if the words weren't as appropriate to the occasion that had brought us together. In other circumstances, mixing up songs like that would have been ludicrous, but now nobody found any cause for ridicule in it. All these rough fellows were suffused with the seriousness of the moment: they grasped something of the mystery of death, which is not after all a complete destruction; they had vague feelings that they were coming in contact with another form of life, one that must exist when the body dies. They sensed somehow that Gamle Hans wouldn't actually disappear in the waves but would pass on to another life, one that they didn't know and couldn't comprehend. They all felt in their unsophisticated simplicity that the ordering of the impenetrable things rested with a higher power, with God, whose sovereignty they also recognized in their hearts without reservation in situations like this. And that is why they dearly wanted to sing a sacred song that sounded like a hymn of praise to the Almighty; which words were sung exactly didn't matter as much. The song that rose up out of that circle of hard men was indeed an acknowledgment of God's omnipotence, and it came from the depths of their being, so that for all its clumsiness it still made a deep impression. The entire drama, for that matter, was very gripping, and I can still see it clearly now, years later — and not only because a resting place was being prepared for one of the sailors in the wide waters on which he had roamed all of his life.

Nature took care to provide a powerful setting that was wholly in harmony with the mournful event. The wind died down, as if it were holding its mighty breath before the majesty of death. But the sea ran high, and the storm-laden clouds hung heavy in the dark sky. Scattered beams of sunlight pierced their way with difficulty through the somber deck of clouds, and flowing tongues of fire lapped over the backs of the waves. It was a picture of fantastic and ominous beauty.

The midpoint of the grand, impressive scene was formed by a group of silent men and the bier with its sad cargo, over which fleeting glances

---

1. Van der Does identifies the tune by the title *'t Hijgend hert der jacht ontkomen*, which is the sixteenth-century setting of Psalm 42 from the Genevan Psalter. Of course, the author's Norwegian shipmates would have known the tune by other words. This melody was very well known throughout northern Europe, not only as a Calvinist psalm but also as a Lutheran chorale (set to many different texts); it was as a part of the Lutheran repertoire that it found its way into Scandinavian culture.

fell, while the heavily heaving ship seemed to wish to be free of its sorrow-
ful burden.

When the wind had wafted away the last sounds of the song, Captain
Larsen gave a short speech. Our leader, who considered himself the father
and protector of the men who followed him, was visibly and deeply moved.
He too had lost a comrade and valued seaman with the death of Gamle Hans.
Undoubtedly it was a certain feeling of solidarity with the simple seamen
that made him use their pithy dialect when he remembered Old Hans's good
qualities, and with true compassion he spoke of his wife and children, who
would be left behind in poverty and loneliness. With moving words he com-
mended the widow and the orphans to the care of the Almighty.

Thereafter Larsen asked again to have a psalm sung. But it didn't flow
right this time, either, even though Nicolaisen, our song leader, did his best.
Things improved when once again the tune of "The Hunted Deer" popped
up, a melody everyone could sing along with, even though the tune had to be
fiddled with a bit, and even though the same words were repeated for all the
different verses. That didn't matter; the men wanted to sing a final farewell to
their dead companion, and better with inappropriate words and the wrong
tune than not at all. After that Captain Larsen read the burial service, ending
with these words: "For dust thou art, and unto dust shalt thou return, and in
the earth shalt thou be buried." With this he took a scoop of sand and sprin-
kled it over the dead man's bier. Out of a feeling of piety the men had filled
the sand chest with Norwegian scouring sand, which they had managed to
locate somewhere after a long search. And thus was Gamle Hans buried, if
only symbolically, in Norway, his fatherland.

Then Larsen gave the bearers a nod. While the ship leaned over, they
raised one end of the hatch that served as a bier, and the shroud holding its
sad burden glided down through the open cargo-gateway, which for Gamle
Hans was the threshold of eternity. It was as if the sea had been waiting impatiently for her due. As the body fell, a wave rose high up underneath, and . . .
plunk! . . . Old Hans was committed forever to the waves. May he rest in
peace!

No one moved, and the reverent silence remained unbroken. There
wasn't a man there who wasn't deeply aware of the presence of a power before whose might his own flourishing life was like grass before a prairie fire.
All those men stood there with taut faces and stared ahead with unseeing
eyes, filled with distant, serious thoughts. No one had peeked curiously over-

board when the long, flag-covered parcel shot out to sea. They weren't thinking of Old Hans anymore — that was past. Their thoughts had turned inward, and with the eyes of the soul they saw their loved ones in the far-off
fatherland. These were holy moments.

No sound disturbed the sacred silence other than the sighing of the
wind and the splashing of the waves, which made the silence seem even
greater.

Then with great gravity the captain began the "Our Father."

With this, the spell seemed to be broken. Everyone returned to reality.
There was a nod to the bridge, the telegraph rang, and the engines began to
turn again. Soon the ship resumed its course; life resumed its rights. The men
spread out and made themselves busy with whatever things happened to
come up. Nobody felt like working anymore that day, nor was it demanded.
The name of Old Hans wasn't mentioned much afterward, and everyone
worked out for himself the thoughts and emotions that had been awakened
by the sad events.

It is customary that the belongings of a deceased sailor are sold among
the crew, with permission of any rightful claimants. But nobody had any desire to buy Gamle Hans's poor possessions; they were put in his sea chest and
kit bag and stored away. There wasn't a man onboard, however, who didn't
gladly sign over something of his earned wages to the account of his former
comrade, so that his widow would not immediately be in want.

CHAPTER TWENTY-NINE

Around Cape Horn

Running before the storm

Twenty-three days and nights from New Zealand to Cape Horn, and almost without exception they were stormy. Especially during the last portion of this great crossing we ran into genuine Cape Horn weather, which is to say, storms out of a westerly direction, accompanied by rain, snow, or hail, in whichever form precipitation happened to fall. For the entire time we couldn't perform celestial navigation; the heavenly bodies hid themselves. It wasn't very pleasant making dead reckoning in that weather and having to run along such a dangerous coast as that of Tierra del Fuego. Birds appeared in steadily greater numbers; that meant we were nearing land. But we saw no signs of this yet in the ocean. It still presented the same picture of mighty, rising seas, of majestic, living mountains of water with wide, breaking combs that left long white placards of foam behind on the flowing backs of the hills. The sea is at her most beautiful this way, even though someone who suffers from seasickness would adamantly deny it.

I freely admit that we on the *Ross* counted ourselves lucky to have our course running before the storm, the most favorable position in such screaming weather. This was the case only because we hadn't taken the westerly route home from New Zealand. On that route, in the "Roaring Forties," the wind and storms wouldn't have given us a helping hand but instead would have been against us, undoubtedly making the trip home take longer. The sailors made jokes about it as they stood looking at the powerful waves that came rolling up behind the ship, calling out, "Hurry up, lazy Rasmus! [another shipmate]. Give it another push." But they agreed with each other that a less pleasant water ballet would have to be performed on a ship that was forced to fight against such a sea.

The wind and sea didn't always come from directly behind us. As long as they did, the ship glided fairly easily along the rolling hills and dales of the ocean and usually took on little water. But it was a very different story when the wind whipped up and the sea ran more or less across our path. Then the *Ross* heaved and tumbled like something possessed. Not much came of our work under such conditions. On deck, Neptune reigned supreme and took care that nothing could be done in the way of cleaning, painting, chipping away rust, or other such tasks that usually filled our days. The men were kept busy in the tweendecks, where it was dark and stuffy because the air shafts had been removed. It was far from pleasant working there. Have you ever tried to paint an iron bulkhead that one moment dives away from your brush and the next moment slams into you? Not only did all the bulkheads have rude and irritating manners like that; all the struts, ladders, beams, and everything else onboard was equally ill-mannered. The whole day men fought against heaving, slamming, swinging objects. This was true even at meals, where we had to try to keep our balance with plates and mugs in hand so as not to lose their contents. Knives and forks we put in our pockets or in the seam of the table leaf so as not to have to keep chasing after them. The benches were fastened down firmly to the legs of the table and onto the supports because our seats often sailed full speed leeward, men and all, if the ship suddenly leaned over particularly far. This hugely amused those who had been able to keep their balance!

The sea seemed to have it in for those immovable benches. Several times she pushed the *Ross* so tremendously hard that the table legs broke from the weight of the full benches that were attached to them, so that every-thing — tables, benches, dishes, and sailors — rolled leeward in one con-fused pile. It was amusing to hear how curses crackling like rockets shot up out of the wriggling, soup- and juice-splattered chaos, out of which individu-als tried to work themselves free with mush in their hair and porridge in their boots.

ON THE Pacific Ocean we had no other company besides a few albatrosses that faithfully followed the ship, unhindered by storm or heavy seas. Other birds announced the nearness of land hundreds of miles in advance. The first to appear were the sprightly black-and-white Cape doves, followed by the silver-gray petrels, skimming gracefully over the waves.

We were nearing the notorious Cape Horn.

No other name has such an unfavorable sound to the seaman's ears —

Helpless

even today, although ships seldom pass "Cape Stiff" anymore. Cape Horn developed its bad reputation in the grand old days of sailing ships, and it was well earned. The heavy storms that we too experienced around the Cape are normal for those parts; days without a westerly storm are extremely rare. It was a mighty struggle for sailing ships to round the Cape, heading against wind, sea, and current on their way from the Atlantic to the Pacific Ocean. The ships wrestled for weeks, sometimes months in a row with the dangerous waters, while the sailors were exhausted by murderous work on the flooded decks and often ended up in no shape to work anymore, done in by cold, exhaustion, and misery. Human lives were often lost, and more often sails, rigging, and spars. The helpless ships with their worn-out crews were then delivered over wholly to the mercy of the elements and driven far off their course by the storm. Usually the men managed to keep sailing until the sea died down or they were driven outside the storm area. Still, many a ship wasn't so lucky and got the worst of it in the bitter battle against the Great West Wind. And many were the ships that were battered to splinters at the latitude of Cape Horn by the merciless seas. Indeed, so many ships sank there and often so horrible were the tales of the seamen that the feared cape was avoided. To this day the memory remains alive, and the name of Cape Horn is still pronounced with respect and fear.

When we estimated that land was near, we dared not steam ahead at more than half-power. Fortunately, the long-hidden sun finally broke through the clouds for a moment between two hail showers, so that we could finally make a proper reckoning.

That same afternoon we spotted our first land: Ildefonso, a high cliff lying forty miles west of Tierra del Fuego. We didn't see much more than a few bare rocks that poked up now and then out of the dashing surf. The island was quickly blurred by the smoking surf and disappeared in driving snow showers. After that we saw no further land. It was in the dead of night that we passed the fearsome Cape — in a galloping storm.

As soon as the *Ross* entered the lee of the land, it came into calmer waters and wasn't slung to and fro so violently anymore. It was nighttime, and except for those who were on watch, everyone was in bed. But the sudden quiet was so striking that it woke everyone up, and they rushed to the deck to see what unusual thing was happening. We had gotten so used to being handled like a toy by the turbulent seas that the sudden calm seemed ominous. The men who quickly came on deck thought there had been a catastrophe, since we were so close to the invisible, feared cape; at the very least they expected an even more unbridled explosion of the power of the waves. The quiet was reminiscent of the striking stillness that reigns in the center of a cyclone — except here it was the sea that came suddenly to rest, while the wind kept howling through the rigging with undiminished force. (In the center of a typhoon it's just the other way around.) For a moment the men expected something terrible to happen, until they understood that the *Ross* had just entered the still water on the leeside of the land.

The following morning, the west wind had also let go of us. Already early in the morning the sun shone glad and clear and spread a silver gleam over the barren, snow-covered mountains of Tierra del Fuego, which was etched against the western sky with its capriciously notched comb. The last remnants of the storm clouds drifted away to starboard over the rock massif of Isla de los Estados.

Le Maire Strait, which lay between Tierra del Fuego and Isla de los Estados, was quickly behind us. Now the land turned back to the northerly course that we were following, and the Atlantic Ocean lay open before us. About eight thousand miles still separated us from our final goal, a matter of another good month of sailing.

The sea charts for the waters around Cape Horn swarmed with Dutch names, remembrances of the time when our country was a great sailing nation and her sons had a very important share in the broadening of the knowledge of our globe.

As if by magic, the weather took on another, wholly mild character. At the latitude of Rio de la Plata we reached the warmer Brazil current, and with it the temperature of the air rose markedly. Luxurious days followed, full of warmth and sunshine. The long, happy days ended like a banquet every night in a glory of rich, glowing colors. They left behind the wide, peaceful water dreaming under the silvery light of the waxing moon, which covered the night like an awning with a gleaming, subtle beauty, fairy-like and at the same time melancholy.

In the tropics one gets ample opportunity to slake one's thirst for light and warmth. Soon life onboard was organized along tropical lines again. The men reduced their clothing to a bare minimum, and soon their bodies sported the colors of lead-red paint and vermilion; later their torsos looked as if they'd been chiseled out of mahogany. There were no more closed doors or porthole sports; instead, the men tried to increase their supply of fresh air

Hosing down the deck

as much as possible and tried to outdo each other in thinking up ingenious but useful plans. The morning deck-washing became a water festival. The fellows took delight in splashing each other until they were good and wet, just the way we as children sprang under the spray-cart, squealing with delight, and in the summertime taunted the men who sprayed the street until they aimed the stream of water at us, which was of course the point in the first place.

In the tropics, cabins and bunks were avoided as places to sleep. Men slept everywhere there was a good chance of catching a breath of fresh wind: on the tanks, hatches, boats, and awnings.

THE TRIP HOME was no different from the final leg of any other sea voyage. Few unusual occurrences broke the monotony of the days, and the general conversation was stale and soporific. Luckily, at the latitude of Montevideo there was a change in the conversation when we came into wireless contact with other whalers, all Norwegian ships. They were returning from the hunt near South Georgia and around the South Shetland Islands and coming to Buenos Aires or Montevideo to take on coal. It appeared that in general our colleagues hadn't been any more successful with the whale hunt than we had. It had been a poor hunting season in the far south that year.

The next sensation was coming across the first ship that we had seen on the high seas since the Cape of Good Hope. At night there was always a man standing watch in the crow's nest, but he almost never got to see anything that was worth the trouble of reporting to the bridge. Then one fine evening the watchman struck two bells, meaning that he had seen a light to starboard, and everybody came on deck to see the ship. There was nothing to see other than two small points of light, which grew clearer and then disappeared behind us. That's all one sees at sea of "ships that pass in the night."[1] Under normal circumstances no fuss would be made over a ship sailing by. The great interest that those simple points of light generated made it clear how solitary our journey had been.

Up to this point we had crossed unsailed seas, but now we found ourselves on the heavily traveled route from Rio de la Plata to Cape Verde. We felt like we were back in the inhabited world. The ships we came across furnished steadily new material for conversation. Sometimes somebody recognized a ship that we spotted, or we saw another boat from the same line, or we guessed where they had come from and where they were going. Always there was some connection leading to a story or a dispute, so that the conversation didn't falter.

The southeast trade-wind blew only weakly. We quickly overtook and left behind a three-master that was sailing on the same course, whereas a ship like that under full sail would easily have been able to keep up with our ten-knot speed with a stiff, sustained trade-wind. They are growing rare, these great sailing ships, and that's a pity, because there are few things that are as beautiful in form and movement as a great ship in full rig.

The evenings below the equator were poetic, one and all, full of sultry life, mystical in mood and abundant in color.

The beauty of the grim, cold ocean is so completely different from that of the warm, tropical sea. In the far south the ocean is grand and powerful, hard and raw, cold and gray, while the seas between the tropics have a decidedly friendly character. The deep blue waves don't go frighteningly high but push playful, dancing white heads against the far, open horizon and catch sparkling reflections of the beaming sun and the cheerful blue-and-white sky.

---

1. The author quotes the phrase in English.

Three-masted ship in full rig

A TROPICAL evening at sea.

A mild, cool breeze blew, making little whitecaps on the dark blue waves; the sun had already come close to the horizon, and though not entirely below it yet, it was already veiled in the mists above the ocean's surface. It sank lower and lower like a bright yellow ball of light until it was hidden, twinkling like gold that gradually grew dimmer. I stood still, lost in contemplating the clouds that floated in steadily changing splendor above the horizon. When an exuberant light radiated over the nearly black sea, I noticed that the whole expanse of the heavens was shot through with a purple glow. In the western sky, up to the zenith, a luminous procession of rose-red clouds floated in the clear azure. One could scarcely call them clouds; they were so fleeting and transparent that in the full sunlight they wouldn't have been visible. Moments before that, I hadn't noticed them; the firmament had been a perfect, soft blue dome that vaulted unbroken from one end of the horizon to the other. When the sun had nearly covered its course along the taut blue sky and disappeared, its last searching rays caught the most rarefied mists that floated in the atmosphere and revived them with a soft, rose-red glow, as a farewell to the tiring day.

Soon the sun sank, and the tender red in the sky grew deeper and warmer in hue until the whole outstretched sky glowed like fire and a purple fleece spread over the darkening sea.

Immediately after the blazing glory had reached its peak, the splendid play of color vanished. The glow of the clouds first paled high in the zenith.

The flaming fire quickly gave way to a cold blue that already spoke of the night that now took possession of the world and pulled its dark mantle over the sky. The eastern horizon dozed away in the falling evening in a vague half-darkness, pushing the lingering red out ahead of it into the west. There was almost nothing left of the exuberant splendor of color but a swipe of sultry carmine in the spot where the sun had sunk below the horizon. The last spark of flaming red was quickly extinguished. The light lingered for a moment above the separation between air and water, and the colors blossomed again for a moment, but much less brightly and not as passionately as before. Soft purple mingled with pale orange and tempered emerald, which, as with a delicately rendered pastel, blended unnoticeably into faint cobalt and even higher into the violet-tinged black of the evening.

Gradually the day had given way to night. Venus stood shining in the same place where a welter of fire and color had swarmed shortly before; the great white planet already laid down a faint, twinkling path of light over the black water. On the other side of the sky, the moon looked like a gleaming metal shield that hung in the heavens. It too was reflected in the sea with a wide band of playful, flickering lights that gamboled over the dancing waves.

One by one the stars freed themselves from the dark vault of the night. First the very largest came hesitantly into view. Then the smaller ones dared to show themselves, encouraged by the success of their larger sisters. And soon the whole sky was strewn with innumerable twinkling lights, although they didn't dare sparkle all that exuberantly in front of their mother, the moon.

All nature breathed calm and peace. Even on the crowded ship the silence of the night had descended undisturbed. The men had gone to their rest, except for those who were on watch. The bustle of work was hushed; only the wind whispered, scarcely audible, and the waves rustled softly as they skipped around the bow in a light cadence. The heartbeat of the ship sounded muffled and regular as clockwork in the engine room. All these sounds had the peaceful, dreamy rhythm of the night. On the deserted decks everything gleamed as if the whole ship was covered with fine silver dust that drifted down with the moonbeams. A rare, wonderful light lay spread out over things, a delicate wash that softened contours, blurred forms, and made the colors flow into each other. But the shadows were deep and black. It is precisely that vagueness which gives moonlight its charm; there's something mysterious about it because the power of imagination fills in what one guesses rather than really sees in the wavering light. The measureless space of sky and water that you feel around you at sea spurs the imagination to still greater activity, since not a single object checks her free rein.

On the ocean the moonlight had taken the entire visible world completely in her possession — the wide water and the whole arch of heaven. The broad path of flowing, sparkling silver laid down by the moon over the sea swelled calmly on the rocking waves; only close to the ship was it broken by the bow wave, which tore the silver ribbon into flashing strips.

Calm and sure, the bow cut the faintly rolling waves and threw the water aside in a wide band of foam, white as freshly fallen snow in the white light. Murmuring and swirling, the restless water glided past the ship's flanks so regularly that the peace of the night was only heightened by it.

A few times the calm was disrupted by a school of flying fish which, frightened by the approaching ship, popped up out of the dark water as if by magic, with a rustling sound of fins that crackled over the waves. Their smooth, wet bodies gleaming in the sudden light, the fish zig-zagged in all directions in front of the ship, like a swarm of shooting stars, then fell back one after the other with a light splash into the sea. As they disappeared, the rhythm and the stillness were restored.

AT ABOUT twenty degrees south latitude, the southeast trade-winds kicked in and accompanied us to the equator. After passing Fernando de Noronha,

The silver beam of light

we found ourselves in the doldrums, the equatorial band of stillness that separates the northeast and southeast trade-winds.

Following the usual route, we sailed along the Cape Verde Archipelago, but without seeing much of the volcanic islands. The atmosphere was too full of water vapor, so the tall, volcanic cone peeked out above the thick layer of clouds only for a few moments.

The northeast trade-winds kept up until the Canary Islands, which are thought by many scholars to be the remnants of the mysterious Atlantis, swallowed by the sea. I had sailed past this group of islands many times before, but always at night; I had never really gotten a good look at the famed Peak of Tenerife. And this time I didn't get a much better one. Far in the distance the top of a standard eruption-cone could vaguely be seen, but it quickly vanished in the night and the mist.

With the chase-boat crews that had come onboard in New Zealand, the *Ross* had really become overcrowded on its way home. There also wasn't enough work for all these hands, even if the whole ship — from capstan to aft peak, and from crankcase to mast-top — had been scoured, scraped, stoppered, sculpted, and slathered with paint. And so with no objection I received permission after we passed Cape Horn to do what I wanted to: my own painting, naturally. While the impressions were still fresh, I developed some of the sketch material that I had collected in the polar region. I also painted for Captain Larsen a large canvas of the *Ross* in the pack ice.

The painting was quite large, so I could hardly work on it in the dark, stuffy cabins or in the professor's cramped laboratory. In any case, it was nicer to sit on deck in the fresh breeze and paint. There, of course, the painting attracted a good deal of notice and provoked a fair amount of critique, most of it far from constructive. For example, it was considered to be an incomprehensible stupidity that the ship was painted rather small in the middle of the wide expanse of the pack ice. Jack Tar thought that this was simply beyond crazy. If you're painting a ship — well, then the first thing you do is make sure that you clearly see the ship, with all its ropes, stays, and portholes complete! Who cared about all that wretched ice, where you never saw anything but misery anyway? "No," said Iver, "I don't get it at all; it doesn't look anything like it!" He was standing with his nose smack up against the canvas to see whether all the blubber grooves were on it, but to his annoyance he saw nothing more than a few smears of paint. And Hauge meant well when he said, after having observed it thoughtfully for a long time, "Bill, you're

Destructive criticism

good with an oar and a hammer in your hand, but this I would quit if I were you; it's never going to amount to anything. If I were you I'd just sign up again as helmsman, like Ouwe asked you to." Another one, clearly less well-disposed, cried out, "God Almighty, look at 'im scribble that mess on there! Nothing but lousy ice — you can't see a d----- thing of the f------ ship. You call that art? Looky here! A kid could do that! The ship's boy paints like that too! Whaddya say, Oernolf?"

Yes, in general the gentlemen critics didn't speak well of my work.

AT THE LATITUDE of the Canary Islands, we received a wireless order to go to Rotterdam and unload our cargo of oil there.

At daybreak on June 7, 1924, I greeted the Fatherland in the form of the stumpy towers of Den Briel, which showed up in the east against the growing light of a summer day. It was good to see the low dunes and the wide beach of Hoek van Holland again; the dikes, the green meadows, and all the familiar spots along the New Waterway.

The *Ross* was moored in Wilhelmina Harbor in Schiedam, where large tanks awaited the oil that we had obtained with so much effort in the Antarctic Ocean. It was a lucky accident that the voyage ended in Schiedam, where I was living at the time. Coming from the *Ross* right out of the polar region, I would be able to go straight home, where the smells of saltwater and oil that I brought with me wouldn't detract in the least from the joy of reunion.

Once back in Holland, I took leave of the ship without delay, and also the many friends who stayed behind with it. I gave especially heartfelt good-byes to Captain Larsen, Captain Kaldager, and the two scientists.

Captain Larsen went back with the *Ross* that same year to the Antarctic, where, sadly, he died in the pack ice. Great respect for this noble, brave son of the Vikings and admiration for his deeply felt humanity led me to ask Mrs. Larsen if I could dedicate this travel story to the memory of her husband. Unfortunately, I was never able to meet him again after our parting. But when later I held an exhibition of my polar paintings in Norway, I often had more opportunities to talk about Larsen and his work with Mrs. Larsen, who had retired to her estate near Oslo. It did her good to hear how he had always been respected as a man and as a leader.

For years I stayed in contact with Dr. Kohl, who also wrote a book about our modern Viking journey. But I lost his trail after he left for Central Africa.

Captain Kaldager and I often met in Surabaja when he lay in the roads there with his ship — not a whaler anymore.

WRITING THIS travel memoir while living in Malang, I was often struck by the extreme contrast between the natural scenes I was describing and the richness of the tropical environment that smiled on me as I wrote. While I was trying to convey what an Antarctic blizzard was like, I saw the crowns of the fruit-laden coconut palms shining in the bright sunshine and the tops of the high bamboo stalks, fine as lace, waving next to them in the sultry warmth of a tropical morning. And the same day on which I recounted the desolate desertedness of the land of the Pole, where not even humble mosses can live, I saw the king of the night blossom, the cactus with its huge, beautiful flowers, a sublime example of the sumptuous splendor with which Flora has adorned the tropics.

Polar Explorers and Other Nautical Figures

—⟨ΦΦΘ⟩—

When Van der Does wrote this book, the Heroic Age of polar exploration had only recently ended, and most of the people he mentions were
still household names. Because this is less true now, these brief
sketches have been included in this translation. Sources of information
include the *Encyclopedia Britannica*, Roland Huntford's books *Shackleton*
(1984) and *The Last Place on Earth* (1999), and two encyclopedic books titled *Antarctica*, one issued by Reader's Digest (1985) and the other by
Firefly Books (2001).

Amundsen, Roald (1872-1928): Norwegian explorer and one of the greatest figures in the field of polar exploration. As the leader of an expedition on the *Fram*,
he — along with four companions — was the first to reach the South Pole (on 14
December 1911). In 1898 Amundsen was a member of the *Belgica* expedition,
which was the first to overwinter in Antarctica. From 1903-1906, commanding
the *Gjøa*, he was the first to make a voyage through the Northwest Passage. He
died in 1928 while attempting to rescue fellow polar explorer Umberto Nobile
near Spitsbergen.

Baerentsz[oon], Jan Willem [Willem Barents] (c. 1550-1597): Dutch explorer
who was one of the most important early Arctic explorers. On a series of expeditions to discover the presumed Northeast Passage from Europe to the Far East, he
first discovered the island of Novaya Zemlya, and later, after being trapped in the
pack ice, overwintered on that island, a member of the first European party to
survive an Arctic winter. The Barents Sea is named after him.

Balleny, John (19th century; dates unknown): British sealer and whaler. In 1838-
39 he made the first crossing of the Antarctic Circle, and the first landings south
of it on a group of islands south of New Zealand that now bear his name; he also
pioneered a route toward the Ross Sea.

Bellingshausen, Thaddeus [Fabian] (1778-1852): Russian explorer who led the second expedition to circumnavigate Antarctica (1819-1821). He discovered and named Peter 1 Island and Alexander 1 Island. An area of Antarctic waters called the Bellingshausen Sea is named after him.

Borchgrevink, Carsten (1864-1934): Norwegian explorer. Serving as second mate on Henryk Bull's 1894 expedition on the *Antarctica*, he discovered the first plant life ever found in the Antarctic (lichen) and claimed to have been the very first to set foot on the continent. In 1898 (on the *Southern Cross*) he led the first expedition that intentionally overwintered in the Antarctic. In 1900, making the first sledge journey atop the Ross Ice Shelf, he reached 78° 50′ S, a record for that time.

Bowers, Henry Robertson (1883-1912): Scottish-born lieutenant in the British Royal Indian Marine. Joined Robert Scott's *Terra Nova* expedition despite his lack of any previous polar experience. Though without skis, he was added to the polar party as the fifth man at the last minute. He, along with Edward Wilson, was the last to die with Scott during their disastrous attempt to return from the South Pole.

Bull, Henryk (1844-1930): Norwegian-born Australian who led an 1894 Antarctic whaling expedition funded by Svend Föyn. Bull's party made the first recorded landing on the continent on 24 January 1895, at Cape Adare.

Drygalski, Erich von (1865-1949): German geographer and glaciologist. He led the German Antarctic expedition of 1901-1903, sailing on the *Gauss*. The ship was trapped in pack ice for a year, and the crew was forced to overwinter near an ice-free volcanic peak that Drygalski discovered and named Gaussberg.

Duke of the Abruzzi, the [Luigi A. G. M. F. Francesco] (1873-1933): Italian mountaineer and explorer whose exploits ranged from Africa to both poles. In the *Stella Polare* (the rechristened *Jason* of Carl Larsen's Antarctic expeditions of 1892-1894), he voyaged to Spitsbergen and reached 86° 34′ N, a record for that time.

Evans, Edgar (1876-1912): Welsh-born petty officer in the British navy. He volunteered for Robert Scott's first Antarctic expedition. On the second expedition, he was the first to die — on 17 February 1912, on the Beardmore Glacier — during the party's attempt to return from the South Pole.

Filchner, Wilhelm (1877-1957): German scientist and explorer. Sailing on the *Deutschland*, he led the German Antarctic expedition of 1910-1912. Although they failed in their attempt to cross Antarctica, they entered the then-unknown Weddell Sea, charted the Luitpold coast, and survived being trapped in ice for nine months.

Föyn, Svend (1809-1894): Norwegian whaler whose invention of the explosive-tipped harpoon, and methods of mounting it on steam-powered whale-catcher boats, revolutionized whaling. He sponsored Henryk Bull's 1894 Antarctic expedition.

Gjertsen, Frederick (18??-19??): Norwegian naval officer who served as second mate on Roald Amundsen's successful South Pole expedition of 1911-1912 and also as the ice pilot/second mate on the voyage described in this book.

Heemskerck, Jacob van (1567-1607): Dutch explorer and, later, admiral. Captain of Willem Barents' 1596-1597 voyage to the Barents Sea in search of an Arctic passage to India, he survived overwintering on Novaya Zemlya with Barents' crew.

Hudson, Henry (c. 1565-1611): English navigator and explorer. Sailing variously for the English and the Dutch, he tried to find routes from Europe to Asia via the Arctic Ocean. The Hudson River in New York and Hudson Bay in Canada bear his name.

Larsen, Carl Anton (1860-1924): Norwegian explorer and whaling captain. His polar experience began on the *Jason*, bringing Fridtjof Nansen to his famed crossing of Greenland. From 1892-1894 he made two whaling voyages to Antarctica, also on the *Jason*, during which he charted large stretches of coastline (including the Larsen Ice Shelf, named after him), became the first man to use skis in Antarctica, and discovered petrified wood on the Antarctic peninsula, the first fossils found on the southern continent. A whaling captain by 1885, he was captain of Otto Nordenskjöld's ship, the *Antarctica*, during the expedition of 1901 and part of its dramatic rescue in 1903. He also pioneered whaling industries on South Georgia Island and in the Ross Sea. Captain of the voyage described in this book, he died later the same year that this expedition ended, at South Georgia Island while on his next whaling trip.

Mawson, (Sir) Douglas (1882-1958): Australian geologist and explorer. As a member of Ernest Shackleton's 1907 Antarctic expedition, he sledged to the Southern magnetic pole on 16 January 1909 and was a member of the first party to climb Mt. Erebus. He later led the Australasian Antarctic expedition of 1911-

1914, as well as a commonwealth expedition of 1929-1931. His explorations enabled Australia to claim over 2.5 million square miles of Antarctica.

Nansen, Fridtjof (1861-1930): Norwegian explorer, scientist, and statesman. In 1888-1889 he made the first crossing of the Greenland ice cap, and from 1893-1896 he led the first expedition to drift through the North Polar pack ice in the *Fram*, a ship specially built for this purpose. Subsequently he put the *Fram* at Roald Amundsen's disposal for the expedition that ultimately reached the South Pole. For his later international humanitarian work he was awarded the Nobel Peace Prize in 1922.

Nobile, Umberto (1885-1978): Italian aeronautical engineer and Arctic aviation pioneer. He designed the dirigibles *Norge* and *Italia*. In 1926 he flew over the North Pole from Spitsbergen to Alaska in the *Norge* with Roald Amundsen and the American explorer Lincoln Ellsworth. In 1928 Nobile crashed the *Italia* on the ice north of Spitsbergen. He survived, but seventeen lives, including Amundsen's, were lost in the attempt to rescue Nobile and his crew of seven.

Nordenskjöld, Otto (1869-1928): Swedish geologist and explorer. He led the 1901 Swedish Antarctic expedition, during which his ship, the *Antarctica,* was crushed in the pack ice in 1903. The crew divided into groups and got lost, but they were all dramatically rescued in a marvelous series of chance encounters.

Oates, Lawrence "Titus" (1880-1912): British army officer. An aristocratic cavalry captain, he joined Robert Scott's *Terra Nova* expedition as a paying volunteer. On the return trip, when his illness threatened to delay the entire party, he went out into a blizzard on 17 March 1912 in an apparent act of self-sacrifice.

Ross, (Sir) James Clark (1800-1862): Scottish officer in the British navy who made magnetic surveys of both polar regions and discovered the Ross Sea and the Victoria Land coast of Antarctica. His ships for his Antarctic expedition of 1839-1843 were the *Erebus* and the *Terror,* the names he gave to the two volcanoes on Ross Island at the northwest edge of the Ross Sea.

Ruyter, Michiel Adriaanszoon de (1607-1676): Dutch national maritime hero. Rising from humble beginnings, he became admiral of the Dutch navy and led it to its historic peak as an effective fighting force supporting the Dutch Republic's Golden Age.

Scott, Robert Falcon (1868-1912): British naval officer and explorer who led two expeditions to Antarctica: the National Antarctic Expedition of 1901-1904, sailing on the *Discovery*, and the fateful, fatal *Terra Nova* expedition of 1911-1912. On the second expedition, Scott and his crew arrived near the South Pole in January of 1912 — a month after Roald Amundsen. The demoralized Scott and his four companions — Henry Bowers, Edgar Evans, Lawrence Oates, and Edward Wilson — all died on their return journey, victims of exhaustion, bad weather, and lack of food.

Shackleton, (Sir) Ernest (1874-1922): Anglo-Irish Antarctic explorer. An officer on Robert Scott's expedition on the *Discovery*, he commanded the British Antarctic expedition of 1907-1909, during which he led a party that got within 97 miles of the South Pole. On a third voyage, sailing on the *Endurance* (1914-1916), he planned to cross the entire Antarctic continent via the Pole, but the ship was trapped, crushed, and sank in the pack ice of the Weddell Sea. Shackleton led a dramatic two-year, 800-mile trek to get help, and eventually his entire crew was rescued.

Shirase, Nobu (1861-1946): Japanese army officer and explorer. From 1910-1912 he led two expeditions to the Ross Sea on the *Kainan Maru*. When he landed at the Bay of Whales, he met members of Roald Amundsen's expedition. He also led a party that climbed the Ross Ice Shelf and sledged to 80° 05′ S as Amundsen and Robert Scott were completing their own polar journeys.

Wilkes, Charles (1798-1877): U.S. naval officer. From 1838-1842 he commanded an exploring and surveying expedition that entered the Antarctic Ocean. Following the Antarctic coast for over 2,000 kilometers (1,250 miles), he determined that Antarctica is a continent. He also sighted new land at several points in the area, which was later named Wilkes Land in his honor.

Wilson, Edward (1872-1912): Scientific illustrator who accompanied Robert Scott on both his Antarctic expeditions. During the second one, he led Henry Bowers and Apsley Cherry-Garrard on a hunt for penguin eggs in 1911 that Cherry-Garrard later immortalized in a classic book titled *The Worst Journey in the World*. An even worse journey was yet to come: along with Bowers, Oates, and Scott, Wilson died during their disastrous attempt to return from the Pole.

Glossary

aft in the direction of the stern of a ship

aft deck the deck of a ship, open to the elements, behind the main mast

aft peak the highest part of the hull, or deck, in the stern of a ship

afterdeck typically a raised section of the deck of a ship, located near the rear or stern of a ship

Agulhas windstream the winds accompanying the warm, northward-flowing stream of ocean water found off the east coast of southern Africa

amidships the center of the deck of a ship, neither forward nor aft. In steering, "amidships" means to be aligned along the centerline of a ship.

anchor flukes those points or projections of an anchor that are intended to dig into the seabottom

anchor shanty a chant or song typically sung by crew members during the effort of raising a ship's anchor

Antarctic Circle the parallel of latitude at 66 degrees and 30 minutes South, beyond which the phenomenon of the "midnight sun" can be observed

Antarctic Ocean properly, that part of the Southern Ocean south of the Antarctic Convergence (which divides the cold southern water masses and the warmer northern waters); the Antarctic Ocean has its own characteristic temperature, salinity, and marine life

astern in, toward, or beyond the rear, or aft, end of a ship

athwartships sideways — that is, extending not fore-and-aft but perpendicular to the long axis of a ship or boat

ballast tanks compartments filled with water, fuel oil, or air, used to control the bouyancy of a ship

battens boards used to tauten the canvas covers that are added to hatch covers to render them especially waterproof in stormy conditions

"before the mast" metaphorically and historically, the province on shipboard of the crew members who are not officers

Benguela current the cold, southward-flowing stream of ocean water found off the west coast of southern Africa

block and tackle on shipboard, a pulley and the ropes belonging to it

boiler kettle *See* oil boiler

bollards vertical posts on the deck of a ship or a pier around which mooring lines can be wrapped

boom a spar extended from a mast, used to hold the bottom edge of a sail in place

bosun or boatswain the petty officer assigned to supervise the ropes and rigging of a ship

bosun's chair a wooden seat suspended by ropes in which a sailor sits to work while hanging in the rigging

bow the front or forward end of a ship

brash ice small or rounded pieces of ice formed by the break-up of other kinds of ice

breakers the breaking waves formed when ocean waves encounter the shallow water around land

breeches buoy a device, riding on a pulley running along a horizontal rope, by which a person can be moved above water from ship to shore

bridge the raised structure of a ship from which the officers command it

bulkheads on shipboard, the walls or vertical surfaces that divide compartments of a ship internally

bully beef canned beef preserved in its cooking juices

bulwarks the parts of the hull of a ship extending upward above the level of the uppermost deck, forming a solid wall in place of a railing at the edge of a deck

bunkers the compartments in which coal is stored. To bunker coal means to load these compartments.

cabin boy a young crew member acting as servant for the officers sharing the cabins

cable locker the compartment of a ship in which cables (mooring and anchor lines) are stored

cablemaker the crewman assigned to turn stored rope or line into cables used in mooring the ship

calf-ice ice recently formed at sea, still in loose or uncemented form, and not so thick as to impede navigation

capstan a large drum on a vertical axis on the deck of a ship, used to wind in or out a heavy line such as an anchor cable

chart room that room or compartment of a ship in which nautical charts are stored and consulted

chase boat (from the Dutch *jachtboot* or hunting boat) a smaller boat, dependent on the mother ship, that goes in search of whales and from which whales are harpooned

clamps devices attached to an anchor chain after it's hoisted into a ship, to keep the anchor in its raised position

clews the lower corners of sails

crow's nest (Norwegian *tönne*) a partially enclosed platform on the foremast, particular to whaling ships, affording the lookout some protection from wind and weather

davits the structures by which a boat can be launched over the side of a ship

dead reckoning a method of navigating a ship that relies on course direction and estimated speed, used when clouds or weather render celestial navigation impossible

deckhand a crew member assigned a role or task on the open deck of a ship

deckhouse a room or enclosure built onto the top deck of a ship

derrick on shipboard, a crane attached at its base to a mast, used to raise and lower cargo over the side of a ship

dogwatch a shortened or curtailed watch, a period of time in late afternoon during which a part of the crew spends a shorter-than-usual time on duty

doldrums regions near the equator noted for the near-absence of winds

drag anchor a device floated behind a ship to keep it from drifting or to maintain its heading into the wind

drift ice loose pieces of ice found in relatively open water, generated by the breaking up of pack ice

dry dock a dock in the form of a basin in which the hull of a ship can be supported, from which the water originally floating the ship can be drained; used for inspection or for repairs to the hull

Dunkirk bottom a ship from Dunkirk in northern France

engineer the officer in charge of the engines of a ship

fathom a length or depth of six feet

first mate the officer ranking below the captain in the nautical hierarchy of command

five-masted bark a sailing ship with five masts, whose forward masts are square-rigged and whose aft masts are rigged fore-and-aft

flensing the process of stripping the layers of blubber from a whale carcass

flytende kokeri (Norwegian for "floating boilers") the mother ship or factory ship, fitted out with oil-processing equipment, around which a whaling operation at sea is centered

foredeck the deck of a ship, open to the elements, ahead of the forward mast

forepeak a compartment located at the far forward end of the ship

foreship that part of a ship farther forward than amidships

foretop a platform on the forward mast of a ship, used for work or as a look-out

forward hold the large compartment in the front portion of a ship used for storage of cargo

four bells two hours into a watch (a watch lasts four hours, with bells struck every half-hour to indicate time's passage)

frost smoke the haze of ice crystals floating in the air above the water's surface, formed by the freezing of water vapor

full rudder, full speed astern a command to turn the rudder to one side to its maximum possible extent, and also to operate the propeller in order to slow or reverse the motion of a ship to the maximum extent

funnel a smokestack of a ship

funnel stays ropes or cables extending from the deck of a ship to the upper end of the smokestack, used to strengthen it

galley the kitchen on shipboard

gangway a walkway extending fore-and-aft on a ship, or from ship to pier

Great Ice Barrier the British name for the Ross Ice Shelf, so named because its cliff-like seaward edge formed a barrier to navigation

Great West Wind the predominant wind in the Southern Ocean, which encircles the globe uninterrupted by any land mass

hard to starboard turning the wheel so as to steer a ship as far as possible to the right

hardtack a form of very thoroughly baked bread, hard and dry

harpoon cannon the gun-like device by which a harpoon is fired at a whale

harpoon line the rope by which a harpoon remains connected to a chase boat

hatch an opening in a deck that gives access to the holds below; also, the covering over it

hawse-hole the aperture in the hull of a ship through which anchor cables (or hawsers) pass

hawser a particularly patterned rope or cable, typically used for mooring or anchoring a ship

heave the vertical motion of a ship, in which the whole hull rises and falls

heave to to cease to make progress over water and instead to use propulsion only to maintain a ship's heading relative to the wind or waves

hold the interior of a ship below the decks where cargo is stored

hull the waterproof steel shell of a ship

ice floe a large, flat sheet of ice formed by the freezing of surface water; also called an ice field

iceblink the lightening of the sky over an ice field

ice pilot a knowledgeable person who advises the captain in steering through icy regions of the sea

ice-sky the sky above a body of ice, indicated by its contrasting brightness or color

Jack Tar slang for a jolly sailor

jackstaff a flagpole on which a "jack," ensign, or flag is displayed

keel the backbone of the hull of a ship, extending fore and aft along its centerline at the bottom of the hull

knot one nautical mile per hour

ladder-way the steep staircase by which crewmen travel from one deck to another

launch that boat of a ship reserved for the conveyance of its officers

lee the sheltered area extending downwind from an object

lee shore land on the lee side of a ship, which constitutes a significant danger during a storm

leeside that side of an object facing away from the wind and thus somewhat sheltered from it

lookout that point high in or on the forward end of a ship affording a lookout or ice pilot the best view of conditions ahead; also, the person assigned there

masthead the top or highest accessible point on the mast

meridian altitude the height of the sun above the horizon at noon, read by sextant and used to compute the latitude of the ship

mess table the table at which a group of crewmen eat their meals

mother ship in factory-ship whaling, the ship to which chase boats return for supplies and other things, and the place where whale carcasses are processed

nautical mile a distance of 6,076 feet

noon watch that period of duty starting at noon and lasting until four P.M.; also, that portion of the crew assigned to duty during that time

oil boiler (oil kettle) the steam-heated vessel in which whale blubber is cooked to extract the oil

oilcloth canvas rendered somewhat waterproof by an oil treatment

old salt a veteran sailor (from the many salted provisions he has eaten)

outrigger platform a raft floating by and attached to a ship's side, where work can be done

pack ice the massing of older ice into a nearly continuous and relatively rigid layer floating on the sea's surface

painter the rope attached to the prow of a boat by which it can be towed or moored

pancake ice small, circular pieces of ice with upturned edges

parallel (of latitude) an imaginary line running east and west on the earth's surface, parallel to the equator

"penguin-deck" the area of the ship most crowded with the crew and the crew's quarters (by analogy to the busy, congested nesting grounds of a penguin colony onshore)

pilot the locally knowledgeable person who advises a captain upon entering or leaving a harbor

pitch the rocking motion of a ship in which the bow and stern alternately rise and fall

Plimsoll lines the markings painted on the bow and stern of a ship's hull, indicating the depth to which it has settled into the water under its load

poop deck originally, the highest deck in the rear of a sailing ship; also, the afterdeck

port the left side of a ship looking forward

powder house the specially secured compartment of a ship in which gunpowder and other explosives are stored

prow the forward end of the hull of a ship

quartermaster a petty officer assigned to a ship's course, compass, or steering

radiogram a telegram sent by wireless telegraphy

rigging the various ropes helping to control the masts and to support them and the spars of a ship

road a partly sheltered area of water near a shore in which vessels may ride at anchor; the word is typically used in the nautical phrase "in the roads"

"Roaring Forties" that part of the Southern Ocean between 40 and 50 degrees south latitude, known for its strong winds

roll the motion of a ship in which one rail rises as the other falls

roller a wave that steepens and breaks, especially near the shoreline

sail room the province of the sailmaker, where he makes sails, awnings, etc., and where sails are stored

sailcloth the heavy canvas used to make sails

screw the propeller of a ship

scull to propel a boat using an oar extended aft

scupper hole an aperture at deck level in the bulwarks of a ship, through which water on the deck can drain overboard

sea chests the containers in which crewmen store their personal belongings

second mate the officer ranking below the captain and first mate in the nautical hierarchy of command

ship's papers the offical registration documents of a ship and its cargo

skiff (from the Dutch *schiff*) a lightweight boat that is shallow or flat-bottomed, used in shallow water

skipper slang for the captain of a ship

sloop a sailing vessel with one mast bearing fore-and-aft sails

sloop deck one of the upper decks of a ship, open to the weather and hence to seawater coming onboard

slop chest the "company store" on a ship where crewmen can buy supplies such as tobacco and clothing from a designated officer

sounding the process of determining the water's depth by lowering a weight on a line; also, the depth found by this process

South Polar current the generally eastward-flowing stream of ocean water that surrounds the Antarctic continent

Southern Cross a prominent constellation visible only from southern latitudes, consisting of four bright stars in the pattern of a cross

Southern Ocean that body of water encircling Antartica and joining with the southern extremities of the Pacific, Atlantic, and Indian Oceans

spar a wooden pole used above decks to extend the sails of a ship or, more generally, to support the rigging

starboard the right side of a ship looking forward

stem [as in "stem to stern"] the nearly vertical framing post forming the front of a ship

stern the rear end of a ship

steward a crew member seeing to the needs of the officers

stoke room the compartment in which coal is fed into the combustion chamber of a steam engine

swell the vertical rising of water due to wave action

tabular iceberg an iceberg with a flat upper surface

tar sailor, short for "tarpaulin"; this usage came about because a sailor wore clothing made of this material — heavy canvas treated with tar for waterproofing

telegraph on shipboard, the signaling indicators by which commands on the propulsion of a ship are passed from the bridge to the engine room

three-master a sailing ship with three masts

tiller the lever attached to the top of a rudder by which it can be rotated directly

tönne. *See* crow's nest

trade winds the steady winds found in regions north and south of the equator

tramp steamer a freight-carrying ship following no fixed route

trimming loading the cargo on a ship so that the weight is properly distributed

try-pot (predecessor of the oil boiler) an iron cooking vessel in which whale blubber was cooked to extract the oil

tweendeck or 'tween-deck from "between-deck," the sheltered space below the uppermost deck of a ship

two bells the signal for being one hour into a watch

wake the trail of disturbed water left behind a moving ship

watch the period of time during which a group of crewmen (also known as "the watch") is on duty on a ship

watch below (as opposed to the "watch on deck") that part of the crew not currently on duty, though liable to be called in case of emergency

water-sky the sky above an area of open water in an otherwise ice-filled area, indicated by its contrasting color

windward being in or facing the direction from which the wind is blowing

wireless station/installation the radio transmitter/receiver system

zenith the point in the sky vertically above an observer